Author's Note

First A Dream, my life's story, arrived from the printer in time to fill stockings for Christmas 2002.

The book was written for my children, grandchildren, and their descendants for generations to come. I also wrote it to pay tribute to thousands of talented people along the way – at CMH and in banking – who share my passion for business.

The 15,000 copies were supposed to last forever. They'd gather dust in relatives' closets and company storerooms for decades, I thought.

They sold out.

Thanks to the newspaper serialization and Warren Buffett's numerous endorsements in the media, they are all gone.

First A Dream raised directly and indirectly $800,000 for charity – and I am delighted that professors and students all over the country found the business lessons useful.

The book has meant a lot to me. It's been great fun.

With all the *Happenings* attributable to the book – and the supply gone -- I decided to write several new chapters for *a new edition.*

This *New Edition* is about those *Happenings.*

After Mr. Buffett read my book, he called up and bought CMH. This simple, straightforward sale was derailed and within inches of crashing -- and burning. Miraculously, we managed to get it back on track.

That's just one of many *Happenings.*

If this is your first time with *First A Dream,* please turn the page.

If you've read *First A Dream,* thank you. Now turn to Chapter 21. That's where the new Happenings begin.

What Friends Say About Jim Clayton's
First A Dream

"Jim is from Henderson, Tennessee. That's my hometown also. How can you go wrong with a successful man who rose from the cotton patch? They all have that 'get up and go' about them. You will admire him as I do after reading *First A Dream.*"

Eddy Arnold

"First a Dream is a stimulating book that offers deep insight and practical business lessons. Jim's warm, honest, down to earth style is evident in his writing."

Art Linkletter

"Under Jim's tenure, Clayton Homes became the premier lender in manufactured housing–with a portfolio of $5 billion. His leadership is equally successful in banking. *First A Dream* captures a great American success story. The BB&T board is fortunate to have Jim as a member."

John Allison
Chairman & CEO, BB&T Corporation

"Each century of our country's history has produced a few entrepreneurs who have invented and evolved their organizations while changing their industry. Jim's tenacity in building CMH has influenced all of us he's touched."

Wilma Jordan
CEO, The Jordan, Edmiston Group, Inc.
Former President and COO *Esquire* Magazine

"It's been said that whatever your mind can conceive and believe, it WILL achieve. What you believe yourself to be, you are! Jim Clayton's story is all this and more. A real page-turner. He proves that to accomplish great things, you must not only act—but also dream."

Wink Martindale
Radio, TV Personality

"Not everyone can be a Jim Clayton but everyone, in or out of business, can benefit from Jim's inspirational life story. Jim is much more than the embodiment of the American Dream. He is an 'American Do-er!' who shows us how we can do it too!"

H. Wayne Huizenga
Chairman, AutoNation, Inc.

"Jim Clayton amazes me. He is a premier leader in manufactured homes and in banking. Yet, he still takes time to inspire other entrepreneurs with his warm, yet honest approach to business in *First A Dream.*"

Louise Mandrell

What Friends Say. . .
(continued)

"If you seek success in business and life, read *First A Dream*. Jim's leadership has transformed the manufactured housing industry, just as it has the lives of us fortunate enough to have been associated with him."

William A. Schreyer
Chairman Emeritus, Merrill Lynch

"Selling lemonade on the corner, building manufactured homes, or whatever you dream...to make things happen...read the powerful lessons in *First A Dream*. Horatio Alger from cover to cover!"

Ed McMahon
Television Personality

"My friend Jim Clayton has through hard work, determination, and courage, made the American Dream come true in his life. What impresses me the most, though, is that he has achieved great success without getting the 'big head' and forgetting his Tennessee heritage. *First A Dream* will be an inspiration to all who read this powerful story."

John Duncan
U.S. Congress

"*First a Dream* is a great American success story and details Jim's leadership and business savvy—the foundation for his remarkable success in automobiles, housing, and banking. I only wish I had read this as a lad."

Harold 'Red' Poling
CEO Ford, retired

"What a tremendous achievement it is to be listed with the *Forbes* 400 who have achieved the ultimate reward in business. *First A Dream* by Jim Clayton is his story of helping people and his need for help—from other people and from a higher power. His story flows with simple and easy to adapt lessons for life and for business."

Robert Schuller
Senior Pastor, The Crystal Cathedral

"Some years ago, Jim Clayton happened to run into 'freedom and opportunity'...and many efforts later we have another of our country's remarkable stories of success...read on and see."

Dan Evins
Founder and Chairman Cracker Barrel

"Jim makes his money the old fashioned way—he earns it. What a gifted entrepreneur and writer. I ordered *First A Dream* for my managers."

Jim Moran
Toyota Distributor

NEW EDITION

Jim Clayton

FIRST A DREAM

With Bill Retherford and Amy Nolan

Visit our Web site at www.claytonbank.com
E-Mail: dream@claytonbank.com

Printed in the United States of America

First Printing: November 2002; Second Printing: November 2004

ISBN: 0-9726389-0-3

LCCN: 2002096009

CREDITS
Production Manager: Jim Wells
Book and Text Design: Graphic Productions

To mother, for constant reassurance, devotion and love;

Kay, for love and unselfish support;

my amazing children, Karen, Jimmy, Kevin, and Amy;

and in memory of my father, who left us too soon.

Contents

Contents

Introduction

This book has been in the making for twelve years. Like most of the challenges faced by entrepreneurs, this project took longer, cost more, and involved far more decisions and risks than I could have imagined—and I loved every minute of it.

In writing *First A Dream*, I drew from the same fortitude and determination instilled in me as I was raised, under the most difficult of circumstances as a sharecropper's son. The work ethics demonstrated on a daily basis by my parents provided the foundation for any accomplishments attributed to me, hopefully including this book.

Believe me, along the way there was plenty of indecision. Just deciding how to organize the book was a huge undertaking. Many of the decisions were made, and then promptly changed again and again, during many midnight brainstorming sessions. So many people contributed, and I am so grateful for their wisdom, inspiration, and perspective. Though the organization of the book would change—some days hourly—

the purpose always remained the same.

I penned my story to demonstrate that hard work and commitment does pay off—if you balance it with faith in God, concern for others, integrity, a passion for learning, and a positive mental attitude. By dreaming dreams based on sound values, and sometimes-realistic expectations, and working hard while remaining focused, we can succeed, and accomplish most of the important goals we dream for ourselves.

The book, I hope, will inspire and educate. By writing down the practices and principles that have served me well, it provides one more opportunity to express my beliefs—*just in case you might have been sleeping while I was preaching.*

One of the topics that I have been preaching for decades to staff, kids, and grandkids, are the *Three A's*. I use it in every business, or church seminar, workshop, or sermon I deliver. The following is a condensed version of a very practical easy to facilitate lesson that can be delivered by any speaker in six or sixty minutes:

The first "A" stands for *Action*. We have to have action in all areas of our lives. The action must be positive and plentiful—lots of it. Henry Ford could demand plentiful action. But today, businesses, teams of all types, churches, and even families, enjoy positive action over the long term, only if the motivation level is high and attitudes are positive—voluntarily.

The second "A" stands for *Attitude*. If we have positive attitudes we are likely to provide positive action. However, like action, we can't over the long term effectively demand positive attitudes.

The third "A" stands for *Atmosphere*. If we have a positive atmosphere, or environment, then we will be more apt to have positive attitudes and the resulting positive action. Of course, positive action produces positive attitudes, which produces a positive atmosphere.

Throughout my life the *Three A's* have hovered overhead:

With parents who provided, despite hardship, a positive home atmosphere; at Finger Jr. High, with 10 grades in four rooms; at Chester County High for two years, where terrific teachers had great attitudes; at my first job in Memphis; all during my undergraduate and law school experience at Memphis State and at the University of Tennessee; and especially during my adult career with extremely positive people in the automobile, manufactured housing, and banking industries where the *Three A's* were always present.

It's my pleasure to introduce you to some very special *"AAA"* people and organizations, in the pages that follow.

I hope you get the message from *First A Dream* that I truly believe: *Money can't buy happiness.* In speeches I pause and then add, *It sure can help you look in a lot more places.* It always gets a chuckle. But for many people, money creates a whole new set of problems. One thing for sure, money cannot buy a rich life. *That* must be derived from being aligned with wonderful family, friends, and colleagues. Purpose in life, kindness to others, maintaining strong values, working hard, and playing harder is indicative of a rich life.

I also want you to know that this book, though about the richness of life, will not make more riches for me. All proceeds will go to charitable causes in the communities where we live and work that Kay and I have supported during our lifetimes— and through our foundation, long after we're gone.

I suspect this life is not a dress rehearsal. It's probably the real thing. We must enjoy it, while helping others enjoy it. After all, it could be the only chance we get. Believing there is life in the hereafter, it's difficult to imagine a merciful God giving us another life if we did not enjoy this one. In fact, if this life isn't full of love, laughter, giving, and living—who would want another one?

With the love and understanding of family and friends, I've managed to pack in enough living to last several lifetimes—and

I've been able to make my dreams come true. May you do the same, and perhaps, in some small way, it would be my dream that this book, and my life, will inspire you to dream while living every day to the fullest.

I hope after reading *First A Dream*, you'll more fully believe that ordinary folks like me can live extraordinary lives.

CHAPTER 1

Pickin' Cotton

The country was in the depths of the Great Depression—four years running with no signs of letting up—when I was born on a dirt farm in McNairy County, Tennessee. The region was ailing anyway, even without a Depression, and we surely lived in one of the poorest parts. Just north of the Mississippi border and about 100 miles east of Memphis, Finger was a tiny town with less than a hundred people. We lived four miles of dirt road from there.

Our place sat on a patch of clay and sand that passed for farmland. We could only envy our neighbors further south—those farmers in Alabama and Mississippi who lived and worked the rich, black dirt of the Delta. We had about 160 acres of worn-out earth. Most of it wasn't even usable. The rest was marginal—truly terrible ground.

What's more, we didn't even own it. Dad was a sharecropper, "farming on the halves," which meant the landowner furnished the land and half the mules, seed, and equipment. We sharecroppers supplied the sweat and energy to plant, cultivate, and harvest the crops. The landowner, our grandfather, received half the harvest.

Sharecropping was a tradition dating back to colonial times, and there is no known record of a sharecropper getting rich.

Our home was a log cabin. I was born in one of its two rooms in 1934. Mother was only 19. It was lucky for both of us that I came along in March. Dr. Tucker rushed there in his new, black Model A Ford Coupe just in time to accommodate my arrival. A few weeks earlier, and those dirt roads could've been snowed under. Then Dr. Tucker would have had to ride his bay mare the four miles from Finger to deliver me.

Dad paid the good Doctor two chickens, three gallons of shelled corn, and one home-cured country ham to bring me into the world. The year before, he and Mother grossed only $100 the whole year, so there wasn't a whole lot of cash to go around.

My parents named me James Lee Clayton after my grandfathers, James Nute Browder and Ernest Lee Clayton. Everyone called me Lee. My only sibling, Billie Joe, was born 21 months later. His birth marked the beginning of a close, personal, and later professional bond, which has endured nearly seven decades. We called him Joe, and this time Dad was proud to be able to pay the doctor $12.50 *cash*.

By then, we had moved to another log cabin—the main house. We were still on the same land, still sharecropping for my grandfather, and only a few hundred yards from the old home. At least this place was larger—about 600 square feet, minus all amenities. No electricity, no running water, a tin roof, and a floor made of oak planks featuring ever-widening cracks. Eventually, we could sweep the dirt and dust through the cracks and watch it float to the ground below us.

There was no insulation to speak of, so the cabin was like an icebox in winter and an oven in summer. The main room served as our bedroom, where all four of us slept about eight feet apart on two beds. Joe and I had a hand-me-down mattress with coil springs; Mother and Dad had a mattress made of feed sack and filled with duck feathers.

For light, we had two windows by day and a kerosene lamp by night. The lamp was used sparingly because kerosene was so expensive. We wouldn't have a phone for another three years.

There was a dresser, mirror and wash basin, a rocking chair, and Mother's sewing machine, which doubled as a table for the battery-powered radio. The other room had an extra bed for guests squeezed in next to our pump organ, which Mother played frequently, filling our house with gospel music.

The kitchen area had a wood-burning cook stove and a small dining table with round hickory limbs for legs.

There was no bathroom. In fact, we didn't even have an outhouse. I know this sounds bizarre, but the only privacy we had was behind or inside the chicken house. It was incredibly primitive, and we had to watch out for the roosting hens overhead. During the cold months, we'd bring out the "thunder bucket" kept under our parents' bed. Someone had to empty it every morning. I would entice my brother Joe to take my turn by taking care of his wood-carrying responsibilities.

With all the beds in the same room, it was a challenge for my parents to find some private time. When it was possible, it would likely be Sunday afternoons after church and the midday meal, and sometimes on Saturday after work was done.

Joe and I didn't know exactly what was going on—but we knew something was up, because our parents would suddenly insist that we go out and play, a command rarely heard during the work week.

Once we were out, we'd see our parents cover up the window with a blanket. Naturally, we wondered what the big mystery was. A couple of times, we tried to spy, and my parents verbally hustled us away and made additional efforts to ensure the blanket was snug and secure.

Our barn was about 50 yards from the house. Its population fluctuated over the years—a couple of cows, a couple of hogs, and up to 20 chickens. Our fresh water was from a well just beside the kitchen door; my brother and I drew from it half a dozen times a day for meals and dishwashing.

We took baths on Saturday, heating the water in a kettle over the fireplace. All four of us took turns using the same washtub and the same water. The first one in got a really good bath. The last one got a mud bath. To us, there was nothing unusual or unsanitary about bathing ourselves in second-hand bath water just once a week.

Even something as mundane as drinking a glass of milk was preceded by a process that could charitably be described as labor-intensive. As a five year old, I'd be up at 5 A.M. to milk the cows and bring the two-gallon pail back to the house, where Mother would strain the milk, removing any bits of dirt and debris that had dropped in. (Our cows, constantly thrashing and tossing their tails during milking to chase away flies, invariably inserted surprises like loose strands of hay into the pail.)

Then she packaged the milk in half-gallon jars for Joe or me to carry up the hill, past the barn, down the hill, and through the meadow, to finally deposit them into a cold spring. Later, at suppertime, we'd go back for the ice-cold, refreshing milk.

There was some shortening of this process in winter, when we skipped those last two steps. The house would be so cold that we wouldn't need to use the spring as a refrigerator. Of course, we then had another problem—keeping the milk from freezing.

My brother Joe and I had to walk four miles to school in the winter when the roads were not passable by the school bus. Plow shoes were purchased in the late fall and used for school, church, and work in the winter. The shoes, especially the soles, were well worn by the time spring arrived. In the summer, we went barefoot everywhere—by choice, if not of necessity.

It would be some time before we got a tractor. Dad, proud of his team of mules, did the heavy groundbreaking from sunrise to sundown. Mother, Joe, and I helped out with the lighter work by clearing growth from the fields and by keeping feed and fertilizer ready when Dad needed to refill the spreaders.

Cotton was our money crop and was labor intensive. The planting process required plowing the land before carefully forming rows to receive fertilizer and seed. At age five, I was proud to have Dad promote me to a position of responsibility. Watching me from a distance, after he had given me a half hour of on-the-job training, Dad continued to operate the cottonseed planter using the larger mule, Ned. My assignment was to artfully employ the reins to command Nellie, our slightly smaller mule, up and down every other row. Chained to Nellie's harness was a 12-inch-diameter log that leveled and firmed two adjacent rows with each pass.

Compared to fetching seed and fertilizer, dragging the rows was a significant promotion. Learning to control the mule with few commands was challenging and interesting. After a time, I had little to do but follow. Of course my interest ebbed and flowed and boredom would set in at times.

Being five years old, occasional detours from Dad's grand plan should have been expected.

Once, when Dad left the field for a load of fertilizer and seed, I decided to relieve some boredom and inject some fun and creativity into the work. Stopping Nellie for a short rest at the end of the field, I placed my foot on her right trace chain, grabbed hold of her collar, and pitched myself up onto her back. Nellie didn't seem to mind at all. I was having a fine time taking in the view—sky, clouds, trees—it was a much better view than Nellie's rear end. Smelled much better too.

Dad had gone quite a ways, but not far enough.

"I'd better not *ever* catch you doing that again," he yelled, as he jerked me down from Nellie's back.

With him, one warning was usually more than enough. You thought carefully about trying Dad twice.

Dad never paid me for helping in the fields, but after learning the ropes, I would sometimes plow for Uncle R.C., Dad's younger brother. He gave me my first pay-for-work opportunity—and my first feeling of self-worth that comes from being paid for work performed. Just as important, Uncle R. C. would always acknowledge a job well done, giving me a lasting sense of pride.

The pay for one day's cotton-row dragging—25 cents.

D ad was born in 1911, and his parents named him Cratus. I'm not sure how he got that one, because nobody in our family had it before, nor have they since. The year before I came along, he graduated from high school at age 20. This instilled in him a hunger for learning to be shared with his boys. For farm families, such accomplishment was unusual, since most thought formal education was useless, a frivolity that got in the way of plowing, planting, and harvesting.

My mother, Ruth, the youngest of 11 children, was a more typical case. She left school after the eighth grade to cook for her brothers and sisters who worked in the fields.

At age 16, Mother first met Dad at an All-Day-Singing-and-Dinner-On-the-Ground event at New Church, the Methodist Church halfway between Finger and Adamsville. She rode, as usual, in the back of her Uncle Riley Talley's logging truck with others from Oak Grove Church. Dad traveled from Finger by horse. Since she was too young to be allowed to go out with Dad, he would write letters and see her at church events.

Dad began to date others, but as Mother became 17 and eligible, she and Dad saw their relationship blossom.

On Valentine's Day 1933, Mother received a letter from Dad, as he would write her occasionally between weekends. Her brother, seeing the letter and recognizing it was from Dad, chased her.

Determined to keep Dad's writings private, she stuffed the letter in her mouth.

Herman, seeing that Mother was adamant about keeping the contents secret, pressured her into revealing that she and Dad were planning a wedding.

"I am the oldest, and I'm getting married before you," he said.

"No way," said Mother. "There can't be two Ruth Browders in

this family," she said, referring to Herman's fiancée, Ruth Pusser.

Their double wedding on Saturday, April 29, 1933, resolved the debate.

Interestingly, several years earlier, Mother's sister Evie married Luster Pusser, Ruth's brother. Ruth and Luster were aunt and uncle of the legendary Buford "Walking Tall" Pusser. Every year the Browder-Pusser Family Reunion at Chickasaw State Park near Henderson is well attended.

Mother was pretty, with black hair, shorter than Dad but with a large, healthy frame. Dad was medium height, mostly bald with glasses, lean in his early years but heavier as he got older, topping out at 200 pounds. That was probably from the very rich meals we ate. "Cholesterol" would not be a common word for decades, and a normal breakfast for us was saturated with it: fried chicken, country ham, lots of biscuits covered in gravy, and molasses. It was by far the biggest meal of the day.

A typical day for the Clayton children began before the sun rose. First, breakfast. Then everyone was off to the fields to tend the crops, mostly cotton. Mother would leave the field a little earlier than the rest to fix the family dinner. Then it was back to the field and, after 14 hours, the family would head for the house.

Dinner, more often than not, was cornbread—hot, crusty, and crumbled into a large glass of milk—along with black-eyed peas, corn on the cob, potatoes, and tomatoes, all grown in our fields. On Sundays, we'd have fried chicken, pork—thanks to our hogs—or maybe a rabbit or squirrel. Exquisite desserts, often coconut cake or apple pie, were not uncommon. One thing was certain: We never worried about food. We knew we would always have, as we liked to say, three hots and a cot.

Funny thing about Dad and Mother—I never saw them argue. Ever. They seemed to instinctively understand each other's roles, respected the boundaries, and got along amazingly well. They never bellyached about boll weevils, bad soil, droughts in August, or rainouts in April.

While Dad was certainly not the backslapping sort—the phrase "happy-go-lucky" did not apply to him—neither was he a grim or angry man, dissatisfied with his place in life, or agonizing over the struggles he had to endure. "No-nonsense" might be the best way to describe him. He was stoic, not resigned—there is a difference—highly regarded in the community, and well liked and respected.

Indeed, around the neighbors, Dad seemed to lighten up a little bit. He enjoyed socializing at Sunday afternoon get-togethers with relatives, was always available to sit up with a sick friend, and even sang hymns in the Methodist Church with Mother, Joe, and me. He did a pretty good bass.

At home, Dad was quite intense, completely focused on the farm. Nearly everything else was irrelevant, and a dim view was taken of any fooling around. He was not a screamer, but he didn't have to be. His peach tree switch spoke volumes.

It hissed through the air, climaxing with a crackling snap as it hit ground zero. Dad's switch was long and thin, but tough and deceptively strong, and so flexible it seemed to wrap around you—almost eerily so—as though it had a sadistic mind of its own. I got switched a handful of times a year, certainly not often.

Not finishing a work assignment on time, or doing it wrong, or messing with Dad's tools could be a capital offense. Subcontracting work to Joe was a misdemeanor. Heaping praise on us was definitely not Dad's style, and I don't remember getting a compliment from him until I was in high school.

This was not the case with Mother. Joe and I always knew she adored us. Mother liked the way we looked, the way we talked, everything. She loved to show us off every chance she got.

Even with such unconditional approval, Mother managed to be an effective disciplinarian, albeit using methods less draconian than Dad's. It was an extraordinary circumstance for Mother to whip us. She was a negotiator. Besides, there were always those four magic words: *"I'll tell your Daddy."*

Mother's capacity for work was staggering. She could out-pick anybody in the cotton patch, sometimes up to 300 pounds a day. That was truly wretched work, backbreaking yet demanding the utmost delicacy—and an extraordinarily sensitive touch.

When the cotton matures, it pops out of its boll (the protective case) and hangs there. But you can't just grab it; you'll cut your fingers on the razor-sharp burs that are everywhere on the boll. Wearing gloves was only workable if the ends of the glove fingers were cut out to allow for "feel"—defeating the purpose.

Mother could pick two or three cotton bolls at the same time. She had been picking cotton since she was a little girl and had developed strong and efficient fingers. She had the perfect touch and was able to sweep her hand around the cotton stalk, slide her fingers safely between the razor sharp burs, and firmly pluck the cotton. She would hold the treasure from half a dozen bolls in her hand before stuffing the huge wads of cotton into the bag that she dragged across the ground behind her. She would pick, carry to the wagon, weigh, and empty six bags, totaling 300 pounds—all in one day.

A bale of cotton weighs about 1,200 pounds. Once the seeds are taken out, it might weigh only 500. In a good year, our farm might produce six bales, eight in an excellent one. That's 3,000 to 4,000 pounds of cotton. (By comparison, the fertile, level, and easier to tend Delta farmland would produce four to five times as much for each acre.) Prices varied a bit from year to year, but on average, Dad may have received about 20 cents per pound.

Do the math: That's only $600 to $800 a year. Then, after settling up with my grandfather—remember, he got half the income—Dad's annual take for the cotton was $400 or less! Even back then that was miserable compensation.

Break it down further and it sounds even worse. When you count up all the hours Dad worked at the farm—and he was a sunrise to sundown man—he made about $8 a week, just over a buck a day, about 10 cents per hour! Add in Mother's time, Joe's time, my time—and it was even less.

Remember—that was a *good* year.

With a bad crop—and we had them every five years or so—the number of bales might be cut in half. The U.S. government wasn't much help either. More than 60 years later, my Mother is *still* fuming over President Roosevelt's presumed solution to the rock-bottom cotton prices, which were at record lows.

Plow up part of the crop, the government declared. Plow *up* the crop? Yes, and while you're at it, slaughter some of your hogs too. We'll even pay you to do it.

The idea, of course, was based on the laws of supply and demand. Less cotton meant higher prices for the product. Fewer hogs meant pork prices would rise. There was some logic to it, certainly. But as far as my parents were concerned, it seemed sinful, almost insane. Plow *up* the crop? If this is the New Deal, they said, deal us out. Roosevelt was elected four times—overwhelmingly—but he did it each time without the votes of Dad and Mother, and probably every other farmer in West Tennessee.

No wonder Dad did everything possible to pull in extra cash. For years, he worked one day a week as a bookkeeper at the Chester County cattle auction. He was great at that, because he knew animals and prices. It also gave him an excuse to socialize with all his farmer buddies.

He'd also cut timber on the farm and sell it raw to the railroad company to use as crossties. Mother sold extra eggs and chickens. They'd scrimp and save any way they could. Neither Dad nor Mother smoked or chewed, although most everyone else did. To my parents, tobacco was a waste, and not using it was another way to cut costs.

In fact, hardly anything was store-bought. Our clothes were made out of feed sacks. Really. We would go to the general merchandise store in Finger, walk down the rows of feed sacks, and shop for our new clothes.

The sacks were actually a good quality fabric. Some of them

even had patterns and designs. The manufacturers did that on purpose, even competing a bit to produce the most attractive sacks, because they knew many of their customers made clothes from the fabric. Shirts, skirts, whatever we needed, Mother could do anything with her old sewing machine.

Joe and I had few toys. We never had a bike or the opportunity to develop our skills at baseball and other sports because we had to work all week long. That didn't stop us from creating our own toys. We crafted slingshots from automobile tire tubes and made forays into the "wild west" in a red wagon we shared. Dad purchased the Western Flyer wagon—cleverly disguised as a toy. No doubt, he saw its practical use as a work tool. We, in fact, did use it for several monotonous trips to the woodpile each day to carry the wood used in cooking and heating our home.

"Hey, Lee—get wood!" *still* rings in my ears.

I always felt we had something better than toys, anyway—our farm animals. We loved the calves, cows, and hogs, even the chickens, and really got attached to them. There were numerous dogs over the years. Trixie was the all-time wonder dog, a stray that wandered in, and it was wonderful when she had puppies. For years, she'd deliver a large litter and supply our community with the finest in squirrel-hunting dogs.

Normally we didn't notice that we didn't have much, with one exception—Christmas. Even then, it wasn't a time to splurge, and holiday pickings were always slim.

As part of the Yuletide ritual, Joe and I took what toys we had and put them by the fireplace—our wagon, a couple of home-made slingshots, and a few other trinkets. This way, it was explained, Santa Claus could see what else we needed.

Such a display, I thought, seemed unnecessary. One look at our situation and even the most obtuse Santa would be pretty much clued in. Still, we put out our things and hoped for the best.

One Christmas in particular stands out, and left us wondering what Santa's problem was, since all he left us was one apple, one orange, and two sticks of peppermint candy. Mother told us, gently, that Santa must have thought we already had too much, certainly more than many others. We should be grateful for what was given us.

I got the point, but as I sucked on my already disintegrating peppermint stick, her well-meaning lesson went down as hard as castor oil.

Remarkably, through all of this, Dad somehow managed to swing it so he could buy a car. Keep in mind that in our part of West Tennessee, cars were clearly a luxury. Except for Doc Tucker and the mailman, no one around us had one.

Dad was an extremely good manager of what little money we had. He started with a 1920 Model T Ford, and then moved up to a 1928 Model A. Dad was able to minimize the expense since he was a natural born mechanic and enjoyed performing the maintenance himself. It would be hard to imagine anyone else keeping a family car operating well for such a small amount of money.

Thanks, Dad, for these business lessons, which we apply daily at Clayton Mobile Homes. Aircraft maintenance comes to mind, but in computer manufacturing equipment and all over the company, these lessons on buying good used equipment and maintaining well is applicable.

I can see Dad now beaming with pride as we cruised down a country lane on a lazy Sunday afternoon. He had a special habit of slightly curling his fingers into his palm, extending the thumb up, and lightly shaking his hand three times when meeting or passing our neighbors.

Dad would not hesitate to delay his work to help friends and relatives—even if they were "transportation-challenged." Once, he dropped everything to drive a neighbor all the way to Tallahassee to be with family during an emergency.

Even today, a trip from West Tennessee to that part of the Panhandle is a long haul—about 500 miles—but back then it was like going to Mars. I remember thinking, *Would he make it? Would he ever return?* While Dad was away, Joe and I pondered what sort of pitfalls he might encounter on such an exotic journey, and we were all relieved when he triumphantly returned from his daring adventure.

Dad's generosity with the car, however, did not extend to me. I was confused and couldn't understand his attitude when I volunteered to help as he serviced the car or farm equipment.

"Go on, get on out of here. You'll mess that up," he would say.

It was unclear to me why Dad would then enthusiastically require participation and support when we worked in the fields.

"Come on, let's hoe these rows," he would say, with acceptance and encouragement. Yet, it was rare for him to display any enthusiasm for my involvement when he was interestingly tinkering with the Ford.

His "look but don't touch" attitude toward the car baffled me. I couldn't understand why he could never say, "Come on, let's fix this car," or "Let's change that tire."

Already, I was dazzled and endlessly fascinated by automobiles or any type of gadget.

That was a pretty good gauge of my perceived relationship with Dad, at least a good part of the time: distant, cold, confounding, and focused on the farm. Part of it, of course, was Dad's preoccupation with keeping us out of poverty. There wasn't time, and certainly money wasn't available for niceties. He was immersed in the business of survival and didn't need a little kid wasting his time, screwing up his tools, or scratching up his car.

This was very normal in the rural South. "Touchy-feely" was not in vogue. Parents weren't buddies with their kids. They didn't josh around with them. They didn't quiz them about their hopes, fears, and dreams. Displays of affection were virtually nonexistent. You might get a slap on the wrist, but never a pat on the back.

Nobody, at least no one we knew, regularly kissed or hugged their children. Even my grandparents, though kind and amiable to us, were as reticent as anyone about expressing their feelings, even to their grandkids. When Joe and I were very young, the grandparents would encourage us to climb up onto their laps and ask us to recite our ABC's, or tell them about how school was, or the like. Other than that, the "affection well" was bone dry.

That's just the way they were brought up. It was a normal behavior pattern that had been passed down by their parents and grandparents. Of course our parents cared for and loved us.

My Uncle R.C. was, and still is, a totally great guy. He gave me my first guitar and my first paying job. Never one to verbalize his feelings, somehow I knew he really cared. I felt like he considered me special—that he thought I would be a special person someday. His scheduling of a trip to town for supplies on my first day in school was certainly special to me. He introduced me to my first-grade teacher, Ms. Mattie Lou Ward, and made sure that I was comfortable before he left for the store.

I didn't resent Joe because he seemed to be Dad's favorite. It didn't affect my relationship with him at all, then or later. I'm very proud to say that my brother and I have always been extremely close. Mother says we had a couple of squabbles when we were very little, just minor skirmishes. But I don't remember any of them. In fact, I don't remember ever having harsh words with Joe, to this very day.

When we were young, I was very protective of him, and when he got into trouble, I hollered louder than he did. One sub-freezing night, we were thawing out by the fireplace, all four of us. Move too far away, and that frigid house would turn you into a human Popsicle. We sat in front of the fire, the way you might sit in front of the television, except that every few minutes, when really cold, we'd rotate ourselves to keep our backsides toasty.

One evening Joe jumped from Mother's lap, intending to rush across the hearth in front of the fireplace to join Dad. On the way he tripped over the fresh kettle of hot water, which was sitting on a layer of hot coals. As he stumbled, he fell flat on the hearth as the kettle tipped over. The steaming hot water spread quickly, soaking Joe's diaper and feed-sack pants. He screamed bloody murder.

According to Mom, I yelled even louder.

"Please don't let my brother die!"

I'm not sure to whom I was yelling. God? My parents? The latter were tearing off Joe's drenched clothes while trying to separate the boiled skin from the fibers. They were so frantic and concerned I really thought he might die. Over several months he recovered. Even now I can still see his tortured face and hear his horrible screams.

When I was six, I started first grade at Finger Junior High School, which consisted of grades one through ten in four rooms all taught by four teachers. There wasn't an elementary school in McNairy County. Remember, in this community, education wasn't a priority. I'll be forever grateful that Dad, unlike his mother, made finishing high school a non-negotiable goal for Joe and me.

College was never mentioned.

Ms. Ward taught me how to read and write, and I think a lot more. I was lucky to have her—sweet, tolerant, patient, yet completely in charge. Instead of trying her patience, every student tried very hard to please her.

I knew I was Ms. Ward's favorite student. Later on, I would learn that each of her students felt the same. She had the ability to stay in tune with each person.

A tornado is a war of the elements. They are truly terrifying. Imagine the apocalypse, multiply by 10, and you'll have a rough idea of what it's like to be in the midst of a tornado: a black swirling, twisting funnel, roaring toward you, eating up everything in its path. Trees ripped from their roots. Houses tossed like matchboxes. Cars and cows torn to pieces. People swallowed up whole. What a horrible way to leave this earth.

Our county was on the fringe of Tornado Alley. Usually, we'd hear of two or three tornadoes touching down every year, though not necessarily in our vicinity, perhaps in a neighboring county. That changed one spring day.

I was in the second grade; Joe was in first. We were riding home on the school bus. Five minutes earlier, the driver had let Susie Walker off. She was a classmate, six years old, and one of our neighbors. We noticed that her mother Inez was waiting at their mailbox. Mrs. Walker seemed frightened. She had seen the dark storm brewing and heading our way, building up fast.

As the bus approached our mailbox, suddenly we saw the spinning black cloud chewing up the sky. I could see mattresses, washtubs, and a section of tin-roof from a neighbor's house exploding from the innards of the twister.

Braking the bus to a stop, our concerned driver rushed us off the bus and down the hill toward our house.

"High tail it home, boys, as fast as you can go. It's really bad," he yelled, frantically.

Joe and I ran for the pasture gate. It wouldn't budge. Desperately, Joe slithered under the gate while I swung over the top rail. The path of the tornado was paralleling the narrow lane to our home. It appeared the center of the funnel would miss, but the outer third of the storm would soon enfold our home—hitting about the time we arrived.

I quickly climbed through a barbed wire fence to run through the pasture. Looking back, Joe had decided to run on the muddy road. He was only a few yards behind.

As he saw me looking back, Joe screamed, "Run, Lee, run! The world's coming to an end!"

Mother ran out, grabbed our arms, and practically threw us through the door. By that time, the twister was spinning over-head. The three of us dived under a bed as the roaring sound became as loud as a locomotive from ten feet.

A massive limb from the peach tree—the one where Dad got his switches—crashed into the house. A wooden pole supporting our radio antenna that was embedded deeply into the ground twisted from the earth and spun across the grass, finally splinter-ing into toothpicks.

Suddenly, the roaring stopped. The calm that followed was eerie. We were all right. Mother helped us from under the bed, looked out the window and said, "Oh, Lord. The Young's house is gone." They were our closest neighbors.

Mother was concerned for Dad. This was his day to work at the cattle auction, and he should've been home by now. Did he survive the twister? Was he dead? Maybe an hour later—it seemed like an eternity—I saw Dad hurriedly walking over the hill toward us, an axe over his shoulder. We all ran out to greet him, and this was one time we were emotional. We were so glad to see him alive.

"There are trees all over the road," he said. "I couldn't make it here with the car. Had to leave it."

After making sure we were okay, he grabbed his saw and lantern, and headed back to help clear the road.

Our neighbors went door to door, checking on everyone. A lot of people were hurt; we took them to Finger Junior High School, which served as a temporary makeshift hospital. Everyone pitched in to repair the considerable damage.

Only one person was killed. It was Mrs. Walker, our neighbor, who had collected her daughter just moments before Joe and I got off the school bus. They found her body the next morning, just yards from her house—still clutching little Susie, who was dazed, confused, and distraught, but very much alive.

It probably sounds like we lived under extraordinarily harsh circumstances. It has been said that the American farm from the days of my youth had, for the most part, barely progressed beyond Biblical times. I'll vouch for that. Younger people, I know, can't relate to log cabins, kerosene lamps, and thunder buckets.

But even in that time and in that place, I learned that certain concepts are ageless, no matter what century we're in. Self-discipline. Willpower. Perseverance. Realizing that disappointment is not defeat. Knowing that problems often present opportunities. Obstacles may get in the way—for us, it was boll weevils, droughts, accidents, and tornadoes, among others. But the human spirit can triumph over these things. Adversity breeds resilience and can build character. It is possible to survive, even prevail.

As a boy, I could never articulate these things. As a man, I was able to look back and apply these hard-won childhood lessons to my business and life. Telling others to "work hard" and "never quit" may sound obvious and cliché. But it's a wonderful foundation for running a farm—or a Fortune 500 company.

Dad never preached hard work and perseverance—he just did it. Not long after the tornado struck, he purchased the farm from my grandfather for $1,500. Somehow, with that broken-down lump of soil, he and Mother had sold eggs, timber, and enough cotton to pull it off. They had accomplished an extraordinary feat.

We were no longer sharecroppers. We were landowners.

I'll never forget one morning just before sunrise when we were finishing breakfast. Dad, in a rare, expansive mood, pointed out the window and said, "Lee, if you work hard, save your money, finish high school, and buy yourself a mule—I'll give you a second mule—and that cotton patch out there—that'll be yours." He went on to say, "That way you will have it better than me."

It was a generous gesture. I nodded, even smiled, as I gazed out the window at that scraggly scrub of real estate. But even then, I knew somehow, I'd never be a dirt farmer.

Dad was a good man in so many ways. He struggled; he worked very hard; he never gave up. He tried to do the right things, tried to set a good example, and almost always did. If nothing else, he had worked like the devil.

Other things—like dreams and a vision—were not qualities in abundance on a red clay dirt farm in McNairy County during the Depression. Problem was—and maybe this was my trouble with him—Dad's vision for me never got beyond the cotton patch.

CHAPTER 2

Dreams

D ad didn't know it, but in those days, I really did have a dream, and it had nothing to do with a cotton patch. Instead, it went something like this:

I'm standing on center stage, performing at the Grand Ole Opry. Singing. Picking my guitar. Promoting my latest hit record. Awash in adoring fans. Bathed in bright lights. Drenched in applause. There I am, the consummate entertainer, taking it all in stride, totally at ease with my fame and fortune.

Then I'd wake up.

I probably had that dream on a Saturday night. That's when WSM, the Nashville radio station, boomed out its weekly Grand Ole Opry extravaganza live from Ryman Auditorium. The station's signal—50,000 watts broadcast on clear channel—tore though Tennessee and much of North America. I tuned in every week, along with millions of others.

Understand that Opry entertainers ranked slightly higher than movie stars and royalty, particularly in the South and Midwest. If on some miraculous evening, Clark Gable and Hank Williams both showed up at your doorstep for a fried chicken dinner, Hank would get the breast, and Clark would get the wing.

In short, anyone on the Opry had it made: Chet Atkins, Kitty Wells, George Jones, Red Foley, Jim Reeves. Thanks to the Opry connection, they got the high-paying gigs, everything from conventions to county fairs.

But my favorite of favorites was Eddy Arnold. His career had caught the tail end of a comet. Though he was still on the way up, he was already famous, and fast becoming a megastar.

All of us in McNairy County felt a kinship to Eddy because he was a hometown boy. He grew up near us, in Five Points, a tiny town much like Finger, about ten miles northwest of Henderson.

Eddy started out with nothing, no contacts and no hand up. In fact, he started out just like me—a kid on a cotton farm who undoubtedly had a dream as he learned to sing and play the guitar. We appreciated the way Eddy never tried to bury his dirt-poor heritage. Indeed, he gloried in it, apparently, considering his nickname was "The Tennessee Plowboy."

Within a couple of years, Eddy would hit the Billboard charts for the first time. Eventually, he'd have 28 No. 1 singles. He'd be the first country entertainer to host a prime-time network TV show. Ultimately he'd sell 90 million records. He would become, arguably, the greatest singer in the history of country music.

But even then, though in his twenties, Eddy already had a measure of fame, considerable wealth, and a growing reputation as a shrewd businessman. He was one of us—still in touch with his roots—confirming that any of us can find a way out of the cotton patch. His growing success was an inspiration to me as I shaped and nurtured my dream.

Eddy's high profile also helped me visualize my goals, which then were as grand as they were generic. Basically, I wanted to be recognized (respected) and I wanted to be rich (secure). Eddy already had all of that, and more. He started out on my level, and I knew I could do it too—somehow it would happen—but I knew it would be up to me.

Uncle R.C. got me started on Eddy Arnold. When I was seven,

R.C. was only 16, younger than Dad by 13 years, but already working some sharecropper land—and married. His wife, Annie May, was only 15. (They're still together, now married more than 60 years.)

R.C. was more approachable than Dad, not nearly as set in his ways, though he was quite responsible for his age. I never had a nickel of my own until R.C. hired me to help him plant cotton and corn. He paid me a quarter a day, good money for a kid my age.

Both R.C. and Annie May loved to pick—and loved Eddy Arnold almost as much. The two of them sang duets while they played Eddy's songs, along with hymns and standards. By the time they got around to "You Are My Sunshine," I was hooked.

R.C. showed me the G, C, and D chords, Annie May loaned me her Sears Silvertone guitar, and I took it from there—learning by ear and strumming until my fingers bled. Later, the fingertips on my left hand calloused over, and I could play for hours, painlessly. First I learned classics like "The Wildwood Flower," a country-music standard that any good picker ought to know.

I discovered a family of farm hands who lived close by, with three kids who loved to sing. On the economic ladder, they were probably a rung below even us, living in a small tenant house and working part-time in exchange for rent. They also worked as day laborers on nearby farms. There were two brothers about my age, and a little sister, Francis, who could really yodel. The brothers played bass, fiddle, or mandolin. Francis sang, and I played guitar. We played mostly at church and school fundraisers. Heck, we'd play anywhere they'd let us.

Dad didn't care for my new hobby—he didn't like much of anything that wasn't focused on farm results—but he didn't interfere, either. That's probably due to Mother. She really loved music; we were Methodists because of it. The local Church of Christ did not allow instruments during services—no piano, no harp. The singing was a cappella. Mother was certain that Jesus loved music, and it thrilled her that I took up guitar and sang.

In fact, Mother joined forces with Grandmother Clayton, who also relished my picking, to prevail over Dad.

Their relationship was an uneasy and conditional alliance at best, akin to a cat and mouse teaming up to outsmart the dog. Mother and Grandmother Clayton disagreed on everything from child development to church dogma. Both were strong-willed and outspoken, though Mother often held her tongue out of respect. But they were in cahoots on this one, and together they served as loyal and effective lobbyists for my picking. If they didn't quite win Dad's approval on the matter, they did succeed in obtaining his silence.

The war touched all of us, isolated as we were. But I was so young that my memories of it are quite dim. I don't remember Pearl Harbor. I do remember Uncle R.C. going off to war, and how upset, frightened, and sad everyone was when he left—terrible feelings that never really dissipated until he returned. (Dad received a deferral because he raised cotton and food, which supported the war effort.)

All we had were bursts of news from the radio, plus the newsreels we'd see every few months at the State Theater in Henderson. Still, even as a second grader, I knew my parents harbored a deep hatred of Hitler, Mussolini, and the Japanese.

Over halfway through the war, when I was 10, we had an addition to our family that would change our lives forever. It wasn't human. It wasn't even living. It was short and squat, maybe four feet high, not particularly attractive, noisy, and the color of steel gray. But with it, Dad quadrupled his income.

It was a Ford tractor.

The Ford 8N cost about $600, and it was loaded. Its three-point hitch was a revolutionary feature—for the first time, a tractor's universal three-point connection system accepted implements from other manufacturers. Ford built the 8N very close to the ground so that it wouldn't tip over on unlevel terrain. The driver got tossed around less, with a better ride and less fatigue.

This may not sound like a big deal to you, but back in 1944 on a dirt farm in the South, it was a mechanized marvel, the 20th Century arriving at our door, admittedly years behind schedule.

Dad was able to get the tractor with a little assistance from the federal government—those same bungling bureaucrats who were the brains behind the plow-up-your-farm fiasco that my parents so detested.

Not that the government gave us any money, or even a loan or a discount. By this time, Dad had barely enough money to buy a tractor anyway. But wartime meant most everything was rationed, from grits to gasoline. Factories cut back on consumer goods to create a massive military machine—70,000 Navy ships, 6 million tons of aircraft bombs, 40 billion rounds of ammunition.

Next to that, tractors took a poor second, and like peaches and pork chops, the government rationed them too. You had to get special dispensation to get one. Through the Farmer's Allotment Program, Dad qualified.

His timing was perfect. The farmers' sons who were depended on for the hard farm work were off at war. Hardly anyone was available to plow and tend the fields, except the deferred, like Dad and the older men and young boys who were not eligible for the draft. Our tractor was the only one for miles around, and it did the work of six men and a dozen mules. During 1944, many of our neighbors who desperately needed help gladly paid us to plow their fields.

That tractor ran 24 hours a day. Literally. Dad would drive all night until sunrise. Mother subbed for him during breakfast. Joe and I took turns mornings and afternoons so Dad could get some sleep. (In farm communities, school recessed for planting time.) About nine at night, Dad would come back out and start the whole process all over again.

Dad charged 50 bucks a day, a very fair price. His income rose to about $2,000, his best year ever (until he joined Clayton Homes Inc. in 1966).

It was enough to buy a bigger and better house, even enough to move us into town. Dad wasted no time. Before the end of 1944, right after planting, we moved to Finger. I was still 10 years old.

To us it was truly the Big City, with a cotton gin and even a pool hall. Church was two blocks away, school was four, the post office was five.

There was a hardware emporium, run by Guy Bishop, who was also the local undertaker. Harris Dry Goods sold shoes and clothes. Uncle R.C., back from the war, owned the general merchandise store, with a filling station out front. It was the most popular hangout in town, admittedly a distinction won by default. Still, what fun it was to see R.C. in his store, running the show, shooting bull with his buddies, telling tales and cracking jokes while he peddled his limited inventory—baloney and cheese, feed and seed, eggs, milk, and Royal Crown Cola.

Despite the similarity in names, our Uncle R.C. did not (unfortunately) create, manufacture, or own RC Cola. His relationship with the product started with a coincidence in name and ended with his selling *twice as much for a nickel too*, as the cute jingle went. Royal Crown was then and remains today a popular brand, especially in the South. All us country boys bought RCs because they came in a bigger bottle—12 ounces for a nickel. The standard line at the store, undoubtedly repeated millions of times over by Southern boys of my generation: "Gimme an RC dope and a MoonPie."

The move to Finger and the new home was a wonderful new beginning for all of us. We purchased the new home from Dad's Uncle Johnny Clayton, one of Grandfather Clayton's eight brothers, for $3,600. Now we had a white painted frame house, not a log cabin, with a living room, kitchen, and three bedrooms. For the first time, Mother and Dad had a bedroom all to themselves.

Finally we had electric lights—just a 100-watt naked bulb dangling from a beaded chain in each of the five rooms—but it seemed a miracle. Never again would we have to smell and fuel a kerosene lamp. We still didn't have running water and used an outhouse, but when Dad sprang for a refrigerator and a used electric range, we felt we had arrived. (With the range, it meant the never-ending request to get wood was history.)

An enormous barn was out back, with a loft so large it could hold a Boeing 737. Around the barn was our pasture of 11 acres, where we kept the two cows and several hogs.

We grew our cotton on new farmland about three miles away, just north of us, on 30 acres that were far more productive than our old fields. Dad got a deal on the land just before the move to Finger—land prices were exceptionally low then, about $200 per acre. He leased an additional 30 acres adjacent to the new land.

Our move to town didn't help win over the neighborhood kids. All along, Joe and I had been treated like outsiders, which I guess we were. The city kids had bicycles. We didn't. They had lots of free time. Not us. We envied their store-bought clothes. Our shirts were still homemade from feed sacks.

Not only did their parents make more money—they had *salaries.* Most of them worked at the train station, post office, or bank, or at the Brown Shoe Company, which was 15 miles south of us in Selmer, our county seat. Those were sophisticated and glamorous trades, compared to dirt farming.

The city kids frequently would remind Joe and me that we were dirt farmers in subtle, but sometimes direct and more pointed ways. At first, we weren't in the clique at all. But over the six (seven for Joe) years required to graduate from the 10th grade at Finger, we were increasingly included.

Sure,we felt left out at times, but we were too darn busy to let their haranguing bother us much.

This is where our front yard comes in. It was huge, big enough for a ball field, which is precisely how the neighborhood kids used it. *They wouldn't let us play ball in our own yard.*

Ultimately, we scuffled, forced to fight for the privilege to play there. Joe and I acquitted ourselves well enough to earn a spot as "extras." We could play, but only when they needed someone to fill a position.

At first, we didn't do as well as the other kids. Sports didn't come easy to us, since we spent all of our time working the fields, not playing ball. And while it's true that friendships eventually did develop, it was slow going.

This is not to say these were bad times. On the contrary, even if my self-image briefly shrunk a bit, my world became larger. Opportunities to work and make money were out there.

During winter, I built fires in the four classrooms at Finger Junior High before school; on Saturdays, I swept the place clean. I did the same on Sunday mornings at the Church of Christ. After school, usually on rainy days, I helped out Uncle R.C. at the store. During the cold months, I made $1.75 a week for these chores—a quarter a day from the school, and a quarter a week from the church. The work for Uncle R.C. was strictly barter, my services in exchange for an occasional RC and MoonPie.

In whatever spare time I could find, I sold flower seeds door-to-door. Seed selling was a school activity. Kids did it to raise money for books, paper, and library paste. I always exceeded my quota. Rose bushes and pine seedlings were the easiest for me to sell, and relatives made up a large portion of my clientele, at least in the beginning.

To entice us to sell, there were rewards. The more you sold, the more prizes you won. Actually, the seed company gave us a choice between prizes or free products.

I weighed my options carefully. Did I want a toy car (instant gratification) or free seeds (deferred compensation)? This decision was more consequential than I ever knew. Without realizing it, I was setting the tone and shaping a philosophy that would characterize the rest of my life. I chose the seeds. It was my first attempt to become an entrepreneur.

Plowing the money back into my business (if you'll pardon the expression) was a smart move. I got to keep all the proceeds from those extra seeds, so it really increased my cash flow.

But I learned something far more profitable: Forgo those things that give you momentary satisfaction. Look at the long-term. Defer profits for something more substantial. Pass up the plastic toy car and invest your capital. Plant the right seeds. One day, you could buy a new luxury car. Or better yet, start your own seed company.

Ironically, the move to Finger—which precipitated so much conflict with the city kids—was also a catalyst. It ignited my ambition and drove me to make something of myself.

That's why I was taking on every odd job in sight. Making money, I thought, would deliver my two primary goals: recognition and wealth. Already, it seemed to be working. Even with only a few dollars in my pocket, I felt more on par with the neighborhood kids, not just financially, but in a social sense as well. I began to squirrel away cash, and even opened up an account at the Home Banking Company in Finger.

Dad had mixed feelings about my freelance work since it cut back on my time at the farm. But he was glad I made the money—maybe even secretly pleased that I seemed so industrious, though he never said such a thing, at least not to me. Besides, he was too busy stewing over my spending five bucks a month on a radio repair correspondence course, offered by the National Radio Institute, and advertised in a *Superman* comic book.

The course taught me how to take a radio apart, change speakers, replace vacuum tubes, improve sound, and enhance reception. I treated our radio like a battery-powered Guinea pig. Before long, we could pick up a lot more stations, and soon, I was doing this for friends and relatives. Even so, Dad seemed to think I was wasting my time.

If only he had known about one disaster. It was a Friday afternoon, and I was in boy genius mode, masterminding a brilliant scheme to pipe beautiful music throughout the house.

Since the new electric range had replaced our old wood cook

stove, I made use of the obsolete stovepipe and flue, and finagled a speaker into the hole that was in the ceiling. It fit perfectly. I wired the speaker to the phonograph and put on a 45 rpm of Eddy Arnold. I tested it at low volume.

Eddy never sounded better.

Then Mother came home. Company was arriving soon, and she was in a hurry, already rushing around the house, cleaning up. Of course, I didn't tell her what I had done. Instead, I set the volume high. Real high. I hit the power switch, thinking this would be a wonderful surprise for Mother. It was.

Eddy hadn't finished his first lyric line when a cloud of black soot billowed out of the hole. For a moment, we were in a fog. The powder went everywhere, blanketing the kitchen—walls, chairs, table, floor, and us—with Eddy still blaring in the background. Apparently, I had turned the volume so high that the vibrations from Eddy's voice loosened the soot embedded in the stovepipe.

I was too humiliated to realize it then, but I was ahead of my time. This, I should have surmised while watching the soot shower the room, was merely a test version of a brilliant marketing stratagem—a prehistoric version of the massive pyrotechnics that one day would thrill millions at rock concerts throughout the world. Visual effects of this caliber wouldn't be part of the show for another 30 years.

Mother was stunned, but remained grimly focused on the arrival of company, which was imminent. We wiped up the mess, which was difficult. I learned that black soot tends to smear into a stubborn goo when you add water. At least we got things reasonably tidy before the guests showed up.

If Dad had witnessed this fiasco, he would've gone off—and switched me to the tune of "Cattle Call," or worse, "Nearer My God To Thee." But Mother never told Dad the story, at least not for years. For that alone, I am forever grateful.

In 1950, I graduated from 10th grade at Finger Junior High— and we had options. Which high school should I attend? There was Bethel Springs High, to the south in McNairy County, or Chester County High, to the north in Henderson.

Academically, Chester County was the better of the two, with some of its graduates actually going on to college. Frankly, that made no difference at my house. College was never discussed or even mentioned, other than to say it was too expensive and a waste of time. Dad's unwavering support for higher education ended with high school.

Instead, it was a matter of convenience *and* academics that prompted the decision. Mother had been working at the Salant and Salant shirt factory in Henderson as a seamstress for four years and would remain there until she had completed 17 years. She had seen the new Chester County High School being built across town. Mr. Averitt, the plant manager, discussed the strong academic program at CCHS and urged her to send me there. That resolved the dilemma. I'd drive her to the factory in the morning in the '37 Model Ford, attend classes, then pick her up after school.

This decision pleased me, but for a reason other than taking Mother to work. I thought Chester County High was Eddy Arnold's alma mater. Most people think he graduated from there. Eddy assured me at his 84th birthday celebration at the State Capital Building years later that he grew up in Chester County, but graduated from Pinson High School. Living on the county line, he was closer to Pinson than Henderson and could ride the Pinson school bus to school.

I was never an honor roll student, but I was good enough, made mostly B's, and managed to keep up with my farm chores and the odd jobs. I'd drop Mother and four of her colleagues off at 6:45 in the morning. An hour later, I'd taxi four teachers and my third cousin, Sharon, to school.

For this, I got 25 cents a person each week, but some of that was spent ("lost" might be a better word) at the pool hall in Henderson, an early morning excursion into the shady realm of small-stakes gambling jammed in-between the two rounds of my shuttle service.

Very small stakes, mind you—about a nickel or dime a game. Mother knew I went there, and tolerated it, probably because the two brothers who ran the place were genuinely nice guys, friendly and above-board, despite the iffy reputation that pool halls had at the time. She probably guessed that I was not always playing just for fun, as she must have known a dime-a-game wager was the norm. She never brought it up.

The summer of 1950 was filled with lots of hard work on the farm, repairing radios for gas money (I turned 16 in March, and Mother would let me have the Chevy from time to time), entertaining at fundraisers, and dating Bobbie Jo Maness. Mother had told me about her friend, Elizabeth Maness, and Edith's cute, sweet, and bubbly daughter who was a cheerleader. For the first time, I was in love.

Bobbie's mother thought we were the perfect couple, never hesitated to say so, and had us practically married from the moment we met. She was like a second mother, feeding me wonderful meals and treating me as though I could do no wrong.

Bobbie Jo and I dated all through high school, and continued the relationship even when I went away to college. She and her whole family were a joy.

We were blessed with great teachers at CCHS, and A.C. Jones was my favorite. To refer to A.C. as merely a schoolteacher, and stop at that, is like saying Eddy Arnold was just a singer. It leaves out so much.

A.C. was a remarkable man. He was a taskmaster, even a perfectionist, and he was relentlessly upbeat. He got me on the debate team, got me involved in social activities like the Future Farmers of America, and got me some interesting singing gigs with my guitar.

"You can do it," he always said, no matter what challenge I was facing at the time.

The debate team traveled all over Tennessee and won the state championship. Those playing gigs took me to square dances, hog calls, county fairs, and church socials all over the area, from Nashville to Memphis. A.C. introduced me to Freddie Melton, another guitar player, who was to become a constant companion. He and I split the collection money—sometimes nothing and sometimes ten bucks or even more. (The recent top country song, "She Was," was written by Freddie Melton's son Jimmy about his parents.)

All of these experiences increased my confidence. A.C. soon became the first true mentor in my life. He loved country music. Would he have given me the time and encouragement if I had not been a guitar picker? I think he would. His wife Alma was my typing instructor, and the two of them became my lifelong friends.

Chester County High had a reputation as tough and disciplined, with zero tolerance for any shenanigans. James Williams was the principal, and I knew him already, since he worked with Dad during summers at the cattle auction. Mr. Williams was stern, strict, a devout member of the Church of Christ, and he ruled Chester County High with an iron hand.

His religion was definitely part of the grand plan, even on prom night. He let us dance, but only at a distance—arm's length—and you could touch a girl's hands but nothing more. Touch a girl's waist, and you were in deep trouble.

A.C. and Kathryn Baker hosted debates by the Future Farmers of America and the Future Homemakers of America, respectively. Teams from schools in our regions competed before judges, with each team debating parliamentary procedure as defined by *Robert's Rules of Order*. (How did A.C. know that I would need that experience as chairman of CMH?) On this particular occasion, our school had won both the FFA and FHA competitions, and we were ready to party.

After the competition, there was to be a social hour with square dancing in the new CCHS gym. The visiting teams were unaware of the local rule that the boy was not to put his arm around the girl's waist during the "swing your partner" call, and resorted to their "back home" dance behavior. Seeing the fun, Bobbie and I adapted to their swings. A.C. and Kathryn were busy with refreshments at the time and conveniently did not notice as others joined in. It was great fun!

But Mr. Williams, always on the prowl during school social events, suddenly stopped the music. The next thing we heard was Mr. Williams saying, "The party's over." He shut us down. A.C. and Kathryn were embarrassed since they were in charge. We were distracted, but within 15 minutes, most of us were down at the darkest corner of the football field, where Mr. Williams' rules were not applicable.

I always felt that going overboard with religion often back-fired. Like Mr. Williams at the party—it seemed to provoke, even magnify, the precise behavior that was supposedly so sinful. Mother and Dad, moderately religious people, said grace only when we had guests. We went to church every week for a while after getting charged up at our annual revival—then, gradually, we'd backslide to just once or twice a month.

Our Methodist church was very hardcore fundamentalist, with lots of hellfire and brimstone, preachers who hollered, end-less warnings about eternal damnation, and ongoing condemna-tion of smoking, drinking, dancing, playing cards, going to movies—anything, it seemed, that had a reasonable expectation to be remotely enjoyable or amusing.

I did go down the altar at New Church at the age of 12 at a revival meeting, but frankly, I don't remember much else about that moment. I suppose that was my salvation experience. After that walk down the aisle, they baptized me (sprinkled, not sub-merged). This offended Grandmother Clayton, who wanted me dunked, and prompted much debate between her and Mother.

Even then, I had a real problem reconciling the contradictory concept of a God who loves us, but would cast us into hell if we weren't saved—especially since so many Christian denominations seem to have a different spin on salvation anyway.

One thing they seem to have in common—each one has the Truth, no one else. It still bothers me, these all-knowing people, claiming a personal pipeline to God Almighty, waving their version of the Bible in one hand and a collection plate in the other.

At our Methodist church and at Chester County High, our African-American friends did not attend, even though a number of black students qualified to attend our school. I never saw a black kid at Finger Junior High either. Segregation, of course, was still in practice, especially in the South, and it would sadly continue for years. There was a small African-American school in Chester County, Vincent High, just outside Henderson.

We enjoyed getting to know the black farm workers. Some of the workers were our neighbors, and we became fast friends and playmates. Once in a while, Dad would provide some work by the day on our farm for our newfound black neighbors. My parents had none of the prejudice of the time, and Dad treated all field hands exactly the same, black or white. In fact, perhaps knowing their hardships, he went out of his way to be kind.

When in the fields, Dad insisted all of his workers, white or black, drink out of the same dipper and water bucket. In those days, even public water fountains were separate, with one labeled "White" and the other "Colored." It was interesting to see some white people go to considerable effort to keep from touching the common gourd dipper.

Dad's one lapse was his use of the word "darkies," but I know for a fact that Dad never meant that in a disparaging way, and probably thought it was an enlightened, maybe even edifying term. Sadly, when compared to the usual epithets that many whites used when referring to blacks, it was.

That said, I can honestly tell you that I never heard of the Ku Klux Klan while growing up.

Before leaving this topic, I want to share an article that I wrote for the Summer 1998 *Clayton NOW* quarterly newsletter. I think the article clearly conveys the Clayton family and corporate cultural views on equality and diversity.

Remembering Rory

In our small, red clay cotton patch in West Tennessee back in 1940, I picked cotton with my 6-year-old best friend and neighbor, Rory. He and his family were sharecroppers just like us.

August would inevitably find us under a hot summer sun picking cotton. To quench our thirsts, we all dipped the same gourd dipper into the same oaken water bucket. Dad saw no reason to take two buckets to the fields, but a short distance from our tiny farms in the little town of Jackson, Tennessee, we would have had to drink from separate water fountains: one labeled "Colored" and the other labeled "White." Those water fountains would remain that way for another 25 years.

For our African-American neighbors, this was just one injustice of many that they were forced to endure. I can remember a Christmas when Rory's family rode the Greyhound to visit grandparents in Memphis. They sat in the back of the bus—no choice. That's the way it was during those years.

Memories of Rory, his family, and those times flooded back the other day as a friend recounted a recent, jarring experience. I'd like to share his story with you.

My friend, a respected Chief Executive Officer of a NYSE corporation, received a call from an analyst whom he had not seen in many years. The caller told him of an event that had happened several years earlier.

To this CEO, the analyst said, "While visiting your company with an Orthodox Jewish investor, one of your corporate officers remarked, 'Our company never hires Jewish people; we only hire good Christians!'"

During their phone conversation, the analyst noted how the remark had made him sick to his stomach.

"As a result of that awful manager's ugly comment, I've not bought your stock or that of any company who's hired him since."

My friend's experience gave me pause to reflect upon the richness and depth of perspective that diversity has brought to our company. But why share these ponderings with you? Well, I'm troubled when I consider how much further along we could be on the journey.

We need talent, all brands of talent. We need unique individuals with unique talents worthy of development to the fullest. When we go recruiting, we must use the glasses with the strongest filters—those that make us blind to political, religious, racial, and other differences. Sure, we can be discriminating when determining if a potential team member shares our values. After all, we should be "singing from the same hymnal." Our value statements are our hymnal.

In examining our value statements, we see three values directly relevant to the issue at hand. They urge us to:

- Emphasize our strengths in a positive environment.
- Respect and protect the rights and dignity of one another.
- Embrace and leverage change as a strategic advantage.

Our values must guide our actions. We can transform and transcend damaging, learned biases. My vision is to attract greater diversity as our company continues to grow. We must do a better job of attracting and keeping team members who can enrich our culture. It is the right thing to do. It is what works best, too.

Every person deserves the support, respect, and kindness called for in Clayton Homes' value statements. At almost every gathering, we state this credo in unison: Our lives work only to the extent that we are willing to keep our agreements. Let's fully recognize that our values require us to keep our agreements, all of our agreements.

Can we agree that individually, and as a company, we will examine our thinking and actions while making sure that we manage our natural biases and prejudices in such a way that we never discriminate? Agreed?

If you ever hear one of our people say or do anything that

amounts to discrimination, report it to your manager. Should you find your supervisor is involved in such an act, immediately call 877-858-HELP (4357). Your anonymity will be respected.

Yes, we have come a long way; however, we all must pitch in and uphold the values of Clayton until that perfect day when Clayton achieves zero discrimination.

When Rory's father answered the call to serve his country during World War II, his family moved, and we never saw each other again. I would give my next paycheck for a visit with Rory. What a great playmate and friend.

How good and pleasant it is when brothers live together in unity!
—Psalm 133:1

Hesitantly, I asked, "Dad, could I borrow the car for a few minutes?" I shifted my weight from side to side. "Malcolm needs a ride."

Dad liked my friend from school a lot, but he was still wary about loaning me the car. The dirt roads weren't good when dry, but after the downpour earlier that day, the road could be slick and muddy. That car was his pride and joy—shiny, spotless, and in mint condition.

"You can take him a mile down the road, that's all," he said.

The first mile of the journey went well. I took pity on my friend, who still had four more to go before he made it home. *It'll be fine*, I thought. *I'll go a little further. The road doesn't look as bad as Dad said. He'll never know. I'll just drive a little faster to make up for the lost time.*

Nearly two miles into the trip, I rounded a sharp curve and did not see the slick spot. I lost control as Dad's car skidded off the muddy road, plowed into a briar thicket, and flipped *on its side*.

Malcolm was flat against the right door, and I was on top of him. We both seemed to be fine as we climbed out the driver's door—now the top of the car.

It could've been worse, I guess, but the car's right rear fender had a big dent, and there were several little scratches.

This can't be happening, I thought. *How, in God's name, am I going to tell Dad?*

Two loggers stopped by and helped us upright the car. It seemed fine mechanically. Malcolm walked east as I carefully drove west, the long mile home. As I drove up, Dad came outside. He walked around the car. Saw the dent. Saw the scratches. Then he walked around it some more. He said nothing.

I was dying. Squirming. All I could say was, "Really sorry, Dad. Really, *really* sorry." The defense rests. To be sure, I was more than a bit reckless that night, but my intentions were good. True, I realize the "road to hell" is paved with "good intentions." But if the roads around Finger had been paved, this hell I was going through wouldn't have occurred.

Dad didn't scream. Nor did he lecture. He didn't whip me, and if there was ever a time, this was it. Instead, without saying a word, he turned around and walked back into the house.

It would have been better if he had just thrashed me good. But he left me in limbo to contemplate the horrible punishment he would conjure up. What he did was worse than a whipping.

He simply kept driving the car—without fixing the dent.

Every time I saw it—which was virtually every day—I had to relive that terrible night. I was enormously relieved, some months later, when he traded it in for a 1940 Chevrolet sedan.

Usually, traumatic stories like this mellow with age. Sometimes, they even become a cherished part of family lore—an always reliable source of amusement at family reunions, Thanksgiving dinners, and Christmas get-togethers, no matter how many times the tale is told. That happened with the soot story. Mother will tell that story at the drop of a hat, even today.

The '37 Ford story was not to be told. Not later, not ever, not even decades down the road. Dad never found it amusing. In fact, neither he nor I ever said another word about it.

CHAPTER 3

Memphis Blues

That dream of standing center stage at the Grand Ole Opry stuck in my mind and replayed time and time again. I told Bobbie Jo about it—Mother and Grandmother Clayton, too. They were too kind to laugh or make sport of my ambition. If anything, their comments were encouraging. But down deep, I thought they were just humoring me—indulging the hopeless fantasies of a country boy, even though my picking was clearly more than a passing fancy. I had been at it for nearly 10 years.

I was 16 and entering the 11th grade when I got my first big break as a performer. WDXI, the radio station in Jackson, only 25 miles away, had a live program on Saturdays called the *Farm and Home Show*. The show had been popular for 25 years, running from seven in the morning until one in the afternoon. It was exclusively for local performers who would carve out half-hour blocks for themselves within that six-hour slot.

Though all this was news to me, the revelation that I could be the star of my very own radio program thrilled me. It didn't hurt that WDXI was no "teakettle" station—it was a 10,000 watter, reaching Nashville, Huntsville, the outskirts of Memphis, and into Mississippi.

It was also the station that provided the springboard to Eddy Arnold's early career. He too began on the *Farm and Home Show.* I decided to audition.

It helped that I knew "Uncle" Tom Williams, the producer and general manager of the popular and profitable radio show. His son, James Williams, was my high school principal and worked part-time with Dad at the Kenneth Woods Cattle Auction at Henderson. Uncle Tom had dropped by the office at the Sale Barn when I was there with Dad. I remembered him well and thought he would remember Dad.

Along with his other duties, Uncle Tom booked the talent for the Saturday shows and was an on-the-air announcer. He was, in effect, the Ed Sullivan of West Tennessee.

Tom was friendly, well respected, and willing to give me a chance, 11th grader or not. My audition went well, and he told me I could have my own half-hour show, provided I'd bring in some sponsors to help pay for the air-time.

To me, this seemed more than reasonable. I landed two sponsors immediately—Junior Tolbert, an old family friend who ran the general merchandise store in Finger, and Charlie Skinner, one of my uncles who operated a popular general store and the post office in nearby Montezuma. Each commercial was "a dollar a holler," sixty seconds for a buck.

Eventually, I sold half of the show's eight spots, with Tom Williams taking care of the rest. I was not paid for performing, nor did I receive a commission for selling the commercials. Later, I learned there were actually two ways to get your own half-hour show on the *Farm and Home Hour.* First, like Eddy Arnold, you had to be talented. Since I did not meet that qualification, I had to go to rule two to get on the air. Fortunately, Uncle Tom's second route to stardom—selling spots for a dollar a holler—was workable for me.

So it wasn't like WDXI took advantage of a young kid, having me work for free and all. I considered myself lucky, pay or no pay, to be the "star" of my own radio show at age 16.

I was my own producer, account executive, assistant engineer, chief copywriter, and transportation captain, with the chance to learn lots of new people skills. Shoestring operations offer tremendous opportunity. You have no choice but to learn everything.

I brought in the members of my original band, Francis the yodeler and her two brothers, Bobby and Dennis, along with my buddy, Freddie Melton—and basically copied other programs. We'd do maybe eight country songs like "I'll Hold You In My Heart," "Red River Valley," or "Back In The Saddle Again," then close with a hymn like "Old Rugged Cross" or "Rock of Ages." I did the chatter, introducing the songs and read, with some ad-libbing, the commercials.

The station and Uncle Tom provided a comfortable, informal atmosphere. Unlike most newcomers, I was rarely nervous. After all, I was already a reasonably seasoned performer with dozens of credits, even if they were just church socials and county fairs. Even the sophisticated gadgetry at the station didn't intimidate me, since I was already halfway through a correspondence course on radio theory and repair.

The experience at WDXI would grow into a college meal ticket for this "cotton picker."

We'd start the show with our theme song, "Lamp Lighting Time Down in Dixie," something I'd written a year earlier. I'll spare you the lyrics. The band would begin picking in the background, while our staff announcer Wink Martindale (remember the popular network game show host?) boomed out, *"And now, from Finger, Tennessee—Lee Clayton and the Dixie Plowhands!"*

Wink Martindale was, and still is, one of the most personable people on the planet. Being one of TV's most popular and long-running game show hosts, I think he's done more shows than anybody, about 20 at last count: *Tic Tac Dough, Gambit, High Rollers, Debt,* and *Trivial Pursuit,* to name only a few.

I'd watch for Wink through the studio glass to give us our

cues, and after the show, he'd motion us back to chat in the control room. He was exceptionally nice to everyone, especially Mother, who enjoyed all the flattery and attention Wink bestowed upon her.

I didn't know the term then, but WDXI became my "loss leader." Maybe I didn't make any money from the program itself, but it brought in other work and gave me a certain cachet. The people running those church socials and county fairs heard my show and suddenly saw me in a special light, as a star in some cases. No longer was I some ordinary, amateur singer-picker. I got my first taste of celebrity recognition, and I loved it.

Incidentally, WDXI had staff musicians on hand to accommodate their "stars." We could bring all our own band members, part of a band, or the station would furnish basic musicians—keyboard, guitar, and bass. At a moment's notice, they'd play backup for any of the Saturday morning performers.

There was a staff lead guitar player, a little older than the rest of us, who was awesome. Obviously, he could outplay anyone in our band blindfolded, so I asked him to play with us each Saturday morning.

We developed a great rapport, and he was extremely accommodating, even though I was a rank amateur. Like me, he was a sharecropper's son. His dad made his first guitar from a cigar box with a broom handle and bailing wire as basic components. Now he had a quality guitar and could he make it talk. Like Wink Martindale, he was a class act.

Within five years, this fellow became one of the original recording artists at Sun Records in Memphis. He sang with Elvis Presley, Johnny Cash, Roy Orbison, and Jerry Lee Lewis. In 1956, he scribbled out a song on a potato sack and called it "Blue Suede Shoes." His recording of it sold 2 million copies. He became one of the great fathers of rockabilly music. Jackson, Tennessee, his hometown, named the convention center and a highway after this star. The Beatles idolized him.

That man, who was so good to me, and who supported my show with his remarkable talents every Saturday morning for two years, was the great Carl Perkins.

More than 10 years had passed since that horrific tornado ripped through our community and killed one of our neighbors. In March 1952, it would happen again, and this time it would be much worse—the Storm of the Century.

It hit on an unseasonably humid Friday night. Bobbie Jo and I were at a Chester County High basketball game, double-dating with a buddy of mine, Donald Smith, and his girlfriend.

As I left Donald at his home after dropping off his girlfriend— they all lived in Henderson—a violent electrical storm was lighting up the night sky. Bobbie Jo, in particular, became quite frightened. As I said my goodnights to her, I reached for one more kiss as she said, "Lee, please hurry home. I am so scared for you."

The tornado struck just after eleven o'clock while I was on the way back to Finger. I had left Bobbie Jo's house just in time, and I often wonder if the few extra minutes I wanted to spend with her might have placed me right in the path of this monster of a storm. Bobbie Jo's comment could have saved my life.

The storm cut right through Henderson, destroying a large residential area. They called out the National Guard; the Red Cross opened a shelter for the homeless.

Bobbie Jo and her family were lucky to be alive. The tornado's eye missed their house, but the outer edge of the storm was so strong that the back corner of their home was demolished. Many of her neighbors had it much worse. It took days to find all the bodies, and there is nothing sadder than to see a parent wandering amidst devastation, looking for a missing child.

That storm killed 24 people. One of them was Donald Smith— both his parents, too. His death devastated our class. It was especially hard to accept his death since I had dropped him off at his house literally minutes before he died. That house was obliterated, and Donald and his parents were gone.

Weeks later, someone found an envelope with Donald's name on it lying on the ground in Humphries County, which is 75 miles from Henderson. Inside the envelope were Kodak negatives. A local photographer developed them and found pictures of his family and neighborhood friends that he had taken the weekend before his death. The storm had taken his envelope that far.

As soon as telephone service was restored, a call came in from Eddy Arnold offering support. Eddy suggested a benefit concert, with all proceeds going to the local Red Cross. The *Chester County Independent* called it a "splendid gesture" from a famous entertainer who remembered his hometown.

Being a huge fan of Eddy Arnold, I was thrilled to be asked to serve on the show committee. Once again, A.C. Jones, always thinking of me, had a hand in that. He knew my familiarity with sound systems and music production would be helpful.

But my excitement at the prospect of meeting Eddy Arnold was tempered by the terrible tragedy that was making such an event possible.

Finally the day of the concert came, and they assigned me to be Eddy's assistant during the rehearsal and sound check. He seemed in great spirits, and somehow managed to be glamorous and down-to-earth at the same time—just another good ole boy, cutting up and clowning around with the guys in his band.

Eventually, there was a break in the action and a chance to slip in a word, and I had to say something to him—anything. So I said, "Mr. Arnold, I sure hope you're gonna do 'I'll Hold You In My Heart Tonight.'" That was one of Eddy's best, the No. 1 country record in 1949, and one of my personal favorites.

And he said, "Heck, I haven't sung that song since I recorded it. I don't think I can even remember the words."

His response left me reeling—*he couldn't remember the words?* Why, *I* knew them by heart. I knew *all* the words to *all* his songs. Still do, more than 50 years later.

And that was it. Eddy went back to rehearsing. It certainly

wasn't a disagreeable exchange, but I could not get over him not knowing the words to that great hit.

I guess if I had my way, we would've sat down for a nice, long chat—ideally three or four hours—time enough to discuss, in detail, my hopes and dreams. I wanted to click with him, maybe even experience, if only for a moment, some of the camaraderie he had with his band. I was so envious of his confidence and the ease in which he went about all the details in rehearsing for a show.

After all, we had a lot in common: two dirt-poor West Tennessee plowboys turned musicians, although I'd concede to Eddy the edge in talent. As I watched him kid around with his pals, I felt like an outsider, my nose pressed against the proverbial window. So close and yet so far.

It was no fault of Eddy's, but our two-sentence conversation left me aching. Did that moment challenge me to press harder for success? I think so. Eddy and I would have our three-hour chat on his 84th birthday, May 15, 2002, in Governor Sundquist's chambers in the State Capital.

Mother and Grandmother Clayton loved the radio show. They always offered suggestions and told me how good I sang. Uncle Charlie Skinner, L.E. Talbott, and the other sponsors seemed pleased with their sponsorship. I would call them each week to ensure that my copy was consistent with their inventory, flyers, postings, or other ads.

Bobbie Jo never missed a show either, in person or by radio. Sometimes her cheerleading commitments kept her from making the 15-mile trip to the WDXI studios each Saturday.

Dad never said much to me about the radio show, though I knew he listened some Saturdays if bad weather kept him inside.

There was a brief moment when I wondered if things were warming up between us, when I happened to overhear a conversation at the Finger Service Station. Dad, who thought I was outside, got into a conversation with a neighbor who asked if I repaired radios. Dad said, "Lee's really good at fixing most anything that can go wrong with 'em."

Yes, Dad finally gave me a compliment in a roundabout way.

That was all it was, but I can't begin to describe the good feelings that washed over me when Dad said that. He didn't think I had heard him, and I surely didn't bring it up to him later, so afraid was I to break the spell.

Maybe I was craving a repeat performance of this warm, fuzzy moment on the day I decided to personally upgrade Dad's old green Chevy pickup. Believing he had confidence in my radio knowledge, I thought he would enjoy having news, music, and my Saturday program in his truck. During our lunch break under a big oak at the edge of the cotton patch, I went to the truck and quietly fastened a used radio neatly in the dash. It worked perfectly. I couldn't wait to tell Dad his good fortune. Wrong! He felt violated, saying, "If I'd wanted a radio, I'd have bought one."

Of course, I didn't ask permission first. Didn't think I needed to. Besides, like the aborted plan to pipe beautiful music through the house, I wanted this to be a surprise. Once again, it was.

Based on Dad's reaction, someone passing by would've thought I had spit on the car. He became upset the moment I mentioned the radio and went into a rage when he heard my defense argument. Darn, I should have found a more appropriate stage for this scene, because Dad had to take only six steps to reach the peach tree. With one pass, his Barlow knife cut a man-eating peach tree switch, and it was pointed at my young butt.

Now *that* draws the line, I thought. Here I am, in high school, driving, dating, and earning my own money. I was even a *radio star*. No way he was going to switch me, especially for my well-intentioned act.

"You're not gonna whip me now, and you're never gonna whip me again," I said, with some bravado. True, I said it while I was running from him. That may not sound particularly courageous, not exactly on the order of Churchill telling the Germans to go to hell, but considering that I'd never talked back to Dad in my entire life, this was the ultimate defiance.

Dad made a couple of token efforts to chase me down, but barefoot and 130 pounds, in the freshly plowed field, I could easily stay out of peach-tree-switch range. Out of breath, Dad yelled, "Come back here and take your whipping like a man."

I failed to see the correlation between the two.

Finally he gave up, went back to work, but lectured me later as we rode home, making it painfully clear that if he wanted a radio in his truck, he sure didn't need *me* to install one. He'd take care of it himself, and frankly, *he didn't want a radio in his truck anyway.* Me, I was still in a defiant mood, though not defiant enough to ask if I could turn on the radio.

As to the old Chevy truck, I removed the radio before going to bed and made sure Dad never saw it again. He would trade the truck for a new Chevy pickup soon after I moved to Memphis. Yes, the truck would have a deluxe, pushbutton Chevy radio.

In fairness to Dad, he was having a rough time on the farm then, even rougher than usual. The cotton crop had been mediocre for two years straight, and the boll weevils were eating us up. They would depend more and more on weekly paychecks—Mother's from the shirt factory, and Dad's from the cattle auction.

Just as bad, hog prices had crashed. By that time, I had a small herd of my own, yet another Future Farmers of America project sustained with a loan from Grandfather Clayton. As luck would have it, my animals became ready for market precisely when hog prices hit bottom. After I paid off the loan to my grandfather, I had $20 in profits for a year of work.

Grandfather Clayton waived the 3 percent interest charge.

For me, at age 18, it was the final straw. I knew when I was nine that I didn't want to be a farmer, and my experience over the last nine years confirmed that I wasn't cut out for that career path.

As I saw it, there were three ways to escape—join the military, move to Detroit to build cars, or become the next Eddy Arnold. I knew the final option would take some time, a lot of luck, and a vast enhancement of my musical abilities.

Some of my buddies had signed up for the service, and I was leaning toward the Air Force when Mother bluntly told me she was unequivocally opposed to the military solution. She urged me to find something else, something closer to home.

I got my diploma at Chester County High's graduation cere-monies in June 1952, wearing a used suit bought at the second-hand store. The next day, I said goodbye to my family and Bobbie Jo, borrowed the family car, and took off with a classmate, Billy Joe Naylor, the vice president of my graduating class. We were headed for the Big City: Memphis. I wanted to appease Mother, but only if I could find a job that distanced me from the farm.

Most of all, I wanted to get away from that woebegone dirt farm. Even Dad, who once had such high hopes to hitch me to the cotton patch with my own team of mules, understood.

The state unemployment office was a big help. By the end of the first day, I'd been interviewed four times and had two offers. One was a welding job, with a good company, good bene-fits, and good pay.

The other was with the local utility, Memphis Light, Gas and Water. It paid a quarter an hour less, but the open slot was for my specialty: repairing radios. More specifically, fixing the two-way mobile radios that the line trucks and other vehicles used to com-municate with headquarters and staff members in the field.

It wasn't quite my dream job, but I took it. The company hired Billy Joe, too, in an administrative desk job in a building near mine on Walnut Street.

Next was a place to live, and we found a room at a boarding house for nine bucks a week, which included three meals a day—scrambled eggs and toast for breakfast, a bowl of stew for dinner, and peanut butter and jelly sandwiches in a "poke" (brown bag) for lunch. Then, we made a quick trip back home to pack our belongings and tell everyone the good news. Dad and I went car shopping, and he loaned me half the cost of a green '41 Chevrolet coupe, priced at $245.

Already, I had digs, wheels, work, and would soon have money. Joining the Air Force was forgotten, and Billy Joe and I had found that this leaving-the-nest challenge was working out pretty well. Little did I know.

On my first day at Memphis Light, Gas and Water, I found myself working in the basement garage of a utility building three levels down. This really was starting at the bottom. What had happened to the air-conditioned offices and repair benches where I was interviewed?

Surrounding me, in the damp dingy basement were piles of dusty old radios, cables, microphones, transmitters, and receivers, many of which were rusty. My supervisor deposited a five-gallon can of carbon tetrachloride beside the boxes along with a huge box of rags. My job was to clean every item down there with that highly toxic chemical.

Now I got it: my new job description was "rag wiper." Actually, not even that—I was a trainee. Someday, I thought, I'd be a *professional* rag wiper.

It was dark, dirty, dingy, depressing, and good that I did not know how dangerous it must have been. For eight hours a day, I was in this underground garage with no ventilation, breathing in those poisonous fumes.

OSHA was not in existence and wouldn't be until President Nixon signed the bill into law on December 29, 1970. Naturally, I had no gloves or face mask. Every now and then, I'd actually wonder if the farm wasn't better than this. Any such thoughts, however, I'd attribute to temporary delirium caused by the chemical. (And can you imagine what a plaintiff attorney would do with a case like this today?)

Harsh as it was, the work hours were good. That part, at least, was like a holiday to me. Five days a week, eight to five, with weekends off, a snap compared to the farm. I felt like I had lots of spare time and like I had to be busy every minute learning or earning money.

Dink, one of the guys at work, was moonlighting, repairing TVs in his garage, and I helped him out a couple times a week. A honky-tonk club 50 miles from Memphis was short a band member, so I auditioned and won the three-nights-a-week gig.

The band was fun and profitable, and I made 20 bucks a night. I knew honky-tonks could be trouble, but this one seemed quite tame. I'd been chatting during breaks with a young lady who came each Saturday night. She was petite, dark-haired, cute, and sweet. I enjoyed the attention, and I suppose she was beginning to like me. She was with a group and danced with different people.

She came up as usual during the break, and we danced to Jim Reeves singing "Four Walls." Our eyes remained locked as I strapped on my guitar, took to the stage, caressed the microphone, and began singing "Careless Love" to her.

Love, oh love, careless love. See what love has done to me.

Suddenly my attention was diverted by a dark, hulking figure emerging from the shadows and heading my direction—her boyfriend. How could I believe this beautiful, young chick would not have a boyfriend? How naïve! Up until that moment, I didn't know he existed. Apparently, he had seen our flirting. He looked perturbed. In fact, he was mad as the devil.

What's more, he had a long neck Budweiser bottle, half full, in his hand, pointed directly at me. *He's gonna pop me upside the head*, I thought, and I raised my guitar just in time to cover my face.

I was okay, but the guitar wasn't; he gave it a six-inch long crack. A shame too—it was a Martin D28, a darn fine instrument. His beer bottle remained intact. I wanted to remain intact too, so within two minutes, two band members and the bouncer escorted me to my Chevy. Jim had left the building. I was back the following Thursday night with the cracked D28. We were both back on Saturday, but did not speak. The big bully never came out of the dark corner all night.

I also sold vacuum cleaners for a while, door-to-door in the evenings, when I wasn't repairing TVs or playing honky-tonk. I realize that vacuum cleaner salespeople have a reputation for over-the-top, aggressive behavior reminiscent of the way a shark circles and ultimately devours unsuspecting prey. But believe me, there is another species even more aggressive, and that's a vacuum cleaner sales manager.

The guy who recruited me was good, real good. He explained two pay plans, and offered me the right to decide between the two. Either take a cash commission, right after the sale or get a higher commission. There was one catch: commission payments would be made monthly as my customers paid their installment payments. His chart showing higher commissions and the monthly income available to me, an 18 year old, was impressive. I took the annuity payment commission plan and sold a bunch of Rex Aire (now Rainbow) vacuums right away—Mother and Uncle R.C. were two of my early customers.

After building up a nice residual, I eagerly looked for the monthly commission checks to roll in. I got a couple, and then they stopped. I called the company, thinking there must be some sort of mistake. There was, and I had made it.

They waved the contract at me and suggested I read the fine print. I discovered that any month I didn't make a sale, I wouldn't receive a residual commission check. In order to be paid for my previous sales, I'd have to sell vacuums forever. My friend, the sales manager, never mentioned this glitch in the contract.

I guess they thought it was a clever little trick to play on naïve and trusting kids, who typically worked more than one part-time job, juggled their schedules to increase cash flow, took people on their word, and, yes, failed to read the three-point type buried in their work agreement. I had counted on that income; I was cheated out of hard earned commissions, even on my Mother's machine.

I hope management at CMH will always remember the lesson

from this story—how important a creditable pay plan is to any worker. That one incident had considerable impact in shaping our business standards. I'd remember my anger, years later, when I was designing the commission programs for my salespeople. There's no small print, no "gotchas," no murky language. The program doesn't allow for "wiggle room," and everyone is paid in full and on time.

Frequently you will hear a salesperson say, "I left that company because they *pencil your pay*." Translated, this means the salesperson did not receive the compensation expected. At CMH, we make it simple. The salesperson calculates the commission, gets it approved by the manager, and transmits the pay summary to bookkeeping. The paycheck will be to the penny the amount requested, unless an error is found. In that case, bookkeeping and the salesperson will reach a new agreement in time for the pay request to be corrected. In conclusion, the salesperson can't have unrealized expectations or surprises as to compensation received.

In turn, our salespeople must treat our customers the same way. They are required to go to great effort to avoid the appearance of the slightest impropriety. If it means disappointing the customer in any way, I'd rather not make the sale. In fact, the sales academy teaches that a sale in which the customer will be disappointed must be aborted. Refusing a sale is far less of a problem than making the sale to a customer who will regret their purchase.

Despite the debacle with the vacuum cleaners—not to mention the monotonous dust wiping at the utility company—it was a wonderful summer. I even managed to keep the Saturday radio show going, though at a different station, one closer to home.

KWEM was in West Memphis, just across the Arkansas border. Once again, I was in a long block of shows hosted by local performers looking for a break. I still did the program for free, but at least I didn't have to sell the commercials.

One footnote about my time at KWEM: I met this guy who was on one of the Saturday shows, one that aired a couple hours before mine. He was a singer, but not the headliner.

He'd be leaving as I came in, and we'd say hello in the hallway. We never struck up a long conversation, much less a friendship— he seemed shy, quiet, and remote, not really approachable, and definitely not charismatic. Frankly, he barely registered with me.

He was Elvis Presley.

Elvis may not have made much of an impression on me, but a guy named Bill Elliott did. Bill was a colleague at Memphis Light, Gas and Water, an electrical engineer, a few years older than me, and on a fast track with the company.

Bill was bright, affable, and the only guy in the shop with a college degree. He knew what that could mean to my earning power. We talked a lot. Not surprisingly, he talked me into college.

Until Bill came along, the thought never crossed my mind.

The first item on Bill's agenda was for me to obtain my license as a Radio Operator with the Federal Communications Commission. With Bill's coaching, I was ready for the test by the next quarterly testing event in Memphis. I passed and soon received a raise in pay as a result.

Bill, on Saturday morning, gave me a tour of the Memphis State Campus, where we saw a neat and well-maintained facility. We went back on Monday at lunch and worked out a schedule. I'd go to school in the morning taking pre-engineering classes, then work at the utility company in the afternoon. In September 1952, I moved out of the boarding house into a brand-new college dorm. Actually, it was a suite with four bedrooms, one large bathroom, and a shared living room that even had a TV.

It became obvious that my "To-Do" list was way out of control.

College classes, my homework, the utility company, the TV repair job, the honky-tonk, the radio show. Plus, every other weekend I was still dating Bobbie Jo, who was finishing up high school in Henderson, *and* beginning to see another girl, Peggy, who worked for the phone company in Memphis.

I had not gotten around to disclosing to either of the girlfriends that I was seeing someone else. In fact, I was expending considerable energy making sure it stayed that way. Within three months, it was clear that the candle I had been burning at both ends finally disintegrated. By Christmas, the right side of my face began twitching. Uncontrollably. And it wouldn't go away. Then suddenly, a few weeks later, the twitching moved to the right eye, and the side of my face became completely paralyzed.

It was as if half of my face had *died*. I'd flick my right cheek or pinch the skin on my face, and I wouldn't feel anything. I couldn't move the right side of my mouth; I couldn't smile; I couldn't close my right eye. I'd have to use my finger to lower the lid every few minutes; otherwise, my eye would be dry and uncomfortable.

For the first time in my life, I went to a doctor, actually, several doctors, along with some chiropractors. No one had a clue or offered any kind of therapy or treatment. They all acknowledged some kind of mysterious "nervous disorder" was at work, but that's as far as they got with a diagnosis. About all they could suggest is that I get more rest.

My condition made that easy. Because of my frozen face, I became a social recluse. I remained in school and kept my job at the utility company. I stopped playing honky-tonk. I quit the Saturday morning radio show. I saw way less of Bobbie Jo and Peggy—after all, I couldn't even kiss them.

The time off to relax and rest worked, but the paralysis remained for six forlorn months. By the following June, the twitch in the eye was gone and most of the paralysis. Over a few months, my face returned to normal, with all of the feeling intact.

Whatever it was (and it has never been diagnosed), I have sporadic recurrences of that numb feeling and even a slight twitch to this very day, in the same area on my face. It doesn't happen often, just when I'm really exhausted from travel or work. It's my signal to take off for a long weekend.

By the summer of 1953, Bill Elliott, by now my unofficial mentor, was nudging me to raise my educational and career expectations upward.

I had done well at Memphis State in drafting (how many floor plans have I drawn using these skills?) and in calculus, physics, chemistry, and liberal arts courses.

Bill asked me to consider applying for an electrical engineering degree at the University of Tennessee in Knoxville since they would accept all my credits from Memphis State. By alternating quarters between classes at UT and work at MLGW, I could finance my engineering degree without debt or having to work much, if any.

The co-op, work at MLGW, and study at Old Miss program had served Bill well. His third promotion in two years was announced just before I left.

What a mentor!

Bill also pushed me to get my first class radio license, required by the FCC to operate and maintain transmitters at commercial television and higher-powered radio stations. This, in particular, was a superb idea as TV was sweeping the country, absorbing engineering talent, and leaving a void in radio.

Only five years prior to this, television was a novelty, with barely 20,000 sets in use, all of them on the East Coast. Now nearly 200 TV stations were on the air, and that number would double by the end of 1954. A first class license would virtually assure me of a job in this exciting new industry—at a comfortable pay level.

I knew that the test, administered by the FCC, was really tough and rarely passed on the first attempt. I was running out of time to study, and would not have an opportunity to retest for several quarters. Quite a few of the guys I worked with at the utility company had tried and failed, all except Bill who "aced" it the first time. Mr. Dobson, our department manager, sat for the license two times in the 14 months I was there. When I left, he still had his second-class license, which met FCC requirements for all MLGW transmitters.

With Bill's help, I studied hard. By late summer, I was ready.

At 8:00 P.M., I boarded a train for New Orleans, got to the Federal Building at 8:00 A.M., finished the test by two that afternoon, took a tour of Bourbon Street, and rode the train all night so I could be back at work the next morning. No one knew I had been gone except Bill. A week later, my license arrived in the mail.

This, I thought, would be my meal ticket. About the same time, the University of Tennessee accepted my application. I packed the Chevy, left Memphis, and moved 400 miles to Knoxville. On my first day there, armed with a fresh first class license, I got a job as a transmitter operator for WNOX, a 10,000-watt radio station. I filled a slot left vacant when their engineer moved to WATE-TV. I took note of that fact.

I loved Knoxville at first sight: the lakes, mountains, rolling hills, and all the greenery. I was thrilled with the UT campus. Having arrived right in the middle of Rush Week, I was fascinated with all the attractive people on fraternity row.

Upon meeting Bud Pennington and Jim "Smooch" Daniels, I kept coming back to the Sigma Phi Epsilon fraternity. The rush list had me down as "James." All I heard at each frat house was "Hey, Jim." Not one time was I called Lee. In fact, for 50 years now I have been called Lee only when visiting Finger. Mother and Dad adapted to the naming after we exchanged a few visits. Joe helped facilitate their adjustment to my new identity.

I joined Sigma Phi Epsilon.

Meanwhile, that tangled web I wove with Bobbie Jo and Peggy was about to unravel.

Bobbie Jo graduated in June from CCHS, and I tried to entice her into joining me in Memphis and getting a job. Instead, she insisted on "having fun" with her friends for the summer. In September, as I moved to Knoxville, Bobbie Jo moved to Memphis, which triggered a most unfortunate scenario involving comedy and tragedy.

Bobbie Jo went to work for the phone company.

That's right—the *phone company*, where *Peggy*, my secret paramour, was employed and working in the *very same building!* The two still didn't know about each other. Both assumed I was their exclusive steady. I was sweating this one out as coolly as possible. "Brazen" might be another way to describe my behavior. I tried to sweet-talk both of them into visiting me in Knoxville, on separate weekends, obviously. Both agreed. This led to my undoing.

Peggy made a passing mention to a colleague about going to "see Lee in Knoxville," and her friend said something like, "Y'know, there's another girl who works here one floor down— she's got a guy in Knoxville too. You should talk to her. You could drive up together."

Uh-oh.

Bobbie Jo and Peggy did get together, and what a remarkable coincidence it was, discovering that their boyfriends had so much in common. Both named Lee. Both in Knoxville. Both at the University of Tennessee. Both taking classes in electrical engineering. Both played guitar. Both drove Chevys. Both grew up in Finger. . .hmmmm.

It took them maybe two minutes to figure out what I had done; I doubt they even had to compare Polaroids of their respective boyfriends. Soon, my phone rang. It was Peggy. She got right to the point.

"Lee, are you sure you really love me?"

"Oh yes. Yes, I do, Peggy. I really, really do."

Then another familiar voice came on the line. To my horror, the voice belonged to Bobbie Jo.

"Lee, *say that again.*"

I really don't remember anything about our conversation after that. To this day, it's a total blank. But I do know that I've never felt so embarrassed. Peggy never spoke to me again.

Bobbie Jo and I had a terrific weekend in Knoxville as I introduced her to the fraternity brothers, toured the campus, and showed her the TV station. I think both of us expected the relationship to blossom from this point. After all, we had a history together. She forgave me, and I was so grateful that she gave me a chance to apologize and make up.

It's a long way from Knoxville to Memphis. I would not see this wonderful person again for 25 years, and that was only for a quick lunch.

I met Mary Shelton on a blind date set up by a fraternity brother who was dating Mary's housemate. Like Bobbie Jo, she was pretty and intelligent, a freshman who had been a high school cheerleader. She was from a very religious family in Manchester, a little town about halfway between Nashville and Chattanooga. Her father was a Studebaker car dealer there. Her brother, Joe Powell, was an Oldsmobile car dealer in McMinnville, and Roger, her youngest brother, was attending Baptist Seminary in Louisville, Kentucky.

Mary was studying home economics, made very good grades, and loved the frequent social events sponsored by my fraternity. We had a great time going to movies, dances, and picnics.

It wasn't long before I gave her my fraternity pin and introduced her to my parents.

CHAPTER 4

Flying High

It was the spring of 1954, and even though I'd lived in Knoxville for half a year, my hectic schedule would not permit sightseeing. But now, with college classes on break, Mary visiting family in Manchester, and the eerie silence of an empty frat house, I finally had a day with nobody around and nothing to do. So I hopped in the Chevy and headed south toward the Smoky Mountains with no particular destination in mind, just out and about, exploring.

Driving south outside of Knoxville, I was soon near Alcoa looking straight ahead at the Smoky Mountains, gorgeous and lightly covered in a white haze as though wrapped in faded gauze—when something even more riveting caught my eye. It was a billboard: *See Knoxville By Air—$5—Cherokee Aviation.*

Never in my life had I been in an airplane. Not even near one. But I was curious to see what it was like, and I'd just gotten paid. Why not *really* see the countryside?

Turning toward the hanger, I saw a little yellow Piper Cub parked on the tarmac, and my casual curiosity gave way to downright enthusiasm. I think Bruce Powell, the pilot, sensed he had a live one, because he instantly made a second offer.

"For only ten dollars, you can have a flying lesson," he said.

Bruce's self-assurance, a carryover from his fighter pilot days during World War II, was infectious. I gave him a ten and climbed into the cockpit.

The Piper Cub was a two-seater, 65-horsepower, 1946 model. As I settled in, Bruce told me to press and hold the brake pedals; then he spun the wooden propeller by hand. I glanced at the mysterious gadgets on the tiny instrument panel, which were smaller than a car's dashboard.

While we taxied out, Bruce gave each of the gadgets a name: altimeter, air speed, turn, and bank. When we reached the start of the runway, Bruce pushed the throttle forward; we accelerated to 65 knots, and I felt the tiny wheels break from the pavement.

Within six minutes, we were at 3,000 feet, and Bruce surprised me by suggesting I take over the controls. A moment later, he casually said, "You're flying," like there was nothing to it.

It's hard to explain, but somehow, even though all this was new to me, I felt right at home in the Cub. Like I belonged.

After some demonstrations from Bruce, I did my first 90-degree right turn. Bruce said it was perfect, but reminded me to watch my altitude.

"We dropped 400 feet during that nice turn," he said, laughing. "Now how did that happen, Jim?"

Gotta watch that altimeter, I told myself.

Flying, I quickly learned, meant constant multi-tasking, not unlike managing a business. Making timely decisions, absorbing and assimilating information. I'm told the average F-16 pilot can process data from five different sources simultaneously. A Top Gun can do seven.

Obviously, I wasn't anywhere near either level, but I'd always been a quick study—I like to think so, anyway—so within 15 minutes, I was climbing, descending, and yes, even able to turn while maintaining altitude.

That hour wasn't enough for me, but my thin wallet brought

me back to Earth. I knew I couldn't afford regular lessons.

"Aren't you full-time at the University of Tennessee?" Bruce asked. He pointed to the fine print on his company flyer. Full-time students got a discount: 10 hours of training and two hours of college credit for $120, less than half the regular cost. I signed up.

After my sixth lesson, Bruce climbed out of the Cub, but told me to leave the engine running. I thought he just wanted to check something out before shutdown. Then he shouted over the roar of the engine: "It's all yours. Time to solo."

Uh-oh, I thought. I didn't think I'd be doing this so soon; Bruce said I wouldn't solo until my 10th lesson. Suddenly, that large runway, used by the big airliners every day, looked very small.

And intimidating.

I wondered if I was ready for this.

For a brief moment, my mind flashed on all the things that could go wrong. Then I thought of something Bruce had told me. With just me in the plane, the little Cub, which weighed only 800 pounds, would blast off like a rocket—lifting off quicker, climbing faster, and gliding further.

I'm glad I remembered. That plane practically jumped into the air. It was like flying a hot rod.

Climbing past 1,000 feet, I saw Bruce on the ground, and pointed the left wing tip toward him—one pilot saluting another. I landed without incident, took off again, landed again. Piece of cake. Breaking the boundaries of gravity, doing what human beings thought inconceivable just a few decades before, was an unforgettable experience.

Bruce endorsed my student license. Now I could fly solo, albeit with some restrictions. I couldn't carry passengers or fly in questionable weather. I couldn't go up at night either, unless my airport was in sight throughout the flight. Even during the day, I always had to fly within a 50-mile radius.

Already, I was anxious to go to the next level, and get my private pilot's license. With that, I could fly anywhere in North

America, even at night, with passengers. But to get the license, I'd need 40 hours in the air, and it would get very expensive. There had to be another way.

First, I checked the classifieds and saw an ad: *Good airplane—$895*. Turned out the owner was Sam Poston, an infamous character throughout Tennessee, reportedly a bootlegger who kept dry Knox County awash in illegal alcohol.

Supposedly, Sam used the plane to make his rounds through the state, and he made a great living at it. Nationwide, Prohibition had ended in 1932, but in little pockets throughout the country, religious fundamentalists applied whatever political pressure they could to keep the counties alcohol-free—precisely the kind of scenario that kept bootleggers in business.

This incongruous coalition, the Baptists and the bootleggers, had successfully lobbied to keep legal liquor business out of Knoxville and the surrounding area for more than two decades.

It didn't stop anyone from drinking. It did mean higher prices for booze, availability at all hours, and lots of sales to underage kids. I doubt that Sam or his colleagues requested picture I.D. from customers. This was a point the Baptists chose to ignore.

Anyway, Sam was currently doing time—presumably, an occasional cost of doing business—and for the time being, he no longer needed an airplane. His 1947 Model Ercoupe, 85-horsepower with two seats side-by-side, though now sitting in weeds taller than itself, was in excellent condition, mechanically sound, and met all FAA requirements.

Clearly, the price was right. Only one problem: I didn't have anywhere near $895.

I did, however, have a brother and some buddies who were intrigued with the idea of a "flying club." Joe, who'd graduated from high school in 1953, had spent most of the last year attending business school in Nashville. Now that he'd joined me in Knoxville, he was anxious to sign up, and we talked six friends into pooling funds and buying it together. Each of us put up $120, an amount everyone could easily afford.

Now we owned an airplane.

The other guys were revved up at first. Later, they'd learn just how much work was required to obtain a pilot's license, and didn't want to put in the time. Except for Joe, none of them became pilots, and only two of them ever took lessons. For a time, I was really the only one flying the plane on a regular basis, and for all practical purposes, it was mine.

My expenses were minimal. Instructors were only five bucks an hour, and gas was 23 cents a gallon. Considering this little plane ate less fuel than many of today's sport utility vehicles, my flying was inexpensive. The Ercoupe got 30 miles to the gallon.

Within a few weeks, I'd logged the 40 hours, including a required three-legged, 150-mile, cross-country solo trip, taking off from Knoxville, landing in Crossville and Chattanooga, and then returning to Knoxville. With an FAA examiner present, I passed the written test and the flight check certification.

Now I had my private pilot's license.

Naturally, one of my first trips was to Finger, over 400 miles and nearly four hours away. Since I could take passengers, I brought along Jack Rockwell, one of the partners in our little flying club. Jack was just about to start taking lessons himself. This trip, I thought, would certainly spur him on.

The flight west was real nice—lots of fun, no problems, and right on time. Descending towards Finger, it thrilled me to see the town landmarks. The cotton gin, Uncle R.C.'s store, Grandpa Clayton's place, the Home Banking Company, three churches, our old farm—memories of my childhood from a new perspective.

Finger was once my whole world, and now, from up here, it all seemed so small.

When I saw the old home-place and the ball field out front where the neighborhood kids gave me so much trouble, I felt a certain vindication. I thought triumphantly about how far I'd traveled in only two years—and I don't mean the flying lessons.

And I couldn't help but think: *Dad, look at me now.*

I descended even further, pointing the left wing at the ball field. The plane was at 800 feet as I began to circle the town. My turns tightened, and I could see little pockets of stick people scurrying out of the little buildings, looking up from the fields, trying to figure out what this crazy pilot was doing.

Jack was wondering the same thing. "Jim, what the hell are you doing?" he asked.

"Just trying to get a little attention," I laughed. I've always craved attention. Some people think an entrepreneur is motivated solely by money. It ain't necessarily so. Recognition is at least as significant to many entrepreneurs. To this day, I get a kick out of it if someone says, "I hear you fly gliders, helicopters, and jets." If I have the time, I'll give them an earful.

On that day, I was the talk of the town when all of Finger learned the Clayton boy was a pilot.

We touched down a few miles from Finger at the airport in Jacks Creek, a tiny non-paved landing strip that had its heyday during the war, when the military used it for practice landings. The family picked us up, and during a fried chicken lunch at my grandparents' place, I fielded questions about my flying.

Then it was Grandfather Clayton who said, "Who's gonna ride in that thing with him?"

Joe, of course, was up for it. Dad avoided the question. Mother, true to form, jumped right in. She'd never flown before, and if she was nervous, she didn't show it.

It was a wonderful visit, and I had the unspoken but unmistakable impression that Mother and Dad were proud of my accomplishments. In fact, Jack and I had such a good time with the family that time got away from us, and we got back to the airport late.

Jack was apprehensive. He knew we'd barely get back to Knoxville by dark, and he knew my night-flying experience was practically non-existent.

I assured Jack that the flight back was a cinch. All we had to do was go east, and look for the same checkpoints we used to get us to Finger—mountains, rivers, cities, power lines, railroads—then confirm them on our map, note the time between each checkpoint, and adjust for the tailwind. This was, and still is, standard operating procedure for a VFR (visual flight rules) pilot.

We were experiencing a textbook flight on a gorgeous spring afternoon, cruising at 7,500 feet to take full advantage of the 30-knot tailwind. As we approached the next checkpoint, the Cumberland Plateau near Crossville, we saw the land rising. Jack checked the map, routinely searching for a valley with a stream flowing through its middle.

The valley was there. But the stream winding it's way through the valley was missing. "No stream," said Jack.

No stream? *There had to be a stream.* The map said so. If what we saw below didn't match what was on our map then this couldn't be the checkpoint, not the right valley. We were off-course. Either we had drifted too far north or too far south. Now I was the one who was apprehensive.

I deviated from my flight plan, which was pretty silly, considering it got us to Finger successfully.

"Let's find Highway 70," I said, turning south. Finding such a prominent landmark, I thought, would get us back on track. Jack estimated we'd see the highway within nine minutes.

When it didn't show up after 15, I said, "Must have been north." After 20 minutes of flying north, and no highway in sight—you guessed it—we turned back south, figuring we didn't go far enough the first time. We flew and flew, but still no Highway 70.

We were, as Grandfather Browder might have said, "chasing our tails."

The sun, behind us, was now rapidly approaching the horizon, and the shadows were somehow making surface detail look strange and different. But there was one object that remained quite perceptible: our fuel float gauge. We'd wasted a lot of gas fumbling around, and now the gauge was touching bottom on every bounce.

We were lost and running out of fuel. Daylight was dwindling away with every passing second. We forgot about finding Knoxville. Now, we had to land somewhere, and soon, or the plane would land on its own.

We descended to 800 feet, for a closer look at a stretch of road below us, a two-lane blacktop road winding its way down the valley. But a power line hugged the road as far as we could see.

Slowing to 80 knots, we followed the road south. Up ahead, we finally saw a gently sweeping curve encircling one side of the valley with no traffic. Here, the power line, mercifully, departed from the road and continued straight across the valley and out of our way. This would have to do.

I cut the throttle, setting up a glide with speed at 68 knots while descending 500 feet per minute. The wings banked 20 degrees and rolled out over the road. We touched down at 60 miles per hour and slowed to an easy stop.

I looked at Jack. Like me, he was shaken, but okay.

"That was good, Jim, real good," he said.

Within minutes, we were surrounded by onlookers—kids on their bicycles, farmers on their tractors, entire families riding up to us in their pickups. They seemed to appear almost out of nowhere. Since it was sundown, most were just now leaving the fields after another hard day of labor. They'd caught our opening act while on the way home.

The first farmer to arrive seemed surprised not to see any blood or mangled metal. He asked if everything was all right, and told us we were near Huntsville, Alabama. An airport was minutes away.

Jack and I were stunned. We were off-course about 50 miles south. To this day, I have no idea how we wound up there.

One of the farmers had a half-full, five-gallon container of gas on his John Deere. He gave us every drop, and we thanked him profusely as he poured it in. One woman, a schoolteacher, unfolded a map and showed us the exact location of the airport.

As we prepped for a quick departure—there was almost no daylight left—we asked everyone to move down the road about 400 yards. We'd need that much space to take off. But this crowd barely moved at all, 50 yards at most. No doubt they were enjoying the show and were not about to give up their front-row seats.

I started the engine, as Jack kept waving the crowd to move back. Reluctantly our audience retreated several additional yards and stopped.

I don't think our fans understood just how critical the situation was, for them and for us. Now my appreciation for their earlier assistance was turning to anger. That curve in the road—our airstrip and our lifeline—was vanishing in the darkness. Some of the people in pickups had already turned on their headlights. We had to go. Now!

Ironically, the two factors that could have killed us, almost no gas and almost no daylight, now would work in our favor. Without a tank of heavy fuel, the plane was lighter; with the cool, dense air of early evening, engine performance would improve. I knew that if I held the brakes, easing the throttle to maximum power, we'd have all 85 horses from the first inch of take-off.

We hit 65 knots, flying speed, even sooner than I thought. I could lift off with room to spare.

All those people looking for a thrill were *still* standing in the way, risking their lives, and ours, as they refused to give us some space. Looking straight ahead, eyeball to eyeball with the crowd as it grew larger and larger in my windshield, I felt I owed them my best effort. Roaring down the road with speed increasing, I slightly eased the stick back and lifted off to less than one foot above the pavement. To the spectators, it would appear we were not airborne and unable to take off and climb.

If they want a show, I thought, *I'll give 'em their money's worth.*

With speed at 105 knots and increasing, I lifted off at only 100 feet from our fans. Pulling the stick back against my belt buckle, I saw an unforgettable image just before the nose of the plane blocked my view. Finally realizing their curiosity had placed them in imminent danger, they began leaping off their tractors, diving into ditches, jumping off mules, and scurrying helter-skelter in every direction, certain I had become a Kamikaze pilot.

Once in the air, I leveled off the plane, and within ten minutes, we had landed at the Huntsville airport. Jack and I looked around for a beer to celebrate our survival, but like the mysterious missing stream, we couldn't find that either.

We did, however, find a motel, and for once, a cheap mattress felt good.

By the way, Jack never got around to taking those flying lessons. Can't imagine why.

How do you know which way to go if you don't know where you are?

That was the crux of the problem on our flight back from Finger. But such a question applies to more than just an airplane ride. A business, a family, a relationship, or an individual all need a plan to reach the desired goal. For whatever endeavor a human being is engaged in, an anchor is needed—reference points—to provide directions to the destination, along with the time and resources required to get there.

For example: Flying east from Nashville at 150 knots per hour? Then you'll definitely be at or very near Knoxville in one hour. Selling 10 widgets with an average margin of $100 each? Keep overhead and operating expenses at $800, and you'll definitely have a net profit of $200 before taxes.

Of course, that assumes you stick with the plan, instead of impulsively changing the plan along the way. With the widgets, you might lose control of expenses or allow the sales staff to tinker with price.

Allow that, and suddenly your plan has lost its way, and your projected profitability may quickly nosedive into insolvency. That's like fiddling with a working plan in mid-flight, as I did on my way back from Finger.

On that trip, I had all the facts at my fingertips. My flight plan was packed with plenty of detail to get us to our goal. But I abandoned it the moment I got into trouble.

Never mind that the plan worked fine on the flight west to Finger that very morning. Never mind that it was working fine half the way back. Forget that hundreds before me had used a similar plan, so it was tried and true. Forget that I'd thoughtfully reviewed the plan just the day before, and found it satisfactory.

With all that going for it, I should've had enough confidence in my plan. But the second the plan seemed not to work, I threw the plan out the window, and let my "feelings" take control.

Call it what you will—impulsive behavior, "seat-of-the-pants" decision-making, emotional response, what your "gut" tells you. Some business people pride themselves on these "qualities," but to me, it's all just thrashing around, like flying in circles.

Abandoning a well-thought and well-researched plan is an act of desperation that occurs just before a crash-and-burn. Stay with the plan.

A bad plan is more likely to work than no plan at all.

If I'd always acted on my feelings, there's probably a time or two I would've jumped off a building.

Instead, it's good to put emotions in the proper perspective. Recognize that in the course of a single day, you'll segue through dozens of different feelings. Shrug off some, laugh at some, and minimize reaction to them. Chart your course with strategic planning. Think of a business plan as your map, with a timeline and checkpoints to follow en route. When something goes haywire, don't scrap the plan. Instead, expect some variables along the way and adjust for them, just as a pilot adjusts for unexpected winds.

Incidentally, with that lesson learned, I haven't been lost, off-course, or behind schedule even once since that fateful afternoon in 1954, and I've flown 11,000 hours and 3 million miles, enough to circle the Earth 100 times.

I can't say my business or even my personal record has been quite that impeccable. It's been a little bumpy at times, but it's been a good ride.

Pilots call it a "deadly spiral." Aviation lore is filled with horror stories about the spiral. You could say a deadly spiral is to a pilot what a rattlesnake bite is to a hiker. While it's certainly possible to survive such a scenario, it's surely one you'd prefer to pass up. Indeed, when John F. Kennedy Jr.'s single-engine plane dropped into the Atlantic during the summer of 1999, a deadly spiral coupled with vertigo was the culprit.

After only a few months of flying, I'd already given most of my buddies a ride in the plane, all except Bud Bennington, my fraternity president. Bud was a veteran of the Marine Corps, a legitimate war hero. He received a Purple Heart during the Korean conflict, but he scoffed at the suggestion of going up with me.

"I have an aversion to flying in junk planes with half-assed pilots," he said.

Of course, we all kidded him about his fear of flying, and "chicken calls" would frequently echo down the halls as Bud would approach. After seeing others survive a flight with me, and growing tired of the chicken calls, Bud gave in.

Arriving at the airport, he took one look at the Ercoupe and backed out again, mumbling something about the dubious prospect of flying in a "tiny tin can."

It took a half hour of persuasion plus the promise of a pint of Jack Daniels afterwards before Bud changed his mind. I assured him that nothing could possibly go wrong, and besides, he didn't want to hear any more chicken calls.

He relaxed after takeoff, marveled at the local landmarks down below, and even started chattering about how we had to take his girlfriend Paula up for a spin. Me, I wanted to show off for my friend, the war-hero-turned-fraternity-president. I wanted to test his newfound confidence in my plane and me.

So when I spotted a little cumulus cloud off to the east, I decided to fly into it. Regulations strictly forbid a VFR pilot from getting anywhere near a cloud, but I could not resist. Let me remind you that I was 19 years old.

A little bump from an air pocket, and we were out of the cloud instantly. Bud loved it, and pointed to a bigger cloud, just to the north. A bigger air pocket this time, a bigger jolt, but again, we were in the clear within a few seconds. Bud wanted more, and I was happy to oblige.

Off to the northeast, I saw a larger cloud, a white fluffy mass beckoning us to fly right in. I went straight for it, and as we got inside, the cloud seemed to swallow us whole. Instantly, this massive, enchanting white puff shape-shifted into a swirling, claustrophobic clump of gray.

Even worse, a frightening procession of jolts, called wind shear, battered us back and forth, up and down. Bud was visibly shaken; there was no whooping and hollering this time. I told him to hang on, that we'd be out of the cloud in a minute.

By now, I was flying blind. It was so dark that I couldn't see much of anything. But I could see the altimeter, and to my horror, it was *unwinding*—going counterclockwise. Even to this rookie pilot, that meant one thing.

We were descending—fast.

What to do? I reacted impulsively, and pulled back on the control wheel. Normally, if the plane's descending, and you want to regain altitude, that's what you do. But this time, the more I pulled, the more the altimeter unwound, faster and faster. *If pulling back on the control wheel makes the plane climb—and I'm pulling back—then why does the altimeter say I'm descending? What is going on?*

I had my answer when we finally broke out of the cloud.

Looking up, to the right, I could see the Tennessee hills, and, yes, the river too. *How did land get up there? Where is the sky?*

We were flying upside down and descending in a deadly spiral!

In the cloud, it *seemed* as though we were flying right side up, but that was a false perception.

This was vertigo—a spatial disorientation dreaded by pilots. The balancing apparatus in the inner ear is unable to distinguish between position and motion when flying. A steadily turning airplane feels just like one flying straight; the coffee remains level in your cup, you sit upright, everything appears to be right side up.

The brain expects the eyes to resolve the inner ear's uncertainties, and so once a pilot is deprived of visual references, he is soon helpless without some kind of exterior reference as to which way is up—in this case, my only reference would be visual—and only after leaving the cloud.

I learned then that my seat-of-the-pants feelings have to be ignored in the cockpit. The only data that matters is from the navigation instruments or outside visual references. My instinctive reaction of pulling back on the control wheel to stop our descent caused us to lose altitude even faster.

Once out of the cloud, I knew, from reading and from a brief lesson on instrument flying, what I had to do. First, I moved the throttle to idle, and began to approximate the textbook procedure for recovery from a deadly spiral.

The first step is to point the nose straight ahead using the rudders while making no attempt to level the wings or the nose. Since the Ercoupe did not have a rudder, we would go to the second step and level the wings using the stick. Now, at least, we were flying right side up, but still descending fast.

I knew we couldn't just aggressively pull back on the wheel to stop the descent. To do so during a high-speed dive could cause the wings to fold and collapse.

Rolling the wings to level with moments to spare, I moved to the third and final step in this life saving process. Easing the nose up and level with the horizon, the altimeter pointer stopped at 1,200 feet. We had lost little more than 1,000 feet in the cloud.

Bud, a basket case by now, had seen his life flash before his eyes—upside-down, no less. He couldn't wait to get out of that plane, and I don't recall him thanking me later, either for the ride or for the well-deserved pint of Jack Daniels that followed.

But we remained good friends. Bud moved to Houston and became a very successful sales rep in the oil well industry. His girlfriend Paula, the Sigma Phi Epsilon sweetheart, became his bride. I saw them frequently over the years and watched their three wonderful daughters grow up.

Bud died of pancreatic cancer in 1992. At least once or twice during all those years, we got a good laugh from our death-defying adventure.

But he never flew with me again.

The most difficult adjustment that you must make as you acquire flying skill is a willingness to believe that, under certain conditions, your senses can be dead wrong. If your business is in a deadly spiral and in a situation that takes more than just a course correction, it's even more imperative to resist the urge to rely on impulse.

With so much negativity swirling around, realize that your sullen perception of things may not square with reality. Take action, yes, but knee-jerk bloodletting usually won't work. Dramatic gestures, like massive layoffs, or cutting the advertising budget to zero, could well add to the problem.

During that horrific nosedive, I was desperately trying to recall fragments of information from the instructional manual that I'd skimmed—something, *anything* that might get us through.

I remembered one piece of advice pertinent to my situation.

The last thing you should do, the book said, *is the first thing you feel you should do.*

In other words, during predicaments when you've lost all sense of direction, don't trust your senses; don't act on impulse.

Same with your business. If you've lost all sense of direction there, don't react on a whim. Instead, take your feelings out of the mix, gather all the data you can, analyze what you've got available, consult with your experts, engage your reliable sources and resources, and identify the root cause of the problem through rational thinking, not raw passion. Stick on a Band-Aid to stop the bleeding, and then figure out the long-term fix.

I know this advice almost goes against human nature. It's natural to respond instinctively, spontaneously, and emotionally. But *natural* doesn't always mean *desirable*. Remember that cyanide, arsenic, earthquakes, and salmonella are also natural. Planning, organizing, controlling, and delegating are unnatural to most of us, but that's what works in business.

Successful organizations, whether a Fortune 500 company or a Mom and Pop corner grocery, use these principles. Either through education, experience, or instinct, these companies tend to make these principals part of their culture.

Shoot from the hip at your peril—you may wind up shooting yourself in the foot.

In flying, you follow the basic rules of navigation. In sales, you follow the basic rules of communication. It's not that complicated.

Funny about the lessons in life and how they, sometimes literally, strike you out of the blue.

Just before I took up flying, I snagged an engineering job at WTVK, Channel 26, the ABC-TV affiliate in Knoxville. It was a step up from the radio station, with better pay. Still, WTVK was a small outfit back then, UHF television, and it took a lot of maintenance just to stay on the air.

This meant plenty of overtime for me, since they kept the station running with minimal staff. I was happy to get the extra pay, even happier to help Joe get a job there, too.

Normally, my hours were four in the afternoon until midnight, so I clearly recall *American Bandstand* as background noise while I worked. I also remember *Ozzie and Harriet, Make Room For Daddy, You Asked For It,* and *The Lone Ranger,* all of which ran during prime-time.

The ABC network didn't offer its affiliates a lot of programming back then. For quite a few years, its daytime schedule was bare until the afternoon; WTVK filled the mornings with a hodgepodge of talk, cooking, and entertainment shows. Naturally, I migrated toward the musicians and singers who frequently appeared on these programs. That's what got me into trouble.

My immediate supervisor at the station was Joseph Broyles, the chief engineer. At first, he was impressed with my eagerness, drive, and technical abilities. But as I began to socialize with the performers, he started to complain.

"If that kid would keep as sharp an eye on the transmitter as he does the girls in the studio then we wouldn't be off the air so much," he'd growl.

I told myself there was more to it than that. The musicians frequently invited me out for a drink after work or to dinner at Regas, then Knoxville's finest restaurant. (Even now, with Mike Connor as principal owner, I still love to go there.) But I don't recall that they invited Broyles, and maybe he took it as a snub.

At my pink slip meeting, to Mr. Broyles's credit, I didn't detect any sense of gloating on his part. In fact, the unpleasant business of canning someone seemed difficult for him. We talked for about an hour until he finally let me go.

For me, it was a lesson in employer-employee relations, a humbling one. The warning signs were there. I just ignored them. Like my deadly spiral in the plane, my senses were dead wrong. Naturally, I navigated toward the musicians. I was a musician myself. As a result, I nose-dived straight into unemployment.

Luckily, I had plenty of friends at WATE-TV, Channel 6, Knoxville's NBC affiliate; many were refugees from WTVK. On their recommendations, I got an engineering job immediately.

WATE was a much better station with higher pay and state-of-the-art RCA equipment. Instead of *American Bandstand* during the afternoon, I'd catch *Howdy Doody*; in place of *The Lone Ranger*, there was *Dragnet*. It wasn't long before Joe joined me there, and he soon began directing many of the station's local programs.

I even remember my exact start date at WATE—March 7, 1955—but only because of something monumental that happened two days earlier.

Mary and I got married.

CHAPTER 5

Married. . .And Mobile

Mary was already planning a June wedding between spring and summer quarters at UT. This would coincide with my scheduled vacation week at WTVK-TV. Time off with pay and between quarters, what a perfect time for our wedding and a weeklong honeymoon. We couldn't wait.

My getting fired sure sabotaged Mary's wedding plans, and with the new job I would not get a paid vacation all year. Being practical, and at the risk of seeming impetuous, I suggested we get married immediately. She agreed.

We were married at the First Baptist Church of Knoxville on March 5, 1955, the weekend before I started at WATE. Joe was my best man, while Mary's best friend from first grade, Barbara Rogers, was her maid of honor.

We moved into a cozy, but tiny upstairs apartment off North Broadway halfway between the campus and my work. My pay at WATE allowed us to remain in school, and our grades improved immediately. Mary was a good student anyway, but now she made A's with regularity. Me, I'd been making strictly C's, but I began getting a few B's.

I'm not suggesting that marriage is key to making the honor

roll, but it worked for us.

Toward the end of the year, I was at Regas having dinner with Roger Hamilton, an engineer with RCA. He told me about a new TV station under construction in Memphis. WREC would be state-of-the-art, with first-rate studios, a top-notch control room, and the finest RCA equipment available. With offices inside the Hotel Peabody, a landmark in downtown Memphis, it was scheduled to be on the air by mid-year.

The station needed a team of engineers to install and operate the RCA studio, control room, and transmitter equipment. Roger, who'd be supervising much of the work, asked if I would be interested in a temporary or permanent position. He knew the owner, Hoyt Wooten, a member of a prominent and very wealthy Memphis family. I was assured the pay increase would be significant. I told Roger to put in a word for me.

Within a week I got a call from Mr. Wooten's assistant, and Mary and I flew down. Roger was right; the station was everything he claimed. It was the Taj Mahal of television stations. The salary offer was excellent, and in addition to paying moving expenses, they'd even let us have a room at the Peabody until we found a place to live.

Mary and I had dinner in the hotel's elegant ballroom. Guy Lombardo and his orchestra were playing there that night, just a few weeks before their annual New Year's Eve appearance on network television.

The Peabody housed one of the originating stations for the NBC Network's radio show, *Saturday Night Dance Party*. In late June we would have our farewell party there as the announcer said, "From high atop Hotel Peabody, overlooking downtown Memphis and the mighty Mississippi—live—it's NBC's *Saturday Night Dance Party*, featuring tonight the famous Guy Lombardo Orchestra." What a place to start and end our terrific six months in Memphis.

With the orchestra in the background, Mary and I discussed

what a move to Memphis would mean. The experience and the pay would be good, but I'd have to postpone my degree; so would she. We made the decision happily, knowing we'd enjoy the break and change of scenery, and could return to school later.

We moved over the Christmas holidays, and I started at WREC-TV right after New Year's Day in 1956. Mary got a job at Southern Bell, ironically, at the same building where I'd had the infamous three-way call with Bobbie Jo and Peggy earlier.

The Hotel Peabody treated us like royalty, and we relished the splendor. The station paid all expenses, including our room, amenities, meals in the restaurant, and 24-hour room service.

Eggs Benedict for breakfast? Sure. Filet Mignon for dinner? Certainly—maybe for lunch, too. The Peabody's cuisine was exquisite, especially for two college kids who still thought "dining out" meant hamburgers and pizza. Mary and I lived it up, along with a dozen colleagues also staying at the Peabody, and our search for a permanent place took a low priority.

This is a classic case where an organization allows the door to the company safe to crack open, then steps aside, only to learn that the whole world now has unlimited access.

It seems Mr. Wooten had been too busy to write policy and establish a control system for managing relocation expenses. It could be he was too hands-on to properly oversee all the new activity, which is not unusual in the case of a new start-up enterprise. No doubt he had been able to personally monitor every expense account for the successful WREC radio station, but the complexities of his TV station did not allow him that luxury.

Several of us continued to enjoy the gravy train until the middle of March, when Hoyt Wooten happened to see a rather large envelope from the Peabody. Rumor has it that Hoyt fell ill after looking at it, and actually had to go home for the day.

House-hunting suddenly became a priority.

Mary and I stepped up our search, found some nice apartments, but the rents were shockingly high. Maybe we were making good money on this job, but we weren't free spenders. Driving east on Summer Avenue as we looked for an apartment, we saw a beautiful mobile home park. It was nice; well kept, with good security—something Mary liked since I often worked nights.

At the Summer Avenue Mobile Home Park, we would have our own place, good neighbors, a parking place by the door, and no stairs to climb. We especially would enjoy *not* having only those thin walls separating us from apartments below, above, and on either side.

We selected our "home site" on a corner lot, subject to finding our dream mobile home. Like searching for just the right apartment, we found shopping for the perfect mobile home just as difficult. Being able to find the desired size and features at an acceptable price with our limited time was not easy.

Dad had been pleased with our Memphis transition and offered to support us in the move. He and I drove to a plant near Little Rock, Arkansas, during a bitter snowstorm to buy wholesale. Since this was their slow season, they agreed to deliver one of the partially built homes in a week. We quickly set up Mary's dad, the car dealer, as a temporary mobile home dealer.

Not bad. But arriving back at the Peabody, there was a call from a mobile home retailer who was referred to us by the manager of Summer Avenue Park.

The retailer was leaving the sales side of the business immediately, and was flushing his inventory as quickly as possible. I told him we already had a deal, and that I was buying from the factory at cost. But he went me one better.

"I'll let you have it for the balance I owe the bank," he said.

Now that was a sweet deal. Since he had owned the home for a few months already, he'd reduced what he owed the bank by about $500. Not only that, but he'd deliver to the park and set it up for free.

There was only one catch—I had to pay him in cash that week. Like I said, he was in a hurry to get out of sales.

I called Dad, and with his co-signature, I got a loan from the Home Banking Company in Finger. (The interest rate was only about 6 percent, but Dad thought this was outrageous. He soon paid off the loan. Later, I'd pay Dad for the note.)

Mary turned that little place into a real home, planting flowers and putting up pictures. Mother and Dad, close by in Finger, visited often, and we'd go see them every month. We really loved Memphis and the job was terrific, with lots of overtime pay.

Nothing had gone wrong until a little piece of paper arrived in the mail one day. It was my draft notice. Unless I went back to college, I'd have to go in the military.

There was a time when I would've been happy to go. Remember, when graduating from high school, I almost joined to support the country during the terrible Korean War. Four years had gone by, and now I was married, launching a career, and ready to start a family. The military just wasn't in the cards anymore, especially three years after the end of the conflict in Korea.

Our six months in Memphis was over, we were out of there—and back in Knoxville.

It was back to the books.

I gave notice at WREC and re-enrolled at the University of Tennessee. It was difficult, leaving that great job, that charming city, but the process of moving itself wasn't difficult at all. We didn't have to move furniture or pack anything in boxes. Canned goods stayed in the cabinets; clothes stayed in the closet; socks and shorts stayed in the drawers; silverware stayed in its compartment. All it took was a little masking tape to make sure doors and drawers stayed shut, and we were done.

In an hour we had the home and all our belongings ready to ship, and within an hour of arriving in Knoxville, Mary was ready to cook dinner.

Moving the home itself was just as easy. Once again, we called on our friend, the retailer who'd sold us our home. By now, he was full-time in the service and transportation end of the business. In one day he moved everything for us at a great price, without a scratch, to a nice little mobile home park on Sutherland Avenue, near the University, and populated mostly by students.

I almost took an engineering job with WBIR, Channel 10, Knoxville's CBS affiliate. But I opted instead for a mysterious little job with the University, offered through the College of Electrical Engineering and affiliated with a never-to-be-named government agency.

My laboratory office, a little travel trailer surrounded by a big fence, was parked in a cornfield 15 miles out in the country. Three enormous satellite dishes were nearby, ranging from 12 to 20 feet in diameter.

Our supervisors, cryptic from the start, told us our job was top-secret. We couldn't bring anyone out there to visit, and we couldn't talk about what we did. I know, I know—it sounds like something out of *The X-Files.* Cue the spooky music.

Actually, it would have been difficult to communicate what I did anyway since our supervising professors would not explain what we were doing, who we were doing it for, or why we were doing it in the first place. I had the impression we were tracking meteorites in the atmosphere.

The dishes were motorized and remotely controlled from inside the trailer. Every hour, I'd point the dishes to a different spot in the sky. We'd dial in some esoteric coordinates, take some ambiguous meter readings, and that was it. It was a truly easy job, offering plenty of study time, which is the reason I took it in the first place.

I wouldn't know anything more about that project for another 30 years, until someone brought up the subject at a University of Tennessee College of Engineering fundraiser. There I learned the University had received a government agency grant. The objective was to establish a system for "bouncing signals" off meteorites as well as the Moon and some of the planets in the solar system, probably Venus, Mars, and Jupiter. We were one of a dozen sites like this located around the globe. It was the government's first tiny step towards the creation of a satellite-tracking program—all from that little camper out in the middle of nowhere.

Keep in mind it was the summer of 1956, more than a year before Russia launched Sputnik, the world's first artificial satellite. NASA wouldn't be in existence until late '58, another two years.

But the "space race" had already begun, even if under a cloak of government secrecy. Manned missions weren't quite off the drawing board yet, but unmanned rockets and satellites were already in the advance planning stage. The technology was not available to track whatever man was able to send into space yet. Obviously, the success of these missions would be dependent on effective tracking of the space vehicle whatever the cargo. The data we gathered, apparently, was part of that early research.

Me, I just studied my engineering books while they tracked their imaginary Sputniks. By fall, a nighttime position became open at WATE radio as a transmitter operator for four days each week. Sunday night, my shift would involve performing routine maintenance on their downtown studio equipment, the same studio control console where Tennessee Ernie Ford and Archie Campbell had originated their popular shows.

Toward the end of 1956, with graduation looming just ahead, Mary and I decided to start a family. We began looking around for a new place to live—something bigger and nicer—but not once did we consider anything but a mobile home. As we searched, we already knew we had someone to buy our current home, Tom and Mary Benson, who have remained lifelong friends. For many years, Tom was commissioner of agriculture for our state.

Elkhart, Indiana, was the birthplace of the manufactured home industry with more factories located there than anywhere else in the country. I visited Don Jackson, a retailer in nearby Tullahoma, a man Mary's dad knew. He was about to make a buying trip to Elkhart. I offered to drive him there for free in my new '55 Studebaker and pay him a small fee for his time in helping me select a new home at factory cost.

He agreed, and I bought a brand-new 1956 Richardson for $3,900, including $400 freight. I spent another $600 for the cost of the Elkhart trip, including the $200 I paid Don Jackson. Not a bad deal, and far better than if I had gone directly to a dealership.

I did not know about "packing" invoices, or "over-billing."

Twelve years later, as an authorized Richardson retailer, and buying Richardson homes regularly, I asked the sales coordinator to retrieve the file on our earlier Richardson home. From those documents, I learned that my retailer friend had directed the factory to "pack" an additional $500 to the invoice as an "advertising allowance."

That $500 went directly to Jackson. A copy of the check remained in the file.

Like most young entrepreneurs, I didn't have the experience or know-how to protect myself from wheeler-dealers looking for easy pickings. This was my first lesson on over-billing. Sears, for instance, built their business on over-billing. Their buyers were evaluated based on the amount of rebates they could squeeze out of vendors. Instead of asking for a lower price, some buyers actually asked for a higher price to increase the amount of rebate. Because of abuses and price competition, Sears stopped this practice as Wal-Mart became more aggressive on pricing.

Here's how it works: a retailer buys a $30,000 home from the manufacturer, but asks the manufacturer to add a pack, or rebate, to the invoice for $5,000. This could be labeled as marketing support, display materials, or even furniture package. The invoice has now grown to $35,000.

The manufacturer, after receiving payment, rebates the $5,000 to the dealer.

The retailer takes out a loan in the amount of the inflated invoice from the inventory lender. This is called "floor planning." The manufacturer normally is required by the inventory lender to take the home back and pay the loan if the dealer defaults. Notice the manufacturer has assumed an obligation to repurchase the home at a price that includes the extra $5,000. The manufacturer, believing the retailer will sell and pay for the home, sees little risk. All of this works well until the industry enters one of its "correction" phases. The industry is cyclical, and after increasing capacity to accommodate seemingly endless demand, it periodically experiences a painful adjustment period like the current one, which began in 1999.

I jokingly say in speeches, "I have six years experience in our industry," then I pause and add, "six times." The point is that I have been through six industry cycles of six years each.

Historically, the industry becomes euphoric at the first sign of increased sales. Look at the graph below, indicating the upturn in 1991. Lenders rush in after seeing that CMH earns more than $100 million after tax each year, also because they believe the higher yields will offset poor underwriting, aggressive advances, and weak servicing. The lender looks like a hero for three years as the portfolio builds. Early warning signs are ignored because the next

Industry vs CMH Homes – Shipments (000s)

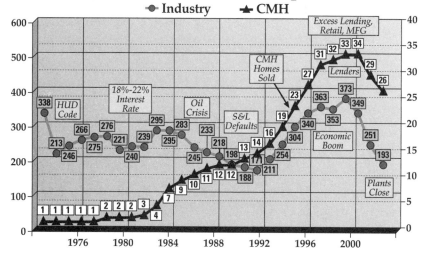

downturn is still three years down the road.

Imagine how painful it is for the manufacturer to have to repurchase and then resell one-year-old homes when half their plant capacity is idle. In all previous down cycles up to now, the manufacturer did not have the liquidity to honor repurchases late in the cycle, leaving the lenders to "take their medicine." This may cause some lenders to leave the industry, never to return. Others return to the "hog trough" after about seven years.

Before continuing with my story, let's look at customer financing on the same over-billed home.

Since the mortgage advance is normally determined by the invoice amount, this lender, too, is advancing $5,000 more than their underwriting guidelines allow.

Is that legal?

The answer is, probably not. If the manufacturer who certifies the accuracy of the invoice knew, or should have known, that the lenders would rely on the invoice, then they could be liable for fraud or conspiracy, in my opinion. Likewise, the retailer who may have initiated, and is likely to have benefited, may have criminal and civil exposures. Fortunately, appraisals have become more available recently.

For a customer, being able to fund the lender's initial cash requirements may be their greatest challenge. A salesperson willing to cheat may be tempted to get creative in documenting the required cash payment, while the customer may simply not have the cash available. There are a number of standard jokes in the industry about tricks that are used to "fake" the buyer's down payment. We hear about $1,000 allowances for broomsticks; car titles from wrecked cars used to document a $5,000 trade allowance; used homes traded in for $4,500 and then sold back to the customer for $1. The more brazen method would involve simply writing in an $8,000 cash payment on the contract, when the buyer actually paid $1,000.

Why would a lender continue to accept applications from dealers who compromise legally, morally, and ethically? There are a lot of answers to this seemingly simple question. One short answer could be that the people in the field offices have production quotas, and their bonus programs are based on volume of loans originated.

It is also thought that lenders who left our industry one or more times permitted a culture to thrive that encouraged underwriting and compliance deviations to be ignored. In effect, the losses experienced resulted from their nontraditional lending and compliance guidelines. At CMH, our retail people frequently show us approved applications from other lenders, which our credit department would not approve. However, for more than a decade, we did have a very aggressive lender who pushed the envelope on terms, down payments, advances, and rates.

"A rising swamp covers all stumps," is just as applicable in our industry. In this down phase of the cycle, we are rapidly draining the swamp. This exposes the *excesses:* the weak, the unstable, the undercapitalized, and the poorly managed.

As I write this, one of our long-term competitors is reported to be at the brink of bankruptcy. Another has negative net worth after deducting the goodwill on the books.

Guess how much goodwill CMH has on the books? None! How much equity? As you can see from the graph below, over $1.2 billion, which is more than all other public companies com-

Shareholders' Equity
$ Millions

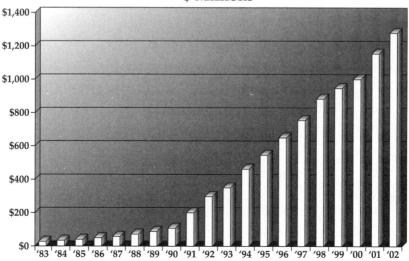

bined in our line of business. For the last two years, Clayton Homes has earned more than the rest of the publicly traded retailers and manufacturers in this industry combined! At our fiscal year-end in June 2002, CMH achieved its 28th consecutive profitable year, as the manufactured housing industry experienced its third consecutive year of declining shipments.

Let me get down off my soapbox and return to my story.

I received my electrical engineering degree in June of 1957—the first Clayton to graduate from college. This was a major event in our family, and my parents and grandparents were extremely proud. So were my teachers from Finger Junior High and Chester County High, particularly A.C. Jones. The fact that it was an electrical engineering degree, a highly technical and difficult discipline, made it even more impressive.

Mother and Dad drove up for the ceremony, and this time, it didn't matter that Dad didn't say much; the big grin on his face told the story. By this time, Mary was pregnant with Karen, who was due in October. We had a wonderful day, taking pictures and celebrating.

With my degree, it didn't take long to find a job. Bell's Western Electric made an offer, as did the Wind Tunnel at Tullahoma. I decided to hang on to my night slot at WATE radio, and take a day job with the Tennessee Valley Authority. I was an engineering trainee who did nothing but busywork. It was incredibly boring.

So this is why I went to college, I thought.

While finishing up my schoolwork, I'd been looking to unload the old Kaiser I'd been driving. I'd bought it because the full-size, four-door sedan was clearly more car for less money. But as I attempted to trade, the dealers only laughed. The Kaiser was out of production, and it was hard finding spare parts. No one, not even my brother-in-law, an Oldsmobile dealer in McMinnville, wanted it.

I ran a three-liner in the classified ads: "Must Sell Car To Pay For College." I hoped for the best. It pleased me to get two offers, both at the asking price.

I sold the Kaiser to one of my callers, but didn't want to leave the other guy hanging. I had a friend at work who had been trying to sell his Studebaker. He rushed it over, and we closed the sale in a few minutes for $250. My friend couldn't believe his good fortune and gave me 50 bucks for the favor.

I'm on to something here, I thought. *This is a great way to make some money on the side. If only I had more cars to sell.*

I started spending time on Clinton Highway, which featured almost as many used car lots as beer joints. I got friendly with one of the dealers, and he invited me to a car auction, which was kind of like the cattle auctions I attended with Dad when I was a kid.

For a while, I'd pay him $10 for each car I bought using his license. I'd find an old Chevy, buy it for $200, fix it up, run a classified ad, and sell it for $300. After expenses, I made about $50 profit, which, in those days, was not bad for a few hours of work.

I kept advertising in the classifieds and stuck with the line "Must Sell Car To Pay For College," which was true. At the time, I was still a college kid, and I sure needed to sell the car. I was paying two college tuitions. (After graduation, with Mary pregnant, I changed the line to "New Baby—Must Sell.") I didn't tell anyone a sob story, but I didn't offer a blow-by-blow recital of the car's history, either.

Soon, I could purchase cars at the auctions myself. I networked with other dealers, and bought some of their old trade-ins that weren't selling. I developed quite a network that way, and made sure I was always cordial and on time, making quick and decisive offers on those cars I could use. I did not waste their time. I'd park each new purchase at home, and show it to prospects from my ads at a nearby supermarket or movie theater.

I spent most of my weekends and off-hours from my other two jobs in this manner. In a few weeks, I was making more money on a good week selling cars than I was at TVA and WATE combined.

Soon I was thinking, *wouldn't it be great if I could sell more than one car at a time?* I partnered with Joe, who was still at the TV station, along with six of my fraternity brothers. They became my first sales team.

I kept buying cars, placing ads, and making repairs. I let them take inquiring calls, show the cars, and close the sale. I'd pay them $50 for every car they sold. After expenses, I'd make just over $50 profit. Soon, I was buying two or three cars at a time.

This cookie-cutter approach to the car business worked better than I could've imagined. Some of these guys sold a car every week. It wasn't long before our gross profit was $6,000 a month! My net was about $2,000, good money for almost anyone then, but especially for a kid in his early twenties.

From my early childhood, when I was doing odd jobs, building fires, and selling seed, I knew that really listening to our buyers was essential. I taught my team to talk less and listen more. We sincerely tried to find a car that exactly fit the needs and desires for each prospect. Rarely would we experience a case of buyer's remorse, where we would have to do an exchange or refund.

If the sales staff knows that the owner will not accept customer abuse, then the salesperson is not likely to create such a dilemma.

Sometimes, especially in the car business, there are salespeople who are fast-talking, manipulative, forceful, and downright intimidating, who care only about making the sale. They're not really concerned about the customer, and will sell them anything to make another commission.

Exhibiting this sort of glad-handed disdain guarantees an unhappy customer. For the record, unhappy customers, among other things, are far more likely to cause problems after the sale, and far less likely to make loan payments. It's for this reason I believe that introverts, those with a quieter, more thoughtful approach, sell more than extroverts do. Introverts listen better.

That's possibly true even for big-ticket items—*especially* the big-ticket items.

John Lewis is a salesperson for Cessna Jet Aircraft based in

Charlotte. He's one of the best salespeople I know, plus he's a good friend and a great jazz guitarist. Talk about an introvert; John is off the scale. His sales technique is extremely low-key, almost passive. It's also extraordinarily persuasive, apparently, since his customers always return for more. I'm one of them. So far, Kay and I have personally bought three Cessna Citations from him, including one on order scheduled for delivery in 2003.

Even though we were selling lower priced vehicles, most sales could not be completed until the buyer found a loan. At closings, I would have the opportunity to meet their lender. After receiving my check, I would give the lender my card and thank them for being so helpful. Turning to leave, I would ask, "Would you like to have applications on good future customers of mine?"

One lender, who gave me a resounding and enthusiastic "Yes," was Fenton Kintzing.

A loan officer at Valley Fidelity Bank, Fenton, in his thirties, was always prospecting for good business.

I don't think either one of us realized that a lifelong friendship would evolve from such an inauspicious beginning. And it's unlikely in the extreme that Fenton thought some part-time wannabe car salesman would become his most profitable account in just a few years.

It didn't take us long to work out a very efficient mode of operation. I'd pre-screen my customers, weed out the dubious, and send the desirables over to Fenton. In turn, he'd interview and credit check them, inspect the car, and, if the car and the individual's credit were approved, Fenton's long-time, highly professional assistant Lois White would then take over the loan closing.

While Fenton and I chatted over a Coke, Ms. White would prepare the documents and have my buyer sign. I would have my check and be on my way in a half-hour, knowing I had a real friend and supporter in Fenton.

Fenton was good, and I do not remember ever disagreeing with him on the merits of a loan application.

In many ways, Fenton was a godsend. Customers who independently shopped for financing often encountered lenders who steered them to other dealers. Yikes! That really spoils a salesman's day. With our "pet banker," we didn't have that problem.

What's a pet banker? A pet banker is a banker who does whatever you want.

Now, let me assure you, I knew never to make an unreasonable request of Fenton. With that premise in mind, don't you think he should have accommodated my every request? Now, that I'm a banker, I teach the pet banker lesson to my team. If we have a reasonable customer, we should make every effort to accommodate their request. This requires us to anticipate customer needs and help them keep their expectations realistic. Proactive relationship management and support is likely to keep customers believing that we are, in fact, their pet bank.

For years, Fenton would stop by every week to chat. Early on, he encouraged me to increase margins. Plainly, he would say, "You are selling too darn cheap. Charge a little more." He added, "Your cars are worth more. You are buying better cars, and your people are reconditioning them well. You can get a bigger profit margin, still beat the other dealers, and with good service, your customers will be happy." He also reminded me that with my almost non-existent overhead, I could make a nice bottom line.

It was music to my ears, and I raised my prices. I began making $250 profit on each car, not just $100. I was able to price under my competitors with the fancy lots, but remain low enough that my customers got a real bargain. Since the cars remained affordable, customers had lower payments, which they tended to make on time. Fenton, observing my responsible clientele, became even more interested in supporting us with his lending services.

After a few months, he was so confident that he authorized me, informally, to be a closing agent for the bank. Essentially, I was a deputy loan officer, and could now offer "on the spot" financing and closing, which allowed us to facilitate a "quick loan close" in our own office just like our larger competition. Fenton continued to do the credit check, and I took over responsibility for the interview and the car inspection functions.

As our relationship grew, so did Fenton's confidence in me. He soon gave me a $25,000 line of credit to fund additional inventory. This meant more and better cars. He also made us officially an indirect dealer. Now we could process and close every facet of the loan, except for the credit approval function.

Adding straight to our net profit was the finance income Fenton now shared with us. This was the best part and would ultimately make us the most successful lender in our industry.

Incidentally, the fact that Fenton independently controlled credit approval separated automatically the function from the sales staff. In doing so, we established a "Chinese Wall" between the credit and sales departments that could never be compromised. In doing so, we kept sales and credit functions separate.

Let me illustrate the importance of this: Eight years ago, after recognizing that Clayton and Oakwood, the two original vertically integrated companies, were the "Street's Darlings," Wall Street began to pressure our friends at Champion, Fleetwood, Cavalier, Southern Energy, and others to become vertically integrated, too. These manufacturers were compelled to rush out and buy their own retail sales centers. The bidding started. Suddenly, the small "Mom and Pop" sales centers, historically valued at little more than the land they sat upon, were now priced from $2 million to $5 million.

Not being able to buy sales centers fast enough, Champion, Fleetwood, and the smaller manufacturers began to build theirs from scratch. The goal was to own more sales centers than CMH and Oakwood.

In the meantime, Oakwood outbid CMH for the Schult factories and their retail subsidiary. We offered $18 per share, and Oakwood paid $22.

Carl Koella, our vice president of investor relations, and I were telling the Street that acquisition prices were two to five times our cost to build, and completely unworkable. Our competitors were buying anyway. We watched them laugh at us for being conservative, much like the kids did when Joe and I could not play ball well enough to compete.

My Grandfather Browder would say, "Wherever you dream about going, whether it's getting a driver's license, graduating, getting married, buying a home, taking a vacation, or whatever, when you get there—*there you are!"*

Our competitors wanted the margins, the loyal distribution, the dependable finance source, and the cash flow. Their shareholders demanded this. We made it look so easy. What they did not know was that developing expertise in manufacturing, retailing, lending, insurance, and communities (real estate) is very hard for any company to accomplish. However, to integrate the distinctive cultures normally found within these disciplines, if even possible, will take years. I believe it is completely impossible unless the organization is very small.

Oakwood, Conner, Mobile Home Industries, and others, some say, did not keep the sacred "Chinese Wall" in place. It is so tempting to become aggressive when sales are needed. Since 1999, when production began to slow, these "Johnny Come Lately" integrated companies were whining about lenders being too tight. They were wrong. The fact is the industry and these companies sold so many homes from 1991 to 1998 largely because lenders were euphoric and overly aggressive. Down payments went down to 5 percent or less. Terms stretched to 30 years. Credit underwriting became reckless. Now the industry pays the piper, as foreclosure rates and inventory are the highest in more than a decade.

Want the rest of the story? Take a look at the chart on the next page. See how many sales centers and factories have closed in the past three years.

"He who has the last laugh has the best laugh," my Grandmother Clayton used to say.

Store and Factory Closings

COMPANY	STORES	FACTORIES
Clayton	28	0
Fleetwood	109	16
Champion	164	19
Oakwood	216	22

Numbers as of October 2002, based on company news releases.

But back to my story. I felt like I was scratching the surface of a gold mine. *This is almost too easy*, I thought. On that point, I was right. As an "embryo-entrepreneur," I did not know what I did not know. No fledgling entrepreneur does.

If I had even the slightest idea just how difficult it would be, from the gut-wrenching heartaches, to the hard work and the long hours—a grueling combination that every successful entrepreneur can identify with—I probably would've remained a guitar picker. Or maybe a seed salesman.

It wasn't easy keeping the car business going with my job at TVA. I couldn't take sales calls there. Instead, Mary worked the phones at home, updating me throughout the day.

To my colleagues at work, I tried to keep a reasonably low profile about my moonlighting. But as the business gained momentum, I'm sure they overheard my occasional conversations with Mary, and I did sell cars to a couple of TVA employees. Some of the staff workers concluded (correctly) that I was making quite a bit of money on the side, and it seemed to annoy one or two who worked on the floor. Nothing breeds resentment like success, especially if the other guy isn't getting his share.

There was, apparently, some animosity from a few of the car dealerships around town. They'd heard about this upstart kid through the grapevine, and like most gossip, it was exaggerated. *Some college boy is selling loads of cars from his front yard.*

I never found out who "ratted on me," but one rainy afternoon, an examiner from the State Motor Vehicle Department paid a visit, and it was obvious he wasn't looking to buy a car.

Determining on the spot that I was operating an illegal car dealership, the examiner found that I'd failed to comply with a long list of licensing and regulatory requirements. State, county, and city violations would command fines—big ones. I knew I didn't have a leg to stand on.

It was obvious that arguing with them would be self-defeating, so I became humble and listened intently—admittedly, a difficult act for me. I acknowledged my ignorance; I assured them my goal was to obey all laws; I thanked the examiner for bringing this to my attention, and apologized for inconveniencing the various departments and their staff. With appropriate meekness, I asked him to assist me in becoming a fully authorized, licensed, and registered automobile dealer.

Within moments, my adversary became my mentor. They'd forgo the fines if I acted quickly. This meant that I had to immediately meet the requirements of the department, which included an office, a sign, a phone, and a service bay. Then upon paying the taxes and fees, I would be an official used car dealer, licensed by the State Automobile Commission.

And it meant a full-time commitment to the car business.

Now Mary and I had a choice to make. Should I give up that safe, easy, but boring government job with TVA for the risk of becoming an entrepreneur? At TVA, I had security, a pretty good salary, paid vacations and—this was a huge consideration since Mary was pregnant—health benefits.

But already, I was making far more selling cars than I did with TVA, and that was in my spare time. It was logical to think I'd do even better full-time. And I was certainly having a lot more fun.

It was an easy decision for us to make. Really, it didn't have anything to do with the regulators breathing down my neck. All they did was speed up the inevitable. Sooner or later, I would've gone that route. I quit that dull job at TVA, let go of my night shift at WATE, and called on my friends at the neighborhood Texaco station on Kingston Pike, a few blocks from the house.

I knew the two owners of the station since I bought most of my gas there, and they made me an offer. A tiny office, the use of one of their two service bays, access to their pay phone, and parking slots for up to 10 cars, all for sixty bucks a month. Agreed.

I put up a sign, "Jim Clayton Autoland," and pinned my dealership licenses on the bathroom wall. (These days, you won't find those tacky licenses and permits on CMH office walls. In my view, there are only two ways to display such items: in a frame or on a framed bulletin board. And yes, I know there's language requiring them to be displayed conspicuously, so file them where you can display them quickly should a bureaucrat audit you.)

Joe joined me part-time, and my frat buddies continued to freelance. With their support, sales doubled. Now we were selling about 20 cars a month.

Entrepreneurs can't stand to be "taken." Imagine my horror when I was!

I bid on a beautiful 1956 Ford Fairlane at the Lenoir City Auction. The price quickly reached my $500 limit, but the car was so new that I couldn't turn it loose. A few more bids and it was mine at $725. I couldn't wait to show it to Joe and get it on display.

A professional dude in a pin-stripped suit and dark wool topcoat came in at 10 o'clock the next morning as I was placing my classifieds. I didn't know him from a cord of wood. He was a fast talker and commenced to impress me with his name-dropping.

He dabbled in a lot of things, he said, including car sales. By sheer coincidence, he had a hot customer, someone looking for a car right now.

"She trades every two years," he said. "When she trades in, she buys only from me. She trusts me."

Superficially, the guy seemed smooth, but I should have sensed the slipperiness beneath the polished surface.

He glanced over at my 1956 Ford two-door sedan, only two years old and my best car, and said, "This is exactly what she's looking for. Believe me, I know. She'll love it. I just need to show it to her. She'll pay full price."

Sure, I said. Why not bring her down and let her check it out?

"She'd never do that," he said. "She's very shy and private."

Of course. But he offered a solution. He'd drive the car to her place and let her have a look. How unreasonable was that? He promised to pay me promptly, right after delivering the car to her.

"After all," he said, "you hang on to the title until she pays you in full—cash."

You already know the rest of this story. I let him drive away with the car. He never came back. Two weeks later, the Knoxville Police located that beautiful little Ford, filthy and scratched, with a lot more miles on the odometer. Once again, I was naïve, but I was also greedy. I'd counted on a big profit from the car, and when this crook told me what I wanted to hear, my judgment took a sabbatical.

It's so easy to be snookered, particularly when you're an inexperienced entrepreneur starting out and eager to do business. Believe me, there's no shortage of con artists out there. They'll sell you an inferior product; they'll talk you into hiring them; they'll urge you to lend them money they can't possibly pay back—all as they wave money in your face. You end up with a product you can't use, an employee who can't perform, or an invoice that's impossible to collect.

I've been there more than once.

No matter the scam, it's ultimately about surrendering control. When I let that guy drive off with my Ford, I surrendered control.

Starting a business is tough and risky for anyone regardless of experience. It's especially tough on the beginning entrepreneur since there's normally no one to provide a second opinion, no staff of experts in sales, marketing or accounting, and no board of directors. Instead, it's just *you*—alone in the office—a one-man band struggling to meet payroll, win the contract, and beat the competition. The powerful urge and impatience to make a sale may win out over your better judgment, common sense, and rational thinking.

Having a partner or a mentor can be invaluable. Someone you can bounce ideas off, even on an informal basis, is priceless.

We all need a person who's there to challenge our assumptions and question our wisdom. I can't begin to tell you how important my relationship with Joe Clayton was and is. Joe not only provided wise counsel, but I went about my workday making decisions consistent with our discussions. After all, I did not want to disappoint Joe, nor he me.

In our company, we've taught the 90/10 rule for decades. It works this way: The manager of a sales center is expected to make 90 percent of the decisions. For the other 10 percent, the manager is to collaborate with the regional manager, their peers, or anyone in the organization who may have expertise in that area. We have an open door culture. Of course, a new manager will want to consult with others on far more than 10 percent of the decisions.

Which decisions are in the 10 percent category? Anything that involves unusual risk, special skills, or subject matter outside the manager's expertise should be considered a 10 percent item.

For example, suppose a manager wants to buy advertising to increase home sales, but does not have advertising experience. First, he or she must be at the point where they recognize: *I do not know—and I know that I do not know.* Thus they will happily ask for assistance, and at CMH, they're likely to receive excellent support.

That could be the regional manager, but it could also be someone from anywhere in the company. Our organization is so vast, there's likely to be someone who knows which advertising medium to choose and which message would work—and they're only a voice mail or e-mail away.

This philosophy has translated into a wonderful support system not only for our managers but for everyone in the company.

Incidentally, if a team member can't recognize the decisions that are 10 percenters, they're likely to lack good judgment in other areas.

When we recruit from other organizations, they are likely to have the attitude, "If I am the manager, then I make all the decisions." They better change fast. Clayton's is all about people helping people.

Most entrepreneurs don't have dozens of experts to call on at a moment's notice, but you can use the 90/10 rule on a small scale. Start by using a partner or mentor as your resource. You will be amazed as your decision batting average increases dramatically.

One footnote about the stolen Ford: Since that incident at Clayton Motors, the salesperson always goes along on the demo. Not only does it eliminate the possibility of the rare scenario described above, but it also gives the salesperson more time to get to know their new potential customer.

Some lessons seem so obvious, don't they?

CHAPTER 6

Volvos &
Volkswagens

Karen was born in October 1957, and she was such a good baby. She didn't cry much, usually slept through the night, and quickly became the sweetheart of our mobile home park.

The park was such a quiet and close-knit community. We barbecued together, went to movies together, and watched each other's homes. Everyone knew everyone, and if Mary and I needed a night out, Karen had plenty of babysitter volunteers.

Spending long days at the Texaco Station, now called Autoland by more and more people, I'd take my friendly competitor to lunch on Friday. I loved chatting with Raymond Norris, who ran a nice, well-displayed used car dealership right next to Autoland. By now, Raymond was a legendary figure in used cars. He was successful, well known, and respected in the community, and the sponsor of *The Mull Singing Convention*, a long-running gospel music program on Sunday morning TV.

Raymond was one of the really good guys in the business, loved by his peers as well as his customers. I had first met him at the Lenoir City car auction. Months earlier, when I was buying cars one at a time, I had picked up a few of his trades. Yes,

Raymond was a competitor, but he was also a friend and mentor.

I'd been at Autoland for about six months when, in the middle of 1958, Raymond shocked me even before we ordered lunch by saying, "I'm shut'n her down." I couldn't believe he was closing his lot next to mine. Having already leased the land next to Autoland for a restaurant, he offered to sell me his second dealership, the one on Clinton Highway, for $1,800, a great deal.

Raymond didn't charge for the dealership's "goodwill"—that is, the customer loyalty that any ongoing business brings to the table when it's up for sale. I just paid for the land, the sign, and the office furniture.

This was a chance to bring together all the skills I had learned from months of operating without inventory, staff, and other resources. Operating out of a tiny corner of a Texaco station, though profitable, was certainly limiting my upside potential. By contrast, Clinton Highway was fast becoming home for several new car dealerships. More and more people were shopping the various dealerships before making a buying decision.

Raymond's place, Norris Motors, was in an excellent location, in-between Malcolm's Drive-In Restaurant and McConkey Drugs. Both had been landmarks for more than two decades. I bit and bought. I closed Autoland and called my new place Clayton Motors. Raymond soon retired, though he later bought a motel, about eight miles down the road.

I'd need at least 25 cars on the new lot. With the larger inventory, and a good sign out front, we'd have an effective display, our primary marketing tool. That many cars would triple our inventory, and we could not rely on classifieds for sales. Now the traffic would be coming to us. Clearly, we needed staff—salespeople and mechanics.

Joe quit his job at the TV station to join me full-time. I found other staff through—where else?—the classifieds. One of the first was Carl Cole, our mechanic. Carl was in his early twenties— quiet, serious, cooperative, and honest—and someone who listened well, not only to me, but also to our customers.

Carl would remain a valued team member until he retired.

With most of the dealerships in town advertising heavily, I knew I needed a hook, something to make us stand out from the competition. We would advertise on radio, of course, but I didn't want the same old pitch. One of our salesmen, Ramsey Kerney, a professional musician for years, scribbled out a clever little jingle for me: *Buy your cars where the prices are slim. Go to Clayton Motors—and ask for Jim.*

I recorded my own commercials, always tagging the jingle at the end. I'd go to WIVK, a popular country station, with my guitar late at night when I could spend more time in their studio. I would record the commercial over and over trying different phrasing until they were distinctive. They did not have to be good, but they did have to "rise above the clutter."

I'll always be grateful to Jim Dick, the WIVK owner, who was so accommodating. Thanks to Jim, I carried a key to the station for 25 years with full access to the studio and record libraries.

When the commercials aired with that little two-line jingle, the response was instant. I was amazed at the name recognition those spots brought to us, and I was amused when I'd hear kids, as they wandered around the lot with their parents, singing and humming the tune.

By late '58, with sales up and better cash flow, we began to add TV to our advertising. During a taping session at WBIR-TV, I noticed that a guitar had been left behind on the set of Cas Walker's long-running, live morning show. Our camera was down, so while the crew fixed it, I picked up the guitar and started clowning with George Blevins, our new salesperson.

"See Jim Clayton on the Clinton Highhh-way," I sang, as I strummed the guitar. George double-dog dared me to sing the jingle in the commercial.

It caught on. People kidded me about being "the singing car salesman." It was fun and more successful than the radio spots.

Once again, I learned the power of thinking out of the box. Sure, it's easy to copy the competition. But doing business like everyone else means you'll get results like everyone else, which is usually average. For me, that's completely unacceptable.

We ran our spots on all three local stations including WTVK, the one that canned me a few years earlier. Most of our commercials were under $50 a play, and we bought a lot of $20 time, like during the late night movie.

That's inexpensive by today's standards, even in a small market, but back then, I was wondering whatever happened to "a dollar a holler."

After appearing night after night in their living rooms, even from inside an electronic box, people felt like they knew me. I mean, really knew me, like I had a personal relationship with them. They'd walk into the dealership and say, "Where's Jim?" I was like an old friend. Because of TV, they trusted me, and if you're selling something, that's about as good as it gets. I can't begin to overstate how much credibility those television commercials gave us.

Most markets then had only two or three commercial TV stations, making it easy to reach a large audience. Today this kind of mass exposure would cost a fortune. With cable and satellite, anywhere from 100 to 200 channels are all competing for the viewers. With the audience fragmented, a Johnny-Wants-To-Sell-Lots-Of-Stuff tends to get lost in the electronic muddle.

With the media landscape parceled this way, it's tough for our sales center managers to make effective media buying decisions. They can be easily seduced by a polished presentation and a low price. A glitzy pitch and a pretty face can sell airtime on even a weak station with poor ratings.

What the media reps may not tell, unless really challenged, is that a competing station may have five or ten times the audience.

Before investing in advertising, we insist the manager get to know the market. What TV channels are our customers watching?

What newspapers do they read? Which radio stations do they listen to?

This information can be simply and easily gathered right at the sales centers using a simple and inexpensive contest. Prospective customers register for a drawing by filling out a brief questionnaire. *How did you hear about us? Radio? If so, which station? TV? Which channel? Newspaper? Was it the* News-Sentinel *or the* Thrifty Nickel? We do this all the time, and the data collected leads to rational decision-making.

Modern digital radio tuners put an end to a nifty little trick we used to use back in the '50s, '60s, and '70s. We'd go to a nearby shopping center, walk through the parking lot, and look through each car window to see where the radio dial was set. We'd log the position on the dials of 100 cars. Almost always, 25 to 50 of the cars would be tuned to one station.

That survey told us a lot about the audience in that market.

One more comment on advertising—I don't think much of the Yellow Pages. Never have.

I will say this for them; their sales force includes some of the best pitch people on the planet. Each Clayton manager gets a pitch from them every year. When it's over, they're convinced: *Gotta get a Yellow Pages ad. A big one. After all, the competition has one.*

Over the years, I've had many arguments over this. Not any more. Now we do our own "consumer test." If the local manager insists, we'll buy a listing in the Yellow Pages, on one condition: He will have to follow our test program explicitly.

A bright red phone is set aside in the sales center office specifically for this test. A new number is assigned to it. This number appears only in a special Yellow Pages ad.

The deal is, if the red phone rings even a handful of times, we'll remove the "yellow handcuffs" and let the manager buy the ad, a small ad with the sales center's main number listed.

We've performed this test half a dozen times over the years in different cities. We've placed large ads, up to a quarter of a page.

But no matter what size the ad, or what city we test, the result is always the same.

That darn red phone never rings.

It was a great '58, until around Christmas. A drunk driver, weaving around Clinton Highway at two o'clock in the morning, slammed into the Clayton Motors used car lot. She wasn't hurt, but our inventory was. In two seconds, she wiped out our display, no less than a dozen of our most expensive cars.

Our body shop couldn't repair all the damaged cars. With much of our capital now tied up in unsaleable cars, we needed a larger body shop to get the cars ready to sell. Our shop foreman, Ed Anderson, and his people worked overtime. Remembering his friend who had just opened his own body shop, Ed made arrangements to have several cars repaired there at reasonable cost. Soon the repaired cars began to arrive back at the lot.

The wreck made the news, and I helped by hyping the story in our radio spots. Normally, we would not advertise wrecked cars, but all the publicity helped us move the repaired cars plus others over the holidays. We turned an unfortunate situation into a marketing advantage. In addition, the favorable insurance allowed us to give our customers some great bargains.

By the end of January, we'd sold all of the repaired cars.

It was a hectic time, but Joe insisted on taking off December 26, and for good reason. He and Dot were married. In what was now developing into a Clayton family tradition, they didn't take a honeymoon until later, either.

Even in those days, we took pride in being different. Sure, we watched the competition carefully and learned all we could. However, the intent was definitely not to imitate. For example, Kaisers and Studebakers, even though they were out of production, had appeal to some customers.

It was a tiny minority, to be sure, but we loved those devotees who'd pay as much for a well-maintained Studebaker as they would for a Ford or Chevy.

That meant a higher profit margin, as we bought them for less. Before long, the auctions and dealers were calling us, knowing we'd buy these quaint cars if they were in good condition.

It was probably my first practical lesson in position marketing—seize a niche that's under-served, and own the market. The fact that we were comfortable selling weird American cars made it easy for us to transition later to selling weird import cars.

Like the singing commercials, the Kaisers and Studebakers were a way to stand out from the competition. It made perfect sense to offer inventory that the competition wouldn't carry. But sometimes, it made sense to go toe-to-toe with a competitor.

Such was the case with Volkswagen.

It is generally known that the Volkswagen Beetle had a tremendous impact on the American car market. Unique in appearance—some might say peculiar—but a good ride, with great gas mileage, outstanding durability, a low sticker price, and the highest re-sale value in the industry. The Volkswagen was so sought after that the manufacturer didn't advertise, and dealers didn't discount; yet there was a six-month waiting list.

In Knoxville, the Snyder Brothers—Homer and Harrison— had the Volkswagen franchise. They sold the Beetles for about $1,850 and offered the standard waiting list. You could stay stuck on their list for about six months waiting for the privilege of buying a VW. As I recall, the Snyders were choosy about their customers and sold for cash only, no loans. They wouldn't take trades, and closed by five on weekdays and noon on Saturday.

I thought Homer and Harrison were passing up a lot of good business, and I saw an opportunity.

Having developed a friendly relationship with some dealers in D.C. and Baltimore, I'd fly up to see them each month in the Cessna 170. I was buying Studebakers, Kaisers, and a few imports from them. On one of those trips I was shocked to learn that Volkswagen was about to allow European distributors to indirectly make available extra cars that would be channeled to non-franchised dealers in the United States. Dealers like us.

The term was "grey marketing." Volkswagen never officially sanctioned it. We were told that the company flat-out denied that grey marketing ever took place. However, we had observed first hand the widespread phenomenon, which became an increasingly significant factor in satisfying the growing U.S.A. demand for Beetles.

Apparently, it worked this way: Volkswagen's parent company in Germany increased capacity and earmarked the extra production for European distributors. In turn, the distributors, directly or through large retailers, exported the excess cars to the States, through brokers who then sold to independents like us.

Despite their denials, I believe the parent company must have known, or could have known, all about the grey market network. Volkswagen of North America, the U.S. subsidiary, must have seen the cars selling rapidly in most major markets. Franchise dealers like the Snyders, angry over lost sales, must have exerted tremendous pressure on Volkswagen to cut off the supply of cars to the grey market network.

A non-franchised guy like me paid more for the Beetles ($1,865), so I'd have to sell them at a higher price to make a profit ($2,150, about $300 more than the Snyders). We also had to provide our customer warranty. It was great that the Volkswagen was durable and required little maintenance.

But, unlike the Snyders, we didn't make our customers wait. In fact, our customers could buy a Volkswagen and drive it off the lot that very day. For that, they'd gladly pay the extra $300. Ironically—and here's the kicker—Volkswagen would sell grey marketers like us all the Beetles we wanted. Yet they'd limit the number they would sell to their own dealers.

Limiting sales sounds strange, I know, but it's not an uncommon marketing strategy. Create the perception of a scarcity with the franchises, and the company stirs up more interest and scares up more buyers. At the same time, create a new distribution channel to allow the independents to buy all the cars they can sell, while keeping the cars scarce at the official Volkswagen dealers.

From what I saw, grey marketing appeared to be a strategy that Volkswagen used effectively for years—maximize demand, control supply—and use the grey market distribution channel to increase worldwide market share.

I started bringing over six Beetles every two weeks. Our distributor shipped them to the port in Jacksonville. Once the cars were unloaded at the dock, and I had paid for them, we'd rush them to Knoxville. Often we had pre-sold the Volkswagens, and would service and deliver them the same day. As sales climbed, I upped my order to a dozen at a time. Soon, it was 25.

Surely the Snyders were irritated to see this audacious little dealer outsell them with their own products. I don't recall ever having a conversation with Homer or Harrison, but I was the recipient of a few angry letters from them.

Let's put it this way: I was not on the Snyder Christmas list.

Publicly, they retaliated in the *News-Sentinel* with enormous ads, and a headline that bellowed, *"Beware of Grey Market Volkswagens!"* What followed was a litany of warnings indicating the mishaps that would befall the buyer foolish enough to purchase a Beetle from the evil, conniving grey marketeer.

Their writings suggested it was illegal for us to advertise Beetles as new when we weren't franchised dealers. (The logic escapes me.) They said our warranty wasn't as good as theirs (I disagree); that our Beetles were somehow "different" from theirs (disagree again); and weren't built to American specifications (they were). The Snyders never named us in print, but readers knew whom they were talking about.

This was free advertising for us. Readers couldn't help but wonder what the heck a "grey market Volkswagen" was. They'd check us out, just to satisfy their curiosity. Unwittingly, the Snyders became excellent promoters for us; the more they ran those ads, the more Beetles we sold. A top-flight, New York ad agency with a blank check couldn't have gotten us more publicity.

It's never smart to shine a light on your competitor, not even a candlelight. But Homer and Harrison flashed a blazing, 10,000-watt spotlight on us for all the market to see.

One downside to an entrepreneur's growth? Growing pains. By any definition, we were becoming a large-volume dealership. But our staff and support systems were straining under the weight of success.

Looking back, it's easy to see that we did not know what we did not know.

As our Volkswagen sales increased, the logistics of transporting them from the docks became more expensive and difficult. Commercial auto haulers were expensive and could not meet our delivery requirements.

Our practice was to hire local people to drive the cars from the docks back to Knoxville. Typically, college students delivered many of the cars. They appreciated the travel and the income.

Usually, I'd fly three of the drivers down in the Cessna. The others would drive down in a station wagon. The trip from Knoxville to Jacksonville was over 500 miles. Frequently, we'd arrive, accept the cars, hop right in, and drive overnight back to Knoxville.

In retrospect, it's painfully obvious this wasn't a good plan.

On one of our Volkswagen hauls, a supervisor somehow fell behind the six young drivers. Along those flat highways of South Georgia, they began to play "tag" while driving. One young man lost control and crashed. As the Volkswagen rolled, the force tossed him through the open sunroof. He died instantly.

I got the news just as I boarded the plane to fly back. I felt a sickening thud in the pit of my stomach. That nice young man was one of the three I'd brought down in the Cessna. What a god-awful, terrible experience, and what a waste of human life. That young man was only 18 years old. The family never blamed me, never filed a claim, but I was haunted by the accident, and swore such a thing would not happen again—never, ever.

While grappling with this tragedy, one of my customers, E.B. Daughtery, dropped into the office with a problem of his own, albeit a much more mundane one. His employer, a trucking company, had just laid him off, and now he couldn't make the payments on the new Volkswagen I'd sold him.

A light went on. I asked E.B. if he wanted a job.

We bought an old but serviceable Dodge "over-the-road" truck and a hauling trailer. E.B. transformed that into an eight-car tractor-trailer rig—well equipped and safe.

For the next 30 years, he drove back and forth every week, from dealership to port and back. E.B. was very meticulous, took care of that old rig like it was his baby, and never put so much as a scratch on it. Our cars came back the same way, without a blemish. E.B. was far more fastidious than any commercial hauler I can imagine. Simply put, he's the best driver-operator I've known.

Owning the rig saved us a lot of money, and with E.B. driving, saved me considerable worry. He retired in 1990. I know he won't mind me telling you that he took with him a profit sharing check worth $261,000—at the time, the largest ever from our company. He deserved every nickel.

By this time, we'd left our first location on Clinton Highway, the old Norris Motors lot, and moved three blocks away to the Tillery Theatre building. Since it was a movie theater, the auditorium had a couple of hundred seats and a sloping floor.

We removed the seats, but the inclined floor wasn't fixable. Believe me, a tilted floor may be great for movies, but as a garage, it's a challenge. Our mechanics had to lift one side of the car before placing blocks and jacks under the other side. It worked, but boy, was that ever a pain.

From the Volkswagen experience, we learned that the demand for import cars was growing in the Knoxville market. Clearly, this was an under-served niche, one we needed to capture.

A representative from Volvo visited, and Joe and I were

intrigued by this little-known Swedish import, even though sales in the U.S. were sluggish. We visited the new Volvo distributorship in Houston, and saw a splendid facility well equipped to service the superb cars. The transmission was smooth, the engine quiet, the braking excellent, and it was roomy and comfortable.

Perhaps Volvo sales were not impressive then, but its cars were, and so was its commitment to the U.S. market. We signed a new car franchise agreement with Volvo. It was our first and maybe our most important.

The response at the dealership was amazing. Maybe the average guy on the street didn't know much about Volvos, but technically savvy people already appreciated them. Scientists, engineers, and researchers from the nearby Oak Ridge National Laboratory began showing up, anxious to buy this superbly engineered car. (ORNL, now under the U.S. Department of Energy, is the home of the world's first nuclear reactor. It's credited for producing the atom bomb.)

The scientists from Oak Ridge bought so many cars that Volvo kept increasing our allocation, four times in one year.

It was nice that some of the smartest technical people on the planet saw the wisdom in buying the great Volvo cars—and from Clayton, too.

So successful was the Volvo alliance, we soon signed another franchise agreement with another import car company. Through the Renault distributor in Norfolk, we became an authorized dealer for the Dauphine, a little beauty made in France.

With Volvo and Renault, we made some not-so-subtle changes regarding our sales strategy with the Volkswagens.

We continued using the Beetles to attract prospective car buyers. But we'd gently guide those would-be Volkswagen prospects towards the Volvo or the Renault. Both models, of course, were conveniently displayed nearby.

There was even a policy: We wouldn't close on a Volkswagen sale unless the salesperson gave a pitch to the prospect on the virtues of our two new acquisitions. We'd do it subtly, but the message was clear.

For example, when an affluent customer had an itch for a Beetle—not uncommon, since Volkswagens remained in vogue— we'd do nothing to dissuade them. But there was nothing wrong with trying to entice them with the Volvo, which was larger, safer, and a better-performing car, though more expensive ($2,450).

On the other hand, if affordability was a concern, we'd steer them over to the Renaults. The Dauphine got even better gas mileage than the Beetle, had more accessories, including a radio, and was less expensive.

Renaults sold for $1,495, about $700 less than the Volkswagens, but gave us a much better profit margin, about $100 per car. The Dauphine also had excellent factory warranty support. (Remember, with the Volkswagens, we had to offer our own.)

With this in mind, we aggressively marketed Volvos and Renaults. We never stepped over the line, legally or ethically, but we did use a few marketing gimmicks to get our point across.

For instance, when customers took the Volkswagen out for a test spin, we didn't exactly take a route that flattered the Beetle's suspension. We knew the speed and the bumps in the road that would bluntly demonstrate any deficiencies. Conversely, we knew the speed and the bumps to avoid that permitted a smooth ride in the Dauphine over the exact same road.

We turned about half the Volkswagen shoppers into Renault buyers. A little shrewd, perhaps, but it wasn't like we were selling them lemons. Renault was, arguably, a better car than Volkswagen and saved every one of its customers hundreds of dollars.

By the end of 1959, our business doubled, and we expanded again. We signed with BMC, the British Motor Company, makers of MG, Austin Healey, Sprite, and Morris. We also picked up Jaguar, Saab, Simca, and Triumph. In 1960, we obtained the American Motors franchise, which included Rambler, and sold those exclusively at a new facility on Kingston Pike.

Joe and I love to tell the Rambler franchise story. The American Motors sales representative watched us sell Volkswagens, Renaults, Volvos, and other imports. He enthusiastically sold his regional people, but the application was pigeonholed in Detroit because we did not meet their capital requirements, but the primarily reason was my youth. I was only 25 years old.

Remember George Romney, who made the difficult decision two years earlier to drop the Nash and Hudson brands—two of the oldest marques in automobiles—to bet the farm on the compact Rambler line? It turned out to be a brilliant stroke. His decision to bet on Jim Clayton, after a two-hour meeting in the fall of 1959, was pure genius too—for about 20 months.

All this expansion meant more money and more financing, but Fenton Kintzing and Valley Fidelity obliged us on virtually every request. I'm sure there were times when Fenton went to the wall for us with Bob Culver and Valley Fidelity's Board of Directors, though he never mentioned it.

Meanwhile, my family was expanding too. In April of 1960, our second child, James Lee Jr., was born.

CHAPTER 7

Bankruptcy Blues

Today, it couldn't be done, but in those days, producing and airing a half-hour program on local Knoxville TV didn't cost any more than three one-minute commercials.

Do the math: That meant we could produce our own once-a-week music show and get literally 10 times the exposure for about the same price.

Once again, I was borrowing an old idea, this one from my high school days, when I produced and performed on the Saturday morning radio program. Like then, I had to find and sell my sponsors, but this time I did not have to go very far to find one. The sponsor was Clayton Motors.

We thought the best way to keep production costs low and viewer interest high was to broadcast a TV version of the old-time talent show. Local singers and musicians, eager for the exposure, would happily perform for free.

It was a tried and true format. For a dozen years, Ted Mack had been doing much the same on network TV with *The Original Amateur Hour,* an enormously popular show.

To make the show more exciting and appealing both to the talent and the audience, we announced with great fanfare that on the season finale, the grand prizewinner would win a brand-new 1961 Rambler. The second finalist would win $1,000, and quarterly finalists would receive $500. Monthly winners would receive prizes from Lynn's Guitars (now Broadway Sound). We called the show *Talent Parade.*

Our contestants, from Knoxville and the surrounding areas, swarmed us. Country singers, barbershop quartets, gospel, folk, rock, bluegrass—I was astounded at the enormous talent pool that applied, and just how good so many of the performers were. Producing a weekly half-hour show would be no problem.

I co-hosted the program, along with Carl Williams, a popular local news anchor. Even from the first show, the amateur performers automatically delivered their own built-in audience. When little Susie from a local high school was singing, it was certain that her parents, brothers, sisters, grandparents, aunts, uncles, friends, classmates, church, Girl Scout troop—everyone who knew her or had even heard of her—would tune in.

The entire process generated lots of involvement for me, our staff, and the company out in the neighboring community. The show became such a well known success that our mechanics, file clerks, salespeople, and other company staff would be constantly asked by family and friends for details about the show.

"How can I get my niece who sings just like Loretta Lynn an audition?" they asked.

The show was all the "buzz." We ran *Talent Parade* in prime time and consistently ranked right up there with even network competition.

Perhaps for the first time in my life, I was beginning to feel financially secure, even though all the earnings were plowed right back into the business. My salary—Joe's too—wasn't much more than a factory worker's.

Still, we had a nice lifestyle. Mary and the children seemed happy, and as a bonus, I was performing on TV every week.

Maybe I wasn't Eddy Arnold, but considering that I'd been a

cotton picker on a dirt farm less than a decade before, I wasn't doing badly. Not badly at all. And I was still in my mid-twenties.

In early 1960, Tom Preston, a new vice-president at Hamilton National Bank, walked into our office. Hamilton National was the largest bank in Knoxville and Fenton's competitor.

Tom was about my age and just out of the Air Force. Like me, he owned a plane and hangared it at Cherokee Aviation. During the first meeting, we talked mostly about his flying experience. Later, I'd enjoy flying with him in his P-51.

Tom's lofty position with Hamilton wasn't due to his financial wizardry or banking experience. What he did have was a grand-father who had owned a large share of the bank, and an uncle, Harry Nacey, the bank president, who was amenable to giving his young nephew a break. He gave Tom an opportunity to develop an installment-lending department at Hamilton National, and supported him with what should have been plenty of capital.

Now Tom could compete with the "Big Two" in town—Fenton and Johnny Cox of the Bank of Knoxville who handled most of that bank's indirect lending. Tom began to relentlessly pursue relationships with businesses like ours.

He made up for his lack of seasoning with a quiet persistence, coupled with a deep desire to make a name for himself. His soft-spoken nature shielded a star pilot's iron will. He certainly had the knack for telling me what I wanted to hear, which then amounted to one sentence: Grow more, and fast.

This was a language not normally used by bankers, at least not around me. Fenton spoke the cautionary dialect of discretion, a vocabulary of vigilance. He'd go to the wall for us, but never let us do anything off-the-wall.

Fenton favored growth, but in gradual stages. Too gradual for us at the time.

In the spring of 1960—as I learned to do rolls and loops in Tom's P-51—I quietly began diverting some business to Hamilton National Bank. First, a little, then more. Tom, ever determined in his polite way, kept pushing. He wanted all of our business, but was persistently patient.

His encouraging words sharply contrasted with what I was hearing from Fenton those days. By now, Bob Culver, president and CEO of Valley Fidelity, was urging him to pull back. *Rein those guys in,* Bob would say, in so many words.

As always, Fenton went to bat for us, but maybe not quite as enthusiastically as before, probably because he knew his boss was right. We *were* growing too fast.

Fenton told us that Culver and the board were suggesting a "growth moratorium" on our portfolio of business for the next 18 months. This meant we would keep giving them business each month, but only as much as our customers were paying off during the period.

That was a disappointment. *Just look at our sales volume,* I thought. *What's the problem?* I compared Tom's eagerness to expand with Valley Fidelity's sudden reluctance. We would need unwavering support to reach our growth objectives. Changing lending partners was becoming an interesting topic of conversation for Joe and me.

It was hard for us to relate to the idea of "life without Fenton." It would be difficult to leave Fenton, our friend, mentor, and financial godfather. We had a great relationship, almost like father and son. I fully realized and appreciated the fact that if it weren't for Fenton, there would be no Clayton Motors. Still, we were confident that Tom could and would deliver the service and support we would need for our little growing empire.

In July 1960, we transferred all of our accounts to Tom Preston and Hamilton National Bank.

Signing an enormous loan package at Tom's office, we shook hands and briefly celebrated our friendship and growing business relationship over a cigar. He gave me a cashier's check for $110,000, payable to Valley Fidelity. I walked over to Fenton's office, wondering how he'd respond, and hoping this wouldn't end our friendship.

Characteristically, Fenton reacted to the news without rancor. He didn't get angry, didn't even raise his voice. But he was sad, and not so much because he was losing my business. More than anything, he seemed to be sad for me.

Fenton, of course, was up to speed on Tom Preston and his various lending activities. He was well aware of how Tom's liberal credit requirements had already taken significant market share from Valley and other lenders. There were tears in his eyes when he said, "Tom's department's gonna get in trouble. I'll give him a year. You'll be lucky if you don't get caught up in it."

There goes Fenton again, I thought, *so conservative, so careful.* Also remarkably gracious, and I was grateful he didn't slam the door on our relationship.

With Tom's liberal financing for our customers and his generous funding of increased inventory, our sales increased every month. True, our overhead, with a larger inventory and a staff of 70, was also growing. The year 1960, with the TV show, larger staff, and Tom's financing, was for Clayton a great year. The coming year would be a blowout for sure—we thought.

By the spring of 1961, a blip showed up on our radar screen. Our moles inside Hamilton National passed along a rumor that Tom's department had been audited.

The audit, said the rumor, turned up irregularities. Something about high delinquency and poor loan documentation.

Not that I paid much attention. Mary and I were on our way overseas, to be wined and dined, honored and feted—my reward for an extraordinary sales year with Volvo, a company in the U.S. barely five years and struggling to meet its sales goals.

The brass at Volvo were treating us to a lavish, all-expenses-paid, two-week trip to Gotenburg, Sweden, the company's international headquarters, where I'd be a guest of honor—the personification of the Great American Success Story. I felt like royalty.

I delivered a speech before 600 of my peers who'd flown in

from countries all over the world. At least a dozen interpreters translated as I spoke; it was like a United Nations of Volvo dealers. Film cameras whirred as I stood there, 27 years old, from the heartland of the most powerful country in the world, the very embodiment of Volvo's future.

With a line eerily reminiscent of the one used decades later in the Kevin Costner film *Field of Dreams,* I told the Volvo executives that "if you build them, America will buy them, and I'll keep selling my share."

They gave me a standing ovation, and I loved every second of it. They were so appreciative of our hard work and efforts to increase Volvo awareness in our region. It was a wonderful occasion for Mary and me. After the speech, they took us all over to Scandinavia, like touring VIPs, to speak at regional meetings.

I returned to the States thrilled and exhilarated, on top of the world. Joe met us at the airport. I thought he'd be glad to see me, but he had a downtrodden look. Something was clearly wrong.

"We have a problem at the bank," he said.

Considering that for two weeks I had been recently identified and confirmed as the "Personification of the Great American Success Story," I was quite unprepared for what was to follow.

We drove directly from the airport to Hamilton National Bank's downtown office. Joe, filling me in on what little he knew, was in a state of disbelief. Still reeling, he told me that Hamilton National called in all of our notes. The bank was demanding immediate payment of all principal and interest—all $275,000 of it—today.

It wasn't possible. And it didn't make sense. We weren't behind on any payments to the bank; we never had been. In fact, within the past month, Hamilton National had loaned us another $75,000 for new Rambler inventory.

In a moment, my world turned upside-down. My triumphant visit to Sweden was already a fading memory.

When Joe and I walked into the bank's conference room, our

two attorneys, Paul Gillenwater and Jim Chambers, were there with our accountant Tom Pannell.

The opposition countered with two seasoned attorneys, a subdued Tom Preston, and the aforementioned Harry Nacey, bank president—never someone to take lightly even under the best of circumstances, which this obviously wasn't.

The meeting was a disaster, a Hindenburg blowing up in our faces. Paul and Jim, very sharp guys, were superb lawyers. But then, they were young, just out of law school. They began telling the bank's veteran attorneys and Harry Nacey what they could and could not do. It was not going well.

This was like rubbing a feather duster in the face of the proverbial 800-pound gorilla. It doesn't hurt the gorilla, only makes him mad, and he'll swallow your feather duster just before he chews you up. I could see the mounting aggravation on Nacey's face.

He listened for a while. Then he suddenly looked at his watch and announced he had to be at the Cherokee Country Club in 20 minutes. And then Nacey said something that made my blood run cold.

"Let's bankrupt these little S.O.B.'s. I can't be late for my tennis match."

The meeting was over.

There's the old story about the young man wrongly convicted of murder. The judge sets a date for the hanging. The man turns to his lawyer and says, "Now what?" His lawyer, busily placing books and notes back in his briefcase, rather nonchalantly says, "Well, Sonny, I'm going back to the office—as for you, they're gonna hang ya."

That was pretty much our position. Lawyers can go back to their offices. But we'd have to live with the consequences.

We'd been thrust into a nightmare, and the night was young.

We soon confirmed that little rumor about the bad audit report. Hamilton National Bank had made a lot of bad loans. The bank regulators found bookkeeping and accounting records that were badly flawed and loan files that contained incomplete or inaccurate information.

Actually, the examiners could've just asked Hamilton National's customers. It was my understanding they'd flooded the bank with angry calls about all kinds of account errors: the wrong due dates, un-credited payments, and incorrect balances.

Harry Nacey and his board decided to terminate relationships with all of their indirect dealers: car, boat, furniture, appliance, piano, and more.

Even while beating our heads in during the meeting, they had representatives on the way to the Clinton Highway and Kingston Pike dealerships as well as our body shop. In hand, they had a court order, bankruptcy papers, and the authority to take over all of our assets.

When Joe and I arrived back at the dealerships, we saw the bank was hell-bent on taking everything, which would wipe out this business we had worked so hard to grow. They seemed in a huge rush to shove us out the door. Their reps took the keys to the cars, every last one.

They even invaded the service department and snatched the keys of our *customer's* cars, those in for an oil change or repair work. (The bank was out of line on that one. We helped our bewildered customers get their keys back, though it took a day.) They also grabbed our mechanics' tools, another mistake.

Jim Shelby, our friend and a certified public accountant, was in our sales office examining inventory records as part of a year-end audit procedure. Darned if they didn't take his adding machine and car keys. He was mad as heck. In fact, when I asked him about it while writing this, he got red in the face and went into so much heated detail that I wished I had not broached the subject. All of those words from an accountant—can you imagine?

They took all of the cash, seized most of the accounting records, and locked up the rest of the assets to hold for a liquidation auction. It seemed cold-blooded, though a few of the bank employees—friends of ours—were kind and sympathetic, even as they carted our assets away.

There was nothing our team could do as they stood around like zombies, clueless as to what was happening to their vocational existence.

The bank wiped us out, just like that. We were whipped and silent. We were history!

Clayton Autoland was gone.

I remember how Grandpa Clayton used to say, "If you have to swallow a frog, don't look at him too long. If you have to swallow two frogs, swallow the big scudder first."

So many frogs to swallow, and these were all super-sized.

Later that night, I talked to Mary, who was stunned, perplexed, but still supportive. I went to bed, thinking my life, for all practical purposes, was over.

I woke up at five in the morning, after a good night's sleep. I felt great, even with bankruptcy hanging over us. Luckily I've never had any problem getting to sleep, no matter what.

My mind was revved up, my thoughts were racing, and I called Joe. By six-thirty, the two of us, along with four of our best people, were at Shoney's on Clinton Highway.

This skeleton crew of six that would launch a new company.

Although we were bankrupt, we weren't powerless. We could think, and we could dream. The Hamilton bank couldn't stop us from conducting business. Legally, we could form a new company, even while working through the nightmare of bankruptcy.

Our company, as we knew it, was gone. But I wanted to go again. So did Joe.

Our attorneys dropped by, sympathetic, but not able to help. They reviewed the dismal process of bankruptcy, adding the cheery note that the bank would probably seek criminal penalties. Then they said, "Guys, we've done all we can for you." We now needed an attorney who specialized in bankruptcy, and they had someone in mind.

At two that afternoon, Gillenwater and Chambers introduced us to Bernie Bernstein. They shook hands and asked us to call if they could help. On the way out, Jim Chambers said, "Forget this month's bill, it's on the house."

Bernie—studious, focused, and always polite—didn't waste any time. As he filed the appropriate legal responses to the bankruptcy, he applied for our new company charter. Clayton Motors Inc. was born.

Bernie patiently explained the difficult, but workable, process of launching a new corporation when the principals are ensnared in the bankruptcy of another company. The major obstacle would be funding the operation. Certainly, no bank would touch us.

First, the new company needed a location. The easiest thing to do, obviously, was to keep operating out of at least one of our current locations. Joe and I could scrape up enough cash to pay rent and turn on the utilities.

But Hamilton National had taken over both dealerships and the body shop. Our leases at all three locations had automatically terminated. It appeared to be an impossible situation for us.

Not really, said Bernie, already earning his pay. All we had to do, he explained, was to contact our old landlords and sign a new lease with them, for the same land, at the same price, at the same terms, in the name of the new company.

A nice thought. But a tough assignment, at least in terms of the Kingston Pike location. It meant dealing with Anna May "Ma" Cain, a formidable figure even in her seventies. She was owner of huge parcels of land in West Knoxville, including the Rambler dealership on Kingston Pike.

I'll never forget meeting her, this very rich woman stooped over a scrub board washing clothes. She could afford an appliance store full of washing machines, and here she was, wearing a feed sack dress! She was a true larger-than-life character, and she wouldn't offer me a new lease. ("I would never get involved with someone who was bankrupt," she said.)

That left the Tillerys, who owned the converted theater on Clinton Highway. They were receptive, particularly when we gave them a check for the prior month's rent, which had been returned by the bank.

We signed a new lease immediately. The old home for Autoland was now the new home for Clayton Motors.

Now we had the delicious pleasure of telling the bank to get off our property. We were polite. Still, the bank was furious.

We made it easy for them, however. In fact Clayton Motors allowed the bank to store cars, tools, parts, and other assets at the dealership. It took them a few weeks to remove them. With all the bank's assets still parked on the lot and all the activity, it looked, to the untrained eye, like business as usual.

To restart, we invested what little money we could raise in a few insurance company wrecks. This gave work to Ed Anderson and his helper while providing some future inventory to talk about to potential customers. As the mechanics retrieved their tools from the bank, we reopened our service department, now reduced to a staff of one: Carl Cole. After the bank auctioned our assets and moved out, all six of us parked our cars at the front of the lot, so the place wouldn't look so empty.

Certainly these were depressing times, but Joe and I spent almost no time moaning about what happened. Both of us tend to be consistently optimistic. I truly believe that every day brings opportunity, even the bad days.

This was not a characteristic I worked to acquire. This, I think, is a gift from Mother. She is the eternal optimist and believes there's good in everything and everybody, no matter how bleak the situation.

Somehow, this wonderful quality rubbed off on her two boys, and I think it's responsible for a good part of our success.

In no time at all, word spread that we were bankrupt. It was on the TV news and in the *Knoxville News-Sentinel* and *Knoxville Journal*—front pages no less—and even on WIVK.

One newspaper article reported that I'd been on a trip to Sweden just before the bankruptcy. This was accurate, of course, but some readers mixed up *Sweden* with *Switzerland*, and concluded that I had been overseas squirreling away money in a secret Swiss bank account.

I'd never been to Switzerland, and my first trip would be a dozen or so years away. I had no inkling about how to set up a "secret bank account" there, or anywhere else. However, the rumor persisted, and in 1991, after a scuba diving trip to Grand Cayman, my then-girlfriend Kay was asked by her friends, "Does Jim do banking in the Caymans, or does he keep it all in Switzerland?" You'd think a misunderstanding like that could be easily corrected, but no matter what I said, people had made up their minds and wouldn't hear otherwise.

That rumor continued to circulate for decades, until it finally faded away. Even some of my newer friends will occasionally nudge me and ask, "Do you still have some of that money over in Switzerland?" Surely they are kidding, but I am never sure.

Esso and Diner's Club dumped me with astonishing speed, even though my accounts were current. In a matter of hours after the court filings, the business community had flagged our credit files. Our name was mud. Our vendors cut us off. Ads in the newspaper suddenly required cash up front. Ditto for TV.

John Hart at Channel 10 understandably canceled the *Talent Parade* program two-thirds of the way through the season, infuriating some of the contestants who had a shot at winning the Rambler grand prize. Jim Dick at WIVK soon followed suit. (Less than a year later, John would be the first media company to support us with an open account.)

Worst of all, the car companies that franchised us—American Motors, BMC, Renault, Saab—dropped us, just like that, as would be expected—*all except Volvo.*

Joe and I love telling the Volvo story, especially because ours is the oldest Volvo dealership in North America continuously owned and operated by one family.

To my friends at Volvo, our premiere franchise, I made the obligatory call and described the events that had transpired since their golden boy had arrived back in the States.

It was a painful and embarrassing conversation, explaining how the star of Volvo's two-week corporate extravaganza—the *Very Embodiment Of The Future Of Volvo In The United States*, no less—was suddenly mired in bankruptcy.

I told them how appreciative we were for all their confidence and support. I tried to radiate confidence, a difficult task when you've just been declared bankrupt. They knew that six new Volvos were on the way to Knoxville. Faced with the dilemma of securing possession of the cars, or allowing us to pay for them and remain their dealer, they quickly chose the latter. The fact that we had recently spent two weeks together in Sweden and had an unblemished sales and service record, helped make their difficult decision easier.

Volvo stuck with us. For that we are enormously grateful. Their support was limited for a few months—at only six new cars a shipment, but that was more than reasonable considering the circumstances.

One other company did not cancel my credit privileges.

My American Express card inscribed with *Member since 1959*, curiously, wasn't cancelled. I had no idea why, and assumed it was some sort of bureaucratic blunder. I saw no need to correct the oversight.

To this very day, that card remains in my wallet.

Many times, I've considered canceling. In my opinion, the annual fee is too high, and it doesn't have universal acceptance. Hard times reveal which of our relationships are truly lasting, though. As I think back to those terrible times, and how American Express and Volvo stuck with me, I just don't have the heart to cut up that card.

I still drive a Volvo, too.

CHAPTER 8

Back In Business

Aside from American Express, it seemed everyone had heard some version of the bankruptcy story within a few days—except Mother and Dad back in Finger.

Joe and I didn't want to hide it from them, but we didn't want to worry them, either, at least not until we understood the issues ourselves. Then we could explain it to them. Before we got our chance, someone felt compelled to call Mother.

"Mrs. Clayton, there's something you need to know," said the voice. "But first, you have to promise never to tell anyone I gave you this information."

Mother agreed, baffled by the strange request, but curious. Then the caller broke the news.

"Your sons have just filed for bankruptcy," he said.

Mother was stunned, then humiliated. To her, bankruptcy was about as bad as first-degree murder. She immediately called us.

We hemmed and hawed, but she insisted on the full story without embellishment. Mother was horrified at the very notion of bankruptcy. To her, it was a vile concept—legal hocus-pocus, a sleazy way to skip out on a debt.

She reminded us that no one in our family had ever welched

on a debt. We assured her we wouldn't be the first.

I'd always wondered just who called Mother that day. I asked her numerous times over the years—so did Joe—but she would not tell. No way! After all, she'd made a promise.

In our family, it became the topic that wouldn't die. From time to time, we badgered and teased Mother about it, asking her over and over who the mystery caller was.

But she'd never tell anyone—not even Dad.

As she was being interviewed for this book, I brought the subject up again.

"Mom, who told you that your boys were bankrupted back there in 1961?" I asked, and went on to tell her the business failure story would not be complete without this detail.

Under my withering cross-examination, and finally amidst considerable laughter, Mother finally caved.

"Well, since he's passed away, I guess it'll be okay," she said. "It was your father-in-law at the time, T. P. Shelton."

Until that moment, Mother's lips had remained sealed, even though my father-in-law had died years earlier! (Incidentally, I'd always had a good relationship with him, and his intentions in calling Mother, I'm certain, were to give Mother and Dad "the opportunity to help your boys," as he told her.)

The moral of the story: Nobody, but nobody, can keep a secret better than Mother—41 years! To her, a promise made is a promise kept. As Paul Harvey would say, "That's the rest of the story."

After calling us, Mother focused on how in the world she would break the news to Cratus. He would take it hard.

She paced for hours, waiting for him to get home. Later, she would tell us that was the longest evening of her life.

By five the next morning, Dad was on the road for the long drive to Knoxville.

Mother called early to let us know that Dad would be in Knoxville by noon. Our anxiety passed when Dad arrived and we saw he was here to help, not to admonish. Later we would hear a mildly worded "I told you so," in the form of a half-hearted reference to our "too much and too fast" business philosophy. But like Mother, he was supportive, though frustrated and scared.

Just how scared wasn't clear until we introduced him to Bernie Bernstein, who was representing our personal as well as our business interests. Dad looked at Bernie and blurted out, "Are my boys going to jail?"

I was amazed to see that Dad had tears in his eyes.

Bernie put his arm around Dad's shoulder, and said, "Mr. Clayton, I assure you that your boys won't go to jail. I'll see to it."

Bernie had a way of inspiring confidence instantly, and I could see the relief on Dad's face. At that moment, I don't know who I loved more—Bernie or my father.

Before he left, Dad gave us a check for $2,600, which cleaned out his bank account at the Home Banking Company. He headed back to Finger, and we promised to keep him posted—and ourselves out of any more trouble.

When those six Volvos arrived from Houston, we had to come up with $8,800 to pay for them. My brother-in-law, Joe Shelton, the Oldsmobile dealer in McMinnville, loaned us the money and took the titles as collateral. We sold the cars quickly, paid him back promptly, and made a nice profit, especially since, once again, we had very little overhead.

The cash from Dad, and the profit from the six Volvos allowed us to pay rent, place some ads, and provide grocery money for our small and devoted staff of four.

Volvo, true to its word, sent us another shipment of six cars.

To generate a reasonable level of traffic and sales, we needed inventory. We needed more than a handful of Volvos arriving every few weeks from Sweden and the few restored insurance company wrecks.

How could we get a significant number of cars on the lot, and how could we do it quickly?

Joe and I knew the bank was auctioning off some of our repossessed cars in another few weeks.

What if—somehow—we could buy back our cars at the auction? Was that legal? We asked Bernie Bernstein.

Sure it was, Bernie told us. After all, only our former business was bankrupt.

"Neither of you as individuals are bankrupt," Bernie explained. He went on to say that our personal credit was unblemished. He assured us that Joe, me, or any of our authorized staff, could bid on behalf of the new company, as long as we had the money.

Money? That was the sticky part, but I had a plan.

When I was in Sweden, I helped strike a sweet deal the night before making my Kevin Costner speech. We were at the elegant home of the president of Volvo for a reception and dinner. During the meal, I was on the president's right, and Tom Downing, a successful Volvo dealer from Atlanta, was on his left.

Tom and I urged the President to sell both of us a new Volvo Sports Coupe, the P-1800, a limited production vehicle that wouldn't be in the U.S. for another year.

We'd driven the Coupe the day before at the factory, and a stunning piece of work it was. We didn't want to wait a year to be able to display it in our showrooms. We wanted it now, pronto. Both of us were convinced that the P-1800 would stop traffic dead in its tracks. The car would be a natural promotional attraction that customers in droves would want to see.

We schmoozed and cajoled. I promised to promote the car on *Talent Parade,* and Tom, a very persuasive and charming guy, said he'd use the Coupe to push the Volvo line to at least one percentage point higher in the Atlanta market share.

Before dessert was over, Tom and I had a deal. Volvo would send each of us a car.

We both wrote checks for $3,700, the factory sale price. The cars were on the water when the business closed.

Now that we were in survival mode, desperately raising cash for inventory and to meet payroll, we did not have the promotional budget to effectively utilize the Coupe as we had originally planned. Instead, we reluctantly decided to turn it into operating cash immediately.

The Coupe arrived during the third week of bankruptcy. Fortunately, Volvo didn't bill the car to the dealership name, but to me personally. This meant the car, at least in my mind, was a personal asset, not a business asset.

That was critical, since any business asset of mine, right now, belonged to the bankruptcy trustee.

Go ahead and accuse me of leaping on a technicality, but I deny this was a matter of legal gymnastics. Volvo's documentation made it plain the car was mine. In fact the company had not reimbursed me for the personal check I issued in Sweden for the car. It was my car.

Sure, the bank could've challenged my ownership. First, they would have to know it existed. Oh, we wanted to show it off so bad, but didn't dare. If their attorneys had successfully argued the Coupe was a business asset, the bank's attorneys, no doubt, would have asked the bankruptcy trustee to seize the car.

At any rate, I paid the $1,200 customs and a delivery fee, and then stored the Coupe in Joe's garage for a few days. Racey Feezell, a well-heeled Ph.D. from the Oak Ridge laboratory, happily purchased the P-1800 for $8,500 cash. This gave us a very nice profit, and over $7,000 of desperately needed capital to invest in additional inventory.

That $7,000 was the kicker. Add that to Dad's $2,600, another $3,000 raised by the staff, the profit from new Volvos, and the small change from the insurance company wrecks, and we could pay our operating expenses and still have cash for the upcoming auction. And it didn't hurt when our friend, Racey Feezell, came through once again, this time with a $10,000 loan.

A few weeks after selling the Coupe, there we were, just faces in the crowd with wads of cash in our wallets and smiles on our faces, at the first of three bank auctions featuring some very familiar merchandise.

Representatives from the bank were there, too, obviously displeased with our cheerful presence and speculating as to what sinister scheme might be afoot.

They didn't have to wait long. New cars. Used cars. Triumphs. MGs. Renaults. Beetles. Parts. Tools. Supplies. And here's the beauty of it; we knew the merchandise, so we had a distinct advantage over other bidders.

As we won bid after bid, you could practically see jaws drop as they watched us—*those poor, bankrupted souls*—buy back our own inventory at bargain prices.

We saw the bank guys whispering frantically to each other. *Is that legal?*

Could they do anything to stop us? No, they couldn't.

We kept bidding, adding a variety of quality used cars at very attractive prices to our meager inventory. To our credit, we were careful not to gloat. Not much, anyway. It was obvious that bidders were unsettled by our presence and especially by our active involvement.

By selective bidding at the three auctions, we bought about 50 cars and were amazed at some of the prices. The average price paid for the cars was a little over $800.

Now you may be asking, after performing some quick arithmetic, just how could we buy 50 cars plus parts, tools, and supplies with our relatively small amount of cash?

Simple. We pre-sold a lot of those cars and paid for them with the buyer's own money.

Think about it; we knew the condition of the cars that the bank had on the block and precisely what they were worth. There was nothing wrong with contacting potential buyers to explain how they could buy a good car and save a bundle, as we took their cash to make a purchase for them and a reasonable profit for us.

Those reasonable profits added up.

As for the cars we took back to the lot, we doubled our money on most of them. This was still a great buy for our customers, and kept our cash flow trickling along.

I received some "sympathy job" offers, mostly in advertising or car sales. Instead, I went back to radio. A little, 1,000-watt station in Fountain City—WROL—had just gone on the air, and they hired me as the station's chief engineer and the host of yet another Saturday morning program. The base pay was $125 a week, plus commissions on any advertising spots I sold.

The Saturday show gave me a chance to promote the business—good publicity, for a change—and the salary was enough to allow me to forego taking a salary out of the new business.

A long the way, we would occasionally sell one of Fenton's customers a car. Of course, the customer would want Fenton to make the loan. After a time, Fenton and I began to talk about the possibility of his being able to support us by making a few loans to our good customers. He agreed to look at a few good applications to allow us to get our foot in the bank's door again.

During this period, one of the interesting reoccurring events was when someone who purchased from us before the bankruptcy would come in or call with a complaint about their car. Most likely the complaint would be about their loan with Hamilton Bank.

It seemed our customers were, in some cases, well informed about our conflict with the Hamilton. In fact, some would come in verbalizing their anger over the bank's poor communications or service in general. We listened to them and dropped a few hints. Soon they would ask how they could get rid of their car and loan.

The customer was delighted to hear that the Hamilton, to our knowledge, was not reporting voluntary repossessions to the credit bureau. I remember a very well known media personality who, upon learning that he could turn his car back to the

Hamilton and would likely not have it reported, immediately took his car to their compound. He was driving a new Volvo the next day financed by his credit union.

With our help, you could almost see the light go on as they pondered the scenario: *Why should I continue to pay for a car I don't like to a bank I don't like? Why not get rid of the clunker and get a better car with a lower payment with a bank that I do like?*

We knew it was highly unlikely Hamilton National would harass them, either with a negative credit report or for further payment. On the very few instances when the bank did try to collect, we'd counsel the customer on how to handle negotiations.

Once the deal was done, the customer would take the old car to the bank's storage lot, home for all of our repossessed vehicles. They'd turn it in and be done with it.

Usually, the bank dropped the matter rather than research the records; it apparently couldn't handle such an undertaking. Instead, they simply added the cars to their auction list, and we'd be at the proceedings to buy them back.

Now, Hamilton National was the one with too many frogs to swallow. For our part, we did our level best to supply them with as many frogs as possible—and the bigger, the better.

The customer could choose to dump the car back on the bank, then drive off with a better car and a lower payment plan with another bank—namely, Fenton's.

An observation: Wasn't it odd how Hamilton National Bank had a disproportionate number of foreclosures from our old customers? Had we sold a bad batch of cars? I absolutely, categorically deny it. Did we service the cars properly? Of course we did.

Were some of our loyal customers, many of whom were friends of ours, so mad at the bank for bankrupting us, *that they wanted to get even—and got a better deal to boot*? I really can't say. It is possible this was the motivation in some cases.

But it was odd.

It was not a pleasant experience, testifying at our own dead company's bankruptcy hearings, particularly when they were held at the intimidating Federal Courthouse building in downtown Knoxville. I had to do it nine times.

Remember, back in the 1960s, bankruptcy was not fashionable. Today, it seems companies frequently consider and occasionally use the bankruptcy courts simply to facilitate a restructuring process. In fact, Kmart is an example of a company that has been in bankruptcy only a few months. They just announced that they will be out of bankruptcy by the first of the year.

It was a harrowing experience, watching the bank's lawyers, buttressed by the trustee Hymie Kern—an attorney appointed by the court—go after the assets of our company.

And it was excruciating to hear the bank's lawyers suggest "fraud" at every possible opportunity, and to chastise us for "not cooperating," while threatening criminal charges endlessly.

Invariably, there was an almost-daily litany of allegations, either we had misrepresented loan applications, or were withholding assets from the trustee, or had overvalued collateral for our loans.

Finally, Judge Clive Bare, one of the nation's most distinguished bankruptcy jurists, closed it out. The bankruptcy would pay 41 cents on the dollar. That is, our creditors got 41 cents on each dollar of debt owed to them.

The payback in cases such as ours was usually five cents, maybe 10, on the dollar. In fact, if creditors got much more than 10 percent, then the bankruptcy proceedings were probably not justified. And there we were, at 41 cents!

All along, those who knew the game, like Bernie, were amazed that Hamilton National had gone the bankruptcy route with us. I like to think that even Nacey, his lawyers, and the bank management finally realized they had made a serious mistake. This seemed to be the case, because the bank appeared to drop plans to use bankruptcy to liquidate the debt of its other customers.

As to the much-bandied-about criminal and civil charges, the bank never filed. I don't think it was because they suddenly became nice guys. I think they realized their books were not in good shape, and it would be embarrassing if brought out in court.

In Bernie's opinion, if Hamilton National had sued us, we could've counter-sued for improperly handling our cash and customer loan record keeping. We were prepared to outline, in graphic detail, just how the bank mismanaged and misapplied our funds.

Joe and I vowed to pay off, in full, the additional 59 percent not covered by the bankruptcy court to all of our creditors—as a matter of honor. It took five years, but as far as we could tell, we settled our accounts with everyone—every car company, every vendor, every supplier—but one. The bank.

Not that we didn't try. Despite all the bad blood between the bank and us, Joe and I repeatedly tried to dialog with them, asking for an accounting of the losses they had experienced.

But each time we approached the Hamilton, they refused to provide us with any records, nor would they discuss the topic, even as they saw us reimburse other creditors.

The bank didn't fire Tom Preston; he was family. But they did demote him. This very gung-ho, can-do star pilot was, as far as banking was concerned, professionally grounded. He kept a low profile for the remainder of his career.

Decades after this debacle, I ran into him having lunch at Regas Restaurant. We spoke warmly.

"Jim, if they had left us alone, we could've worked it out," he said. "Glad you've been successful."

Then he moved on.

It was a nice thing for him to say, and probably he was right. If everyone had responded with a cool head, we *could've* worked it out, probably within a few months, without any loss to the bank, to the creditors, or to us.

Instead we saw such enormous anguish, frustration, pain,

embarrassment, loss of money, loss of jobs and loss of face, for so many people—every bit of it completely avoidable. Why did Hamilton National do it? Why did they drop an atom bomb?

I believed then, as I do now, that the bank at some point decided to let Tom Preston fail. He was far too inexperienced for such a position, and once he got in too deep, support was not made available to save him and his department.

It may have looked like Harry Nacey responded to the call of family. But it seemed he never wanted Tom at the bank, for whatever reason, so it appeared that they let him fail.

That brief conversation with Tom at the Regas was the last time I saw him. He died a couple of years later.

Tom was a good guy. I liked him a lot personally. It's just too bad he didn't stay in the Air Force.

Though I'd never wish bankruptcy on anyone, I will say one thing for it. Go through the experience, and you'll find out who your friends are.

Volvo never gave up on us. They kept sending us six cars at a time, just like they promised, and never reneged. We kept up our end of the deal too and never missed a payment to them. That respect, loyalty, and concern for each other has blossomed into a remarkable relationship that has lasted more than 40 years.

Today, Joe, in his new West Knoxville dealership, is proud to own the oldest Volvo dealership in North America to be owned continuously by one family.

This well-known dealership has benefited far more than just the immediate Clayton family or the Volvo company. I'm certain that thousands of happy Volvo owners in East Tennessee feel they've benefited too.

Grandpa Clayton, who always believed in swallowing the big frog first, also trotted out this little homily from time to time: *"Our lives work only to the extent that we are willing to keep our agreements."*

Business is so much about relationships and people being willing to keep their agreements. Joe and I did. Volvo did too.

On the day Joe and I officially opened the new company, one of my fraternity brothers, Jack Littleton, hearing about our plight, dropped by our dealership and stuffed $500 in my shirt pocket.

At the time, that was a godsend to us.

Jack was a stockbroker with J.C. Bradford, and it was typically generous behavior from him—especially since I hadn't bought a lick of stock from his company.

Tragically, in 1971, almost 10 years to the very day that he gave me the $500, Jack was killed in an airplane crash near Roanoke.

The crash made front-page news because of a noteworthy passenger in the same chartered Aero-Commander—Audie Murphy, the legendary World War II combat hero, who took his fame to Hollywood and became a popular leading man during the late 1940s and early 1950s.

At the time of the crash, Jack was in real estate, looking to Murphy as a potential investor.

Audie Murphy got the headlines. But when I heard the terrible news, I thought of my friend Jack, his kindness, and how he had cast a ray of light on us during one of our darkest hours.

Early on, during that life-changing summer of '61, I approached Joe with an offer. I'd give him half of everything I owned—for a favor. What if I went part-time at the dealership so I could go to law school?

True, "half of everything I owned" wasn't much of an offer since at the time the business was all I had. It was worthless as a bankrupt company. So, Joe got half of nothing. What a deal.

Certainly, I was getting a lesson in what can happen to a small business if the owner does not have adequate legal experience, and I swore that I would never be in that situation again. The bankruptcy fiasco made it clear there were some huge gaps in my knowledge. I wanted to learn the law.

I told Joe that if I could get my law license, we'd never be bankrupt again. (Whenever speaking before a group, I'll bring up this little story. True to my word, since I received my law license, I haven't been bankrupt a single time.)

Joe gave me his blessing, and on that day we formed a lasting and rewarding 29-year partnership—the best brother partnership I have ever seen.

And in the fall of 1961, I went back to the University of Tennessee, this time, to law school.

CHAPTER 9

Law School

Iknow what you're thinking. I just wanted to get away from it all, right? And law school was my great escape? Hardly. It wasn't that I had enough of the car business. I loved it—still do. I wasn't running away from anything. In fact, I wasn't confident that I could be successful in business.

Considering my career options, I explored working for another car dealer in sales and marketing. I thought about moving from WROL to a larger station as an engineer or announcer.

For months, I had watched with admiration as Bernie Bernstein expertly weaved his way around the legal potholes. At every turn Bernie held his own against a small army of bank attorneys. I was fascinated with the entire process, and especially how fast Bernie learned our business. His level of preparation, his attention to detail, and his courtroom demeanor would, over several weeks, make him the most respected barrister involved in our complicated case.

I spent a world of time with Bernie in court, his office, our office, even in his home. Before taking a position on any issue, he required a mountain of detailed research and discussion. It became apparent to me that if I'd had his knowledge and experience then I would have avoided this bankruptcy. The thought persisted. One day, on the way back from the courthouse, I stopped at the University of Tennessee School of Law.

Law school wasn't expensive, even for a guy going through bankruptcy. It was only a few hundred dollars a quarter. I would take classes in the morning, get to the dealership by early afternoon, work until we closed at nine, and then go home to study until midnight.

My engineering job at the little radio station, WROL, remained an important part of the puzzle. It had to, since it was still my only source of income. I managed to do most of the maintenance work on weekends, and monitored the station with a transistor radio during the week.

It was critical that I listen at least occasionally. As chief engineer, I had to make sure we were always on the air. But as a law student, I didn't want my professors to see me with a transistor radio growing out of my ear.

That's why I'd sit in the back of the classroom, as far back as I could, and plant myself behind the biggest guy there. To use a term that would later become significant in my line of work, I looked for a "double-wide."

As the professor lectured, I'd sporadically listen to my radio and verify that the station was transmitting. I don't know for sure, but I don't believe any of my professors ever saw my earphone. Anyway, they never said anything about it.

The "sit-in-the-back-behind-the-big-guy" trick, used by generations of students to accomplish a variety of objectives, also helped me get some sleep. With my grueling schedule, I wasn't getting enough rest. This way I could rest and half doze while keeping the ear without the earphone tuned to the case under discussion. If my name was called, I would shed the earpiece, snap to attention and venture a comment.

Just like on the old television show *The Paper Chase*, the professors called on students to stand up and explain cases, including the points of law involved in the case.

You didn't want the professor to call your name if you weren't prepared. I was often unprepared. But sitting behind ample coverage, I was often unnoticed.

I planned to rush through law school in nine quarters, including summers, and graduate in December 1963. But I had to drop out, briefly, to shore up a personnel problem at the dealership.

Our general sales manager, Ott Ottinger, who'd been with us from practically the beginning, was making major demands including higher salary, a higher bonus, and an increased stake in the company. (He already owned 10 percent.) With me sidelined by law school, perhaps he suddenly envisioned himself indispensable and grabbed for the gusto.

Now it has always been my philosophy to treat top performers like partners. We don't even label our people "employees" or "associates." We're all people, team members. But Ottinger, I thought, was behaving like a superstar.

He did not know what he did not know, and was not interested in learning. That being the case, he was not teachable. More on this later.

Joe and I, still willing to make a deal, countered with more cash, or more stock, just not both. Ottinger, had he taken the deal, would've become a millionaire one day. But he wanted more. We called his bluff and let him quit.

Ottinger had a big job. Someone had to take his place, and I was that someone, at least until we could grow a replacement. I spent the summer of '62 at the dealership, a wonderful summer, actually. Joe and I revved up our sales and increased profits as we continued to recover from the bankruptcy.

There was another reason why '62 was a good year—our third child, Kevin, was born.

I went back to school in the fall, and admittedly I was in the *one-third of the class that made the top two-thirds possible.* And it's a fact that I don't remember receiving any scholastic achievement awards. I made straight C's, just enough to get by.

I probably did my best work in "moot court," and received high marks as the lead attorney in the second-year competition. I really enjoyed cross-examination. For once, it was nice to be the one demanding the answers.

Moot court is where I learned the "pregnant pause" technique, a very effective cross-examination tool, and a great device for salespeople or collection personnel to use. You ask brief, open-ended questions, and then *shut up* and let *them* talk. That's the idea—probe or question just enough to keep them talking, and let the witness make your case.

My partner in moot court was J.M. Clement, the nephew of then-Governor Frank Clement. For two weeks prior to moot court, we honed our oratorical skills nightly at my Rambling Acres house. One night, after a few too many longneck Miller Lites, J.M. got a little carried away, and his zestful oratory became elevated several decibels higher than normal.

Karen, age five, rubbing the sleep out of her eyes, wandered down the stairs from her bedroom. It was near midnight. She came up to me and whispered, "Daddy, what is wrong with that man? Why is he hollering like that? I can't sleep." We adjourned court for the night.

Many young people enter law school thinking they are going to spend their lives in the courtrooms. However, they soon learn that courtroom stage appearances require a relatively small amount of their time. Attorneys spend most of their time researching, strategizing, negotiating, drafting, and re-drafting—all the methodical detail work they don't show on *Law and Order*.

I can relate this to talented performing artists I have known. Because they love to perform and are attracted to the applause, the lights, the fans, and the money, they make performing their career choice. If they are vocalists, they expect to spend their time singing. Instead, they soon find that the travel, administration, marketing, rehearsals, and other tedious and non-glamorous

The Clayton family's "Sunday best," 1939.

The Clayton brothers, Joe (left) and me, preschool, 1938.

Birthplace, four miles from Finger, Tenn., circa 1965.

The double wedding (left to right): Herman and Ruth Browder; Cratus and Ruth Clayton, April 29, 1933.

Dad, weighing cotton in the field, circa 1950.

Facial paralysis (me kneeling center), with Memphis Light, Gas and Water Department, 1953. Bill Elliott, my mentor (behind me).

Singing "Cattle Call,"
age 17.

My college meal ticket – First Class Radio License, 1953.

"The borrowed suit," senior class picture, 1952.

Graduating UT with electrical engineering degree and living in a Richardson mobile home, 1957.

146-B

Sigma Phi Epsilon first place — Cinderella Girl, Jim and Mary, 1953.

In 1953 with my first airplane, a 1946 Ercoupe.

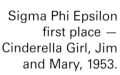

Mother and Dad just after moving to Knoxville, circa 1968.

At WATE-TV studios, 1956.

Jim Clayton Motors, with McConkey Drugs and Milligan Battery on left; Malcolm's Drive-in on right (not shown), 1958.

Dad teaching grandsons, circa 1967.

Mechanics Carl Cole (third from left) and Ed Anderson (second from right), circa 1960.

Moving in day at Tillery Theatre location, 1959.

Jim Clayton Motors on Kingston Pike, the day before the grand opening, 1961.

The "Richardson" at the factory in Elkhart, September 1956.

"The Mobile Home Revolves in the Sky," Clayton's "big sign" for years, circa 1976.

"Claytonville" on Clinton Highway, 1975.

Jim Ausmus's Greeneville, Tenn., sales center Startime lot promotion, circa 1975.

Singing "Going Fishing" to Jimmy (left) and Kevin, 1967.

Jim Clayton Jr. helps his father with a commercial, 1965.

Publicity photo for Startime, 1975 – Look at that mustache!

Startime – a guitar and a smile and The Sisters Four –"always selling," circa 1968.

With daughter Karen on Startime set, 1974.

With Karen in a promo for Startime, 1974.

Talent Parade with Carl Williams.

The family at home Christmas 1974: (left to right) Jim Jr., Karen, Kevin, Amy and Mary.

My children, 1976.

Dolly Parton performed on the Clayton television show several times in the late 60s.

Startime recognizing the No. 1 home salesman, Larry Davidson (left), and the No. 1 car salesman, Bill Fielden (right).

What a team! (left to right) Ty Kelly, Joe Clayton, me, R.C. Clayton, Jim Ausmus (sitting), and Max Everette (standing), circa 1981.

Joe and Jim on Startime, circa 1963.

Celebrating our 10,000th home with Congressman John Duncan at the Maynardville Plant: (left to right) Lowell Woods, Joe Clayton, Duncan, me, and Ty Kelly, circa 1983.

Startime sells homes – even on a billboard, circa 1971.

With my good friend, General Pat Harrison, in his Commerce Union Bank office, circa 1969

"Congratulations to Jim & Joe Clayton" – Valley Fidelity Bank, 1984.

Clayton Motors Shuts Down

Jim Clayton Motors Inc., 4623 Clinton Highway, discontinued business operations last night, President Jim Clayton announced. The company, which handled Rambler, Jaguar, MG, Triumph and Volvo, was organized in December, 1957. It also has an agency on Kingston Pike.

"The primary difficulty stems from the recent recession and inability of our customers to maintain their installment accounts," Mr. Clayton said. "This resulted in substantial repossession losses which were charged to our company by local financing institutions.

"The rapid growth of our company produced an excessive overhead situation, which coupled with a reduced car market, does not permit continuation of business at this time," he said.

Business failure, June 1961

Harold Hull (far left), Fenton Kintzing, me, and Pat Harrison, 1976

Ringing the opening bell at the NYSE: (left to right) David Booth, Rick Strachan, Bill Johnston, me, Kay, and Kevin, August 1998.

At the CMH post on the floor of the NYSE (left to right) Bill Johnston, CNBC's Maria Bartiromo, me, and Kay.

With Joe at New York Stock Exchange on the first day for CMH, Dec. 19, 1984.

Family and Officers at the NYSE, Dec. 19, 1984.

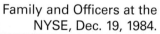

Another incentive trip – Acapulco, 2002.

January managers incentive trip to Las Vegas during
the slow sales season, 1979.

Kathy and Karen with the Kountry Kings Band on Startime, 1973.

Buford "Walking Tall" Pusser on Startime, 1973.

Karen's Startime publicity photo, circa 1975.

Dear Mr Clayton,
Please send me a picture of you and Karen. I would like one of the band if you have any of them. Tell Steve and David and also Stoney I said hi. I really enjoy watching your show on Monday night on channel 6. Tell Steve I would like to hear him sing "My turn to wait" he can really sing it real good and so can the rest of you all

Love Always
Carolyn

I always come and see you all when you are in Middlesboro please come again real soon.

Startime performers received a lot of fan mail, circa 1972.

Ty Kelly's successful "Vegas" model –19th off the line, 1976.

ANOTHER QUALITY MANCHESTER *FROM Clayton Homes*

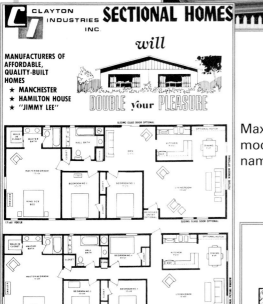

Max Nichols named this model the "Jimmy Lee." Bad name—Bad home, 1974.

Floor plan for our lake house, 2002.

Today's manufactured home, built 2002.

Early single section home, 1975.

Delivering homes for use as dormitories to ease overcrowding at the William Henson Home for Boys, an orphanage on Old Maryville Pike.

activities require most of their time. Most leave the industry after several months.

A number of law students left during their first year when they became mired in tedium. I loved law school and looked forward to the practice of law as a career. Sure, I didn't like detailed research and writing briefs all the time, but I liked the prospect of knowing the law backwards and forwards.

Most of the law school students, like J.M., were younger than me, and still living in dorms, small apartments, or mobile homes. Our modest but larger house, featuring a refrigerator liberally stocked with Miller Lite, was enough to get them to group study with me before exams. Mary, pleased that I was going to law school, fed us, and made everyone feel at home.

They were, and still are, a great group of guys who'd go on to have impressive careers. Along with J.M., there was Bob Ritchie, now the most famous criminal attorney in Tennessee; Wheeler Rosenbalm, a distinguished Circuit Court judge; and Bob Hedgepath, who had a successful career with the Department of Labor. Bob, along with his wife Barbara, would later help me get back into television.

With graduation drawing near, I threw together a research paper at the last minute. Granted it was not some of my best work, and I got a D, my first.

Now, one quarter away from graduation, my grade point average had slipped below the C minimum. To get my degree, I needed a B in at least one of my three remaining classes.

I'd never made a B in law school.

Fortunately, my professors were apparently sympathetic to my predicament. They also appreciated Mary's efforts, as she and I had co-chaired the annual faculty-student social. We had volunteered to help organize the event and mail out invitations. It was a big success, as the attendance and involvement from the faculty, students, and families were much greater than expected.

An impromptu meeting was held in the hallway, and my three

professors discussed my grade dilemma. They knew that I would not graduate without a B in one of the courses. Since they all agreed that I was a worthy candidate for the degree, one of them decided he could justify a B- for the work I'd done in his class.

I graduated in March 1964, with gratitude toward the merciful court. Had the professor who'd graciously given me the B- *really* examined my final paper for his class, he might have reconsidered his generosity and given me an F, probably. As I frantically scrambled to finish the paper the night before it was due, I lost my research notes for the legal bibliography. There wasn't time to reconstruct all the quotes and references I'd used. So, as I listed the page and paragraph of my citations, I guessed on many of them.

I was grateful the professor let that slide, although embarrassed to end my formal education on that less-than-stellar note.

All that was left now was the bar exam. If I passed that, I'd automatically be admitted to the bar, and I could practice law in every court in the nation.

The bar exam is difficult and the casualty rate is high. It's not uncommon for law graduates—some of them very good students—to flunk the exam on the first go-round. But it's extraordinarily rare for a graduate to be denied the opportunity to *take the test*. But that's what was about to happen to me.

Enter Foster Arnett, the senior partner at one of Knoxville's better-known law firms and the imposing Chairman of the Bar's formidable Grievance Committee.

To an aspiring attorney in Tennessee back in the '60's, Foster Arnett, having been president of the Tennessee Bar Association, was not someone to take lightly. His Grievance Committee had the authority to deny, for "due cause," any applicant the right to sit for the bar exam.

Arnett took one look at my application and saw "due cause" written all over it.

He was going to see to it that this "ambulance chaser" was not going to be turned loose on society.

This was his logic, as I understand it: I was a car dealer operating my own body shop; the primary task of a body shop is to repair wrecked cars; a wrecked car is the result of a car wreck; a car wreck frequently injures people; and injured people frequently file lawsuits.

That's all true, no argument there. But then he went on with his reasoning: I'd set up my law office in the Clayton body shop, keep an eye out for the next wrecked car, wave my law license at those injured, and aggressively encourage the filing of a lawsuit. I, of course, would be their humble servant and would happily advise them every step of the way through the legal maze.

Sort of a one-stop shop: *Clayton Sports Cars, taking care of all your post-accident needs: we fix your car and file your lawsuits.*

Never in my wildest imagination had that scenario occurred to me, but Foster Arnett seemed certain his conclusions were correct. Rather, the reverse was true. In law school, I had been ingrained with a number of ethical principles. Among these were: *A dual relationship with a client must be disclosed and carefully handled to avoid even an appearance of a conflict of interest.* And: *At that time, an attorney could not solicit business.*

The Grievance Committee probed my character as well as my business background. In researching the bankruptcy records alone, they had to comb through a room full of documents at the Knoxville Federal Court House.

Arnett and his committee rounded up me and six of my law school buddies who were selling cars for me through the classifieds. Taking us to the law school basement, they placed us in separate rooms to await our depositions. One at a time, the interrogation proceedings continued on into the evening.

One question after another was asked of us: *Were we lying to customers about the cars we sold? Were the student-salespeople directed to misrepresent the history of the car? Were the odometers set back? Were defects concealed?*

The committee members seemed to be grasping for some

speck of evidence to confirm Arnett's suspicions. I thought it was outrageous how he and his team of attorneys orchestrated their investigation with what seemed to me to be complete disdain for "due process." On that day, in my opinion, they violated both the Fourth and Sixth Amendments.

Soon, Bernie Bernstein and a few other noted members of the Knoxville Bar, including Judge L.D. Word (the attorney for Valley Fidelity Bank), U.S. Senator Howard Baker (my good friend who later became President Reagan's Chief of Staff and Ambassador to Japan), and others became involved on my behalf.

They met individually with the members of the Grievance Committee, and convinced them my values were sound. The committee members agreed, and I understand they were delighted to learn that Arnett had elected to finally terminate the investigation.

With approval to sit for the bar exam, I passed on the first attempt, including the section on professional ethics.

For more than 30 years, I drafted, edited, or reviewed every standard form used to transact business at Clayton Homes. All correspondence that involved legal exposure, or would likely develop into a legal issue, always crossed my desk. You might think this would have been impossible, when our company was building, selling, and installing 25,000 homes each year.

Traditionally, legal activity increases along with sales volume. Other companies our size, and not even as large, have expensive legal departments with scores of attorneys on staff. My experience indicates that over 80 percent of legal claims originate because of a failure to deliver customer satisfaction. Therefore, it has always been my conclusion that most of our claims can be eliminated if we simply meet, or exceed, customer expectations.

Our one-person legal department, by acting as an internal consultant and a trainer, proactively eliminated much of the complaint volume by designing forms that were clear and understandable; training the staff to deal with unrealistic expectations;

establishing incentives that rewarded team members who achieved high customer service scores; and requiring the managers who were close to the problem to fix the problem.

That last point was critical. The manager who opened the file, or caused the file to be opened, gathered the data, met with the customer, and ultimately experienced the entire legal process. Getting their hands dirty and keeping them dirty until the customer was happy and sold on Clayton was and still is the manager's responsibility.

After new managers experienced this culture and unique approach to managing legal matters, they were amazed at how effective they could become in self-managing their legal issues. It was easy to see that a team would want to conduct their business so they had no legal issues.

Even today, many of our sales center managers and plant managers do not have legal claims—ever. Immediately after opening a legal file, we contact the attorney initiating the claim. Usually, our young general counsel and secretary of the corporation, Tom Hodges, makes this call. Occasionally, someone in senior management does it.

In the early years, I would do it. Invariably, they'd be caught off-guard. Attorneys are accustomed to hearing from other attorneys, not the CEO of the company.

My surprise call, I discovered, generally paved the way for an early and effective conclusion to the complaint. I'd schmooze a bit, talk a little Tennessee football, and say something like, "We lawyers always have a stack of files on our desks that will be profitable—and another stack not likely to produce much income."

Then I'd say, "I don't see how either one of us is going to be able to retire on this case."

That remark usually prompted a chuckle and the willingness to hear suggestions on how to conclude the matter quickly.

In a situation like this, I'd always remember "Rule Number One." In law school, one professor reminded the class frequently that we could be the best litigators, negotiators, researchers, and brief writers, but unless we remembered Rule Number One, we'd fail as attorneys. Rule Number One can be summed up in three words: *Get the fee.*

That's why, during my conversation with the attorney, I'd offer to reimburse their client for legal fees. While I was always careful to avoid suggesting the amount of the attorney's fee, I would offer to add, say, $500 or $2,500, to the client's settlement to help his client "pay part of your fee for helping them with this matter."

Every time I did this, the amount I paid toward legal costs was exactly the amount billed by the attorney. Isn't it interesting how it worked out that way? However, I would have likely made the attorney mad if I had suggested a specific amount for him to charge his client.

Looking out for everyone's interest and trying to put it together in one package created a "win-win-win" situation—for the customer, for the attorney, and for me. That was our objective.

After some discussion, much of the time I could obtain permission to visit their client, our customer. Obviously, the main reason for the visit was to resolve the legal issue, and most importantly, make our customer happy again. At this point there might be few options. We could fix the home. We could buy it back. We could trade them another home. And we were likely to give our customer the opportunity to choose from this list of "fixes." Attorneys were amazed that we would be so accommodating.

In these cases, we wanted to learn all the lessons we could about how to better build, sell, and service our homes. We insisted that the manager who allowed the customer to become, and remain, unhappy be involved.

We'd document the complaints, make the repairs, replace the product, or in some cases, buy back the product, anything reasonable to make our customer happy and prevent a lawsuit.

The Final Service Letter was originally called the Max Nichols Service Letter, after a former team member and friend of ours.

Max and Jim Ausmus, a consistently successful sales center manager in Greeneville, Tennessee, developed this procedure. It is so logical and simple, and "works miracles."

Max, Jim, and I went to see a customer who could not be satisfied, according to the manager who sold the home. Even after servicing the home, the customer would call again with an even longer complaint list. This had gone on for two years, and the home was long out of warranty.

We greeted the angry customers and asked them to show us all of the problems with the home. "I hope you have all day," said the wife. I assured her that we had whatever time was needed.

With our camera and writing pad, we listened and documented every complaint item, starting from the front of the home, through the living room, kitchen, three bedrooms, two baths, and finally to the master bedroom in the back. We were attentive, understanding, and concerned about each item. We were not at all judgmental as to the validity of the problems. Collecting the facts and building credibility with the customer was our goal.

A third of the way through the process, we noticed the customers were more relaxed, less hostile, and less concerned with many of the listed items. "Oh, hon, don't bother them with that little gap in the trim," the husband would say. Later, he'd say, "Hey, let me fix that. You guys don't worry about adjusting that door."

The customers moved us through the last third of the home much faster. By the time we'd been through the entire interior and had circled the exterior, we were moving at a fast clip. There was laughter, casual talk of kids, fishing, politics and the like, as we continued to make our list and take pictures. Along the way, we would try to see some items that they had missed and add them to the list. That would surprise the customer.

"Is our list complete?" we asked. If not, we would resume our examination of the house. When we reached agreement, we thanked them and said, "If we fix all these to your satisfaction, you would be a happy Clayton homeowner, right?"

Then, in closing, we got them to acknowledge that if every item were fixed, they would release us from any further claims. Then we wrote them a letter that simply stated, "When all items on the list attached have been repaired in sequence (the service person is not permitted to move to the next item until the prior item is repaired and approved with the customer's initials), Clayton is released from any further responsibility."

When Max and his helper went to repair the home, they were warmly received, and the customers appreciated the jackets and caps he had for them. The repairs were started promptly, beginning with the first item on the long list. The customer initialed each item on the list as the repairs were completed. After an hour or so, with five items completed, the husband said, "Here, let me initial number six. I will fix that later."

After two more items were repaired, the customer took the pad again and initialed several more items. Max completed the list before sundown and had all items initialed. He had actually performed work on little more than half the items.

In this case, we learned that the anger started because the home was delivered two weeks late. Living with the wife's parents created family tension that lingered.

We sent their lawyer a check for $500, payable to the customer, to pay toward their legal bills.

That couple referred three new customers to us within a year.

In many companies, such complaints that threaten legal exposure are handled very differently. Instead of inspecting the problem, re-selling the customer, and trying to resolve the problem, the corporate attorneys get involved. Often, they believe the script presented by the company people, ignore any data indicating the product or service was less than acceptable, and respond to the customer by stonewalling.

This makes the customer feel ignored and powerless, and that they have little choice but to file a lawsuit. That's when the company's legal department turns it over to outside counsel and the real ordeal begins.

Outside counsel can often take small matters and bulldoze up enough animosity to guarantee an endless and expensive court proceeding. In that sense, they are like the exterminator who drops an atom bomb on your house to get rid of the termites. The termites are gone, but so is your house.

Now I ask you: Why go through all the aggravation of a lawsuit when you can usually fix things in one-tenth of the time for a fraction of the cost? The approach taken by Clayton's, including the use of the Max Nichols Service Letter, helps keep us from getting trapped in a bottomless pit of legal entanglements. We don't spend a fraction on legal compared to other companies our size.

Thanks to the training they receive from our general counsel, Tom Hodges, and other operating managers, our staff is skilled at handling complaints and correcting problems. They satisfy better than 99 percent of our customers, and save us enormous amounts of time and money.

Communication breakdowns between the customer and the company, what I call "unrealized expectations," are at the root of most legal complaints. With this type of early attention from management, it is rare for anyone from Clayton to spend any time at the courthouse.

Although *Talent Parade* was long gone, at law school, during those all-night study marathons, we'd sometimes stop for a jam session.

Though Bob Hedgepath couldn't sing a lick, he knew songs and loved to listen. His wife Barbara was a gifted vocalist. I'd bring out my guitar when we needed a break, and she would sing.

In particular, they loved folk songs, which were the rage, and we talked about my producing another musical show for television, this one with a folk music theme—a hootenanny.

In the early '60s, that made a lot of sense. Folk was enormously popular then. Peter, Paul and Mary ("If I Had A Hammer") and The Kingston Trio ("Tom Dooley") were at the top of the charts and at the pinnacle of their careers. There was also a popular ABC-TV prime-time show, *Hootenanny*, the first (and maybe last) folk music series, airing on Saturday nights.

When I graduated from law school, I had the time to develop advertising and marketing for the company. *Talent Parade* taught us that music shows with local talent would deliver an audience. I also had fond memories of the way *Talent Parade* made us a household name, generating traffic throughout Tennessee and the surrounding states.

John Hart, the general manager of WBIR, excited for our new success, cautiously approved a new account for us, up to a maximum of $10,000.

I still love the name of the new show: *The Smoky Mountain Hootenanny*. It was an inexpensive show to produce, since local talent would perform simply for the exposure and an opportunity to promote their show dates.

Hootenanny was much less complicated than *Talent Parade*, since it was a straight variety show, not a talent contest. And we could buy 30 minutes from WBIR for about $500. I auditioned and booked the acts, wrote and produced the commercials, and, along with Joe, was in front of the camera.

My daughter Karen, even at age five, could really sing and performed on every show, occasionally singing harmony in a duet with me.

The Smoky Mountain Hootenanny received good ratings, but we missed the broad appeal that worked for us on *Talent Parade*. We had the nagging feeling we were only filling a niche with folk music, however popular it may have been, and not appealing to the widest possible audience.

After six months, we gave the show a new format and a new name: *Startime*.

We still offered folk, but also gospel, some rock, and a lot of country. The audience loved all the pretty young girls featured each week. *Startime* was on from Labor Day through springtime.

The Sisters Four was our answer to the Lennon Sisters. The Kountry Kings Band featured wonderfully talented musicians like Ray Rose on bass, Stoney Stonecipher on pedal steel guitar, Darrell Puett on lead guitar, and Curtis Young, who probably has sung harmony on more Nashville recordings than any other artist.

One of the most popular performers on *Startime* was Kathy Hill, a beautiful, blond 13-year-old with a voice that belied her years. Kathy's aunt, Gene Weaver, was a bookkeeper for WBIR, which gave her more than enough pull to secure an audition for her little niece.

Kathy showed up at the studio with her mother, Katie, who told her to "sing for the nice man." Did she ever. She sang "Young Love," by Sonny James and Brenda Lee's version of "Jambalaya."

Before the audition was over, this kid, a seventh-grader, had run through every song we requested, and did it flawlessly.

During our first season, Kathy Hill became a regular performer. Though everyone on the show got a lot of fan mail, it was always Kathy who received the most. Often, the writer would have a song request, or ask what she'd be wearing that week.

Part of the show's success, I think, was due to our use of highly technical production techniques. With my years of television experience, I knew the equipment and its limitations.

Like the *Lawrence Welk Show*, which was on ABC-TV at the time, all of the singers—including Karen, Kathy, the Sisters Four, and myself—sang background on each other's solo performances. Often, the Sisters Four would sing background for me, and I'd sing harmony for Kathy and Karen.

We'd pre-record the sound of several production numbers with a multi-track audio recorder, and by over-dubbing and pre-recording, we'd have the sound of a 10- or 20-piece band, even though we had only six actual musicians.

One of our musicians might record the same song up to five times on different tracks, using a wide variety of instruments, including the piano, organ, fiddle, mandolin, or guitar (lead, steel, and rhythm). In later years, we'd use a synthesizer.

After everyone left, Ray Rose and I would mix them down, adding echo along with extra instruments and backup singers. The finished product was amazing for a locally produced show.

By the time the production aired, it sounded like our performers had a 12-piece orchestra behind them, along with a group of backup singers. On-camera, we'd lip sync or sing the solo live over the prerecorded sound track.

Today, this level of production is standard operating procedure, but back then, it was unusual and required unbelievable amounts of time.

The show attracted performers from all over Tennessee. They'd drive in to audition for us in pickup trucks overflowing with guitars, drums, and amplifiers.

The good performers often got a shot, although there was never enough time to audition all the talented people who requested to be auditioned. But for those not quite as talented, there was only one way to get a guest spot on the show. They or their family had to buy a car, and later, a home from us.

This, you'll recognize, was the Uncle Tom Williams approach to casting talent. With Uncle Tom, you'll recall, I had to bring in commercial sponsors so I could host my own radio show when I was in high school.

With some of the less-experienced performers, our pre-recording chores became a messy and time-consuming process; we'd tape them at least a dozen times. We hoped they'd sing each word or phrase right at least once somewhere amidst the takes.

We'd pick the best take with the fewest mistakes, then go to work. Ray Rose and I would sometimes spend all night, with scissors and tape, eliminating the obvious by splicing out bad notes, substituting good "takes" of the same note, bringing up the echo, and increasing the level of our background singers. It took a lot of time, but on the air, it would sound great.

On occasion, some performers and their families thought an

appearance on *Startime* would rocket them to the big time. People would call in and tell me they had a daughter who could sing "even better" than Loretta Lynn, and it was tough explaining to them that I couldn't secure for her a record contract or a spot on the Grand Ole Opry. After all, I couldn't even obtain a contract for Karen, Kathy, or the Sisters Four.

Startime usually ran on Sunday nights, but no matter where it was, it consistently ranked higher than other local shows and compared favorably with even the well-known network shows.

The show was a tremendous help to the business. By the end of 1964, our dealerships had reached $2 million in annual sales. (In 35 years the net income of CMH would be $155 million.)

CMH Net Income
$ Millions

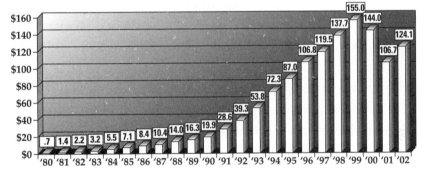

Although *Startime* was a ton of work, it was one heck of a lot of fun. To work with beautiful kids and watch them grow up on the show was thrilling. To be able to get to know Barry Sadler, the Green Beret, and especially Dolly Parton was one of the great pleasures of being associated with a popular television show. Although we normally were introducing up and coming talented kids, these established stars were frequently available.

Nashville stars respected the young talent who migrated off our show and into the bands and recording studios in Nashville. Because of the shows ratings and the quality of the regular *Startime* performers, our show was appealing to the stars.

Already, Dolly Parton was a star, though this was just before she became a "megastar" with her guest shots on Johnny Carson and her starring role in the hit movie, *Nine To Five*. Nevertheless, she was very well-known and had been featured on the popular *Porter Waggoner Show* for a decade.

In fact, she was such a big name, I was nervous at the thought of singing a duet with her. But then I met Dolly, and she was a delight. Polite, fun, witty, sweet—she made everyone around her feel comfortable.

Dolly was on the show to promote for her what she hoped would be a beauty salon franchise that would go nationwide. She and her niece were partners in the venture, and they had already opened up one salon in Knoxville, with another about to start up in Nashville.

Everyone had their picture made with Dolly—me too. She wrote on a print from one of my 49 poses with her, "I love working with you, your show is great! Thanks for everything! Dolly Parton."

Dolly abandoned the salon franchise as her career took off.

Twenty years later, when Dolly was inducted into the Bijou Theater Hall of Fame in downtown Knoxville, I visited with her at a reception and showed her the *Startime* scrap book. She reached for the picture she had autographed years ago, and wrote again, "To Jim, 20 years later 1988, Love, Dolly Parton."

If you've seen any of the *Walking Tall* movies—there were three of them in the 70's, and they were huge at the box office—then you probably remember the name Buford Pusser. He was the now-legendary sheriff who took on the "Stateline Mob" that supposedly controlled much of the criminal activity in McNairy County for decades—prostitution, gambling, bootlegging.

He paid for it dearly—his wife was killed in a mob ambush. He was shot twice in the face and barely survived the attack.

Buford was a true American hero. He was also my third cousin, and we grew up just two miles apart.

We had him on *Startime* in 1974, just before filming began on the third *Walking Tall* movie. In this one, Buford was the star—he would play himself. After all the tragedy in his life, it was good to see him happy and excited again.

But it wasn't to be. Just a few weeks later, Buford was driving along Route 64 in McNairy County when he lost control of his new Corvette. He crashed into an embankment and went through the car's open roof. He died a few hours later.

Rumors have always circulated about his death, and some people still speculate that the Stateline Mob was responsible. It does seem strange that this man, who knew those roads like the back of his hand, wouldn't have made that curve.

Then again, some say he was going 100 miles per hour at the time of the crash.

But was he joyriding—or trying to outrun the mob?

On most everything else, I have pretty strong opinions. But on this one, I don't know what to think. I do know that the accident, and Buford, are still a topic of conversation at the Browder-Pusser family reunion.

CHAPTER 10

Manufactured Homes

f I say so myself, Joe and I were the comeback kids of the car business. Just two years after bankruptcy, our cash flow, credit, and credibility were again satisfactory. By now, in fact, we operated with all bills paid current—no exceptions.

Either of us could've bought big houses and luxury cars, or become jetsetters with frequent jaunts to Europe and Hawaii. But we didn't.

Our lifestyles were so modest that I wouldn't even drive a clean car off the lot for the drive home from work. I wanted the clean cars on display and available for customers, so I'd drive the latest dirty trade-in, even one that was a little beat-up.

As for Mary, she settled on a '49 Ford ('49!) and since it ran well, we hung on to it for the longest time. That was fine with her. Mary was like me, not prone to spending sprees, preferring to keep the purse strings tight. We stayed in our very ordinary Rambling Acres cottage.

We invested in additional inventory, a faster airplane (the Cessna Skylane 182), and became one of the first dealerships in the country to computerize our accounting system. As a sales oriented dealership, having a Daily Operating Control program with an up-to-the-minute inventory system allowed us to effectively sell increased volume.

At day's end, Joe would deliver a Daily Operating Control, or DOC, report. With this up-to-date listing of inventory, cars on order, sales, gross profit, units sold, commissions earned by sales people, and other detailed management data right at our finger-tips, we could manage cash and other assets more effectively.

As sales continued to increase, we added staff selectively. Uncle R.C., after years with the Brown Shoe Company and Liberty Mutual, moved from Finger to join us. His contributions as a senior member of our sales management team over the next two decades would be significant.

Joe and I, with our wives, would take a trip or two to Europe each year, but without exception it was to attend a new product showing by Volvo or Renault, so they picked up the tab.

After the meetings we enjoyed some rest and relaxation time.

To sum it up: if a considered expenditure didn't support the business, we'd be taking a long, hard look before approval. Cash was king then, as it is now.

In researching this book, I spent many hours in personal and corporate archives examining photographs, minutes of meetings, documents, and records. It's amazing how much of it is devoted to legal, regulatory, and tax matters. During my search, I found two large boxes of records on Larry Davidson.

Larry, a good friend and one of our best people, staged a now-notorious blunder at the ill-fated "Renault Obstacle Course."

He was a dynamic sales guy, one of our all-time best direct sales people. He was likable, creative, loved people, couldn't resist injecting drama into his life, and often got carried away. He also had what we call a very low BTL—Bliss Tolerance Level. If Larry experienced more than a handful of good days, he'd find a way to reverse the tide. Some of them were real beauties.

This was one of those times.

Renault had long been ballyhooed as the best-riding car in the competitive price category, smooth and steady as could be. Larry enjoyed confirming this claim by conducting a deliberately rough-and-tumble, dramatic, off-road test drive near the Interstate 75 and Clinton Highway interchange.

For Larry, a little blunder along a country road wouldn't be enough. Instead, he chose a major exchange on a highway, assuring him of a large audience.

He'd warm up by twirling the Renault in 360-degree spirals, do some quick starts and stops, then drive the car smack into a gigantic, 20-foot concrete drainage ditch with 45-degree banks on each side.

It may sound wacky, and today such a demo would not be considered. But at the right speed, the test drive was not perilous in any way to the passengers or to the Renault. Really. But it invariably left a sensational impression with the customer and hammered home the idea that Renault rode well and was stable, even under extremely rugged conditions.

So sensational was the demo ride, that while placing advertising for the week, Larry invited the *News-Sentinel* out to record this thrilling performance for posterity.

Larry convinced me, over Joe Clayton's objections, that this promotion was a good decision. I should have listened to Joe.

Larry, who couldn't wait to impress our customers with a dazzling display of the Renault's prowess, not to mention his superb abilities as a stunt driver, hit the gas a little too hard. All the while, Larry was talking 80 miles per hour—with gusts up to 105. This was not unusual when he was excited.

This time, when the smooth, steady, fail-safe Renault bopped down the 45-degree bank toward the bottom of the drainage ditch, it flipped! Larry was still talking, we were told, as the car rolled over on its side, and landed on its top.

There were seven people in that car, and miraculously, no one was hurt. The newspaper photographer saw it all, and frantically was snapping pictures of our stunned "ex-customers" throughout the run, and as they stumbled out of the upturned Renault.

Once again, we made the front page.

The bad publicity from that one dogged us for months. It was like having gum on your shoe, and poor Larry got chewed out for his overzealous behavior.

Happily, he lived down this calamity and played a big part in our company for the next 20 years or so. We remained great friends, but I cringed every time I saw him get near a Renault.

After years of excellent relations, we began to get a cold shoulder from some members of the Tillery family who had leased us the old theater where we sold our Volvos, Renaults, and sports cars. The grapevine indicated they wanted the old building back to restore and reopen.

At first, it was just little hints here and there. Like during lease renewal, they'd groan about the way we defaced their baby.

Suddenly, anything we added on was a major blemish to the building, no matter how much of a necessity—signs, stairways, or garage doors. If anything, we'd added value to the building.

Actually, I thought what really upset them ran much deeper than a few signs. Instead, I sensed that there was a longing, at least among some family members, to bring back the theater to its earlier glory.

They were ruled more by sentimentality than by business logic. The large theater chains were already choking out the independent operators.

By 1966, a few of the family members finally convinced the others to abandon their notion to re-open the theater. They decided to sell the building and distribute the proceeds. That was fine with us, because by then, we were ready to stop leasing and buy the property.

Let's-make-a-deal time, right? Not even close. The Tillery family would not return our calls.

I guess we put up one sign too many. Joe thought they were just jealous of our success. Whatever the reason, their final answer was a resounding "no."

That meant we'd have to move.

The old Wright Drive-In Restaurant was right across the street, and we started making inquiries. The owners seemed interested, and soon the inquiries turned into negotiations.

But Bernie Bernstein advised that we could take another approach to buying the Tillery. Suggesting that we form a separate corporation for the sole purpose of purchasing and holding title to the property, we would need someone to "front" for the new entity. The Clayton name would not be involved in the closing. A little creative, perhaps, but certainly not illegal.

What should we call the new company? Bernie had a friend, Tommy Hahn, a successful stockbroker in the same downtown building. He was celebrating the birth of his daughter Margot.

Why not? We called it the Margot Corporation.

The Tillery family went for it and hastily accepted Margot's offer. Apparently, they were in such a hurry to close, they didn't ask many questions. Margot was simply one or more "investors" buying the building for "investment purposes," which is about as vague as it gets. They never thought about Margot being ours.

The Tillery deal was owner-financed, which meant we had to make a monthly payment to them for the next 10 years. You can imagine the reaction of the family a few weeks later, when the first check arrived, and Margot's true identity was revealed.

We assumed that if even one of our payments for the next decade were so much as a day late, they'd foreclose with big grins on their faces. Needless to say, we never missed one.

And as for the "real" Margot, that little baby girl who was the namesake for our corporation, she's approaching (should I say it?) age 40.

But like our company, she's aged mighty well and doesn't look a day over 30. We were introduced for the first time last year. We both laughed.

Just as we were closing on the Tillery deal, we got a call from the owner of the drive-in restaurant we'd been negotiating with. Now he was ready to sell. So we closed on that one too.

Now we had two properties. We decided to keep the dealership at Tillery. But what should we do with the drive-in?

As I pondered my problem, I'm sure my thoughts were occasionally jarred by the constant turmoil taking place every weekday morning just a couple hundred yards from us.

It was those Taylor guys again. Gene and Larry of Taylor Mobile Homes. The two brothers were friendly and social, and we guessed they were making a mint. They were delivering so many mobile homes that they caused a traffic snarl on Clinton Highway almost every morning with their deliveries.

Those huge homes were sometimes 10 feet wide and as long as 55 feet; the Taylor staff would block the inbound and outbound lanes as the truck lumbered out of the dealership.

Clinton Highway would back up and quickly resemble a parking lot. It was a colossal mess. And I would think:

This happens every day—darn guys—and I hear they make a couple thousand bucks every time they sell one—10 times what we make when we sell a car—darn guys. Those Taylors sure are doing well. No wonder they're living the high life, real party guys. Just think, every time I see one of those big things pass me on the road, they've made a couple grand—and I see it every day...

Gee, that mobile home business must <u>really</u> be good.

I admit, sometimes it takes me a while to catch on.

I already knew a lot about mobile homes, having lived in a couple. I'd even sold a few of them just to help out some of my law school buddies. After graduation, they'd be ready to move out of their mobile homes into brick, three-bedroom, two-bath, suburban split-levels. We would agree on a minimum price for their old home. Any amount over that price, we shared equally.

While scanning the classifieds, an ad for a used mobile home caught my eye. It was a "10-by-56, like new." The ad went on to state that there had been a "small kitchen fire."

I began to wonder if this little burnt-out home could be fixed up. If so, maybe we could sell it for a little profit. And if it worked, who knows? Maybe we could make a few dollars in the mobile home business too.

Who would have thought that little burnt-out would take us to number one in market share in several states?

CMH Market Share 2002

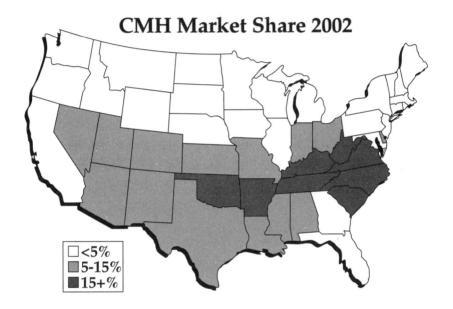

□ <5%
▨ 5-15%
■ 15+%

That small kitchen fire, as described in the classifieds, didn't quite square with the visual inspection.

True, it looked okay from the driveway, but as I approached the house, I saw the smoky windows, and then, when I walked in—well, that kitchen was *roasted*. It had a charbroiled ceiling, melted light fixtures, and black soot was liberally dusted over a ruined carpet.

I bought it for $1,200 and called in the troops—Mother and Dad. They were in town for a few days to see the grandkids, but the way it worked out, they probably saw much more of the week-long family "fix up" project.

The three of us started to work on the damaged but repairable home at the newly acquired drive-in-restaurant. We were joined by a couple of guys who did car detail.

We spent two days and another $800 to re-do the kitchen, re-paint the ceiling, and replace the carpet. The new floor covering wasn't installed before someone driving by saw our "For Sale" sign and stopped. They bought the home for $4,500. Profit after delivery: about $2,000.

Not bad. I was on to something.

If the Taylors—who were high flyers, to be sure—could make a fortune in this business, just think what we could do with the added benefits of our Clayton team management approach. With our experience in cars, the lending relationships, the accounting systems, and a quality staff, surely we could learn the mobile home business, I thought.

Joe agreed to cover for me at the car dealership, while I took a few half days off to explore mobile home sales opportunities.

We stuck with the same formula that worked with the used cars a decade ago: taking the profit; buying more mobile homes, the fixer-upper type; running classified ads; selling the homes; and buying some more. This worked fine for a while, but we knew our limited inventory would only carry us so far. Not many mobile homes out there fit our purchase requirements—up for sale, good quality, and cheap. Besides, the whole process was too labor intensive. Finding and fixing them took a lot of time. While we were off to a good start, we needed to take the next step.

Just as we graduated from selling used cars to new cars, we decided to test-market a few new models of mobile homes. If the Taylors could do it, surely we could too, at least on a small scale.

In May 1966, I flew the Cessna Skylane to Alabama with George Blevins. By now, George had been with us for about eight years, and in the past few weeks, he'd sold a couple of our repaired homes. We were visiting Tidwell Homes, the talk of the mobile home industry. Since the Atlanta trade show, where their new décors were well received, the whole industry had taken notice of this company, along with its colorful owner, Don Tidwell. Just three years ago, Don was a cabinet shop foreman at Frontier Homes, an established player in the business.

Now, as president of his own successful company, he was turning the industry upside-down.

Don was doing something no other mobile home designer had done before. He was using bright, vivid colors for his models—red, blue, gold, and black. This stood in stark contrast to the bland visage offered by other manufacturers, who covered every inch of every wall with dark brown wood panels.

His "Alabama Flash" model was extremely popular, and especially appealing to young homebuyers. The wildly creative designs mirrored his lifestyle, which was just as flamboyant. Don had Elvis sideburns, wore flashy Elvis-type clothes, and even did a pretty good Elvis impersonation.

We hit it off right away. Turned out he grew up on a cotton farm too. I think my college degrees impressed him, and he said, "Hell, I ain't never seen a lawyer, engineer, pilot, and a regular ole country boy all rolled up in one not-so-purty package."

Don had been supplying the Taylors with a few homes each month, but the relationship was strained.

He told us flat-out how fed up he was. "I've had it with Gene and Larry," he said. "They want to tie up my line while they keep Frontier and all the others, too." In other words, he thought the Taylors wanted to keep the hot new Tidwell models off of other dealers' lots. Don wanted someone in Knoxville to market his products aggressively.

Communications had deteriorated so much that just the day before, Don had refused to ship two homes they had ordered.

We gladly volunteered to be Don's dealer in Knoxville and to make Tidwell our featured line. I bought the two homes built for the Taylors, plus another one scheduled to be off the production line in two days.

Don knew, of course, that we were just starting the business.

We had no office yet, no sign, and no relationship with other manufacturers. We didn't even have any gravel.

He told us to take care of the office and gravel, and he'd handle the inventory and the sign.

That said, while standing on the airport tarmac, he sketched out our Clayton Mobile Homes sign, right there on the wing of the Cessna. He drew, on the very top of the sign, a little revolving replica of a mobile home. He agreed to build it personally.

Don and I shook hands. We had a deal.

Now we looked forward to the challenge of persuading Fenton Kintzing to floor plan the new inventory. After all, we knew Don Tidwell would call for payment approval before shipping. The three homes arrived the following Wednesday, along with the sign, and Fenton drove out to take a look.

You could see the reluctance on his face even before his feet touched the gravel. It seemed hard for him to even look at the shiny new homes. He was quick to remind me that with one bankruptcy under our belts, he was too old to go through another.

I spent considerable energy assuring him the mobile home business was just something on the side, nothing more. After all, we had to do *something* with this extra land. "Fenton, I understand your concerns," I said. "But I assure you, there'll never be more than 10 homes on this lot—ever."

Yeah, sure.

Fenton agreed to pay Tidwell the invoice amount of about $16,000, and by that weekend, we'd sold two of them. I called Don on Friday afternoon and ordered four more.

With growing excitement, I carefully and quietly studied my competitor's homes (being an engineer sure helped). I also examined the durability features in the older homes that customers were offering us in trade. While in school, I had been in a few dozen homes of fellow students and friends. Listening to them talk about the features and occasional defects had been a learning experience.

I learned a lot from the Taylors, who advertised heavily, and since they were right across the street, we picked up considerable traffic from them. It's amazing what you can learn about the competition from prospective customers.

I also called on Jackie Williams, an aggressive and innovative retailer, and one of the hottest names in the mobile home business.

Jackie owned not one, but two thriving chains of dealerships—Bonanza Homes and Upside-Down Charlie's—and both were all over the Southeast.

He invited me to an industry conference at the Hyatt in Atlanta. (Jackie's home office was nearby.) I immediately began collecting notes on the procedures used by this dynamic organization. He was charismatic, charming, and interestingly enough, a Mormon, so presumably he didn't smoke or drink even so much as an RC Cola.

At the time, Jackie was widely regarded as the industry's best promoter, and a number of Georgians were urging him to run for governor of the state.

To sum it up, he was an extremely persuasive man. If he had been a TV evangelist, I would have been down on my knees handing him my checkbook.

Jackie was so impressive, in fact, that I was nervous around him. Even intimidated. But I plunged ahead, and he listened to me carefully as I expressed interest in a franchise.

He invited me to an inside look at his operation, so I visited his sales centers and home office where I asked a lot of questions, made some contacts, and learned quite a bit.

To me, it seemed that doing business with Jackie Williams was an expensive proposition. A franchisee had to pay $25,000 up front, plus 6.5 percent on the sales price of every home sold.

For the fee, Jackie was providing a sign, his buying sources, his advertising strategy, and access to financing. But since we already had an attractive and unique sign; already had access to the hottest line of mobile homes; already were masters at advertising;

already had Fenton Kintzing financing our sales—why, I asked myself, do I need Jackie?

Don Tidwell, along with other manufacturers, had assured me they'd sell direct to us at or near the same price. Jackie thought he could be the distributor of choice for the major lenders, manufacturers, and insurance companies. It just didn't happen with us.

I was still interested enough to ask for an invite to Jackie's franchise school, to learn more of the finer points of advertising, selling, training, and recruiting. I needed to learn a lot more than I was able to do by visiting his sales centers.

Jackie was too shrewd for that. First, I'd have to sign a franchise agreement and I would have to pay half the fee before attending the school. I stalled him again and again, he kept pestering me, and soon it was obvious I was just working him for more information. He stopped returning my calls.

Some years later, Jackie went bankrupt when he tried to franchise a tax return service. He made a comeback, however, and at last report was thriving in Atlanta.

Maybe the best lesson I learned from Jackie was that selling a car and selling a mobile home might seem to be somewhat similar, but they were two very different kettles of fish.

At the dealership, we were now moving over a hundred cars a month. With the homes, the best retailer was lucky to sell a hundred homes in a year.

With a car sale, the financing term maxed at three years. A home might have a term of five to seven years.

Although Fenton clearly saw the advantages in financing longer-term loans, I had to be sure he was comfortable with the credit-worthiness of the buyers and the durability of the homes.

Selling a Volvo or a Renault was so simple by comparison.

We'd stick on a temporary license; put some gas in the tank, just enough to get it over the hill to the service station; sign some papers; and wave cheerily at the customer as they drove off. All that might take an hour, tops.

Just delivering our homes was complicated and expensive. We needed a specially equipped truck to haul the home to its site, set it on a concrete block foundation, and hook it up to electricity, water, and sewer. This would take an entire day, even if the site were close to our office.

This went on through what was left of '66 and all of '67—me slowly ramping up the business, and Fenton keeping close tabs. Soon, he agreed to approve orders for six homes at a time. Later, he approved more.

Before long, that "no-more-than-ten-trailers-on-this-lot" pledge was history.

Within a matter of months, Clayton Homes had four aggressive salespeople, a service department, 50 homes in stock, and an average of one sale every day, more than triple what even top retailers were doing. In almost no time at all, it seemed, we were number one in the market.

It was a mysterious phone call from Fenton Kintzing that started it all. He needed an urgent meeting with us later in the afternoon. That's all he'd say.

Joe and I thought maybe Bob Culver and Valley Fidelity's board were again putting pressure on Fenton, for whatever reason, and now it was his job to rein us in, one more time.

Fenton arrived as if dressed for a funeral, which, in fact, he was. They'd held services that day for Cowan Rogers, who owned the Cadillac and Pontiac dealership in Knoxville. Both franchises had been in his family for half a century.

Swearing us to secrecy, Fenton said that General Motors, makers of both Cadillac and Pontiac, was wasting no time and immediately canceling one of the Rogers franchises, but would offer the family a choice—give up Cadillac or give up Pontiac. At the funeral, Fenton learned the family was giving up Pontiac.

To us, this meant two things: the Pontiac franchise was now up for grabs, and half of the Rogers staff would soon be out of work. Fenton wanted us to apply for the Pontiac franchise and hire one of the two experienced finance managers before some other dealership grabbed them.

We applied for the Pontiac franchise, but our application was not approved. Back then it was difficult to obtain a "Big Three" franchise if other new car manufacturers were sold at the same location. Still, it was revealing, and heartening, to discover that Fenton, just five years after the bankruptcy, now believed in us to that extent.

As for the two finance managers from Pontiac, Jim Ausmus and Wayne Countiss, they interviewed with us, and Joe and I were pleased and impressed. In fact, we liked them both so much, we couldn't decide whom to hire. So we hired both.

Even at that early stage Joe and I recognized that we should hire when we could. This eliminated much of the hiring that tended to be based on immediacy.

One night, just after Fenton introduced us to Jim and Wayne, Mary and I invited them along with their spouses out to dinner at Regas. It's important for us to get to know the spouses, too, and all of us had a marvelous time—at least until Mary innocently mentioned our newly purchased Cessna 310, something about how they'd get to fly when visiting, say, Don Tidwell in Alabama.

To Wayne, that sounded like fun, but the look on Jim's face indicated that such a notion was anything but fun. Turned out that flying in a small plane was something he couldn't *ever* do. And his wife Marjorie, quoting a Bible verse from memory, opined, "if God wanted us to fly, He would have given us wings."

Somehow, Wayne and I coaxed Jim to ride the Cessna with us on a quick trip to McMinnville. He did it with great trepidation, reluctantly joining me in the cockpit.

I was careful to explain everything I did along the way, and his fidgety behavior noticeably quieted before the end of the flight. In fact, by the time we landed, he seemed fascinated with the Cessna, and was asking me all sorts of questions.

Later that week, I gave Jim his first flying lesson.

Within six months, he bought his own plane. Four decades later, he's still flying in his own Cessna 310, and now they can't get him out of the damn thing. His home is 65 miles from the office, so he even flies to work much of the time.

As for Marjorie, she flies, too, but only as a passenger, not as a pilot. I keep thinking that's next.

Perhaps one of the most significant additions to the staff at Clayton Homes was, of all people, Dad. He and Mother were still in Finger, still farming.

By this time, Dad was well into his fifties; as a concession to age, he was working the farm less and the cattle auction more. He was only harvesting hay now, which was much easier to handle than cotton.

Dad had always been marvelous at mechanics and could repair or re-condition practically anything. I needed someone like that to help service the mobile homes, particularly to fix up the used ones, the way he and Mother did with that barbecued trailer a year and a half earlier.

They didn't have much reason to stay in Finger any longer. Though Grandfather Clayton lived nearby, Uncle R.C. was in Knoxville by then, and many of Mother's relatives had died or moved away. Why not move to Knoxville, join the boys, enjoy the grandchildren, and help out at the business? We even had a house ready for them, a little brick bungalow near the car dealership.

It was wonderful when they agreed to move up.

Even so, I was a little wary of this new dynamic, and maybe Dad was too. Now *I* was the boss. I wondered if we'd get along, or if it'd be like the old days.

Happily, those old ghosts from childhood past never haunted us. Our uneasy relationship, over time, had resolved itself. In more recent years, we'd had some sitting-by-the-fireside chats, a fair number of in-the-car chats, and the conversations invariably went well.

Maybe it was because Dad had seen us become successful;

maybe he had just mellowed a bit; maybe it was a little of both. But he was much more open and receptive to me, and I remained, as always, respectful.

I remember one conversation: Dad was distressed about the way we'd sweep up perfectly good nails, screws, washers, and other useful paraphernalia that had dropped on the floor during the day—and toss them in the trash, along with the dirt, dust, and scrap.

To someone who never chucked anything that might be used again later, this was colossal waste. He was right, of course.

But what I remember most was the way he brought it up as thoughtful and heartfelt advice, not a scolding lecture.

And I don't think his soft-spoken demeanor was just because I was the boss.

CHAPTER 11

"Too Big To Get Out The Door"

On a warm Saturday morning in early June, I reported to work at the Clinton Highway home sales center, expecting to see my four smiling salespeople, as always. But this time, the place was empty. Nobody home. The whole thing had an eerie Twilight Zone feel to it, but I soon discovered my nemesis wasn't Rod Serling. It was Jackie Williams.

The night before, he swooped down in his plane, spirited my sales staff to the nearest Shoney's Restaurant, seduced them over fried shrimp, and hired them away. He gave them temporary positions at his newly opened Bonanza and Upside-Down Charlie's sales centers, and promised to open new franchised stores for each of them to manage.

Apparently, one of the conditions of employment was for them to maintain a conspiracy of silence, because none of the missing salespeople gave any notice. They were just gone into the mist. They never even called. I wrote some fresh ads for the classifieds.

I sent an S.O.S. to Uncle R.C., who was now sales manager at Clayton Motors, to come over and help out. By mid-morning, we sold two homes.

Not only did we keep the office open, but also, with the help of our spouses and children, produced a record month. Joe, while maintaining his general manager position at the car dealership, covered R.C.'s role. We immediately began training four people to take over the open slots, including George Blevins, who moved over from cars.

None of the four salespeople who left us lasted even a year with Jackie Williams. Larry Davidson, the only one to return, stayed with us for 20 years and remained a dear friend.

By early 1968, I was spending zero time supporting Joe at the car dealership. Clayton Homes was eating my clock, and I have to admit, I was loving it.

In June, Joe and I stopped for a beer after work and held the Big Meeting to "formalize" the role he had been playing very capably. The conversation lasted almost a full five minutes.

"Mr. President, it looks like you're running cars," I said to Joe.

"Sure looks that way," he said, with his sly half-smile.

"Okay, you run cars, and I'll run homes," I said.

The next day, my assistant, June, ordered new business cards. Now Joe was officially the president and general manager of the car division. That was about it. Joe and I never kept score. We simply did what needed to be done, without arguments, drama, or controversy.

I guess that was my first real experience in delegating, the first time I "walked away" and gave responsibility to someone else.

It surprised a few people, in and out of the company, that I could do that. My management style is clearly "hands on." Fenton Kintzing, among many others, thought I was making a mistake turning my back on the automobile business, which had "brought us to the dance."

But I wasn't about to waver. Joe had already eased into the job, and we'd still be fluid. I'd be close if needed, and vice-versa.

Truth be told, I was a little disappointed upon discovering I wasn't needed. Not needed then or later. Joe was good, and everyone—staff, customers, lenders, and factories—were quite comfortable looking to him. It took a few weeks, but even Fenton came around as he saw Joe and his team produce record months back to back.

Make no mistake, all 8,000 of us who get our paychecks from Clayton Homes should never forget that our organization wouldn't exist if not for the dealerships run by Joe and later by his children, Mark, Rick, and Debbie.

Surrendering control to a good leader and watching the team respond is a wonderful experience. For those who think I'm too picky, too hands on, and too distrustful, I'd like to remind them that I've initiated dozens of similar transitions over the years.

It's always amazing what a team with a shared vision and a gifted leader can accomplish.

It was during this period that both our car and home divisions began a dramatic surge in growth.

From 1968 to 1970, we sold 145 new and used vehicles per month. From 1971 to 1973, with the addition of the Lincoln-Mercury franchise, we averaged 310 sales per month, an astounding number.

Meanwhile, the mobile home business grew far beyond any expectations. During that same five-year period, we sold over 700 homes each year—a total of $25 million in sales each year.

In one record weekend, we sold 26 homes. During one record month, we sold 86 homes. This record still stands. No one, before or since, at a single sales center, has ever sold 700 homes in one year (or, for that matter, 26 in a weekend or 86 in a month).

There were lots of reasons for our success: a highly trained and aggressive staff; a state-of-the-art accounting system; *Startime*, a wonderful way to promote the business; a booming and stable economy, particularly good in our area; customer financing that was convenient and quick, thanks to Fenton and Valley Fidelity Bank; and attractive pricing, a strategic decision made possible because our two companies shared much of the overhead costs.

No question, those wildly successful five years gave us

momentum to build a lasting foundation and launched a unique concept that has produced results unequaled in the industry.

In 1968, we began to expand Clayton Homes as we opened a second sales center, Western Mobile Homes. It was on Kingston Pike, and Uncle R.C. managed it.

We also paved the Clinton Highway sales center for $38,000. It might not sound like anything groundbreaking now, but paving a mobile home lot back then was virtually unheard of. They'd always been gravel. The pavement made the sales center more attractive, helped us attract more prospective customers, and supported our efforts to recruit and retrain top-notch team members.

I personally supervised every inch of the grading, compaction, and base and topcoat of the paving. This location accommodates up to 100 homes on display, all of which have access to oil, gas, electricity, and water. No other sales center has offered these amenities. Today, Stephen Bowery, an amazing young man, manages this prime location.

M y son Kevin claims credit for "discovering" Stephen Bowery—and loves to tell this story.

Kevin was at a motor bike race outside Knoxville—in a dirty, dusty cow pasture—when he saw Stephen, a polite 19-year-old getting ready to participate. What struck Kevin was the way Stephen, purchasing a spark plug for the next race, negotiated the price down from $1.19 to less than a buck. You couldn't help but be impressed by how the young man so expertly combined his wonderful "people skills" with a very competitive spirit.

Stephen didn't win the race that day, but Kevin saw a professional young man exhibiting core values, so important at Clayton. The two met that day, and discussed career opportunities. Soon, Stephen was sent to interview with four different sales center managers and a regional manager—but all of them thought he was too young and inexperienced. Stephen did not give up.

He was persistent and kept in constant contact with the managers until he was hired, in June 1990. In no time, Stephen became one of our top 10 salespeople and quickly quadrupled his pay from the two jobs he'd previously held. Within two years, he was the No. 1 salesperson in the company.

After four years in sales, Stephen was promoted to manager of our International location in the very competitive Knoxville environment—and took it from an under-performing sales center to one of the top three in the company. This successful performance provided Stephen with the opportunity to transfer to the original founding sales center on Clinton Highway, which continues to be a top performer. Stephen has been inducted into the Clayton Hall of Fame as one of our most successful salespeople of all time.

And to think he's still only 34 years old!

Within months after opening Western, we'd opened a third lot on Alcoa Highway near the airport; then a fourth in nearby Athens; then a fifth in Middlesboro, Kentucky. And more were on the way.

As we grew, so did the product itself. You'll remember that little Richardson home that Mary and I purchased in Elkhart just a few years earlier. It was only eight feet wide. By the early '60s, about the time I started selling homes, the standard was 10 feet; by the mid-'60s, 12-wides dominated the industry.

Fourteen-wides became popular in most states by the late '70s. We thought 14 feet was as wide as we would ever see, but by the '80s, most single-wide homes were built in 16-foot widths.

We kept up with the technology, the newest models, the décor changes, and the latest innovations with weekly flights to our factories, not only Tidwell Homes in Alabama, but also plants in Indiana and Georgia. For more than 20 years, we never bought from a factory that I had not personally inspected.

I didn't hesitate to give them input. After all, I'd been on the firing line at the sales centers. I knew first-hand what customers liked and didn't like. I knew from our people, particularly Dad, the service and performance shortcomings of every model.

"Those faucets leak," I'd tell the manufacturers. "Those floors crack." "You're ripping the vinyl floor covering." "You're scratching the walls."

Don Tidwell, of course, always listened to my suggestions, and sometimes even implemented them. So did Fleetwood, another prominent manufacturer. But the others weren't as interested. Though they welcomed our business and my recommendations, I felt they frequently didn't have the structure and the processes in place to make the requested changes.

I stopped buying from some of them. Then I began to wonder, *maybe we could do this better ourselves.* Why not build our own?

This thought pattern is familiar to most retailers. Anyone who sells widgets ultimately thinks they can build them better, prettier, and cheaper than their current supplier.

My original plan was to build homes that were nothing like the competition. I had a vision of an earthy, warm, rustic home with décor in early American, very popular at the time. The furniture would include exposed wood frame sofas and chairs, the kind manufactured at a plant in Sevierville, Dolly Parton's hometown.

I quickly found out how difficult it would be to make homes that unique. For any manufactured product, there were only a few Original Equipment Manufacturers supplying the final assemblers or distributors—and, in an effort to control costs, all of us bought from the same OEM vendors.

This is why, today, a Chevy looks much like a Ford.

Even building homes with the "standard" look was going to be a difficult proposition at best. Other retailers had tried, and failed. In fact, the manufacturing operation had ultimately caused the companies to fail.

We did, however, have some distinct advantages over other retailers who had taken the plunge into manufacturing.

I already had an "in" with a number of vendors who sold building materials like plywood and paint, sheetrock and steel, flooring and fixtures. We'd bought materials from these guys all along when we refurbished used homes received on trade, or for our foreclosed homes, which we purchased from lenders.

We also received help from an unexpected source—our manufacturers, who gave us names, phone numbers, prices, and even encouraged the vendors to sell to us at attractive rates.

You may be wondering why our manufacturers would help us. After all, if we built our own homes, they could be cut out of the picture.

But they were familiar with the abysmal track record of other retailers who'd gone the same route, and they knew this was a mammoth undertaking for us. By helping us now, they continued to sell homes to our company, figuring that, eventually, we'd drop the manufacturing idea before we went broke.

Besides, if they were stingy or secretive with the information in their little black books, they ran the risk of offending us, one of their biggest, fastest-paying, and best-servicing customers.

By 1969, Joe had just built a new body shop, adjacent to the main car building. The old rented building we had been using in Inskip, five blocks from the Clinton Highway sales center, became our first factory. You'd never mistake it for General Motors, but the rent was inexpensive.

Dad would be helping us, and Joe wanted to supervise the factory start-up. (He now had Jim Ausmus and Bill Fielden, capable managers, available to run the car dealership.) Joe and Dad recruited Clarence Cole to round out the factory team. Clarence had been a construction supervisor of remodeling crews at site-built homes, and was a fast, skilled, multi-task craftsman. His brother was Carl Cole, our first mechanic at Clayton Motors.

The factory was only big enough to construct three mobile homes at the same time. We quickly created a crude assembly line and adopted, unintentionally, the trial-and-error approach.

One early lesson learned: always make sure the size of the finished product is smaller than the doorway.

The first home, with the aluminum skin, doorknobs, other fixtures on the outside, and other amenities, was 12 feet wide.

But the door width was 11 feet and 10 inches.

When we finished the first home, we triumphantly brought in a tow-truck to haul our new creation to the sales center. We were making a big show of it. Our team was excited about its arrival, on Friday afternoon no less, just in time for the weekend traffic. One of our team members, Jess Haun, even changed our marquee to say, "New Clayton Home, Just Arrived—$3,995."

It was Dad who called me with the bad news.

"We have a small problem," he said. "The home is too big for the darn door."

We had to knock out the wall, which didn't please our land-lord, then spent two days and hundreds of dollars building a larger door.

Over the years, we've had lots of laughs about this. But at the time, it wasn't funny at all.

The homes were simple, cheap, and sold even before they were off the assembly line. Our retail price was $3,995, a little lower than the rest of the industry. Our customers saved significantly on freight costs, the hundreds of dollars normally paid to move the homes from the factory to the dealership. Instead, this was credited to our customers; since we were building the homes locally—just blocks away from the sales center—there were no "freight to dealer" costs.

We soon recognized that we couldn't supply the growing demand for these low-priced homes, not in that tiny plant, nor could we build enough there to make a profit.

Early in 1970, we moved to an old tobacco warehouse on Stockyard Road in Halls, a community in North Knoxville. It was three times the size of our original place. This represented a huge move for us. In a sense, this was the ultimate entrepreneurial start-up, unlike anything we had ever done before—a retailer becoming a full-fledged manufacturer.

If it weren't for our perseverance (some would say stubborn-ness), we wouldn't have succeeded.

One of our biggest challenges was finding capable management who understood production and fast-assembly techniques.

At the beginning, we brought in Jim Early as general manager of the plant. Jim was excellent, a great communicator who was loyal and dedicated. Interestingly, his background had nothing to do with manufactured homes; instead, he was a journalist, and a very good one—he was news director at WBIR, Knoxville's CBS affiliate. At one time, Jim had his own band and TV show on Channel 26, and was one of the first people I met when I moved to Knoxville in 1953.

To us, there was nothing negative in the fact that Jim was new to our industry. Our philosophy, then and now, is that we can teach someone the fundamentals of our business. What we really want is someone with good values, and he had that in abundance.

Only one month after joining us, Jim had a heart attack. Thankfully, he recovered and today runs a very successful advertising agency in Knoxville; our car dealerships are among his clients. If he'd been able to stay with us at the plant, I know he would've done a bang-up job, as he did in helping me produce *Startime* for years, and in placing all of our advertising.

Max Nichols, our factory supervisor, was expert at finding skilled craftsmen who could build mobile homes to industry standards. He also knew how to maintain excellent relationships with them. If there was a problem, Max would take his managers out to the back of the plant, get them a "chaw" of tobacco, and talk through the problem. He is one of the finest small-group managers I've ever seen, and the kind of guy who'd always grab the heavy end of a load.

Lowell Woods, our operations manager, had a résumé full of engineering and management experience, including a stint with the Apollo space program. (He was a guidance control specialist for Apollos 4, 5, and 6.) He was part of a "two-headed" management team with Ty Kelly, who had an extensive background in home building. Lowell supervised production and engineering.

Ty handled sales and marketing. Both were recruited in 1974.

All the books will tell you that co-management doesn't work. The books were right. For several years, Lowell and Ty got along quite well. But eventually, their management styles clashed.

Lowell liked having his hands in the mix and "walked the line" every morning and afternoon. He had a strong need to control. Ty preferred to plan, train, delegate, and share the decision-making responsibility with people at all levels.

Both of them were good, effective and professional, but there was room for only one boss. Lowell left the company, but has remained a friend. Ty stayed with the company until 1999 and retired the same day I did.

Even with the added expertise, not everything worked the way we wanted. Ford had its Edsel; we had our "Jimmy Lee," a low-priced model that Max Nichols wanted to manufacture in 1971. We hoped the Jimmy Lee would be a high-volume, entry-level product. But it wasn't aesthetically pleasing, and there were some quality control issues we couldn't quite overcome—warped floors, for one.

After three years, we finally stopped producing the Jimmy Lee, went back to crafting traditional models, and accepted the notion that our manufacturing center wouldn't see a profit for awhile. On that, we were right. Though the sales centers continued to grow, we wouldn't make money on the manufacturing side until 1976.

At first, it wasn't part of the grand plan, getting into the business of owning and operating mobile home communities. That was simply a deal that fell into our lap.

An investor had built the Green Acres mobile home park only to find very few people who wanted to move in, even though it was attractive and in a nice section of Knoxville. He got me interested, however, at least enough to put a dozen of our homes in the park, completely set up and ready for immediate occupancy.

In appreciation for the new home orders, I took the gang from

Startime, Kathy Hill, the Sisters Four, the Kountry Kings Band, and others, out to Green Acres for a weekend promotion, and true, the people showed up, hundreds of them. They enjoyed the music as they munched on hot dogs and popcorn, and listened to us as we tried to sell the park and the homes. But we still didn't get anywhere. Nobody bought. It took us two years to sell the 12 model homes we placed in this community.

By 1973, only 30 homes were in Green Acres, and the investor finally had enough. He sold it to us at a price that was less than his construction costs. We thought it was still a good idea and a good investment. A profitable park would be reliable, year-round revenue for Clayton Homes and take up the slack during winter months, when mobile home sales were slow.

We still own Green Acres today, and it's one of the finest mobile home communities in the area. It now has 240 sites and virtually every amenity featured by the most expensive apartment complexes, including a pool and playground. (We now own over 21,000 sites.)

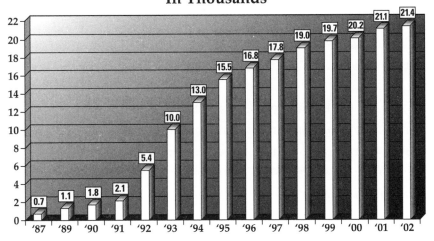

Community Sites
In Thousands

As we began to purchase other mobile home parks, we learned each had its own unique set of problems.

You've seen that movie *A River Runs Through It?* Well, one of our parks, Lincoln Estates, had a creek running right through it. No problem, we thought. Let's reshape the land and divert the flow of the creek around the edge of the park, instead of letting it run through the community. Major mistake.

Water goes where it wants to go, and where it wants to go is where it has always gone. It wasn't too long before walkways collapsed, blacktop crumbled, and fissures popped up in places where the creek used to be. We paved Lincoln Estates twice, at a cost of $30,000 each time, and within a month of each paving, the rains just washed away the expensive blacktop paving, including the base.

We learned, right then and there, literally to go with the flow. Make your plan conform to the land, not the other way around. Either work with it, or walk away.

Spending time with all the seemingly boring details of a business often pays off—and sometimes leads to opportunity.

This time it was a phone call from Lincoln-Mercury in Detroit. They wanted us to consider buying and operating the local dealership, located in downtown Knoxville. It had lost over a million dollars in the last year, but Detroit was willing to offer some excellent incentives if we would agree to build a new facility and revive the dealership.

We flew to Detroit. Ben Bidwell, the vice-president and general manager of Lincoln-Mercury (and later, Lee Iacocca's right-hand man at Chrysler), confirmed the incentive support program—if we brought the dealership up to their expectations. We shook hands and had a deal.

Later, Joe and I flipped a coin to see who'd supervise the Lincoln-Mercury takeover and who'd run the mobile home manufacturing operation at Halls. I got the plant, and Joe got Lincoln-Mercury, but he spent every spare minute helping me at Halls as he planned for the Lincoln-Mercury take-over.

In fact, when the Lincoln-Mercury rep showed up for the final sign-off, he found Joe, in his blue jeans at the factory, on top of one of the homes placing screws in the roof.

It's clear from all this that we were on the upswing of a tremendous growth curve that was building at an impressive rate. You can ride the wave, or you can wipe out.

It's intoxicating, but dicey, with plenty of bumps along the way, as you train your growing staff, conserve your working capital, and maneuver through the shifting tides of the economy. You have choices: you can expand out-of-control (been there, done that), you can stagnate (no fun in that), or you can grow rapidly but responsibly (we chose this).

George Jones, in his song, "Choices," sang: *"I've had choices since the day I was born. I've had voices that taught me right from wrong. If I had listened, then I wouldn't be here today, living and dying, with the choices I've made."*

So far, we'd been growing horizontally, adding franchises to the car business and expanding sales centers with the mobile homes. Now we made our first move toward becoming the most vertically integrated company in our industry.

We began in housing, just like cars, at the retail level, selling homes produced by other companies. We served our customers and shareholders very well on that one level. Then with a huge step back, we began to design and manufacture from scratch the homes we wanted to sell. Now we were covering two levels. We were vertically integrated, but not much.

Owning and operating mobile home communities took us to a third level. Now we were providing our customers with quality sites for their homes and an attractive lifestyle for their families.

When we started Vanderbilt Life in 1973, our customers were offered home, lifestyle, and extended warranty programs with their home purchase. With this toe in the water, we were slowly entering into a fourth level. Little did we know that soon the tail would wag the dog. At the time, financing was a by-product of selling homes. Our emphasis and income was primarily sales. Over the next three decades, financial services—mortgages and insurance—would become the larger source of income, dwarfing even that of manufacturing and retail.

Our financial services began with "family protection programs," which were offered to the primary income provider. If the provider died, Vanderbilt paid the scheduled coverage amount during the early years of the mortgage, when the balance on the home is higher. The family then has the option to reschedule the mortgage for a much shorter term or to significantly reduce the payment amount and mortgage balance.

Through Vanderbilt Life, hundreds of our homeowners have been able to keep their homes, and expensive foreclosures for the company have been prevented.

Owning the insurance company provides significant income for us. In Tennessee, the maximum commission permitted on credit life insurance is 40 percent of the earned premium. Our claims tend to be less than average since younger customers tend to buy more homes, and we underwrite, when permitted, to avoid writing policies for customers with pre-existing conditions.

Vanderbilt writes its policies using the license of American Bankers Insurance of Miami. ABI also provides consulting and compliance services for a small commission, while ceding the premium and the risk to Vanderbilt.

To sum it up, with this partnership, and if we underwrite and adjust claims effectively, we can earn an excellent return on our investment while allowing the agency to earn the appropriate commission permitted by state law.

Vanderbilt Life was so successful that we decided to use what we learned from our long-time finance partners—Fenton Kintzing of Valley Fidelity and Pat Harrison of Commerce Union—to write our own mortgages.

Actually, we had already started such a process. Joe had about a dozen owner-financed account cards totaling about $6,000 on his desk for customers with weak credit who were buying older homes and cars.

Shifting our mortgage company into high gear would take us to our fifth level of service. Or, to look at it another way, our company would realize five levels of income with just one product.

These twelve accounts totaling $6,000 in 1973 would grow to the nation's premier Mortgage Portfolio of 180,000 accounts valued at $4.9 billion by 2002.

Like I say, it was a great time for us.

Mortgage Portfolio
$ Millions

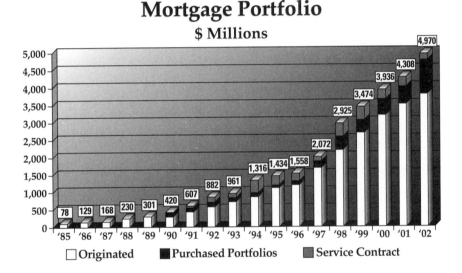

Legend: □ Originated   ■ Purchased Portfolios   ■ Service Contract

On February 29, 1972, the family was finishing up breakfast when Mother called. She'd been crying, which was unusual. Mother never cried.

When she called me Lee, a name she hadn't used in years, I knew something was horribly wrong. She spoke only four words, but it was enough to turn my world upside-down: "Lee, your Dad's dead."

He had a massive heart attack just as he stepped out of the shower, and died instantly. He was only 60 years old. There had been no indication that he was ill, aside from a little bit of indigestion that followed him from time to time. He seemed healthy and fit.

We'd had long conversations about his upcoming retirement. Dad had made it clear that he and Mother wanted to take several trips each year to visit their many independent retailer friends. In addition, he promised to attend all the "new product" shows.

It was indescribably painful to think that this man, who'd worked so hard all his life, wouldn't get a day of his carefully planned retirement.

There were long lines at the memorial service in Knoxville, and the next day at the First Baptist Church in Finger. Coincidentally, the day of his funeral was March 2, my 38th birthday.

The Sisters Four, who were Dad's favorites from the television show, sang at the funeral. Later, our family and friends from Knoxville and Finger gathered at Grandfather Clayton's home. As we celebrated Dad's life, it seemed unusual, watching a father bury his son.

Mary couldn't be there. She was back in Knoxville at Baptist Hospital, about to deliver our fourth child, Amy. It was going to happen anytime, so I kept calling the hospital from Grandfather Clayton's home. Just before two in the afternoon, Mother, Joe, and I left for the service with still no fourth child.

After the beautiful service, I rushed back to my grandfather's home and heard this from a wonderful nurse: "Mr. Clayton, congratulations! You have a perfect baby girl, beautiful and healthy." Amy Michelle had been born at 2:25 that afternoon, during the hour of Dad's funeral and on my birthday.

I'm sure I reflected a bit on the symmetry of it all—the passing of a generation, the birth of another. But the joy for my newborn daughter, the anguish over the loss of my father, my concern for Mary—all the emotion, reflection, and dwelling on life's imponderables—soon gave way to an immediate need. We had to comfort Mother.

It had been pouring rain much of the day, but with the weather beginning to clear, Joe and I piloted the family and friends back to

Knoxville in the company's two planes. Soon, I would be with Mary and Amy.

Only someone who has lost a parent can relate to this brand of pain. It leaves a gnawing void that you can't escape, as emotions ebb and flow through the mind. It's especially difficult for someone with a need to be in control, and Dad's death was an event I had zero control over. Even though he and I were not extremely close—at least until the last several months of his life—I still felt a large part of me was missing.

I found myself thinking of Dad all the time, in a business meeting, on the phone, driving down the road, or while holding my baby daughter. Even today, I can still hear Dad telling a neighbor at Uncle R.C.'s store that I was "pretty good at fixing radios." And I'd love it when he'd brag about the way our homes always fit together because "Jim insisted we do it that way." In his last few years, he had become comfortable with the company, its mission, its people, its products—and with me.

Dad, I wish you could see your company now, along with your two children, seven grandchildren, and 10 great-grandchildren.

CHAPTER 12

Expansion In
A Recession

Not long after Dad died, we held a grand opening celebration at our recently purchased Green Acres Mobile
Home Park. We needed someone to run it, and all of us
agreed the perfect "someone" was Mother.

We were right. Mother collected the rent, kept the books, and
looked after the residents. Anyone who played the stereo too loud
always heard from her, without hesitation.

It was good for the company, and good for Mother.

The year 1973 was one of record growth not only for us, but
also for the entire industry. That year, 600,000 mobile homes
were built, an unprecedented number in the history of the business. With 17 mobile home sales centers in four states—Kentucky,
Virginia, North Carolina, and, of course, Tennessee—we were
active participants in the industry upturn.

The acquisition of the three sales centers of International
Mobile Homes from Fred Langley, owner of East Tennessee Ford,
gave us an even 20, all within our *Startime* TV coverage area.

Fred was our friend, neighbor, and competitor on Clinton
Highway. When he saw how well we were doing with mobile

homes, he jumped into the game, opened five sales centers, and even produced his own television show. But he soon closed two sales centers and probably celebrated when I bought his last three.

Later, as the 1974 recession began, we had twice as many foreclosures from Fred's relatively small number of accounts (200) as we did from our own accounts. Our original 17 sales centers had sold and guaranteed over 1,200 accounts. Ouch!

When a company begins to expand its retail operations, it has to make a critical strategic decision: lease the land or buy it outright. For example, McDonald's Restaurants chooses to lease the land and franchise its restaurants, rather than own them.

We decided there were tremendous advantages to ownership: We no longer had to negotiate a lease with a landlord, or endure rent increases after making property improvements. We didn't have to track, negotiate, and re-document leases. We had fixed costs and control.

In addition, it simply made good sense to go into a market, buy the land when it was priced relatively low, let it appreciate in value, and then sell it for profit. No matter what town we were in, we'd follow a basic formula when purchasing land. We'd go to the edge of town, just past McDonald's and the car dealerships, and choose property that was inexpensive and undeveloped.

Within a few years, what was once the "edge of town" suddenly became the heart of suburbia. Families moved into the area, supporting the grocery stores, fast food restaurants, and gas stations. Suddenly, our land was worth much more than what we'd paid for it.

The very nature of the mobile home business was helpful when we decided to sell the land, since there were no permanent buildings on it. With a larger list of buyers competing to purchase such unspoiled property for car dealerships, shopping centers, or fast food restaurants, we could often sell at a premium price.

The absence of permanent structures on our land also made it easy for us to move our business. After selling the property, we could move our offices and the entire mobile home inventory within a day.

It would probably take another book to precisely describe just how often that real-estate strategy has worked. In '73, we moved a new sales center into Somerset, Kentucky. The land cost $50,000. Five years later, as the community grew, and the shopping centers, fast food restaurants, and Wal-Marts moved our way, the land at the sales center dramatically increased in value.

Our land, suddenly in a high traffic area, attracted a shopping center developer, and we sold the land for $500,000, ten times what we had paid just five years earlier. We moved our inventory, the office, our signs, everything, just a little further down the road where we continued doing business.

Developers have learned that our property is readily for sale at any time. We can practically move overnight if the price is right.

In 1989, when I went on the board and Audit Committee of Dollar General Stores, I was surprised to learn they owned little of their real estate. I urged the CFO to look carefully at the numbers and consider investing in more of the store properties. At the time, I saw a large staff devoted to negotiating, documenting, and tracking leases. Within two to five years, leases tend to expire, and considerable staff attention is required to extend the leases, while keeping rent increases manageable.

Frequently stores have to move from a productive location because rent increases are unacceptable.

When CMH leases property, we negotiate a "90-Day Walk" clause in our agreement. Essentially, this means that while we have a five or even 10-year lease with the landowner, we have an option to "walk away" provided we give the owner 90 days notice in writing.

I realize this appears at first glance to be a one-sided agreement, but when the landowner hears our well-articulated presentation, it becomes an easy sell. With the 90-Day Walk clause, the landowner is immediately paid three months rent along with our notice, should we find it necessary to vacate during the lease period. We also immediately put up a "For Lease" sign on the property and leave it in perfect condition, sometimes even moving well before the end of the 90 days, allowing another business to move in.

This is a markedly different approach than the course typically taken by our often under-financed competitors, who may bankrupt and leave the property unkempt. Landowners know this, and after getting to know us, and after hearing our presentation, are often eager to have the cancellation language included in their lease. Since the SEC requires us to disclose our lease liabilities in our financial statements, it looks better if we are not exposed to long-term leases without an opportunity to cancel. The 90-Day Walk is a "win-win" for everyone.

During the '70s, I was personally involved with most of the property acquisitions. I'd manage the manufacturing plant until four in the afternoon, rush to the airport, and take off in the plane. Within an hour-and-a-half, I'd be looking at property 200 miles away. Often, the landowners were elderly people, who loved nothing better than to talk about their families, particularly the grandchildren. Their stories were always interesting, and they seemed to enjoy the fact that I enjoyed getting to know them and hearing the history of their families and their land.

The fact that I was truly interested in them helped later as we negotiated, because they'd already developed a sense of trust in me. I'd explain how our company's expansion was a tremendous opportunity for them to get a great price for their property with a combination of lease payments initially. Later, if we exercised our option (we always did) to buy their property, they would receive a very large additional sum of money in the form of principal and interest payments. The entire transaction would be structured to minimize their tax burden.

Around sundown, I'd grab a three-piece box of Colonel Sander's crispy chicken on the way to the airport for my trip to the next stop. In an hour or so, I'd meet with another property owner in another state. I've signed many a lease with purchase options late in the evening, arriving back home after midnight.

If the owner wasn't interested in selling, I wrote a letter afterwards, thanking them for their time and reminding them to call me if circumstances change. Believe me, circumstances change. People die, divorce, move, become ill, or simply want a change.

It's reasonable to say that much of the vacant property we liked would be available within three to 10 years. "You remember that property we told you would never be for sale? Well, if you're still interested, you need to get here fast," the caller would say. We would be on our way.

These days, we purchase property very much the same way, though our regional managers tend to use realtors who take them on a tour of the area. Realtors, of course, aren't likely to know unlisted property, but we ask anyway: "Will Mr. Smith sell?"

We'll go visit the property owner to see if we can establish a rapport. If they like us, they might sell months or years down the road or even now, if we are lucky. After all, you don't catch a fish every time you throw in the hook.

The young CMH "Turks" out in the field have become more sophisticated in their approach to buying property. Armed with technology, they research the market, study the competition, examine demographics, look at the local economy, and try to evaluate the political climate. Sometimes, this takes months. But when it comes time to purchase the real estate, it is back to people dealing with people.

In 1973, we acquired Universal Modular Homes, a factory housing company that built low-cost rental apartments using stacked modular units. It seemed to be a good concept. Modular units cost less and require less time to build.

UMH had been owned by local lawyer Bob Worthington and businessman Pat Wood along with U.S. Senator Howard Baker.

(In fact, this was just after Baker had become a national figure in the Watergate hearings, which ultimately led to the resignation of President Nixon a year later.) Neither he nor his partners had the time to develop the operation.

Meantime, at our Halls manufacturing plant, production began to increase, thanks to the systems implemented by Lowell Woods and Ty Kelly.

At the same time, the size and look of mobile homes began to change. Double-wides were becoming popular, and the standard way to build them was to construct both sections of the home separately. The two units would not be joined until they were set up on the retailer's lot or at the homebuyer's permanent site.

Constructing the homes in this manner was indeed faster and cost less, but often the two halves did not fit together. The end walls, floors, ceilings, and doorway openings did not line up without "major surgery" in the field.

The standard tool, which involved a highly technical and precise procedure, was to take a sledgehammer to the protruding member and force it to match the opposite half.

How could you explain this unconventional process to the homebuyer? You couldn't!

Observing all the havoc caused with this kind of construction, we were determined to make certain our homes always fit together properly, even if it cost additional time and materials to manufacture. We re-engineered our production line to join the floors as they were built. From that point the home was built as one unit. The end walls, the roof systems, and the floors were bolted together when set. The home traveled down the assembly line as one whole unit instead of two separate *halves*.

This process required large appliances, cabinetry, tubs, sinks, water heaters, and furnaces to be "loaded" in the floor station. Then the exterior walls and roof system were added. This allowed faster loading and installation of these items and prevented damage to floor and wall coverings.

Using this method, much of the activity after the walls were set was limited to molding, trim, and electrical wiring. It was a more difficult process, but we quickly learned the retailers and prospective buyers were impressed with the increased quality of our homes. The sales advantage was significant and the process of building double-wides as one unit and then literally sawing them apart only after they are completely built was ingrained deep in the CMH culture.

Again my engineering degree paid off.

Because *Startime* was increasingly popular, by now we were syndicating the show to six cities in four states—Winston-Salem, North Carolina; Columbia, South Carolina; Lexington, Kentucky; Jackson and Nashville, both in Tennessee; and of course, Knoxville. In the syndicated version, our commercials were inserted by our local sales centers, though the Knoxville version featured spots for both homes and cars.

TV time was still quite inexpensive then, and our total cost to run the show in all seven cities was under $3,000 a week. In Knoxville, we'd move *Startime* around a lot, and scheduled it at various times on each of the three network affiliates. Sometimes we'd run the same episode on two different stations during the same week.

But with the growth of our company, I was increasingly required to focus on recruiting, planning, financing, and administrating as my dreams for our companies continued to grow. As our sales increased, I saw that someday we would be in the same league as the reigning giants in our business: Conner Homes, Mobile Home Industries, and Oakwood Homes.

Watching each of the giants become publicly held companies over several quarters, I was motivated to grow and position our company for a public offering at some point. Accordingly, we began to selectively act and look like a public company over time. Hiring one of the "Big Eight" accounting firms, Ernst & Ernst, to provide us with certified audits, tax, and other accounting services, we immediately began to develop more sophisticated financial reporting. (Ernst & Ernst is now Ernst & Young.)

While performing our first audit, their partners in charge suggested we invite in one of their small business consultants for a two-day overview of our operations. Since the cost was only $1,000, we readily agreed.

The consultant observed our operations while surveying our complete computer, accounting, tax, and reporting processes. We were excited as we gathered to hear his recommendations.

Instead, the consultant simply said, "I really don't think I'm going to be able to help you."

We asked why. Were our systems so good, and serving us so well, that he couldn't add any value to them? Or were we lacking in our accounting and bookkeeping systems? Was it because we were so profitable? Was it because Joe Clayton had personally written the computer software supporting our accounting and reporting systems? They really worked even though they were quite unconventional.

The consultant never told us directly. He did allude to how we were too focused on growing too fast. (I've heard that one before.) It's certainly true that we paid more attention to sales and marketing than to accounting and record keeping.

Though he didn't go into much detail, the consultant clearly gave the impression that if we wanted to become a publicly owned company, we'd have to change.

So we did. We hired additional accounting and administrative staff, and Joe continued to upgrade the computer systems. More and more, our financial reporting began to look like that of the publicly held companies in our industry. We began turning out management reports, balance sheets, and income statements that were comparable to any financial report issued by other large, publicly owned companies.

We also decided to move our corporate headquarters. The house we'd been using next to the car dealership on Clinton

Highway was no longer big enough.

Around this time, while driving out to Green Acres, I saw a crowd gathered near the road. I thought there had been an accident, so I slowed down and discovered what was really going on—an auction of the 26-room Holiday Motel.

I bid and bought. Within a week, that motel became our corporate headquarters. It was unique, to say the least, 26 rooms with 26 bathrooms. It served us well for 12 years.

Our business had grown so much that Fenton Kintzing and Valley Fidelity were now telling us that our loan portfolio was rapidly approaching the regulatory limits for a bank their size. We would need another source to provide customer financing for our growing customer base.

Fenton recommended Commerce Union Bank and his good friend, Harold Hull, vice president of lending, to handle the required additional customer financing. After exchanging visits and meeting Mr. Hull and his two senior lenders, Pat Harrison and Billy Stephens, we happily agreed to begin sending customer loan applications immediately to Commerce Union.

This turned out to be a very happy and profitable relationship for all of us. As we opened our new accounts with Commerce Union, we continued giving Valley Fidelity enough business for them to maintain our portfolio at a comfortable level.

For some time, we had been Valley Fidelity's largest source of business and most profitable account. It would stay that way, and within five years, we'd be at the same place with Commerce Union Bank.

Pat Harrison became the senior vice president and manager of the department a few years later after Mr. Hull retired. General Harrison retired years later after the bank became part of the Bank of America organization. Today, nearly 40 years later, Pat and I exchange e-mails several times each week. In fact, he, his wife Marylou, Kay, and I enjoyed an Alaskan cruise in 2000.

In 1991 Pat, Tim Williams, and I spent a week in Odessa, Texas, performing due diligence on a $110 million loan portfolio from a failed savings and loan. It would require more time and paper than we have allocated for this chapter to detail how complicated this transaction became. This was one of those deals that just would not close. At the 11th hour when Tim was about to lose a $2 million, non-refundable deposit, the General stood up and called all the lawyers to attention. "I'll guarantee it," he said.

With that statement, he placed Bank of America at risk for $20 million. That's all it took. Vanderbilt Mortgage Company made over $40 million on that transaction over the next seven years.

Business is all about relationships and trust. Thanks, General.

For five years in a row, we had sustained record growth. We thought 1974 was going to be even better.

Boy, were we wrong.

The economy did more than go south. It went straight down. Talk about a deadly spiral.

The OPEC oil embargo, the energy crisis, high inflation, high unemployment, bank failures, a horrible stock market—the entire country, and the housing industry in particular, had one of its worst years ever.

Actually, we thought the recession had missed us. Business was at record levels and increasing all through the year, although bad for others in our industry. We talked to an investment banker about taking us public, but decided to wait another year because we expected earnings to increase over 30 percent. That would add significant value to our Initial Public Offering.

However, in the fall of 1974, it hit the fan for us, too.

The sales faucet slowed, then it became only a trickle. That trickle soon slowed to a stop. From then until the fall of '76 was two long, terrible years for our industry.

From '73 to '74, industry shipments fell over 40 percent—from 580,000 to 338,000. They dropped almost another 40 percent in 1975, to 212,000. There was a small recovery in '76, but only to 246,000, not even half of the '73 levels.

It's fair to say we were in crisis management.

When the economy is this sick, a domino effect begins to take over. People become fearful for their jobs, so they hunker down and stop buying. They lose confidence in the stock market, so it continues to plunge. Lending institutions become increasingly wary, so there's less capital available for companies like ours.

Fortunately, we had not gone public the previous year. At the time, it was a decision we made reluctantly. But if we had gone public, we couldn't have received a favorable price for the stock. The Initial Public Offering window had slammed shut in 1973 and would not open for a decade.

Though we were doing far better than many of our competitors—some of them had gone bankrupt, while others closed many of their dealerships—we still had to shut down six of our sales centers, about 25 percent of the total. We also closed the Maynardville plant.

Once again, circumstances changed the way we did business. To handle the recession, we needed help in all areas, in everything from time management to delegating responsibility. But even more critically, we needed a solid plan for the future. We were still making decisions by the "seat of our pants." An economic environment like this is unforgiving; there's no margin for error.

As entrepreneurs tend to do, I was always looking for mentors and expert help. I found it with the Dale Carnegie Management Course. Six of us from the company took the course. The cost was $400 a person, and for us it was a bargain. The course involved six weeks of three-hour classes on Monday nights, plus homework.

Using the business principals learned from Dale Carnegie, we restructured our entire business. Planning, organizing, delegating, controlling, and communicating techniques were applied to every corner of our operations, especially planning. We wrote position result descriptions, formalized strategic plans, and set up a performance appraisal process. We developed our own sales and leadership training programs inspired by Dale Carnegie.

We began holding strategic planning meetings and created "cross-functional" teams to manage credit decisions. We were open with lenders, personnel, our customers, and even our competition; we implemented a variety of procedures still followed by our company today, including "position result descriptions," which identify specific performance standards that our team members must meet.

The one-three-five-year plan implemented in each business segment had specific goals, with specific timetables for reaching each goal. It really kept us focused. No longer could I haphazardly pick up a project while dropping another. This time, we had to stick to the plan. If we did that, the business would be much easier to manage and the results more easily predetermined.

Our plan was the boss.

Yes, we were becoming more and more prepared for life in a public company if the IPO window ever opened again.

Me, I thought the Dale Carnegie philosophy was so powerful that I became a class assistant, then a management seminar leader trainee. Later, I spent a week at their training academy in Hartford. After the training, I taught two classes a year for the next 12 years. I received a lot of satisfaction as I watched scores of business people write their personal and business plans in my class. Occasionally I'll get a call from a graduate telling me how much they grew personally and professionally as a result of that business plan exercise.

It was during my teaching time at Dale Carnegie that I discovered the true meaning behind the old saying, "You don't really learn until you teach."

How do you find the right people for your business? For starters, we always network. Our management is constantly on the watch for quality team members with high potential.

We look for people who already have jobs. We don't necessarily put a lot of stock in résumés. I prefer letters—a two-pager, describing work background, salary history, and career dreams.

Someone who takes the time to write a good letter is likely to have desire and motivation.

After that, we have to make sure a potential team member fits in with the Clayton culture.

For example, to recruit a sales center manager, the prospective team member meets with the appropriate regional manager. If that goes well, there's a second interview with a more senior manager. Spouses are frequently included in the interview process. It is important that they understand and support the long hours and weekend schedule involved in the retail industry. Too, we want the spouse to know the benefits and culture at CMH.

The objective in recruiting is for the process to allow CMH management and the candidate to make the best possible choices. Our batting average is good, but we are not always successful.

When should a team member's employment be terminated?

Some very knowledgeable people will say that the time to pull the trigger is *the first time you think of it.*

What they're really suggesting isn't as harsh as it sounds. Instead, they're saying that most of us will delay the inevitable and procrastinate as long as possible before terminating someone. It's only human nature, since the very person you have to fire has talent and is likeable. After all, you hired them.

About 20 years ago, I had the unpleasant task of terminating a middle manager who just wasn't cutting it. On a Saturday morning, I took him to breakfast to break the news, but instead, we talked family, fishing, and business. We were there for a couple of hours—remember, I liked him, he was a good guy—and I just couldn't bring myself to lower the boom.

After breakfast, I invited him for a drive out to Clinton Highway for a look at our sales center. We talked some more, while I kept trying to think of a productive role he could play on one of our teams. With his pay expectations, there was no fit.

Finally—it was eleven-thirty—I dropped the bomb on him, as gently as I could. He handled it fine. In fact, if I had known he'd take it so well, I would've completed the mission by the time our toast was served.

N o question about it, the recession hurt. But it didn't kill us. In fact, it distinguished us from the rest of the competition. We learned and grew from the downturn, and came out of it tougher and stronger. The recession forced us to restructure and positioned us for a bright future.

What also kept us going during that difficult time was our constant innovation and our diversified sources of income. Other companies like ours ignored potential profit centers like financing and insurance.

We saw a viable market with military veterans, especially those returning from Vietnam, and helped them obtain quality housing. In our five states, Clayton Homes was the only active Veteran's Administration lender, originating and servicing VA contracts worth over $2 million.

What's more—the recession didn't hit our auto division as badly as it hit mobile homes.

True, we weren't setting records, and import sales had dropped a little, but by and large, the car dealership escaped the full brunt of the economic downturn. By 1975, net profits at the dealerships had increased slightly.

In fact, the Lincoln-Mercury franchise was actually earning a higher net income than before the recession. Joe, who turned around that dealership, deserves enormous credit.

By mid-decade, it seemed as though the worst was behind us—at least with the business.

But I had significant issues in my personal life.

CHAPTER 13

Turning Forty

My marriage was in trouble. Mary and I had been happily married for nearly 20 years. We had four wonderful children. She'd been at my side through it all—the early years and struggles, the good times and the bankruptcy.

But now, the children seemed to be our only common interest. I take my share of the blame for allowing myself to be consumed by the business. Maybe I was so busy "doing my own thing" that Mary thought she wasn't needed.

I had created a mind-boggling schedule: expanding Clayton Homes, recruiting the right people, obtaining financing, buying land, resolving regulatory and political issues, supporting our team members, and fighting the recession, all while producing a weekly television program. Business didn't always leave me enough time to be available for Mary and the children.

It was her brother, Roger, a very successful Baptist minister in Nashville, who told me that Mary wanted to end the marriage.

Mary and I separated in the fall of 1974, but we got together again over Christmas. When that didn't work out, we permanently separated in February of '75. But it took nearly two years before the divorce was finalized.

It was difficult for all of us. I moved into a spare bedroom at the Holiday Motel, our new corporate headquarters soon to be renovated. This was a lonely time for me. It was painful to be separated from my family. Amy was only two, Kevin was 10, Jimmy was 14, and Karen was 17.

I was 40—and trying to figure out what went wrong. A friend recommended Gail Sheehy's book, *Passages*, then a national bestseller, and now regarded as a classic.

From *Passages*, I learned that people of my generation, who typically married young and had children right away, were setting themselves up for a crisis at—guess what? —age 40.

That's exactly what happened to us. Mary was 20, and I was 21 when we married. Karen, our first child, came two-and-a-half years later. After that, Jimmy and Kevin came along, two-and-a-half years apart. (Amy, our wonderful surprise, came nine years after Kevin.)

According to Sheehy, as the husband turns 40, he suddenly realizes he won't live forever, and he starts rushing around, trying to effectively use the remaining years to accomplish all his future goals. He attempts to catch up on two or three decades of unrealized goals in a handful of years. That was me, all the way.

The wife, devoted to home and family, sees the children growing up—and panics, knowing they'll soon be gone, one by one. With the husband working much of the time, she thinks that she's becoming increasingly unimportant. Looking back, I assume that must be how Mary saw her relationship with the children and me.

Basically, we were following the patterns of millions of middle-aged American couples. Mary was a good mother and wife. I was a good provider and businessman. Unfortunately, we had developed differing interests.

It was not the most amicable divorce on record. Lewis Hagood, a great labor lawyer, agreed to handle Mary's case because he knew her. During law school, he and his wife were great friends of ours. But Lewis, perhaps experiencing Mary's anger and hurt, was very tough on his law school buddy during the long, drawn-out proceedings.

Fortunately, my relationship with Lewis and his wife Mary survived the divorce, and we remain good friends. They are generous supporters of many philanthropic causes in our community.

Lewis assures me that the Clayton divorce was his first—and his last.

About the time the divorce was finalized, I got a call from Kathy Hill's mother Katie. She wanted me to help Kathy's sister, Beth, purchase a home from Clayton's.

It had been almost three years since I really talked to Kathy. She left *Startime* and moved to Nashville in 1974 after getting her master's degree in communications at the University of Tennessee. She was 24 years old.

After graduation, Kathy pursued a singing career in Nashville, cutting demo records and auditioning. She also spent a summer at Opryland, performing live on stage. Interestingly, while working as a performer, she taught geometry and algebra at a local high school. It's an unusual combination, but Kathy is a versatile and talented person.

She called to thank me for helping Beth with the mobile home purchase, and we agreed to have dinner the next time we were in the same city. Later that week, while returning from an industry convention in Chicago with Ty Kelly, I stopped in Nashville and met Kathy for dinner. The next weekend, we met again, this time in Knoxville, and realized we were more than just friends.

Kathy's companionship meant a lot to me. She understood what I was going through and even understood the business. Her intelligence, beauty, and talent motivated me during a very low period in my life. After Kathy moved back to Knoxville in December 1975, she became the co-producer of *Startime,* and we began running in 10K races together. She also earned her pilot's license. Music, of course, remained a favorite activity.

We continued producing *Startime* together, but with all of our other activities, the TV show was taking up too much time. Also, Clayton's had been opening sales centers where we didn't have TV coverage, and, by the end of 1976, we were convinced we could be successful without the show.

Our Christmas special in 1976 was the last *Startime* show. To this day, we miss it, along with the wonderfully talented group of musicians who became our special friends: Ray Rose, Stoney Stonecipher, Brenda Puett and her husband David Rosson, Curtis Young, Darrell Puett, and the Sisters Four, to name a few.

Even 10 years later, people still told us, "We see your show every week." This told us the medium of television is extremely powerful, and that the residual benefit is very high.

The divorce was finally over in mid-1976, and at Christmas, Kathy and I took the kids and our close friends, Dale and Marsha Teague, to Colorado in our King Air for a week of skiing. We left on December 26th and had a wonderful week. It was such a joy that it became a Clayton holiday tradition.

Interestingly, as we left Aspen, I had to spend two hours de-icing the King Air three different times. Shortly after a successful takeoff, I overheard the controllers talking about the Florida Air crash at Washington National. I couldn't understand why those pilots would take off heavy, with every seat filled, knowing full well that the plane had taken on a load of ice while taxiing and waiting for take-off.

We were heavy too, but we made sure that we didn't have any accumulation of ice as we began our take-off roll. Our flight was uneventful.

That year, as a family and as individuals, we all committed to spend that week together, and we did for over 20 years.

As my personal life evolved, so did our business—particularly our manufacturing arm.

Already, we'd had great success purchasing foreclosed homes from lenders, refurbishing them, then reselling them. But by 1976, foreclosed homes were scarce. I remember Kyle Burnett, one of our sales center managers, laughingly asked Ty Kelly, the manufacturing plant's vice president of marketing, to build him some foreclosed homes.

Behind the joke, however, was a serious proposition. Our company needed an "entry level" home, a "Jimmy Lee" with high quality and more eye appeal. With the recession ending, Ty decided to give it a try. It had to be low-margin and a price leader to attract buyers. It had to be well made, so when our customers were ready to trade up, they'd buy from us again. And it needed to be a "draw" to sell other homes in all price ranges. After all, many of us shop by looking at the low-price items before deciding the higher-price unit with the added features is the better buy.

The rest of us were apprehensive, since Max Nichols and I were still smarting from our experience with the Jimmy Lee. Still, we needed to be able to sell to this under-served market niche.

Ty called our new model the "Vegas." It was clean, crisp, simple, high quality, and beautiful, a 12-foot-by-60-foot home that was amazingly inexpensive—$5,995.

Ty kept the price low when he, along with his purchasing agent, partnered with our vendors, whose sales were down due to the recession. They'd filled their warehouses with "distressed" merchandise—leftover carpet, wall coverings, ceiling materials, aluminum siding, and other materials of all colors and designs. Ty assured our vendors that we'd purchase such merchandise from them, even if it had minor imperfections, as long as the overall quality met standard or higher specifications.

The vendors, who knew we'd provide them with immediate cash, were enthusiastic. Some even made special purchases from their factories and suppliers for us. One of our long-term vendors, Carriage Carpet, bought distressed yarn with a color imperfection and created a double-weight carpet for us at only $2 per yard. We bought several truckloads of this carpet each week at that amazing price.

After just three weeks, Ty asked me to privately view his Vegas prototype at the plant, along with Lowell Woods, Jerry Moses (who, to this day, remains our number one mobile home salesperson) and half-a-dozen foremen. Their excitement was apparent and contagious, and when I saw the Vegas, I knew why.

It had a simple design that was conservative but attractive, with impeccable quality construction; it was equipped with central heat, appliances, light fixtures, furniture, carpet, and window coverings. The Vegas could be delivered and set up on the customer's site for under $6,000, a very low price. We had sold 10-year-old refurbished foreclosed homes for that price.

Frankly, after seeing the Vegas, I found it hard to believe we would make a profit selling at that price. I even asked Ty to recheck his bill of material. He did, and he was right. We could indeed make a profit.

Now came the next hurdle: how do we market this appealing new home? What's the best way to excite our sales force so they communicate that excitement to the homebuyer?

We decided to unveil the Vegas at the quarterly manager's meeting, only three weeks away. By then, Ty could have 50 homes available for immediate shipment, and we'd hide all of them until the meeting.

I thought the best way to introduce the Vegas was to play a little joke on the sales force. The plan was a bit risky, but I figured it would work, and Ty, always conservative, supported me with some reluctance.

The first day of the meeting at the downtown Hyatt in Knoxville, we had three of the homes, in varying colors, on display and locked.

On the second day, at the ribbon-cutting ceremony, Ty announced to the assembly of managers that we had 50 *foreclosed* units now available, and with his newly established "refurbishing team," the homes now looked brand-new. He told them how he kept costs low by buying discounted material. This was why none of the homes could be duplicated, he explained, since it was impossible to re-order those exact materials from distributors.

I took the stage and really laid it on thick. I told the managers about the special mortgage rates, down payment, and terms that were applicable to the new Vegas—a customer could pay as little as $200 per month after a $600 down payment.

Then I said, "As you would expect, there is a limited supply of quality used homes, and after we provide one home per sales center, the rest are first come, first serve."

I left them by saying, "Now it's time for you to see what Ty and his manufacturing team have accomplished for us." With that, they toured the homes, and I reminded them to come back in a half-hour, so we could take their orders.

I followed behind, watching as the salespeople marveled at these supposedly refurbished homes. More than a few of them remarked that they appeared new. Clearly, everyone was excited, and couldn't wait to get the homes to their locations.

Remember, the country was just coming out of a two-year recession. Times had been rough for the company, and particularly for these salespeople, who were commissioned. With the economic outlook finally trending positive, they were hoping to have a good spring selling season. One look at these "refurbished" homes, and they knew they'd be easy to sell.

Once the sales managers were back in the meeting room, it was time to deliver the punch line.

I apologized to the group for "misleading" them about the homes, but not about the price, the availability, or the features. Only about saying they were *used*. "These homes are completely new," I thundered. "Ty will build you *all you can sell*."

The salespeople wildly applauded Ty and his team's marvelous efforts. Meeting adjourned. Now that's a sales meeting.

The Vegas was to our mobile home centers what the Volkswagen was to our car dealership not too many years earlier. It served as "pull-through" for Volvos and Renaults.

Though we no longer call it the Vegas, Clayton Homes continues to offer a low-priced, high-quality model. Now we call them "Dream Homes," complete with microwaves, stereos, TV's, and VCRs. They still serve us well as a "pull-through."

The introduction of the Vegas marked our first incentive awards for our sales managers. The top-50 team members who sold the most won a trip, to—where else? —Las Vegas. It was a wonderful trip. Our team members and their spouses enjoyed performances by Wayne Newton, Roy Clark, and Bill Cosby.

Since then, our incentives have included trips to Hawaii, Acapulco, and Europe.

In 1977, we decided to put Vanderbilt Mortgage and Finance, our in-house, mortgage banking firm, on the map.

It was high time. We wanted to offer loans to our customers for a number of reasons.

Even though we had wonderful relationships with our financing partners over the years, particularly Fenton Kintzing at Valley Fidelity and Pat Harrison at Commerce Union, it was true that other lenders would run hot and cold. CIT, Commercial Credit, GECC, and others wanted all of our business or none.

By now, our operations were so extensive that we were dealing with large lenders like Citibank, General Electric Credit Corporation, Ford Motor Credit, and GMAC.

Sometimes, they'd aggressively offer us credit, and other times, they'd tighten up. Rates could be inconsistent, or they could be attractive. They were always, it seemed, in transition—centralizing or decentralizing, moving their offices, transferring their personnel, changing credit policies, consolidating loans, and creating confusion and frustration.

We felt they regularly made decisions without regard to their borrowers or even their personnel. Such changes were traumatic for our customers and caused frustration, and, yes, foreclosures.

It was March 1977 when we hired Phil Eckstein, an experienced manufactured home lender, to be the general manager for Vanderbilt Mortgage and Finance.

Under Phil's direction, Vanderbilt began to grow. We supported him with recruiting and training programs, along with $300,000 in capital.

Phil and I couldn't have been more different. He was a "big city boy" from Indiana who was controlling, opinionated, and demanding. (Of course, I'm not that way at all.) But he knew his business, and he was dogmatic about thorough underwriting, precise documentation, compliance, and keeping the credit process separate from sales.

I had to referee a few of the conflicts between Phil and the sales staff, and we agreed—only half-joking—that we'd be lucky if the relationship lasted a year. We enjoyed telling that story frequently during the four highly successful years we worked together.

During those four years, Phil—along with Tim Williams, then an administrative trainee, and three other people—grew Vanderbilt from a small company to one with $12 million in receivables. The company developed a robust and creditable lending platform.

In 1978, Phil received authorization from the Housing and Urban Development Administration (HUD) for Vanderbilt to become an FHA Title One Lender.

That same year, the Government National Mortgage Association (GNMA) approved Vanderbilt to issue its mortgage-backed securities.

When Phil left in 1981, Tim took over and ran Vanderbilt until 1995, when he started his own company, 21st Mortgage. Tim partnered with Rich Ray, who had been our CFO for 10 years and had managed our initial public offering.

Would I allow good talent like Tim and Rich to leave and compete against us? No way! Instead, I asked, "Will you cut me in your deal?" I was so impressed with Tim and Rich, and their contributions to our company over the years that we invested in 21st Mortgage. Today, Clayton Homes owns 50 percent of their company.

Meanwhile, Vanderbilt Mortgage has continued to grow at a healthy rate, now employing 640 people. In 2001, it earned $125 million before taxes. It has 160,000 loans totaling $5 billion.

Today, nearly half the income from Clayton Homes comes from financial services. Vanderbilt is a major reason why CMH is the most profitable housing company the world has ever seen.

To think it all started from half-a-dozen ledger cards on Joe Clayton's desk.

By the mid-'70s, I considered our bankruptcy to be ancient history, an old ghost, dead, buried and forgotten. Not quite.

It returned to haunt me yet again during a meeting with Jake Butcher, the new owner of United American Bank.

Actually, United American was a new name. It used to be Hamilton National, the bank that called in all our loans in 1961.

Jake had been a good friend for a long time. He started out as an insurance salesman, and then became a fuel distributor, shipping oil and gas to service stations and large industries all over the Southeast and Midwest.

His father owned a bank in Maynardville and with his help and contacts, Jake bought his own bank in Lake City, Tennessee.

Not long after that, Hamilton National, although still the largest bank in Knoxville, could no longer hide the fact that it wasn't profitable. By 1966, it was ripe for a takeover.

Jake, who by then owned several banks, was ready. He reportedly used all kinds of gimmicks to purchase Hamilton National, like "creating" fictitious loans that he kept moving through his various banks. His brother C.H., who was also in the banking business, assisted Jake.

When Jake bought Hamilton National, he re-named it United American. The inspiration came, he said, while looking out an airplane window mid-flight, and noticing the names written on two other airplanes.

Jake was colorful, dynamic, and moved well in Knoxville's

social circles. His wife Sonia Wilde had been a movie star, appearing in a few films during the '50s, including a Bob Hope movie. They were a very attractive couple.

It's fair to say that a good part of Jake's success could be attributed to his charm and the aura of glamour that seemed to surround him, an image he was careful to cultivate.

But none of that was the subject of our meeting. Instead, Jake reviewed for me a ledger book from Hamilton National's bank records. In it, he found an entry for $106,000 with the reference "Clayton Charge-Off."

Jake helpfully reminded me that Joe and I paid all of our creditors every penny we owed them. "Now I want to give you exceptional guys the opportunity to pay this debt with interest," he said, suggesting 24 payments of $6,000 per month.

I was dumbfounded. Hamilton National never informed us of the loss, even after we inquired. We called them and wrote them in our efforts to pay any claims or balances owed by us. They reacted as if all accounts were settled, and would not discuss a settlement or payment. The bank, according to our sources at the time, did not file a claim with the bankruptcy court.

Fifteen years had gone by since the bankruptcy, well beyond the statute of limitations, assuming there even was one. But Joe and I always wanted to say that even after our bankruptcy, our creditors never experienced a loss.

To this day, I can still say that. So can Joe. We paid United American in full as suggested for the alleged charge-off—every one of those $6,000 monthly payments—and on time.

After that, Jake soon offered me an interesting proposition: an opportunity to buy $135,000 of stock in United American Bank. In less than a year, he said, he would repurchase the stock at cost plus interest.

Not a bad way to get in with Jake and have him support our growing businesses with his booming financial network. I agreed.

Later, he had another deal in mind, this time, for both Joe and me. For every dollar of United American stock we would buy, he'd offer a credit line of $4 to the company.

That sounded like a pretty good offer, too. Joe and I invested $600,000. In return, the company received a credit line of $2.4 million, which we never got around to using.

We were just two of many individuals who bought into Jake's illusion. Many of Knoxville's most sophisticated business people followed suit. Like I say, Jake had loads of charisma and was very persuasive. He even ran twice for Governor of Tennessee, losing both times.

Jake shrugged off the political losses and embarked on another project—the 1982 Knoxville World's Fair.

He was chairman of the International Energy Exposition, a non-profit group of local business leaders dedicated to bringing the World's Fair to the city. He was, perhaps, the fair's "cheer-leader-in-charge," the poster boy.

What's more, his banks—by now, he owned about 20 of them—financed much of the fair. He poured millions of dollars into the project, and turned a rundown part of the city into a fairground that resembled a futuristic paradise. Perhaps the most spectacular structure, the Sunsphere, is still standing.

It's hard to say whether he did this out of high-minded civic responsibility or simply to massage his own ego. With Jake, it was difficult for me to tell where one stopped and the other started.

The Knoxville World's Fair was regarded as a success. During its six months, it recorded 11 million visits. It was the last profitable World's Fair. (The New Orleans World's Fair in 1984 went bankrupt.) Here, the fair did not go bankrupt. The banks did.

One day after the fair closed, the Federal Deposit Insurance Corporation (FDIC) launched an investigation into Jake's banks.

This marked the start of the savings and loan debacle. Soon, the investigations spread nationwide, billions were lost, and thousands of "just plain folks" all over the country lost their life savings. Jake wasn't the only one involved in the scandal, but he was one of the major players.

The FDIC uncovered massive loan fraud at his banks, and Jake, along with his brother, C.H., went to prison. United American closed its doors. It was the fourth largest bank failure in U.S. history.

For the record, the *News-Sentinel* reported that Jake got out of prison in 1992. For a while, he sold cars in Chattanooga. Today, he operates a truck stop owned by his sons in Adairsville, Georgia. He and his wife Sonia are still together, according to the article, though officially they're divorced, to protect her from his debts.

As for us, need I say that our earlier two investments with Jake—totaling $735,000—were gone forever?

CHAPTER 14

Going Public —
Recruiting A Board

In the late-'70s and early-'80s, the economy, once again, went into a downward spiral. Double-digit inflation *and* double-digit unemployment led to the creation of a new economic catch phrase—the "misery index." This was even worse than the recession of '74, particularly to those who lived in the "oil-patch" states: Texas, Oklahoma, and Louisiana.

All over the country, there were fields full of foreclosed manufactured homes, but *half* were in those three states, and our industry closed 90 percent of its production facilities there.

But during that time, Clayton home sales grew, on average, 25 percent each year, consistently improving over the same month from the previous year. Wall Street, the newspapers, and the TV news kept trying to have us believe that we were in a recession, but our managers and salespeople—those stubborn cusses—just wouldn't listen.

In fact, at Clayton Homes, we came up with our own catch phrase: "The country is in a recession, and we have elected not to participate."

There was also another one, heard frequently throughout headquarters and our sales centers: "We don't have time to look under every rock for a recession." (A personal favorite, which I've used many times over the years, is this one-liner: "Economists have predicted 29 of the last six recessions.")

This time, we were prepared and better able to handle an economic downturn. During the earlier recession, our approach to survival and conserving cash was to close half our factories, some sales centers, and to eliminate recruiting.

But when the economy rebounded, and the industry shifted into growth mode again, we lost valuable time. We had to gear up recruiting and training before staffing proposed new sales centers.

So this time, the decision was made to not reduce either the staff or our stores. Keeping most operations open and fully staffed got us off to a flying start when the economy improved. Only one sales center was closed—in Cookeville, Tennessee—and even then we transferred the manager and other team members to nearby locations.

A number of minor adjustments were made. For example, on some of our home models, margins were reduced; some at the retail level, while some prices were reduced at the factory.

Those cuts helped our customers. After all, the recession hit them hard too; by 1981, the prime interest rate reached 22 percent! (For a few months, we actually had to charge that amount on our home mortgages. Surprisingly, these customers paid well.)

My arrangement with Joe—still working beautifully after 20 years—was the best "brother-business" relationship I'd ever heard or read about.

But as we looked ahead, it became clear to us that our equal partnership could become complicated over time since our children were becoming increasingly involved in the company. Joe and I began to talk about splitting up the businesses.

Clayton Motors and Clayton Homes had operated as two autonomous corporations with a common, central service group. To think that it all started from a tiny used car lot back in the '50's; and here, 25 years later, our chief financial officer, Rich Ray, determined that the current value of the combined businesses after allowing for any debt was $15 million.

Joe and I readily agreed with Rich's evaluation. With this analysis, which included an evaluation of all business assets, we agreed to an amicable "divorce."

Rich suggested one of us should provide an asset "wish list."

"You go first," I said to Joe.

For him, this was a no-brainer. He chose the car dealerships, along with the related land and inventories.

According to Rich's analysis, Joe was due $1 million from me. Rich suggested cash and a note, and we quickly struck an agreement. I'd pay Joe $500,000 in cash, plus a "slow note" of $4,500 a month for 15 long years at 12 percent interest.

Joe and I shook hands, and Rich inked it.

Interest rates were high in 1982, so Joe's charge of 12 percent interest was very reasonable. Still, every year or so, I'd send him a check to pay off the note in full, and he'd refuse, sending it back each time with one of his cute little "thank you" notes.

I had to lick a stamp every month for 180 months until I sent the last payment in 1996.

Joe you stuck me for $435,052.51 in interest on that darn high interest note!

But don't feel too sorry for me. Joe's hard bargain did leave me with three manufacturing plants, the 30 retail sales centers, the mortgage company, and the manufactured home communities.

Thanks, Joe, for one of the friendliest "divorces" on record—at least for me.

On a hot summer night in 1982, I sat in the back of a smoke-filled nightclub, drinking a longneck Miller Lite. The band was excellent, and the vocalist was the best I'd ever heard. The packed house loved her; and I would go back, night after night, to see Kathy Hill.

We'd had no contact since a couple of weeks after the opening of the Knoxville World's Fair on May 1. Kathy and I, along with other civic leaders—Jake Butcher, Randy Tyree, Jim Haslam, and others—watched as President Reagan spoke, with the whole world watching on TV, during the fair's opening ceremonies. A couple of weeks later, Kathy and I decided to stop dating.

But now, five weeks before the end of the fair, I was again drawn to her like a magnet. I had not seen her perform since the last *Startime* Christmas special in 1976, but she sounded wonderful, better than ever.

I went back several nights, always sitting in the back of the room, until the manager of the club blew my cover. Upon discovering I was the silhouette behind the smoke cloud, he informed Kathy. Maybe he thought I was "stalking" his star, and expected her to be scared, angry, and upset.

Instead, she called me and said, ever so sweetly, "What were you doing at the club?"

We talked, and began seeing each other again.

The afternoon wedding, held three weeks later at a friend's home in Greeneville, Tennessee, was beautiful.

By 1983, the economy had recovered substantially. For the first time in a decade, the IPO window was open.

Now, investment bankers were lined up to see Rich Ray, our terrific CFO, and promising very high "multiples." (The value of a public company is often measured as a "multiple of earning." That is, the higher the multiple, the higher the evaluation of the company's earnings for its trailing four quarters.)

Rich was ready for the investment bankers with audited financial statements, a liquid balance sheet, and six years of solid growth to whet their appetite.

Now that Wall Street was primed for us, it was time to select our underwriters. We chose Prudential-Bache Securities of New York to provide the national presence and J.C. Bradford and Company of Nashville to provide the local presence.

These underwriters would guide us through the complicated legal and financial maze to an initial public offering and a worldwide market for Clayton Homes stock.

Dividing up this responsibility between two underwriters is fairly common. To Bradford, the regional company, we were the proverbial "big fish in a small pond." Their local offices would place Clayton stock with loyal, long-term individual investors. Prudential-Bache, the national company, would distribute our stock throughout the U.S., Canada, London, and Paris.

Our underwriters hired Will Johnston with Waller Lansden Dortch & Davis as their attorneys; we selected Jim Cheek at Bass, Berry & Sims to represent us. Jim Shelby, then with Arthur Andersen Company, led our accounting team—long before Enron hired them. Harvey Morgan was the principal with Prudential, Tom Wylly with Bradford.

It took two-and-a-half months for the team to draft the prospectus and perform a mid-year audit of our financials. That was tough, and involved a lot of struggling with attorneys and accountants who argued, frequently, over the placement of a comma. Rich Ray did a marvelous job navigating our way past all the glitches with his calming demeanor. He deserves enormous credit for managing all aspects of the IPO.

One "glitch" involved the $735,000 investment we'd made a few years back with Jake Butcher's United American Bank. Tom Wylly, the Bradford principal, led the discussion as data regarding the investment was presented to the underwriting team. This, he said, was clearly a non-operating transaction that should be removed from the prospectus.

With my personal cash, I reimbursed the company for the $735,000. It was painful, but if that "stock-purchase-gone-bad" transaction had been factored into the IPO historical earnings reports, it would've wound up costing me $16 million! Thanks to Wylly and Rich Ray, the $735,000 bank stock asset was removed from the CMH books and replaced with cash—my cash.

Thanks Jake!

In early May, it was Luke Simmons, the managing partner at Bradford, who said, "Hey, Jim—what about your board?"

"What board?" I cleverly replied.

"Your board of directors. Every public company has a board of directors."

Actually, I was aware that I needed a board. But I'd been so busy with the underwriters, their attorneys, and accountants, I'd barely given it a thought. Besides, until the prospectus has been drafted and accepted by traders, brokers, and a few investors, you really can't be sure the process will reach completion anyway, so there's no need to go recruiting.

But now it was time, so we polled our attorneys, accountants, bankers, and underwriters, and created a list of 30 qualified candidates. I knew most of them, so you'd think I'd visit each candidate personally and sound them out. Makes sense, doesn't it? But that's not the way this dance is done.

Instead, each candidate was "assigned" to a member of the underwriting team who knew the candidate best or to a respected business or political leader who was close to the candidate. These "sponsors" were simply to contact the candidate and indicate that Clayton Homes was going public and needed good directors. They'd add, "If you have any interest, I'll get a package to you."

To get the ball rolling, we decided that I had to get one big player, early on. The most visible person on our list was Wallace Rasmussen, who had an amazing career with Beatrice Foods, rising to CEO and chairman of the board.

When Rasmussen retired in 1980, Beatrice was a $10 billion holding company with 450 subsidiaries: Airstream, Culligan, Dannon, Playtex, Samsonite, and Tropicana, among them. Most of the subsidiaries, at the time, were larger than Clayton Homes.

I'd long been impressed with Rasmussen's life and career. No one had given him anything. He worked his way up. His first job at Beatrice was unloading ice at their dairy plant when they were a small company in Nebraska. Interestingly, by the time he became CEO, Beatrice Foods was headquartered in Chicago, but Rasmussen lived in Nashville, and commuted by train.

Though I didn't know Mr. Rasmussen then, as a board member of Commerce Union Bank in Nashville, he knew our company well. Being their largest user of funds (mortgages for our customers), it was necessary for the full bank board to review our complete financial package each year.

Pat Harrison, our long-time friend there, didn't even have to send him a prospective directors package, since Rasmussen had periodically voted on our loan applications. Instead, Pat simply advised him to talk to me about how to set up a board, along with appropriate committees.

As my breakfast meeting with Rasmussen began, I humbly told him that this huge responsibility—recruiting and chairing the board of a public company—was overwhelming. "Sir, your advice will mean a great deal to me," I said. "How would you do this?" Then I kept quiet and listened.

Rasmussen had a reputation for being abrupt. But at our meeting, he talked for half-an-hour with hardly a pause about committees, compensation, recruiting, stock options, and more.

When he slowed down a bit, I asked him about structuring the Audit Committee, and he took off again, stressing its significance and making it abundantly clear that it must be composed of board members who were completely independent from management.

I took it all in, thanked him for the advice, and asked, "Sir, would you consider helping me set up a first-rate Audit Committee, and would you consider serving as its chairman, just to get us up and running?"

He hesitated a bit, but finally acknowledged that he "guessed a few months wouldn't hurt."

Wallace Rasmussen served more than 10 years. (Later, we would have serious disagreements, but that's another story.)

If you're a salesperson—and all of us are—always remember that we have two ears and only one mouth. Is this an indication that we should listen twice as much as we talk?

During the meeting with Rasmussen, I hardly said anything. But it was obvious that I was extremely interested in him and his career. I reeled in a big fish simply by being a good listener.

We wanted five outside members on the board, and once we had Rasmussen, it was no problem getting the others: Bill Lomicka, treasurer of Humana, Inc.; Jim Haslam, founder and CEO of Pilot Oil; and Harvey Morgan, a managing director of Prudential-Bache, the underwriters who were working with us on the IPO.

The decision to add Morgan to the board was made with reservation. I had planned to add five completely independent and "outside" board members. The gut reaction would be to hire your CPA, banker, and lawyer to serve on your board. But you darn well should already have their counsel—they are on your payroll—so there is no value in having them on your board.

Morgan really wanted to be on our board, and we made an exception that we would regret. We liked his Harvard MBA and his firm promise not to solicit investment-banking business for Prudential. A short look into the future would reveal that Harvey Morgan did keep his promise *until* an opportunity came along for him to jump on his soapbox and pitch his wares.

In an early board meeting, Rich would suggest that a secondary offering of stock, or convertible debentures, would be well received by Wall Street. That was Morgan's cue. The rascal would not shut up; his conduct would be completely without regard for the interest of the shareholders who had elected him.

Just as the proxy statement went out announcing the agenda for the next annual meeting, I called and thanked the opportunistic Wall Street peddler for his support. Then I asked him not to stand for re-election.

Soon Morgan would move on from Prudential, also.

Joe would serve as our fifth outside director. The rest of the board was made up of three company executives: me, president and chairman of the board; Ty Kelly, executive vice president of manufacturing; and Rich Ray, executive vice president of finance.

The excitement was just beginning.

In May of '83, we filed our "preliminary prospectus," also known as the "red herring," with the Securities and Exchange Commission.

This preliminary prospectus contained the essential information that investors needed to know about our company, with one exception—the price of the stock, which would be determined at the offering date and printed in the "final prospectus."

On that day, approximately 1.9 million shares of our stock would be up for sale on NASDAQ.

Along with our prospectus, we had to write and create the slide presentation for the "road show," our 20-city tour around the country to tell the Clayton story. Putting together the road show required enormous input from the investment bankers, lawyers, and accountants.

The road show was one time I happily left the flying to others. Because of the grueling schedule, every spare minute was spent improving the slide show, writing answers for anticipated questions, and planning the next presentation. Ten of us, including the underwriters, were on board our King Air, and Gordon Davis, my daughter Karen's husband, piloted most of the trip.

We began in Knoxville, then made stops in Atlanta, Los Angeles, San Francisco, Minneapolis, Chicago, Boston, and New York—and made our final presentation in Nashville.

Before the road show actually began, we held a mock presentation at Club LeConte in Knoxville. There, our bankers handed me my head. I showed the slides and then opened for questions and comments. In response to the first question, I began my answer by saying, "Well, that's a good question." In the debriefing, the bankers strongly made the point that Wall Street types could care less about how I rate their questions.

Rich Ray, who had been through this before with two other

companies, sat back and laughed. After all, who cares if you think a question is good or bad? Editorials regarding questions from the investors and analyst are not appreciated. Never again would I make that mistake.

In each city, Prudential and Bradford had scheduled every waking moment, or so it seemed. From our plane to the limo to meeting after meeting, then back to the plane—sometimes, it was hard remembering what city we were in because we would be in three or four different cities every day.

Wherever we were, the first meeting was over breakfast at seven o'clock, with 40 or so investors in attendance. Lunch would be much the same, and dinner would be with a smaller group. Between these meetings, we'd do "one-on-ones" at an investor's office or meet with brokers at the banker's local office.

The meetings were similar; I'd present the 20-minute slide show, and then invite Rich to join me for questions. The analysts, brokers, and fund managers were intense and driven, and would try to impress each other by asking harder and harder questions.

Rich and I emphasized the company's success in manufacturing, retailing, and financing, our unique brand of vertical integration structure, our revenue growth, our consistent profitability, and our positioning for the future.

The primary purpose of the road show was to support the brokers who were pitching the stock to their institutional clients. When time permitted, we would make a presentation for retail brokers at the banker's offices. As the road show progressed, the bankers gathered data from their brokers on the reaction from the clients. The take from the tentative orders received by the offices visited and our own observations was that we had a hot deal.

Public Offerings and especially Initial Public Offerings tend to be either hot or cold. If a deal is cold, or even tepid, the bankers are likely to "pull the deal." Since all deals by a top-rated firm for a legitimate company are underwritten "all or nothing," there would be too much risk in taking all of the deal unless there was adequate demand.

Since an economic event could cause institutions to not buy as expected, the underwriters would have to inventory the stock using their own funds. The results could be a large loss if the stock was later sold for less.

It was such a perfect trip. Gordon kept us within five minutes of our schedule as we spanned the continent.

Maybe the presentation that best typifies our reception was with Fidelity Mutual Fund in Boston. We walked into their elaborate and beautifully decorated boardroom, and an analyst whispered to me that Peter Lynch was going to drop in at some point to catch a few minutes of our presentation.

This was like saying God would be attending the meeting. Peter Lynch held the record as the best investment manager on the planet. His books on investing would be blockbusters.

He arrived just as we started, listened all the way through, and then began asking questions. Lots of questions—he spent an entire hour with us. Earlier, they told us he might stay five minutes if we were lucky. To say the least, we were thrilled.

After the conclusion of the road trip, we were in New York for the pricing and the issuing of the final prospectus.

After the market closed on June 22, 1983, Rich and I haggled for over an hour on the price. Rich Ray maintained that our stock should be initially priced at $18 per share. Prudential-Bache thought we should price it at $15.

After an hour or so of intense negotiation, we settled at $16, entered it into the final prospectus, and rushed it to the printer so it could be listed on the NASDAQ the next morning. The investment firms, who had been hyping us to their customers, now called them to firm up the orders that had been promised during the road show. We were oversubscribed. Peter Lynch, along with other investors around the country, had ordered three times more shares than we were offering.

On June 23, 1983, we officially became a publicly owned company. I spent quite a bit of the morning watching the ticker. We'd hired the underwriters as "all or nothing." From the feedback from investors during the road show, we knew it was an "all."

By noon, Prudential-Bache gave us a briefing on the initial trading. It was great news: We were hot, a huge success!

Our stock was attractive to investors. The stock traded up $3.50 a share to $19.50, with 570,000 shares traded, and 1,000 new shareholders gained.

Though it was a wonderful day for all of us, we didn't celebrate or even open a bottle of champagne.

On that day, our company raised $31 million.

The Bradford guys, in particular, couldn't believe I didn't want a party. But I knew they were looking for more business down the road, and allowing them to spend even $500 on us would tend to obligate us to use them next time. Too, the darn underwriters had distracted our management long enough. I wanted to get them back in harness.

At the time the stock went public, I owned 100 percent of the company. After going public, I had given up 20 percent interest. For that, I received $10.5 million in cash and kept 80 percent ownership of Clayton Homes Inc., which had just added $20.5 million cash to its balance sheet (or assets).

Since the value of the company was up to $120 million, I was now "worth" something like $95 million—$10.5 million in my pocket and $85 million on paper.

Just two years earlier, my half of the partnership was valued at $7.5 million.

Now you know why so many entrepreneurs dream about taking their companies public.

We used part of the $20.5 million to repay our minimal amount of remaining debt, increase our working capital, and open a fourth manufacturing plant.

On our next annual financial statement, it was with great pride that we reported to our team members, shareholders, and suppliers that we were a debt-free company.

As for me, all the money wasn't that big of a deal to me—truly. Kathy and I had all the clothes and shoes we could wear. Once you get three hots and a cot, you're doing all right, and anything beyond that is gravy. It did feel good to know that our future and retirements were secure.

Even today, people think I must be in despair when our stock goes down a dollar or when the market takes a drop. Often, that means I've lost millions—on paper, at least—since I own 40 million shares of CMH stock. But I'm not in despair at all. For one thing, you don't really lose until you sell.

But most of all—it's not really about the money.

It was Ray Kroc, the founder of McDonald's Restaurants, who put it best: "I have never worshipped money and I never worked for money. I worked for pride and accomplishment. Money can become a nuisance. It's a hell of a lot more fun chasing it than getting it. The fun is in the race."

I agree.

By early 1984, our shares had become "marginal." That meant a buyer could purchase stock by paying only a portion of the price in cash. In other words, putting up just $100 would buy $200 worth of stock, with the broker loaning the buyer the rest of the portfolio's value.

For us, this was another step up on the credibility ladder.

On December 19, 1984, the New York Stock Exchange listed us on the Big Board. For some of our board members, this represented the pinnacle of success. We were now part of an elite group, one of 1,500 of the most dynamic companies in the world. Some thought, once on the New York Stock Exchange, it meant greater visibility and greater investor interest in our stock.

For several reasons, I disagreed with Jim Haslam, the cheerleader for the move. When listed on the NYSE, there is only one "Market Maker," and that is your specialist on the floor of the exchange. All orders flow through their gate, there on the floor.

On the NASDAQ, we had 10 market makers, including Prudential and Bradford. During lulls in the market, these firms can inventory stock and otherwise support the price and facilitate trades that would not be possible by the NYSE. Note that Microsoft, INTEL, Dell, and thousands of other firms could have moved to the NYSE years ago.

Some would have you believe that the NASDAQ is for hi-tech stocks. Did you ever hear of Cracker Barrel? Dan Evins, my great friend and the founder of Cracker Barrel, chose time after time not to move. He came on our board in 1985. He would have voted with me to stay on the NASDAQ.

Don't let me mislead you here. The NYSE has worked well for us. The point is that there was no need for us to move. There have been times when we would have enjoyed the support of the market makers who traded and inventoried our stock.

There are choices and the obvious may not be the best.

Is that not like life in general? I think so.

Many of us flew to New York for the big day—Kathy, Joe and his wife Dot, my daughter Karen and her husband Gordon, my two sons Kevin and Jim Jr., Ty and Brenda Kelly, Leonard and Linda Stone, Tim and Judy Williams, and Rich and Jane Ray.

The New York Stock Exchange was becoming more user-friendly even at that time. A number of NASDAQ companies were making the transition. To welcome our move from the competition they gave us a two-and-a-half-hour celebratory welcome. For an hour the ticker all over the world welcomed Clayton to the NYSE as our party enjoyed a reception with their senior officers and our specialist. Just before the market opened we were ushered down on the trading floor to our specialist's station.

I bought the first 100 shares of CMH traded on the NYSE just as the market opened. I have the ticket and still have the stock. It was a thrill to watch this prestigious institution celebrate their alliance with us as cameras followed our every move.

CLHO had served us well on the NASDAQ. Now it was time

to take up the new banner, CMH, and make that symbol recognizable in every corner of the globe. What a wonderful moment for all of us.

The future expectations for Clayton Homes seemed limitless. I wish the same could be said for my domestic life. All was not well at home.

Kathy was feeling ignored. As Mary, she thought I was totally wrapped up in the business with no time for her.

She felt that virtually all of my activities were business-related. A trip to the Kentucky Derby, for instance, was just another opportunity to "see the right people."

In that case, the "right people" were Jack Welch, then the CEO of General Electric and his first wife Carolyn. Jack loved hosting the Derby parties for their large customers. (Incidentally, in the 2001 listing of the *Forbes* 400 Wealthiest Americans, Jack and I are side-by-side, with about the same net worth.)

Kathy taught math at Halls Middle School for a time, but in 1983, she returned to the University of Tennessee and got an educational specialist degree in educational psychology. (She already had two other degrees, a bachelor's degree in mathematics and a master's degree in communications.) Her work in educational psychology helped occupy her time, but it wasn't enough.

Even as I look back at all the projects, programs, and responsibilities that we shared, it's easy to see that any attractive and talented woman with Kathy's options would eventually have difficulty coping with my schedule and responsibilities—and she did.

Developing the growth of the business and preparing the company for an IPO was an impossible schedule. In that kind of environment, the demands on a CEO are difficult to comprehend. It takes a very special man and woman to balance the priorities, which are ever-changing.

We separated in June 1987, and the divorce was final in mid-1989. Those divorce proceedings weren't pleasant either.

Growing up and seeing the wonderful example that Mother

and Dad provided, it never occurred to me that I'd be divorced even once—and here it had happened a second time.

Kathy has since remarried, and now has an eight-year-old son. Her *Startime* fans, of which there are many, still ask me if she sings. She does, for friends and family, but now, she spends her time as a wife, mother, and homemaker. She also does volunteer work in the field of education and is an avid runner, having completed the New York Marathon in 2001.

Truly, I wish this lovely, intelligent, and talented lady, along with her family, all the best. Kathy taught me so much and will always hold a special place in my heart.

CHAPTER 15

Coaches, Circles & Bone-Crushing Handshakes

Observing human nature has been a lifelong interest. I've always tried to see and appreciate, what is—the reality of life—instead of dwelling on the why.

An understanding of "what is" can be applied to all areas of our lives. But if we're overly logical, or too analytical, and tend to focus more on "why" or "how"—we may delay or even miss opportunities to apply techniques or programs that we've seen work for others and ourselves.

In assessing an individual's knowledge, intelligence, and ability to function in a given environment, it's obvious that *knowing* is important, but *not knowing* is generally not fatal. Some of the most successful people I know may lack knowledge in certain areas that could limit their success; but they compensate, effectively, because they are quite aware of *what they do not know.*

However, we've all seen people who don't know what they need to know, and *do not know that they don't know.* These people are nearly impossible to help.

But someone who *knows what they don't know*—someone with a reasonable level of self-awareness—*that* individual can be helped, and can achieve success far beyond expectations.

The rule, quoted by respected speakers and writers, follows a common theme: *To know is good. To know not is not necessarily bad, if you know that you know not. But the individual who knows not, and knows not that he knows not, will be difficult to teach and mentor.*

Joe Clayton is one of those who knows what he doesn't know. He's successful, intelligent, knowledgeable, and always welcomes new information and the opportunity to learn more from others. Joe and I have learned so much from each other, and still do.

For decades, I worked with Joe in an environment where we constantly utilized short-cut communication techniques. We said what needed to be said—honestly, quickly, and decisively. The same is true for my son, Kevin, who also has a very keen sense of self and is extremely confident, but not cocky at all. Both Joe and Kevin have a talent for focusing on the content of a conversation, to really listening to what is being felt.

Grandpa Clayton, a wonderful influence, said on many occasions "our lives work *only* to the extent that we are willing to keep our agreements." Kevin and Joe have honored every agreement they've ever made with me, and I'm most appreciative.

It has been such a joy to turn special business units over to Joe and Kevin. The same goes for David Booth, who is president of retail for Clayton Homes; Rick Strachan, our president of manufacturing; and Allen Morgan, the president of communities. All are accomplished executives who communicate clearly and effectively. They invariably honor their agreements.

Scott Northcut is a former vice president of human resources for Clayton Homes. He left us for the same position at Wal-Mart's Sam's Club (the fact that Sam's hired our vice president of human resources speaks well for CMH). Scott's models the concept that high principles and good moral values (P plus V) are required attributes for team members, and are qualities that we require when recruiting.

Talk about a High "P+V"—Tom Hodges, General Counsel and Corporate Secretary of Clayton Homes, whom I mentioned earlier in the book—was a wonderful find for our company.

Tom, raised in Johnson City, is a magna cum laude graduate of the University of Tennessee—and was president of Sigma Phi Epsilon from 1994-95. He graduated from the UT College of Law in 2000—and was student body president. In October 2000, after an earlier stint at Vanderbilt Mortgage & Finance, Tom served us as Corporate Counsel, before becoming General Counsel and Corporate Secretary in July 2002.

Along with his high values, Tom is a leader who radiates credibility, and who has a keen ability to sense "areas of risk" for the company.

And to think he's only 29 years old.

Tom and Heidi have been married for four-and-a-half years—and they are happily expecting their first child.

High performance characteristics are necessary, but we may compromise on this factor when hiring and during promotion review, since we can teach the technical skills required for high-level performance.

But values are a different story. My experience tells me that high moral and ethical values can't be taught. Team members or candidates either have them or don't. I do realize that we can bring in a thief, and if everyone is honest, and we keep the safe locked, they are not likely to steal—not for a time. They will, though, at some point.

It's difficult to terminate individuals who are high performance but have low values. Most likely, a supervisor without this training wants to compromise and salvage the high performance person, even when behavior issues are apparent.

But my view is this: send the low values person down the road, perhaps to our competitors, sooner rather than later. You are wasting your valuable time teaching a "Low V" your business. But if values are high—and performance is lacking—then investing in this person is likely to produce high returns. I've seen it happen time and time again.

"If it feels right, comes natural, seems easy, and everybody does it," then the beginning entrepreneur will likely be seduced into utilizing that procedure. Team members recruited from other companies will maintain, with conviction and confidence, "that's the way it's done back home." I am speaking generically here, but I completely disagree with this line of thinking.

When I see our people relying on "industry practice," or "the way I've always done it," I am concerned. If my raising questions about the procedure or process are not received positively, then I know we have an ego, self-esteem, or other issue.

Doing it like others do it will at best give you average results, and that is not acceptable. The average company will not be around a few years from now.

In recruiting, I see this type of thinking restrain individuals, teams, and companies from achieving their potential. We don't wait until we need to fill a position before beginning the recruiting process. Recruiting under pressure can lead to serious compromise. Oh, I hate to hear, "I interviewed three people and this is the best one." That is terrible logic.

I want to share with you some actual case studies of outstanding people we have recruited. Recruiting them required a lot of time and effort on our part. In each case, a position was not open when we began the process. They were recruited to "fill the bench." Note, in each case, we found a person with "High V." We were more than willing to teach the "High P."

Incidentally, all of these High V individuals had years of experience as successful coaches.

Near our old headquarters on Clinton Highway, at Powell High School, is the Danny Maples Baseball Field. It's ranked as the best in the state, and named after the man who personally raised most of the construction funds to build the field.

I met Danny when Clayton Homes became Powell High's partner in the Adopt-A-School program. Danny's boss, Allen Morgan, the principal of Powell High, introduced us, and it was obvious Allen was proud of his star baseball coach and driver's education teacher.

Already, I could understand why. While Danny was raising funds for the ball field, he called on me, and asked that I help with the lighting system. Except for that, Danny said, he had the funds to complete the construction.

At the time, I was working feverishly with the local politicians to obtain zoning for our Clayton Estates community on Amhurst Street, but it was a tough sell.

One hour after speaking to Danny, I received a call from a politician, who thanked me for being Powell High's partner in the Adopt-A-School program and for agreeing to fund the lighting for the new ball field. In fact, since I was so civic-minded, he and another politician had decided to vote for my Clayton Estates project. I got the message.

Immediately, I called Danny and confirmed that the ball field would be lighted, and that I'd personally write the check.

I spent $15,000 for Danny's lights, $6,000 for Allen's Adopt-A-School program, got the votes I needed on the zoning matter, successfully built Clayton Estates—and the new ball field was named after Danny.

I recognized that Danny had "High Values" and with persistent persuasion, tried to convince him to become a Clayton team member. It took two years, but I finally sold him on the idea of leaving the school system, joining the retail team as a Clayton regional manager, and quadrupling his income.

Today, Danny is a great coach at CMH, and one of our best recruiters. He has "High P plus V," and teaching him our business has paid huge dividends.

Through the Adopt-A-School program, I became good friends with Allen Morgan and his beautiful wife Phyllis, a former Miss Tennessee. Danny, meantime, began a campaign to get the two of them to join Clayton Homes.

But Allen had another campaign in mind and announced he

was a candidate for superintendent of Knox County schools.

However, while Danny may have been unable to recruit Allen to join us, Allen succeeded in recruiting Danny to volunteer as a fundraiser for his campaign. Naturally, I was one of Danny's first "victims." With my check, Danny raised more funds than anyone else on the campaign team.

Allen won by a landslide and served as superintendent for six years, elected for a term of four years and appointed for two. But Danny never stopped trying to recruit Allen for the company.

On June 2, 1998, Allen Morgan and I got together. It was around 9:00 P.M., and Allen had just come from a county commission meeting. Sitting over my computer until well after midnight, we drafted two press releases, both dated June 3.

The first announced Allen's resignation as superintendent of Knox County schools. The second named him vice president and general manager of the Clayton Communities Group. Coach Danny had finally gotten his man!

Our business was a stretch for Allen. He'd never been exposed to the mobile home business before.

"While Jim and Kevin were reading Chaucer, I was doing my ABC's," said Allen, referring to his lack of experience in the industry. But his values made Allen a very "High Performance" leader at Clayton Homes. Soon, he was reading right along with us.

Before we leave Allen, take a look at his report card. Looks like he passed.

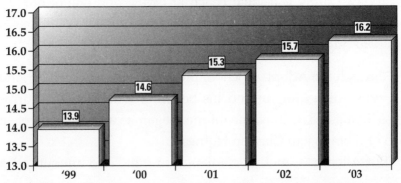

Community Families
In Thousands

From 1992 to 1994, Donie and Shari Wood ran a very successful tennis program at the Cherokee Country Club. Donie was my tennis coach, and after each weekly lesson, we'd chat briefly about the economy or the stock market. I learned he was an experienced investor, and his interest in the business world was growing.

Eventually, I introduced Donie to my son, Kevin, and Ronny Robertson, the manager of our Appalachian plant and a regular tennis partner of mine. The more we got to know Donie, the more we appreciated his values, ability, and experience.

Kevin, Ronnie, and I decided to form a team with Ronnie as the captain. Our mission was to recruit Donie into our leadership, fast-track program.

But that wasn't going to be easy. Donie and Shari, a very talented and attractive couple, were highly regarded at Cherokee. As tennis coaches, their time was constantly booked and their incomes soared. Donie felt they had "achieved their dreams" by having "the most prestigious tennis positions in the country."

For months, Ronny, Kevin, and I talked to them about the CMH culture. They had dinners with us, met with other couples, and asked tons of questions. The travel and incentives appealed to them both, and Shari was particularly impressed with the family involvement at our company.

In January 1994, at a small gathering at our home, Donie and Shari decided they would resign at Cherokee Country Club and join us at Clayton Homes. By the end of the month, after assisting the tennis committee in selecting his replacement, Donie began training at our Appalachian plant with Ronnie, who taught him well. Donie, who came to us with very high values right from the start, learned the business, and is now a "High Performance" recruiter, coach, and inspirational leader.

Currently, he is sales manager at our successful Rutledge, Tennessee, manufacturing plant. He and his four-person sales staff coordinate the shipment of a new home every hour to one of their family of 225 loyal retailers.

I'll never forget when Shari, at my birthday celebration at Beaver Creek, Colorado, in March of '94, announced to us that they were expecting their first child, Nicholas. Since then, they've added two more boys to their wonderful family, Matt and Chase.

Donie's younger brother, Derik Wood, joined us in April 1996. Donie and Shari recruited him away from Princeton Hospital in Orlando, Florida, to join Clayton's.

When I met Les Lunceford, he had just gotten out of the U.S. Marine Corps with a tour of duty in the Persian Gulf and the rank of major. A mutual friend, Al Smalley, had introduced us, and I knew that Al, a very successful, manufacturing entrepreneur, had a great ability to recognize talent.

Marine Corps officers generally have a good social conscience, strong moral fiber, and are persistent, hard-charging goal setters. Les had those qualities in abundance and demonstrated them during his seven-year stint with Clayton Homes. He admitted that he knew very little about building homes, but that didn't bother me. His values matched our core beliefs.

In May 1994, we hired Les and named him special projects manager. He spent a year learning our business and eventually became vice president of human resources. Among other things, he made lasting contributions in hiring, training, and design and content of our leadership academies. During his tenure, our factories realized significant reductions in accident and injury rates and decreases in workers' compensation expenses.

Les left the company in 2001 to acquire his own human resources consulting firm. We are friends, and he remains active in community affairs. He's a great leader, motivator, coach, and problem solver.

I've always been a big fan of books and teaching seminars specializing in the area of self-improvement.

Think And Grow Rich by Napoleon Hill is one book I'd recommend to everyone. First published in 1937, it has been one of the most influential books ever. It teaches a "what is" concept that's fascinating: *What the mind's eye can see and believe can be achieved.* For instance, if we visualize ourselves sitting behind the wheel of a Mercedes and believe owning one is possible, then our subconscious is likely to inspire us to create a workable plan that will achieve the vision of owning one. Visualization works.

I was introduced to a simple but interesting concept while participating in a personal improvement workshop that is typical of the self-awareness groups that began in California and spread east. I took the workshop years ago, in Nashville, with Kathy and Larry and Mary Ann Davidson.

They encouraged us to peel back the layers and take a deep inner look at who we were. Then they confiscated all of our timepieces and locked us in a room. We weren't even allowed the use of a toilet. As the layers "peeled back," facilitators and participants alike accused me of hiding behind my 12-year-old beard. Reluctantly, I shed the beard, but as far as I could tell, I didn't shed any hang-ups.

Still, the workshop exposed us to a number of interesting and helpful tools that I've used personally and in business.

One was the "Circles," a simple concept that can be used to improve communication skills. Every sales training class should include this exercise.

Suppose A needs to communicate with B.

After a friendly greeting, A guides the conversation to subjects that reflect B's interest and won't venture away from "safe topics" until solid rapport is established and confirmed. For example, if A sees golf clubs in B's car, then A throws out a "test probe," or comment, about golf. That may be all that's required to create the desired "circle overlap."

All information provided by A (in this example, a salesperson) must be presented in a manner and at a time that B can accept. In fact, a skilled salesperson never says one word that the prospect can't readily accept. This includes information about price.

A recent experience bearing this out occurred with one of our loan officers at First State Bank in Henderson who was dealing with a high net-worth customer. The officer listened as the customer claimed he'd been offered a loan at a very low rate from a competitor.

"Sir, bring me something in writing to prove you can get that low rate," said the officer.

The customer, furious, threatened to move his accounts into our competitor's bank vault. Believing that his honesty was being questioned, you could almost see his circle shrinking.

When a communication challenge is involved, as is the case with big ticket, direct sale of similar and readily available items, B is likely to be reluctant to open up and share information with A.

In fact, A must assume that B's circle is tiny, and that B may pick it up and run at any moment. So not only must A mention only topics that are readily acceptable to B, but any comments from B must receive a positive and accepting response from A.

A's circle must be large enough that any comment of B's will receive a response of "Fine, fine, fine."

If not, B may choose not to communicate with A, because their attitudes, beliefs, viewpoints, and philosophies are not aligned.

Back at the sales center then, A must begin the sales presentation with non-controversial subject matter—weather, fishing, or the World Series. Price, religion, or politics involve too much risk.

Now suppose a prospect drives up with fishing gear in the back of his pickup, and the salesperson has never fished in her life and has no plans to start.

We certainly don't want our salespeople, in their zeal to "overlap their circle," to lie and say they love to fish. Instead, she can overlap by saying something like, "Y'know, I've never fished at all, but I have an uncle who does all the time. He's always talking about the one that got away."

Instantly, the prospect's circle has enlarged, and, as the presentation continues, the salesperson has more latitude and flexibility. Now they have found rapport, acceptance, and a common ground, enabling larger circles to increasingly overlap.

What is interesting to the salesperson is whatever is interesting to the prospect. To the salesperson, *that* topic is the most exciting subject in the entire world.

Here's another example. The prospect enters, already wary, on the lookout, and saying to himself: *If that salesperson thinks he's gonna sell me a home today, he's in for a surprise.*

Meanwhile, the salesperson approaches, and is, in fact, saying to himself: *I'm gonna sell that guy a home today for full price.*

Obviously, their circles are miles apart. The salesperson has the challenge of enlarging and moving circles to gain overlap. There are two tools to use. The salesperson could pick up his circle and move it to the prospect's circle, so they overlap. But that would mean our salesman has changed his mind. In the above scenario, it would mean he didn't want to sell the customer a house either!

Since this is not permitted in the Circles procedural manual, this is not an option.

The other tool involves the salesperson "enlarging" the circle. This is a critical distinction. By making the circle big enough *to reach out and overlap that of the prospect,* the salesperson can agree that shopping for "just the right home" is great. The salesperson may say, "I, too, wouldn't consider buying until I learned about all the new features available in today's homes."

With a sigh of relief, and a larger circle, the prospect allows the salesperson to continue with the presentation.

Remember how our salespeople enlarge their circles: "Fine, fine, fine," is the response.

"I won't buy your home unless the refrigerator is at least 80 cubic feet."

"Fine, fine, fine. I agree. Everyone needs a big refrigerator these days with bulk purchase opportunities available. Saves lots of shopping trips too. Since Clayton's buys over 100,000 appliances from GE every year, you can select a very large refrigerator at our cost. I'll be glad to go into that as soon as we select your favorite home."

Often, the prospect doesn't say anything more about the refrigerator. It will be our salesperson that brings it up at closing. We will offer to order a large refrigerator for them at cost.

Keeping the circles together also applies to our team members. They must have the same viewpoints, attitude, and philosophy as the company.

The reverse is also true. We don't make decisions about compensation, benefits, or work assignments that our team won't accept. Our circles must overlap as much as possible to increase effective communications; and the more we overlap, the easier it is to communicate openly.

Another powerful concept is "mirroring." Our salespeople are trained to be aware of and to adapt to the tone, style, and manner of our prospects. If they talk fast, we talk fast. If they lean forward in the chair, we lean forward in ours. Whether they're monotone or animated, we do the same. These presumably small nuances are actually wonderful communication tools, a non-verbal way to say, "I understand. We're on the same page."

Even handshakes should be mirrored. Did you ever extend your hand to someone and receive a bone-crusher in return?

For 20 years, Tim Williams ran Vanderbilt Mortgage for us, and he's a dear friend. Years ago he possessed one of the most bone-crushing handshakes imaginable.

At a sales seminar graduation, I made a presentation to our team members, and Tim thanked me as I left the stage. He grabbed my hand and squeezed the heck out of it, saying, "Good job, Boss." My knuckles cracked, and the damage seemed permanent. I thought, "Man alive, has he been doing that all evening?"

The next day, at lunch, after Tim and I visited long enough to develop large overlapping circles, I broached the subject, and took a few minutes to explore the subject of handshakes with him. Within a half-hour, Tim thanked me for supporting him, as he reformed his handshake, and then we sketched the framework for a two-hour course on mirroring. (This replaced the body language module that had never worked.)

Try mirroring a handshake with a friend. You can adapt your handshake to instantly match, or mirror, theirs, whether it's firm, moderate, or dishrag. It's so easy that anyone can learn it right on the spot.

Someone who I will not identify—other than to say he's a very popular, professional person here in Knoxville, a great guy, much admired and highly-respected in the community—also hands out Godzilla-style handshakes. Among his friends, this habit generates considerable conversation about the pain inherent in greeting him and considerable speculation on how to avoid his handshake, without avoiding him, because, except for that handshake, this dear friend is great to be around.

Does he know that he does not know about mirroring handshakes? No! I don't think he is ready to go there.

One final point: How much should a salesperson talk? Earlier, I told you it was the introverts who sell best, because they listen best. So talk just enough to keep the prospect talking. Let them stop talking, and they'll walk. Keep them interested, and they'll "buy or die," right there.

A fascinating exercise we use is the well-known personality profile called "DISC." Each letter in DISC represents a distinct personality type.

A D is a "driver," someone who loves risks, pushes the limits, walks with one toe over the edge, and needs to always be in control. Entrepreneurs tend to be D's—great at starting businesses or relationships—and even better at crashing them. (Can you imagine that some of my friends accuse me of being a "High D?")

I is the "interpersonal" style, someone who is highly social, positive and upbeat, and wants others to validate them. I's are the "cheerleaders" of a team. A "High I" tends to talk a lot, even all the time. As I mentioned earlier, in terms of sales, this can be both good and bad. The I will talk the prospect into buying, and continue talking until they buy it back from the customer.

An S is the "stable" type, someone who follows rules, wants clear direction, and likes doing what is expected. The S tends not to make "seat-of-the-pants" decisions. They are nurturing, the glue that holds the team together, the cream in the Oreo cookie.

A C is the "correct," slower-paced, or task-oriented type. They are analytical. Much like the "High D," they focus on results, but C's tend to overanalyze before making a decision. Most accountants are C's.

There's no right or wrong personality type. DISC will not determine who's likely to be successful, but it will predict how an individual is likely to behave naturally. Actual behavior will depend on various factors including learning and mirroring.

D-I-S-C Personality Types

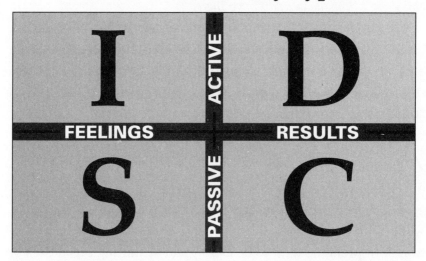

Every sales and leadership academy at Clayton Homes begins with a two-hour presentation on the DISC, the Circle, and various communication topics. These modules, along with numerous courses, are presented several times each year at Clayton University, a 125-acre campus located in a lush, wooded area adjacent to our corporate headquarters. The campus consists of six buildings with several classrooms and sleeping quarters for 75 participants.

When Clayton University began back in 1983 as a sales academy, I taught much of the course. I still facilitate several classes each year. Today, classes are conducted each week on a variety of subjects, and the courses, offered to team members year-round, include topics like leadership, sales, credit underwriting, home renovation, service, and home installation. We also have classes at a facility in Waco, Texas, for our team members who live out West.

Believe me, it's not all book learning. The University offers the kind of physical challenges that you might find on a TV reality show. This includes the "Ropes Course," where 50 people break up into five teams. The groups cross creeks, navigate over rope bridges, climb a wall, and swing from trees. To the individual, some of these exercises may seem impossible; but everyone learns, in the group environment, just how much a good team can accomplish—even under difficult circumstances.

At the end of the course, they are faced with a 12-foot wall that each has to climb. How will they do it? How do they get that first and last person over the top? The teams must figure it all out.

The idea, of course, is not so much to see who can accomplish the physical challenge. We're more interested in other qualities. Who's creative? Who leads? Who follows? Who helps and who watches from the sidelines? Who listens? Who's cheerleading? Who's a stickler for the rules? Who bends the rules? Though we're not grading the participants, we do have facilitators observing behavior. Here we see three kinds of people: those who make it happen, those who watch it happen, and occasionally, someone who doesn't know *what* happened.

Afterwards, during the debriefing, the facilitators and participants replay what they observed, felt, and experienced. To some, it's almost a spiritual experience. They begin to understand how team members, working together, can accomplish what seems nearly impossible. They develop confidence, loyalty, and trust in each other. This bonding can truly be a life-changing experience.

Together Everyone Accomplishes More is an acronym for TEAM.

We've discovered that in meetings and classrooms, people tend to repress some aspects of their personality. But put them on an obstacle course, let them play paintball, give them a challenge, offer them some competition, and in the emotion of the moment, people show their basic inner selves.

It's always revealing to see what's really behind the curtain.

By the mid-'80s, Clayton Homes had expanded to 10 states with the acquisition of Mobile Home Industries, once a powerhouse company that had become mired in bankruptcy.

We purchased 40 of the MHI retail outlets from the bankruptcy trustee for $1.9 million. Now, with 88 retail centers, we made inroads for the first time into the Deep South and Southwest—Florida, Georgia, South Carolina, Louisiana, and Texas.

In so many ways, it was a wonderful acquisition for us. Not only did it bring us into new markets, but also we were able to purchase a considerable amount of MHI's inventory at a discount.

But it was difficult integrating the new company with the Clayton culture.

One general example: at some companies, not ours, it's very tempting for a salesperson to become "creative" regarding down payments. Making the initial investment "easy" for a buyer is certainly the number one way to generate more sales volume.

There have been numerous instances in our industry where a customer will trade in their car to the company, receive $5,000 in trade allowance, and immediately buy it back for $2,000, with $3,000 of the initial investment "manufactured" for the prospect. This scenario certainly makes it easy for the salesperson, whether naïve, disreputable, or just plain greedy, to create a lot of business.

At Clayton Homes, we can't ever compromise our credibility by participating in such schemes. Unethical behavior is not and will not be tolerated. We now sell over a billion dollars of mortgages every year, and investors who buy those mortgages never meet the customers, or see the collateral. The trust and faith enjoyed by our company from so many shareholders, investors, suppliers, and our 8,000 team members is so very important. We must always take our credibility and integrity seriously.

With an acquisition, a few people with the acquired company quickly realize they don't belong with us. That is not unusual as we expect to lose a few people after an acquisition.

By 2002, we would be supplying homes to over 100 sales centers in Texas, Tennessee, and North Carolina.

Distribution Outlets

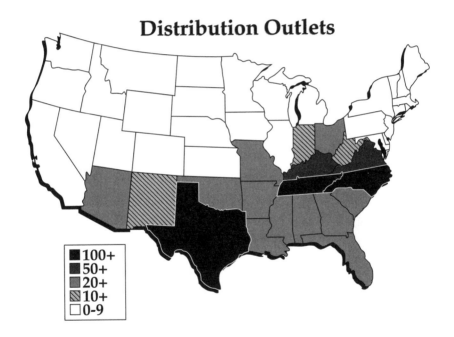

- 100+
- 50+
- 20+
- 10+
- 0-9

Not long after the MHI transaction, we moved into a new building on Alcoa Highway, leaving the 26-room motel that had been our corporate headquarters for 12 years.

The new building was 25,000 square feet, and we built most of it in our Norris manufacturing plants at Bean Station, Tennessee. After construction of the modules, we assembled the building on site, and it went up in a matter of weeks.

My personal favorite feature of the new headquarters was the so-called "Bat Cave" under the building. I'd land my helicopter on the helipad just outside my office and, with the push of a button, the chopper quickly rolled into the Bat Cave underneath. It was a nifty little set-up. My engineering degree paid off again.

In 1988, we began to expand our purchases of manufactured home communities, and during that year, we bought half-ownership of a beautiful park in Wylie, Texas, 20 miles east, as the crow flies, from Dallas. It was called Southfork.

If that name sounds familiar to you, it's probably because you too were a fan of the television show *Dallas*, which was still on the air at the time of our purchase. Our Southfork community was a mile-and-a-half from the actual working Southfork ranch, where the popular TV series was filmed.

Harold Holligan built the Southfork community, and apparently, the *Dallas* production company was less than thrilled over Harold's borrowing the name of the famous ranch. (He even named the streets within the park after the Ewing family and other *Dallas* characters.) Harold ignored all the letters threatening legal action. No lawsuits were ever filed.

It was, and remains, a beautiful community with exquisite landscaping and surrounded by lakes, a jogging trail, playground, picnic area, pool, and tennis court. The enormous clubhouse, 9,000 square feet with huge white columns out front, is framed perfectly as you turn into the community entrance, and is a replica of the neighboring home seen on *Dallas*, only much larger. Inside the clubhouse is a library, along with arts and crafts rooms, meeting rooms, and a kitchen.

Partnering with Harold, we built five more beautiful communities—in Nashville; Knoxville; Greensboro, North Carolina; Kalamazoo, Michigan; and Independence, Missouri. All utilized Harold Holligan's Southfork name and motif. But today, if you visit the five communities built during the joint venture with him, you'll notice the name has been changed to Clayton Estates.

As we planned and built the communities, we had a terrific

honeymoon with Harold, lasting over three years. He is one heck of a builder. After all, he'd built 30 communities by then, primarily in Texas and Oklahoma, with some degree of success.

So Harold did the construction; we wrote the checks; and all was well until it was time to operate these beautiful new communities. Our vision was to sell aesthetically pleasing, larger homes to highly qualified residents, who, in turn, would attract other residents like them. But Harold began to demand a faster "fill rate." Being a developer, he was interested in getting his profit out quick, and did we clash!

Soon the frenzy began. Harold filed legal proceedings against us in Texas. We had no choice but to sue him in Tennessee. The lawyers, insisting that Harold and I not communicate, took over and began the extended battle. The complicated lawsuit evolved into an unproductive and very expensive affair.

After months of legal maneuvering, Harold and I met at the water cooler during a break in depositions.

I said, "Harold, why don't you and I resolve this mess?"

He said, "We need to—these vultures are going to break us."

After the lawyers left for the day, Harold and I met. I knew his home building business in Nashville was booming and guessed he could use some cash. We discussed the matter, agreed on a price, shook hands—and the next day, our general counsel Tom McAdams drafted the agreement for our signatures.

In buying Harold's interest, we were required to change the names of the five communities he built with us to Clayton Estates. But since Harold's terrific ex-partner, Ron Berlin, a world-class guy, owned half of Southfork-Wylie, he could not require us to change that community's name. Later, we purchased Ron's half-interest, and today, we're happy to own this great community of 750 families, called Southfork.

Sharing ownership of the company with their people is something most entrepreneurs want to do.

We recognize the value of ownership in motivating and retaining people, which is why an entrepreneur uses stock, options, and various forms of partnership interest to sell the team members on the future value of their ownership.

A minority interest like this may become worthless, may have some value, or may become very valuable. If the value of the minority interest falls into the first two categories, the resulting disappointment may interfere with the relationship. If it falls into the third category and becomes very valuable, it *seems* like the owner of the minority interest would be greatly, and lastingly, appreciative.

But it doesn't tend to turn out that way. Often, the minority owner wants the cash, and if they can't see, touch, or spend it, they may feel their valuable interest isn't real.

Ott Ottinger, who managed the car dealership back in the '60s, owned 15 percent of our businesses. Uncle R.C. had 10 percent. Ron Cameron, our CPA in the early days and a personal tax advisor for a number of our managers, also owned 10 percent. Over the years, there were others, but none would realize real wealth from their interest. Joe Clayton, who held half of the remaining interest, was the only partner to "leave his winnings on the table."

Today, Joe's car retailers are said to be the richest in East Tennessee. The other minority partners had received their interest without writing a check.

We see this scenario play out in our retail quasi-partnership program. This has allowed several sales center managers to become millionaires. This list includes John Moore, Jim Ausmus, and Stephen Bowery. Their bios are included.

In banking, it was interesting. Some partners developed an "itch to sell" as the value of their minority interest grew. Those that sold before the merger gave up a large part of their gain.

People ask me all the time: What's life like after you make the *Forbes* 400?

The answer: Life is pretty much the same as it was before making the *Forbes 400*. Really, it's not that big of a deal, although I joke that making the list brings me a few more social invitations than I might otherwise receive.

It's interesting how *Forbes* makes up its list of the wealthiest 400. Some of the information they get is available from public records—such as SEC filings, or a company's annual and quarterly reports.

They also call people close to the individual under consideration—accountants, attorneys, banks, anyone who will talk to them—and confirm information they obtain from public records.

The reporters are very clever at getting answers. It's my understanding that, instead of asking point-blank questions ("How much is this individual worth?") they do their research, call up someone in a position to confirm, and ask something like, "We understand a real estate investment that Mr. X has is somewhere around $100 million—is that number a little high, or is that about right? Do we have any reason to believe our information is inaccurate?" Getting this sort of confirmation from a source is easier and more accurate.

In the past, I've been listed next to Jack Welch, the former CEO of General Electric. But in 2002, I noticed that Jack wasn't on the list, and I wonder if he asked *Forbes* not to include him. It's my understanding that it's possible to make such a request, and I might try that to see if it works. For a number of reasons—security and privacy, among them—I'd prefer not to be listed.

When I'm asked about the *Forbes* listing, I speak from the heart when I say, "This recognition honors the thousands of supportive and hard working Clayton people. It's a score card for the entire company and is an indicator of the talent and experience of our team members."

You'd think a guy like me, who has been blessed financially, would be deluged with offers from credit card companies, chomping at the bit to get my business. And I'm sure you can't possibly imagine that a credit card company would *turn me down*. Read on.

In the fall of 1991, I applied for an AARP Visa card. It was the week after I was included on the *Forbes* list as one of the 400 Wealthiest Americans.

One week later, I received a full-page mailing from Banc One—advising me that my application for the AARP Visa had been declined!

I thought this was hilarious, and over dinner with friends, I shared the story—and it was unbelievable how it spread. First, it appeared in "Whispers," a popular column in the local news-paper; then the Associated Press picked it up; local newspapers all over the country published the story; and *USA Today* ran it all over the world. It was even in the *National Enquirer*. It was a topic on local and regional radio and TV; the talk shows got a big laugh out of it.

Suddenly, I was known for being the *Forbes* guy worth mil-lions—who was turned down for a Visa card. Kay and I thought this was very funny, and had a wonderful time with it.

My friend Warren Neel bet me a dinner for two at Cracker Barrel that I couldn't obtain an AARP Visa by Christmas. It was already mid-November. I took the bet—and lost. You wouldn't believe the red tape. They treated me like I'd just fallen off the turnip truck. They sent me another decline notice—this time they indicated I had too many inquiries posted on my credit report.

Finally, I found an *Assistant VP of Something* at AARP Visa who *listened*. When I told him I was the CEO of a New York Stock Exchange company and on the *Forbes* List to boot, he said, "Okay, Mr. Clayton, let me see if I can help you." He thought I was pulling his leg.

He did. In mid-January, 1992, I triumphantly put an AARP Visa card in my wallet, but Kay and I had to take Warren and Annelle Neel to the Cracker Barrel in Branson, Missouri.

I enjoyed that Visa card, and all the jokes that went with it. By 1994, however, I began to carry a BankFirst card from my own bank. Now I carry a BB&T Visa and a First State Bank Master

Card, along with that 1959 American Express card—the one credit company that didn't cancel me during the '61 bankruptcy—to remind me that when the world turns against you, your true friends will be there for you.

I preach to our bankers all the time that we have to be there for our customers.

I always told myself that when I had some cash of my own, I would give back to the community that had made my success possible. When we went public, I owed it to the company and our shareholders, team members, customers, vendors, and lenders to give something back.

I decided to contribute to a cause that, in some small way, would make Knoxville an even more attractive place to live and work. Such investments, particularly in the areas of education and cultural programs, clearly improve the quality of life in the community, making it easier for us to recruit good people.

For example, August 4, 1994 marked the opening of Baptist Hospital's state-of-the-art Clayton Birthing Center. We were privileged to provide the $1 million capital gift that made this possible. From 1957 to 1972, all four of my children were born at Baptist Hospital, but reluctantly, in 1978, the hospital discontinued the birthing facility due to lack of available obstetrician specialists, the difficulty in recruiting them, the capital cost to create the required safety and security, low utilization, and insurance expense.

The Clayton Birthing Center has 12 fully equipped labor delivery suites and a very caring staff. The safety of mother and baby are monitored and secured round-the-clock.

It was an easy decision for us to make the contribution to Baptist Hospital—and we did it in honor of my four terrific children. We feel good when our team members show us their new baby and say, "Our child is a Clayton Birthing Center baby." We like that a lot.

It was Barbara Bernstein who approached me about making a contribution to the Knoxville Museum of Art. Barbara's spouse is my dear friend, Bernie, the talented attorney who saw us through the 1961 bankruptcy and has represented the family and CMH ever since.

Caesar Stair, Bernie's law partner, along with Barbara, "double-teamed" me on Christmas Eve in 1987, and I wilted. They were extremely dedicated and committed to the museum as they laid out its mission, its involvement in education, and the recognition Knoxville and the East Tennessee area would receive as a result of having a world-class museum.

At the time, the Museum of Art was located in an old home on Kingston Pike. Plans had been drawn for a spectacular new structure in downtown Knoxville, but funding had stalled, and the new museum groundbreaking was on hold.

To Barbara and Caesar, I committed a contribution of $3 million for the new building. That included $1 million cash, $200,000 a year for five years, and $100,000 a year for 10 years. It was, at the time, the largest contribution ever to the arts in Tennessee.

In 1988, I was about to speak at a well-attended news conference where we would announce the contribution and the plans for the new museum groundbreaking. Just before I made my remarks, I had a brief discussion with Dr. Alan Solomon, renowned for his cancer research and chairman of the museum's building committee.

He assured me that the museum had enough money with my gift to build as planned, with one exception. There wasn't enough funding, even with my contribution, to build with Tennessee marble. Red brick would have to do. I asked what the difference in cost would be and learned it was about $250,000.

During my remarks at the news conference, I relayed the "red brick" story and agreed that this was a disappointment to the large audience. Then, gesturing to Dr. Solomon, I said, if the building committee could build the new building with Tennessee marble, I, personally, would write a check for an additional $250,000.

The Knoxville Museum of Art would soon be housed in an

Edward Larrabee Barnes-designed building of Tennessee marble.

Supporting our wonderful museum in this manner has been a gratifying experience. But there was a lesson learned, one that may seem awkward to explain, but I will try.

All during the discussions about the gift, even at the news conference, it was the understanding of my family and staff that the naming of either the building or the museum itself would reflect our name. There was no further discussion and the promised document was never drafted or executed.

Two years later, after much of the $3.25 million had been paid—including the $250,000 for the Tennessee marble—I received a call from my good friend, Caesar Stair. He advised me that the name of the building would be on the side away from the entrance and that the name of the museum would be over the door. That sounded good to me as I visualized the name over the main entrance reading "Clayton Museum of Art."

That was the first time we'd heard that the building and museum would have a different name.

Caesar explained that the museum belonged to the people of Knoxville, hence the name: Knoxville Museum of Art. The name of the building: the James Lee Clayton Sr. Building.

But if the Museum belonged to Knoxville, wouldn't the building belong to Knoxville, too? The building certainly doesn't belong to me. What the heck, I did not argue about the name of the museum.

I told Caesar that the building's name must be the "Clayton Building," and I wouldn't compromise, even though my friend said many museums the world over are named in similar fashion using the benefactor's full name. He gave dozens of examples.

But he finally agreed. The building with the name off to the right side of the door, tastefully etched in the stone, is "Clayton Building." You'll have to look carefully to find it.

This way, the building recognizes Mother, Dad, my family, Joe's family, all the people who have supported the various

Clayton enterprises, the people who operate these companies today, and everyone who will support these great organizations in the future. It would be completely inappropriate for anyone to claim credit for this gift and to receive the resulting recognition.

I'll admit that Caesar, who took such a strong position on the naming of the museum and the building, disappointed me at the time, since I wanted all of the people listed above to be identified with the museum and not simply the building. But in retrospect, I'm eternally appreciative of his persistence and our splendid friendship. He actually did me a favor.

The museum had some difficulty during its early years— financial ones, like many other museums. Had my name been on the museum, I would have felt compelled to continually fund the museum's deficits, which ran into the hundreds of thousands. This way, I was just one of many generous supporters who love our museum and wrote checks accordingly.

The lesson learned is to eliminate "unrealized expectations" at the first opportunity. The pledge should not have been issued until the KMA board had approved a resolution authorizing acceptable recognition. It is likely that the name of the Knoxville Museum of Art would be the Clayton Museum of Art had I asked for that board resolution then. An angel was definitely watching over me when the pledge was made. I am perfectly pleased with all aspects of how the gift and recognition have been handled, and I continue to enjoy my relationship with Caesar and all the KMA staff and volunteers.

The important lesson statement from this case study is: Before becoming involved in a philanthropic endeavor, require an appropriate document confirming agreed recognition. The recipient should not accept money or announce the gift until the document is signed. Many times donors require confidentiality, which should be properly documented also.

Kay and I have continued to support the KMA. In addition to my original pledge, it has been our pleasure to add another $1.5

million in annual and event support at various times.

In 2001, the board of the Knoxville Museum of Art asked me to present Caesar Stair with the James L. Clayton award. It's given each year to the individual who has supported the museum through hard work, fundraising, counsel, and leadership.

This had always been a serious presentation—until Caesar won. My presentation to Caesar, written by Tom McAdams—his esteemed law partner, my special friend, and CMH board member—turned out to be a surprise roast, red-hot and pointed.

The audience loved watching Caesar squirm, and I had a ball. Long live Caesar and his support for our community.

Hail Caesar!

CHAPTER 16

"General, If You Ever Need Any Parts, Just Call Me"

Patience may not be my greatest virtue. But I am persistent, even when the odds are against me. In fact, when faced with obstacles, I become even more determined.

An ample supply of doggedness and resolve was required back in 1984, when Kathy and I wanted to join the Cherokee Country Club. We applied, assured that it was an easy process, practically a done deal.

I wish. Instead, it took *five* long years.

Why include this in my book? Somehow, *Forbes* magazine printed a story about a New York Stock Exchange executive black-balled by the Club. As a result, a version of this story has appeared in over a dozen publications, and I'm frequently asked about it.

Here is my story, and I'm sticking to it.

Granted, much of it is based on reports from friends in the club that haven't been verified.

After our first application was posted in the locker room, the secret membership committee reviewed it, listened to members, made inquiry—and gave a thumbs down to the board. Without a recommendation, the board failed to act on our application. In effect, we had been blackballed.

We had submitted excellent "letters of recommendation" from past Cherokee presidents, members of the Board of Directors, and from well-known club members. Still, they turned us down, without explanation.

How strange, I thought. *I'm the CEO of the only publicly owned company in Knoxville. I'm successful, educated, a philanthropist, and an all-around good guy. What's the problem?*

Kathy and I wanted to drop the matter, and actually, I was glad. After all, membership at Cherokee cost $25,000 and dues are several thousand more each year. Besides, I don't play golf anyway, and there are plenty of restaurants, tennis courts, and bars in Knoxville, along with several other good clubs.

But my friends—Jim Shelby, Sam Furrow, Rob McCabe, Jimmy Smith, and other members of Cherokee—said no way. Looking into the situation, they told me the misunderstanding had been resolved, and if we applied again, they were assured that five of the nine-member board would vote for our membership.

So we reapplied in 1986, and once again sent in letters of recommendation from some of the most influential lawyers, doctors, and business executives in Knoxville.

The letters were wonderful. One of our friends wrote that Kathy and I were "able to adapt to any occasion, regardless of the level of social grace required…. They are equally as comfortable in Manhattan or Paris, in a limousine dressed in tuxedos and fine evening gowns, as they are in cowboy boots and blue jeans."

Another friend wrote, "Mr. Clayton is a quiet, introspective person of great charm and consideration for other people." He added, "everyone has an opinion about Jim Clayton, but very few people actually know him."

When the board voted, it was, indeed, five to four—but it was against us. Membership denied.

Our friends couldn't believe that one of the board members changed his vote at the last minute. Now, I had been blackballed two times. How funny. Why not build my own country club?

Seriously, a friend of mine in the hamburger business did just that in a nearby city. He sure showed 'em. Then I remembered—with work, travel, and spending a little time in our vacation homes, we darn sure didn't need that headache.

Frankly, I was not about to apply a third time. Our inability to get into Cherokee, initially a mystery, had now become amusing. My friends were persistent as they insisted we not surrender. My response was, "Guys, it ain't gonna happen, not in this lifetime."

Sam then stated, "Every member supports your application, but two." He went on to tell us that he and others had "beat the bushes" until the opposition was confirmed.

"Will you be willing to pay two old bills from your old bankruptcy?" I readily agreed since Joe and I thought all had been paid almost two decades ago.

Yes, it was the Bankruptcy Ghost, manifesting itself once again after 25 years. Apparently, two members claimed I *still* owed them money, and they didn't believe a bankrupt used car dealer *who screwed them out of money* should be admitted into such a prestigious club.

I couldn't believe it. Joe and I had made a huge effort to pay back every last creditor. We didn't think we'd left anyone in the lurch. Surely, there must be some mistake. My friends at Cherokee identified the two members, and Joe and I went to see them.

Our first meeting was with a successful, well-known businessman whom we had known for years. He said we owed him $275 when we went bankrupt. After filing a claim back in 1961, the trustee paid him the designated 41 percent, just over $100.

For the past quarter-century, he'd never forgotten the amount remaining on the debt, about $165. Neither Joe nor I were aware that we owed him anything. But he thought about it every time he heard my name mentioned, saw me on TV, or heard my helicopter flying overhead.

Let's see—$165 at 8 percent interest for 25 years—about $1,100. I wrote him a check to pay that debt in full, and offered my sincere apologies. He accepted the check, and the apology.

One down. One to go.

Next we met with the owner of a local auto parts company. He said we owed him $3,600 when we went bankrupt. Again, we had no idea this debt was unpaid, and we immediately offered to pay him with interest.

"You just did," was his response.

We kept saying, "We want to pay you," and he would only say, "You just did."

A few days later, he sent me a letter, and it said, "Jim, this is to let you know that as far we are concerned, the debt has been paid in full. We appreciate your offer."

After receiving his touching letter, Joe and I made a $10,000 contribution to a charity in honor of this man's father, who had been a respected member of the Tennessee judicial system.

Finally, in January 1989, with friendships restored, debts repaid, and more than a little arm-twisting from Sam Furrow and Jim Shelby, I applied once more. In the spring, Cherokee Country Club notified me. The board had accepted me unanimously.

One note of irony: By the time Cherokee finally accepted me, Kathy—who originally suggested we apply for membership—had already divorced me!

Over the years, it has been my pleasure to recommend a number of great members to Cherokee, among them: Lars Anderson, president of BB&T Banks of Tennessee; Kevin Clayton, president and CEO of Clayton Homes (my wedding present to Kevin and Chelly); John Kalec, CFO of Clayton Homes; Les Lunceford, human resource consultant and former vice-president of human resources at Clayton Homes; and Dr. Monroe Trout, a retired executive, doctor, and lawyer (a darn powerful tennis player, too).

In 1991, I received a call from the renowned Horatio Alger Association. All I knew about this amazing organization was that my friend and law school buddy Don Stansberry and his wife look forward to the association awards dinner each year. I was surprised when the Association asked me to hold an April date open on my calendar. They promised to call back with details.

The press release listed 10 awardees. My name was listed along with nine distinguished Americans who also were to be inducted. The release went on to explain that the Horatio Alger Association honors the "accomplishments and achievements of outstanding individuals in our society who have succeeded in the face of adversity."

Horatio Alger, of course, was the famed 19th Century author who wrote more than 100 best-selling books. His novels glorified the common man, the value of hard work, and the virtues of honesty and perseverance. The "rags-to-riches" stories inspired millions of Americans, particularly young people. Worldwide, the Horatio Alger books have sold more than 250 million copies.

Since 1947, the Association has honored hundreds of Americans. I quickly found out I was in wonderful company. Some of our greatest leaders in government, industry, and the arts have received the organization's Distinguished Americans award, including Presidents Ronald Reagan and Dwight D. Eisenhower, Henry Kissinger, Oprah Winfrey, Bob Hope, Sam Walton, Ray Kroc, Mary Kay Ash, and Reverend Billy Graham. The list goes on, each name as dazzling as the last—and when I learned who my fellow inductees would be, I was truly overwhelmed.

They included Colin Powell, now the secretary of state, then chairman of the joint chiefs of staff; Fred Turner, the chairman and CEO of McDonald's; Phil Gramm, the U.S. senator from Texas; Harold "Red" Poling, the retired chairman of the board and CEO of Ford Motors; and Stan Musial, the legendary baseball Hall-of-Famer who played for the St. Louis Cardinals.

My induction took place on a beautiful spring evening in Washington, D.C., at the Grand Hyatt Hotel, and it was one of the greatest nights of my life.

I was surrounded by dear friends and family, including three of my children, Jimmy, Kevin, and Amy. (Karen was back in

Knoxville, about to give birth to Chris, her fourth child and my fifth grandson.)

Joe and Dot were there; so was Gordon, Karen's husband, a great pilot in charge of CMH aviation. U.S. Senator Jim Sasser, Congressman John J. Duncan Jr., Tennessee State Senator Ben Atchley, and Knoxville Mayor Victor Ashe were at our table. Also attending as my guest: Senator Al Gore. In little over a year, he would become the vice-president of the United States.

Of course, Mother, now 76, was there in fine form, wearing a lovely powder blue evening dress that she'd picked out months before. As I sat on the dais, waiting for my turn to speak, I looked at her, and for a moment, forgot about all the famous faces in the crowd. This was as much her night as mine.

They gave the awards in alphabetical order; I was the first to speak. Harold Burson, chairman of the Burson-Marsteller ad agency, and Mary Kay Ash, founder of Mary Kay Cosmetics, draped the Horatio Alger medal around my neck.

I had chosen each word of my acceptance speech carefully. After greetings and recognition of my guest, I said, "I would've given my best double-wide not to be first." Then I mentioned that I had something in common with some of the awardees. Fred Turner, Red Poling, and I are all members of the same college fraternity; and General Powell and I share an interest in Volvos.

I noted that one of General Powell's hobbies was restoring old Volvos. "General, I started the oldest family-owned Volvo dealership in North America. If you ever need any parts, just call me."

The crowd roared.

Before closing, I reminded the 1,500 guests from all over the world that I had wanted to be like Eddy Arnold and sing on the stage of the Grand Ole Opry. I paused briefly, looked up and around the stage, and said, "You know, folks, I believe this stage is nicer than the one at the Grand Ole Opry." They loved it.

Afterwards, when I went backstage, the executive director of the Association hugged me and said, "As the first speech goes, so

University of Tennessee 21st Century Campaign celebration with Dr. Bill Snyder, Senator Howard Baker, Kay, me, and Jim Haslam.

Groundbreaking for the new Clayton Bldg., Knoxville Museum of Art: (left to right) Senator Ben Atchley, Dr. Alan Solomon, Buddy Scruggs, and Caesar Stair.

Gift to the Knoxville Museum of Art, 1988.

Clayton Homes chief gives $3M to Fair site museum

By STEPHANIE PIPER
The Knoxville Journal

James L. Clayton, chief executive officer of Clayton Homes Inc., has contributed $3 million to the Knoxville Museum of Art.

The gift will be used for construction and operation of the new 53,000-square-foot museum to be built on the World's Fair site.

The announcement came at a news conference this morning, when Clayton formalized his pledge of support to museum board Chairman L. Caesar Stair III. Stair said the contribution "is the single largest donation ever made to the arts in Knoxville."

"I see the museum and the Fair site as part of a wonderful center city which we have to develop," Clayton told the Journal in an interview on Tuesday.

Knoxville's cultural environment is an important recruiting tool in his business, Clayton said.

"We are a growing, thriving company bringing good people into this area for visits and recruiting purposes, and one of the items on their menu of things to check out is museums.

"I've been busy building a business to the point where we can make a contribution. Now I have the time and the means. In this region which has been so good to me and my family, we have to have a great center city. There's just no reason why we can't be great now."

The founder of the $200 million home-manufacturing company said his work as a board member opened his eyes to the museum's impact on the community.

"I had no idea it touched so many lives," Clayton said. "It's lasting; it's permanent."

He had specified that $1 million of the gift is to be used as an endowment for the museum's operating expenses.

"It's easier to get funds for a building than to get an endowment," he said. "There has been some question about how we are going to pay the operating expenses. A million dollars can pay a significant part of the operating expenses and can give assurance to others who want to make a contribution."

Clayton said he hoped his gift would stimulate other large donations.

"One of the reasons we're making a contribution of this size is that hopefully it will motivate other organizations to become more involved in the museum and development of the center city," he said.

Clayton founded Clayton Homes Inc. in 1966. The company builds, retails, finances and insures manufactured homes.

Stair said Clayton's gift brings the fund-raising total for the new museum to $6.7 million. The city of Knoxville and the Tennessee General Assembly have also pledged $1 million each for the building. The fund-raising goal is $9.5 million, which includes actual building costs and expenses such as architects' and consultants' fees, equipping and furnishing the building, and financing a bridge loan.

The bridge loan is necessary because pledges are payable over a three- to five-year period.

"I now understand the element of 'significant gift,'" said Museum Director Rebecca Massie Lane. "This contribution boosts our fund-raising to the point where I have no doubt about our ability to succeed. It now seems plausible that we will break ground this year and open in 1989."

The museum, designed by Edward Larabee Barnes of New York and Bruce McCarty of McCarty, Holsaple and McCarty of Knoxville, will be built on land north of the Candy Factory. The city deeded the property to the museum in 1987.

JAMES L. CLAYTON: "I had no idea it (art museum) touched so many lives. It's lasting; it's permanent."

Kay and I receive the University of Tennessee Volunteer of the Year Award from Dr. Warren Neel, 1997.

The Clayton Team for many years: (left to right) Rich Ray, me, Tim Williams (standing), and Ty Kelly.

The Manufacturing Trio: (left to right) Jerry Moses, Ty Kelly, and Henry Scott.

With Mr. Sheldon Coleman, of Coleman lantern company, 1984.

Our annual ski trip to Vail with children and grandchildren.

Scuba diving with Kay in the Cayman Islands, a new hobby, 1991.

Skiing with Kay, New Year's Day 1992.

New Corporate Headquarters – 800 team members and not an office in the building – everyone's cubicle is the same size, 1998.

Our "homemade" headquarters – 22 modular units from our Bean Station factories, circa 1987.

Corporate Headquarters at Holiday Motel – 26 rooms and 26 bathrooms –park at your office door. Served us well many years – went public there in June 1983.

I propose to Kay 60 feet under water in the Cayman Islands, Thanksgiving Day 1993.

"The Three Docs" singing buddies, 1999: (left to right) me, Dr. Fred Hurst, and Dr. Warren Neel.

Our Christmas Eve wedding, 1993.

My acceptance speech at the Horatio Alger Awards, 1991 – "I'd give my best double-wide if I didn't have to speak first."

Mary Kay Ash, founder of Mary Kay, presenting me with the Horatio Alger Award.

With my daughter Amy and General Colin Powell at the Horatio Alger Awards banquet. Both General Powell and I were inducted on the same evening into the Horatio Alger Association of Distinguished Americans.

With Mother, Joe, and my children at the Horatio Alger dinner. My daughter Karen stayed home that night to give birth to Chris, my sixth grandson.

Relaxing at my double-wide on the Tennessee River, 2002.

Trailer King

Who better to build a fortune in mobile homes than someone who grew up on the wrong side of the ballfield?

By Monte Burke

UNDER A CLOUDLESS SKY IN Knoxville, Tenn., James Lee Clayton straps himself into his black Bell 407 helicopter and eases the seven-seater off the ground. The 68-year-old cranks up Eric Clapton on the stereo and winds his way between the Cumberland and Smoky mountains. Twenty minutes later Clayton lands the whirlybird at his summer getaway, a cedar-sided joint fitted out with patio furniture straight out of Wal-Mart.

Of his five residences—which include condos in Colorado, Florida and South Carolina, as well as a brand-new 14,000-square-foot house in Knoxville—Clayton says this is his favorite. "I get more thinking done, more work done and have more sex in this place than anywhere else in the world," he declares. "This place" is a double-wide for which he paid $45,000 in 1991.

So not every trailer is inhabited by a chain-smoking couple with tattoos. This mobile-home owner is worth $620 million. He made that money manufacturing, selling and financing homes like this one.

Padding around the 15-acre site on Fort Loudoun Lake, Clayton describes how his hardscrabble beginnings and an early business failure steeled him to survive in a boom-and-bust business. Conspicuous in the history of Clayton Homes is the near absence of leverage or daredevil growth. At the moment, the mobile-home sector is suffering one of its periodic busts, but Clayton Homes is not suffering like its competitors. Its Big Board-listed shares are down only 33% from their alltime high. The shares of Champion Enterprises, the biggest mobile-home maker, are down 90%. Shares of Oakwood Homes, which during the last boom beat out Clayton in a bidding war for another manufactured housing company, are down 99%.

Clayton grew up in rural western Tennessee, the son of a sharecropper. His father borrowed money for seeds, fertilizer and tools, money to be repaid from the proceeds of the cotton harvest. The whole family pitched in to make ends meet. "Picking cotton is one of the most horrible—and boring—things you can do," Clayton recalls.

Clayton's mother worked in a shirt factory next to a baseball field. When Clayton and his brother, Joseph, showed up to play, they were always chosen last. "We weren't as good as the other kids because we were working in the field all day while they were

From sharecropper's son to mobile home mogul: Jim Clayton and his double-wide.

Forbes called me the "Trailer King" — Thanks, Forbes.

From sharecropper's son to the Forbes 400 list, 1992.

My cousin Clayton Skinner (left) with Steve and Billie Lou Ellis, Jan. 25, 2002.

Fred Lawson, Bank First
president and my partner – now
Commissioner of Banking for
Tennessee, 1997.

With First State Bank President
Jack Bulliner, January 2002. He
has been with FSB since 1948.

Bank First Board of Directors, 1998.

James Clayton added banking to amazing entrepreneurial career

By Steve Oden
Managing Editor

Although his fame as an entrepreneurial businessman arose from success in the manufactured housing industry, James L. Clayton is no stranger to banking. The founder, former CEO, and current chairman of the board of Clayton Homes, Inc., acquired First Heritage Bank in 1993. In 1995, First Heritage became BankFirst.

In 1996, Clayton purchased FNBG and was elected chairman of the board of Smoky Mountain Bancorp, Inc., the holding company. He purchased Curtis Mortgage

and Athens Bank in 1998.

His effort to acquire First State Bank of Henderson started when several local friends and stockholders contacted him about a possible purchase being negotiated by Decatur, Tenn., banker James Ayers.

"I looked at the offer, and it

**JAMES L.
CLAYTON**

See CLAYTON, Page 2-A

Bought my hometown bank after
merging Bank First
with BB&T in 2001.

WE BELIEVE IN BUSINESS

BankFirst

Strong • Local • Quality
Member FDIC

Bank First in
downtown Knoxville,
Tenn. – now part of
BB&T, 1998.

"Black Beauty," my new Bell 407 – what a machine! 2001.

At home on top of Norton Creek in Gatlinburg, Tenn., 2001 – friends and "Black Beauty" – Warren and Annelle Neel, Kay, me, and Margit and Earl Worsham.

Swapping flying stories with Chuck Yeager in Washington, D.C., 1994

My Bell Jet Ranger, new in 1981, pictured circa 1990.

Clayton Board of Directors, 2002: (standing left to right) Tom McAdams, Dan Evins, Joe Clayton, John Kalec, Wilma Jordon, and Warren Neel; (sitting) Kevin Clayton and me.

Clayton Board of Directors, 1991: (standing left to right) Ty Kelly, Joe Stegmayer, Rich Ray, and Bill Lomicka; (seated left to right) Joe Clayton, me, and Wallace Rasmussen.

After this trip in 1988, I joined Cal Turner's Board (Dollar General), and Dan Evins (Cracker Barrel) joined the Clayton Board; (standing left to right) Joe Stegmayer, me, Cal Turner, and Dan Evins; (seated) Nick Baird, Pete DeBusk, and Pete Peterson.

Clayton Board of Directors, 1983: (left to right) Rich Ray, me, Jim Haslam (standing), Wallace Rasmussen, and Harvey Morgan (standing), Ty Kelly, Bill Lomicka (standing), and Joe Clayton.

Eddy Arnold – also from Chester County and my inspiration – at the UT vs. Florida game, 1998.

The Three Coaches, 2002: (left to right) Allen Morgan, Donie Wood, and Danny Maples.

Visiting with Eddy Arnold and Mrs. Arnold in the Governor's office when Eddy received the Key to the State on his 84th birthday, May 15, 2002.

Celebrating 25 years with CMH – me with Carol and Jerry Moses, the world's greatest manufactured home salesman, 2001.

Kay and I introduce friends George and Joann Rothery and Patsy and Wallace McClure to Louise Mandrell (center), after a concert at our theater in 2001.

"Power Lunch" on CNBC, June 23, 1999.

Clayton Homes sponsored a Chet Atkins concert on March 14, 1992.

Senator Fred Thompson, Kevin and Chelly Clayton, and me at a fundraiser at our home, 2001.

Kay and me with Dr. Henry Kissinger during the Normandy Invasion 50th celebration, June 6, 1994.

With Oprah at Alex Haley's farm near Knoxville, 1989.

I have been lucky enough to meet Bob and Delores Hope several times. He is also a Horatio Alger recipient. Pictured here in Beaumont, Texas, 1994.

Alex Haley and Fred Langley at my home, 1986.

Maren, a "firecracker" baby born on July 4, 2000, is the apple of her granddaddy's eye.

Three of my seven grandsons – Craig, Corey, and Chase Clayton, 1999.

Grandsons Flynt, Kevin, Reed and Chris, 2002.

The Old Timers in 2001 (from left) Jim Ausmus, John Moore, Eddie Venable, and Jess Haun – each with 30-plus years at CMH.

Singing with Mother, 1990.

Today's Appalachia plant, 2002.

The first plant in Halls, circa 1983.

The Clayton men: (left to right) Jim Jr., me, and Kevin, 1998.

goes the whole night. It's going to be a great night."

And it was.

Later, Senator Al Gore asked me to introduce him to General Powell. As we wove our way through the crowd, the General saw us coming toward him, pointed a finger at me, and said with a big grin on his face, "Jim, if you need any parts, *you* call *me*. I got more parts than you got parts."

Sure General!

General Powell later told me that during his many family relocations, there had been parties in his neighborhood celebrating the "mechanic" moving away, indicating the extent of his hobby. As to who had the most Volvo parts, since he was the chairman of the joint chiefs of staff with the might of the U.S. military behind him, I guess he is right. The General would likely know where to find more Volvo parts.

Mother was so pleased to meet Stan "The Man" Musial. After all, she and her brothers, along with Grandfather Browder, loved the St. Louis Cardinals.

The Horatio Alger Association has a 50-year tradition of offering financial assistance to underprivileged kids who only ask for a shot at the American Dream.

I'm proud that CMH has provided thousands of dollars in scholarship money through the Association, prouder still to see the impact a college education can have on a young life. I'll never forget how Bill Elliott, my mentor at Memphis Light, Gas and Water, encouraged me to continue my education. Thank you, Bill. I get to take my turn now.

Each year, Horatio Alger presents two outstanding high school seniors from each state and commonwealth with a $5,000 college scholarship. A year after my induction, I had the pleasure of presenting this award to Chad Smith, then a senior at my old alma mater, Chester County High School.

Chad's family was so poor that their home didn't even have running water or indoor plumbing. But with the Horatio Alger scholarship, he received his degree from the University of Tennessee, and now is deeply involved in medical research. While in school, Chad spent a lot of time with Mother and our family. We remain good friends.

Through my association with Horatio Alger, Clayton Homes began a summer internship program for high school students. We pay them, but I like to think that the experience and what they learn is even more valuable. During their internships, I always spend time with these bright kids, emphasizing the power of setting goals, positive thinking, time management, and other subject matter from the various Clayton University courses.

The clock is ticking. Why waste even one second? The first time I computed the numbers in the Average Life Span chart below, I couldn't believe it. I rechecked them for accuracy. To think that when I was born, I had an average of only 960 months to live.

Average Life Span

Years	80
Months	960
Weeks	4,160
Days	29,120
Hours	698,880
Minutes	41,932,800
Seconds	2,516,000,000

Recognizing that I've already lived 816 of my allocated 960 months definitely motivates me to spend the remaining 144 months in a meaningful and productive manner. For example, in writing this book, I had to make a decision to spend a large part of several months to accomplish the task.

As to the "average" time we have on this Earth, we are all created equally, and assume we'll live to near age 80. (Actually, the insurance companies currently forecast 75 years for men and 79 for women. Who says men and women are created equally?)

But in whatever time we have, how can we be happy? How

can we be more productive?

The answer: we must logically plan, prioritize, focus—and live our plan. Decisions as to what we really want, and what we'll be required to give up are determinative.

Most time management experts stress prioritizing activities, using a version of the following labels and definitions:

Class A activities: Those activities that if, and only if, performed within the planning period produce the desired results.

Class B activities: Those that support the Class A activities. For example, if we do not prospect (a B activity), we won't be able to close the sale (A). Along with prospecting, other examples of Class B items are advertising, training, and ordering inventory.

Class C activities: These activities do not relate directly to the desired results. Relaxation, spiritual pursuits, family time, and other personal activities are C's.

CMH, in its Time Management training, substitutes "Hi-Po" (High Priority); "Lo-Po" (Low Priority); and "No-Po" (No Priority) for the classes A, B and C, respectively. The definitions are the same.

Most of the time management books and seminars teach similar concepts, and most are very good. One in particular that I like is the concept of the "Squares." This model is easy to teach and remember. It's part of the culture at CMH and now at my banks. Here's how it works:

Start with a sheet of paper and divide the space into four equal squares. The top left-hand is the Crisis Square; the top right-hand is the Planned Square; the bottom left-hand is the Urgent Square; the bottom right-hand is the Insignificant Square.

The two squares at the top—the Crisis and Planned squares—relate to important activities, while the two squares on the bottom—the Urgent and Insignificant squares—are associated with unimportant activities.

Looked at another way, the two squares on the left—the Crisis and Urgent squares—tend to be "immediate," and "require attention now," while the two on the right—the Planned and Insignificant squares—are "not immediate," and "do not tend to require attention now."

To be even more specific, here are the types of activities that seem to match the criteria for each of the squares:

Crisis Square: Those items that are "important" and "immediate." Actually, we must plan, train, and manage to minimize the amount of time spent here. To spend significant time in this square indicates we are crisis managing. The entrepreneur likes and becomes quite good at managing on impulse. The adrenaline junkie loves it here.

Planned Square: Those items that are "important," but "not immediate." This is where the organization's vision and strategic plan is formulated—*proactive* decisions, instead of *reactive* ones are made here.

Urgent Square: Those items that are "not important," but "immediate." This includes unscheduled meetings, phone calls, unplanned interruptions at the office—by definition, things that must be dealt with "at the moment," even if they're not related to the achievement of desired results.

Insignificant Square: Those items that are "not important" and "not immediate." This includes "escape activities"—busywork, watching TV, going through junk mail, or hanging around the water cooler.

Entrepreneurs tend to spend far too much time in the Crisis Square. We react fast; we make quick decisions; we find problem-solving "on the fly" fun and challenging. The adrenaline flow becomes addictive.

This behavior helps the embryo entrepreneur start a business successfully. However, all too soon, as the organization moves up the growth curve, turnover, disappointed customers, frustrated lenders, vendors, and other supporters are likely to limit growth—and can destroy the organization.

In order to maximize our effectiveness, especially as leaders, we must spend as little time as possible in the Urgent and Insignificant squares. This can be accomplished through structuring, planning, training, and delegating. Items in the Urgent Square are hard to escape, but possible to minimize. The Insignificant Square is almost completely avoidable.

Whether you're running a business or a ball team, the Planned Square is where much of the leader's time must be spent. It's also where a board of directors should be. The Planned Square means planning, preparation, and prevention; it encompasses training, recruiting, relationship building, and values clarification. The Planned Square activities can drastically reduce the amount of time spent exposed to the Crisis Square.

Personal analysis leading to self-awareness can help us understand which behavior patterns work for us, and which work against us.

All of us have our own quirks and idiosyncrasies. Time spent in the Planned Square can help us identify those behaviors we need to keep, and those we need to discard.

Here is an idiosyncrasy of mine: It seems that I can't have a good week unless I complete three activities before going to work on Monday morning.

First, my car must have a full tank of gas. I'll likely to be too busy during the week, and it's stressful to be low on gas. Second, my shoes must be shined. I will look and feel better. Third—and this one's not so quirky—my activities for the week must be scheduled, prioritized, and planned. This keeps the subconscious from having to make "on the fly" time management decisions all week long.

As for calendars, I've preached for years that *one* is a challenge to maintain; two or more are impossible. Years ago, I took a lot of heat when I cancelled our annual desk calendar order, and gave our team members Day-Timers. Pulling those desk calendars was like pulling teeth, but how many old fashioned, ring-type desk calendars have you seen well managed? None, I bet. I still carry a

Day-Timer, but now depend largely on my Palm Pilot.

Down through the years, I've tried hundreds of time management recommendations. Most did not work for me, probably because I didn't believe in the technique enough to invest the time to properly implement it. But the "red-yellow-green" folders for the executive assistant did work for me, and still does. It helps me keep a clean desk, and it helps the executive assistant become more decisive and confident.

Here's how it works: Tina Adkins, my executive assistant for 15 years, opens our mail, scans it, and places each mailing in one of three folders. Let me share the type of items she will place in each folder:

Red: Here, Tina places mail that she wants me to handle by nine o'clock tomorrow morning. That's my promise to Tina.

Yellow: Tina places mail that she wants me to process by nine o'clock in the morning on the second day. If I haven't handled the item by tomorrow at 9:00 AM, she will move it to the Red file, giving me the agreed second day to process.

Green: Here, I can take a week. This is primarily reading material. During my last 10 years as CEO, Tina placed the more important reading material in the Green file. She kept a special travel or weekend briefcase for reading material that she thought I would like to scan, but could disregard if needed.

With this system, Tina has the authority to delegate the mail to me, pre-prioritized by her. I've enjoyed this system for 25 years. Kevin and other CMH executives use this as well.

She also would assure you that our follow-up system is invaluable, yet so simple. At the office store, purchase a "1-through-31 accordion," or collapsible file for $15. Request the combination "1-through-31" packaged with January to December sections in one file. Mine is called Fast Sorter. This terrific tool keeps the clutter off the desk and out of our minds. You will keep thinking of ways to benefit from this system.

Here's just one example of how I've used it over the years. In the 1970s, I managed all the real estate transactions for the company. For instance, I'd lease five acres for a sales center and get an option to renew the lease in five years. In addition, we would receive an option to buy the land at the end of 10 years with seller financing for another 10 years.

My presentation to the owner would involve adding lease payments for 120 months, plus a down payment at the time of purchase, plus another 120 payments for the mortgage. The total received by the owner would amount to $700,000 over time, while the cash price was only $200,000.

On my flight back to Knoxville, I'd dictate a letter to renew the lease at the end of five years. The letter, with details for closing the sale and loan, would also be dictated.

How satisfying to have Tina hand me a well-drafted letter properly prepared years earlier, ready for my signature! Imagine how much time it would take to collect all that data 10 years after signing the contract. Note: The letter was prepared while we had access to all the information, a Planned Square activity.

For this transaction, the letters for the future are initially filed in the last compartment of the system, labeled "Future Years." This pocket is sorted only on December 31 of each year. Those items for the upcoming year are spread February through December. January items are placed in the 1-31 section. The February items are spread to that section on February 1.

The results from this system are amazing, and I can't imagine not having this system, with an assistant or solo.

Back when she was growing up in Knoxville—and watching me sing and play guitar on *Startime*—little did Tina Adkins know that one day, she'd be my secretary and personal assistant.

That wasn't Tina's only early "connection" to Clayton Homes. As a 1980 graduate of Powell High, her principal was Allen Morgan—today, our Vice President of the Communities Group. Among other things, Tina was on Powell High's track team, and part of its mile relay (which *still* holds the school record).

Tina joined Clayton Homes in 1984, after four years with First Tennessee Bank. In 1986, she began working with Rich Ray, our CFO, and with our Board of Directors—handling SEC filings and assisting with our annual report and proxy statements.

Today, along with supporting John Kalec, our CFO, and Carl Koella, our Vice President of Investor Relations, Tina helps me manage my day-to-day activities—my calendar, mail and phone calls.

She is wonderfully efficient, a pleasure to work with—and capably supports the team.

In 1990, CMH initiated one of its most successful products ever. We called it BUBBA—Buying Under The Bi-Weekly Budget Advantage. Over the years, this mortgage program has saved our customers millions of dollars.

BUBBA is easy, fast, with no checks to write, no mail to send— and a 20-year loan can be repaid in 12 years.

It works this way. Instead of paying a mortgage once a month, BUBBA homeowners pay half the mortgage every two weeks, or bi-weekly. Instead of paying a $400 mortgage on the first of the month, a BUBBA participant pays $200 every two weeks, electronically, through a no-fee checking account.

In the early years of most mortgages, the vast majority of the payments are for interest, not principal. If you have a mortgage that's $400 a month, you're only paying about $400 in principal for the entire year. By paying bi-weekly, the homebuyer pays 26 payments of $200. The extra $400, from the 24th and 25th payments goes directly to principal—with all interest stopped on the extra principal for the life of the loan.

Over a period of years, this adds up to thousands of dollars saved in interest payments.

The homebuyer will never receive a delinquency notice, never pay a late notice, and will not have a bad credit report, since the money is withdrawn from the accounts electronically. To our knowledge, we are the only mortgage company in our industry with the systems to support such a unique program.

It's always a joy to see such a "win-win" program launched. To market BUBBA, we discovered Bubba Cola, a now discontinued canned soft drink. It was a natural. To promote the name Bubba, we shipped several cases of Bubba Cola to our sales centers. Sales center managers kept a Bubba six-pack on their desks.

Also, while throwing the name around, "Bad Bart" Mize got a new name, "Bubba" Mize. Tim Williams, president of Vanderbilt Mortgage, made Mize president of the Bubba Mortgage MBU (Million Dollar Business Unit) and charged him with the responsibility to track, coordinate, and market the concept. I tagged him with the nickname Bubba, and it stuck.

Today, Bubba Mize works with Tim Williams and Rich Ray, our partners at 21st Mortgage.

Both the BUBBA mortgage and Bubba Mize have been very successful. The BUBBA loan now comprises 30 percent of our mortgage business and was our very first MBU.

I'd like to take credit for the MBU idea, but it was really my son, Kevin, who developed the concept for CMH.

Basically, anyone in our organization with an idea for a new product or service can make a presentation to senior management to sell the concept. The idea must be able to produce a net profit of $1 million a year by the third year. If the program is approved, CMH will support the concept with start-up capital, a full-time staff, and a board of directors versed in accounting, legal, marketing, computer systems, and administration.

The MBU's have been a wonderful incubator for new Clayton products and is an excellent showcase for developing talent. Over the years, we've created a number of them, like specialty financing for raw land, lottery winning buy-outs, and home security monitoring. At Clayton Manufacturing, Kelly Williams, a fraternity brother of mine, runs the commercial division. There we supply modular buildings to be used for everything from bank branch offices, beauty shops, classrooms, eyeglass clinics, in-plant offices, event restroom clusters, construction trailers, and other specialty buildings. Kelly rents, leases, and sells for cash. Long-term mortgages are also offered at attractive rates.

I love the MBU's because they give our team members the chance to run their own businesses as Joe and I did in the early days—but with the risk minimized. Being able to showcase talented team members in a relatively safe environment is exciting. The MBU program reflects the Clayton entrepreneurial culture.

The first time I met Kay Montgomery was back in the early '80s, years after my divorce from Mary.

I'd been dating Mary Anne Shoopman, one of the Sisters Four from the *Startime* program, and Kay was a close friend of hers. Kay and a companion double-dated with us a few times during the 1982 World's Fair. I remember thinking that she was the epitome of southern refinement—and a very nice, kind, and attractive person. The Fair ended; Mary Ann moved to Nashville; and I would not see Kay again for nine years.

Through the 1980s Kay would cross my mind from time to time. I heard she was engaged, and assumed she got married. But in 1991, I got a business call from a friend of Kay's, and in passing, I asked how Kay Montgomery's marriage was working out.

"Heck, Kay never got married, and probably never will," he said. Apparently, the engagement didn't work out.

I wasted no time getting in touch with Kay, and was extremely pleased that she remembered me. Our first date was at Naples, a local Italian restaurant popular with the locals. I walked in a couple of minutes early and was shocked to see a large crowd staring in disbelief at the lounge TV. Kay arrived a few minutes later. Neither of us was aware that the Gulf War was underway. It was January 16, 1991, and the Gulf War was being televised live!

Kay had never married, had taught school for 13 years, and on a lark, interviewed for a flight attendant position at Piedmont Airlines. Of course, she was hired. She flew with Piedmont, and then with U. S. Air after the merger for over six years. I think that hectic schedule helped her prepare for life with me.

We dated for three years.

On Thanksgiving Day in 1993, Warren Neel and I flew our children, along with Kay, to Cayman Brac in the Cayman Islands for a long weekend of scuba diving. I had commissioned a professional underwater photographer to make the descent to 60 feet with us—allegedly to take a group picture.

We all dived in the 80-degree water and were soon making our way down through the shimmering turquoise. Gathering for the picture on the ocean floor I kept my arm around Kay, keeping her attention on the camera. Only Flynt Griffin, my grandson, knew the real motive for the group picture.

While I kept gesturing for everyone to give attention to the camera, Flynt rolled out an eight-foot banner that read, *Kay, Will You Marry Me? Love, Jim.*

I gave her an underwater marker—and she checked the "Yes" box a dozen times. From my wet suit jacket, I brought out a diamond engagement ring and put it on her finger.

Now, when I tell the story, I laughingly claim that I bought a small diamond at first, but as I considered the possibility of losing the stone in the sand, I went back and bought a diamond large enough to be found—even in the sand.

Back on deck, the Captain had a Dom Perignon toast all set for the group celebration.

After completing two dives and lunch, Kay and I relaxed on the pearly-white, sandy beach. Thinking I'd want to drag out the engagement as I had the courtship, she asked "Well, when?"

But much to her surprise, my immediate response was, "Just as soon as you can put it together." She had us married in six weeks. The wedding was at noon on Christmas Eve at Cherokee Country Club. Over 100 of our family and friends were present. Her father Harry gave her away.

CHAPTER 17

Board Members:
Care And Feeding

It should have been the best of times. In 1993, *Forbes* magazine named me to the *Forbes* 400 for the second year in a row. According to *Forbes*, I was number 330 on its annual list of the wealthiest Americans, just before Hugh Culverhouse (real estate and banking) and just after Saul Philip Steinberg (financier).

For 13 years in a row, our sales and earnings set records, and our stock's value had quintupled since 1990. The *News-Sentinel* called Clayton Homes the "darling of Wall Street."

My enjoyment of this success was to be short-lived.

Beginning in 1992, an auditor from the State Department of Revenue was performing a routine examination of our sales tax collections and payments. Such audits, expected every few years, are assigned to the controller and accounting staff of the group being audited to coordinate and support. By offering them access and cooperation, the auditors seem to wrap up their examination in less time, and may even be more understanding when settlement discussions occur. Rich Ray, our CFO, fully expected our staff to provide this auditor with our normal high level of support.

The auditor was staying an unusually long time, but the controller of our retail division, Warren Schede, assured Rich that the audit was going well. We would soon learn this accountant had stonewalled the auditor for months, making her wait for even the few papers he chose to give her from time to time.

Eventually, she had all of Schede and CMH that she could stand. I don't understand why she didn't appeal directly to Rich or me, but exasperated with Schede, she went back to her office, organized her presentation, went across the hall to the revenue department's criminal division, and made her case that CMH was withholding records and interfering with the audit process. The criminal division assigned the case to agent Charles Smith. This would be his last case before retirement.

Smith immediately fired his first bullet, though it was more like a cannon. It took the form of a subpoena demanding over 100 items. An 18-wheeler would have been required to transport the numerous files and records requested. "Burying" the adverse party with a documentation request is an often-used strategy by auditors and attorneys.

This would be one of the longest summers of my life, with lots of "frogs to swallow."

Surely, I thought, this is simply a misunderstanding that can be cleared up quickly. Immediately, I called Tom McAdams, our attorney, while Rich talked to Jim Shelby, from our outside auditing firm. They agreed that the board, as well as Jim Cheek, our SEC counsel, should be informed about the criminal investigation and the horrendous subpoena. I certainly didn't want my board of directors to be surprised by reading this story in the *Wall Street Journal*. A conference call was set for 10 o'clock the next morning.

On the conference call: Jim Cheek of Bass, Berry & Sims in Nashville, our SEC counsel for a decade; Jim Shelby of Ernst & Whitney, our outside auditing firm; Tom McAdams, CMH general counsel; and, of course, all of our board members, including Wallace Rasmussen, the chairman of the Audit Committee. You may recall Rasmussen agreed to serve only long enough to help me get the board and the Audit Committee organized. But now, at age 79, he was in his tenth year with us.

Other directors on the call included Bill Lomicka, former treasurer of Humana, and Joe Stegmayer, CFO of Worthington Steel. (Along with Rasmussen, they made up the Audit Committee. CMH had more public company experience on this committee than most NYSE companies.)

Also on the call were Dan Evins, CEO of Cracker Barrel, Joe Clayton, Rich Ray, Ty Kelly, and myself.

In some detail, I informed the board about the document request and the intervention of the revenue department's criminal division. Rich explained that the retail controller had failed to cooperate with the sales tax auditor, which caused the subpoena. But he assured the board there were no material sales tax issues, and any final tax adjustments would be insignificant.

The board was comfortable with our explanation, except for Rasmussen, the "Boss." (This was the title of an article about Rasmussen written by famed journalist Studs Terkle.)

As it turned out, Rasmussen suggested the Audit Committee, which he chaired, conduct an independent investigation, just to make sure this was a localized problem. He asked Jim Cheek if Bass, Berry & Sims could do the investigation. Jim responded that the firm would be glad to handle it for Rasmussen.

Then Rasmussen asked if the firm had a "good, experienced lawyer familiar with independent investigations who could get on this matter real fast—like Brad Reed."

"Mr. Rasmussen, Brad Reed here," said the voice over the speakerphone from the Bass, Berry & Sims conference room. Reed said he would be glad to handle the matter for Rasmussen.

We had invited only Jim Cheek from Bass, Berry & Sims to join the conference call. Yet there was Brad Reed, stationed "at the elbow" of Jim Cheek, apparently up-to-speed and ready to go at a moment's notice. Rasmussen hired Reed on the spot.

How strange, I thought, strange that Reed was on the line, and strange that Rasmussen would suggest that our own counsel conduct an "independent" investigation. After all, Bass, Berry & Sims had represented CMH in all SEC and NYSE activities for a decade, including Vanderbilt securitizations. We'd paid them hundreds of thousands of dollars in legal fees, making CMH a significant client for the firm. How could they take huge sums of money from CMH and still be considered independent? How could Cheek investigate the executive officers of CMH when he had been, and still was, the CMH attorney for all public company matters?

I passed the ethics requirements in law school. I even got through Foster Arnett's inquiry into the ethical practices of my used car sales activities. Even Arnett and his committee were apparently satisfied that I'd be an ethical attorney, should that become my chosen career.

They taught us in law school that an attorney couldn't be involved in any activity that would create an adversarial relationship between the attorney and his client. Any situation with even the appearance of an adversarial relationship or conflict of interest with the client must be avoided. It just can't be done. I couldn't believe this firm that we trusted and totally depended on to guide us in all such matters would now maintain their independence from CMH.

After all this was a tax and possibly an accounting issue. Why would they not advise us to have Jim Shelby's national firm audit all matters related to the tax issue? That would quickly give Rasmussen and the entire board all the information needed to remain comfortable with the CMH management.

Let's fast-forward to 2001, where, as a member of the audit committee for Dollar General, I watched in disbelief as Jim Cheek made a presentation to our committee recommending that he and other lawyers from Bass, Berry & Sims conduct an independent investigation of Dollar General.

The audit committee chairman, relying on Cheek's advice, had a few days earlier approved a preliminary inquiry into some alleged accounting irregularities. Cheek urged the committee to retain him and his firm to expand the inquiry into a full independent counsel investigation.

Not this time. As I shared information with officers and directors about my experience with his partner, Brad Reed, from nearly a decade earlier, the committee and ultimately the full board hired another firm as independent counsel. Cheek's recommendation to use his firm was rejected by the Audit Committee and Board of Directors.

The ethics issues involved in these types of cases are very serious, and frequently I am asked about this experience by other lawyers and how this could happen. I have not been able to come up with a good answer. Other attorneys voiced concern that a firm would accept an assignment that could lead to an investigation of company officers who had retained the firm for years.

Go to www.bassberry.com/search/index.htm to look at Cheek's bio.

Note that his area of expertise includes corporate and shareholder conflict as well as "internal investigations." The Web site résumé tends to add credibility to the rumors that Cheek had positioned himself to become head of the SEC. Some say he darn nigh got the position. The world of business is very fortunate that he missed the mark, in my opinion.

Again from the Web site, we see that Cheek welcomes assignments such as: "Representation of Special Committees of Boards of Directors of public companies. . . internal investigation. . . ."

Back to the conference call that Rasmussen had taken over, with assistance from Brad Reed. Board members agreed with Rasmussen's suggestion to conduct an investigation of the tax matters. I am embarrassed to admit that I, too, supported the decision. I was naïve, never guessing that the scope of the investigation would rapidly expand and become adversarial and even hostile. Looking back, one might wonder if the script for this meeting had been prepared and rehearsed well in advance of the conference call.

Reed advised that he would need independent accountants to assist with the investigation, in order to protect the attorney-client privilege on information the accountants might find. This arrangement had the new accountants working for and reporting to lawyers rather than working directly for the company and reporting to the board. Our outside accountant, Jim Shelby, was on the call and could have responded to any questions, but the attorney-client privilege would not apply to any information he provided.

The risk of losing confidentiality of evidence gathered is a real risk in some situations. In this case, it was not likely to be an issue, and in fact, never was an issue. We were not trying to hide anything. Any irregularities found by the investigation would be quickly fixed. If we owe taxes, we want to pay them. At CMH (other companies, too), we encounter problems and exceptions all the time. We fix them immediately and go back to work.

In my view, the attorney-client privilege is overused, grossly increases cost, and often interferes with getting matters resolved.

Numerous times Tom McAdams and Bernie Bernstein have privately asked me if I want to take the business risk of disclosure and avoid the effort and expense of protecting the privilege. Knowing that over 80 percent of cases are settled, I say yes much of the time. This means the other side may gain access to some of our confidential files. Heck, we've been required to hand over documents to our opponents on several occasions when I thought the privilege should have applied. In several cases, I, as Clayton corporate counsel, had our staff prepare such evidence at my direction, expecting the attorney-client privilege to protect the confidentiality. Sometimes, the court agreed, sometimes not.

The next day, Brad Reed showed up at our headquarters with Bob Hensley, who would manage the audit for Arthur Andersen, and asked to see me. I was told bluntly, by him, to stay out of the way and not to interfere or question any facets of his investigation. Reed reminded me that not only was he authorized by the

Audit Committee to investigate the sales tax matter, but he also had the authority to look into "any other irregularities" that came to his attention.

It became immediately apparent that the sales tax issue that got him on board was of little importance. He was hunting bigger game in my opinion, and I was not sure it wasn't me. How long would Reed be here? How much would this cost? I did not have a clue.

L et me share some thoughts on independent investigations. Normally, the initial issue is small and immaterial. However, early on the independent counsel may ask his employer (in this case, the Audit Committee) if they want to be informed of other irregularities that may be uncovered in the investigation. It was unlikely the Audit Committee would say, "No, I do not want to know about any irregularities you may uncover." At that point, the door for a much broader investigation is opened.

Ken Starr asked this of the congressional committee that employed him to investigate Whitewater. Was Ken Starr limited to Whitewater issues? No way! He went on to stains, occupants of closets, sexual positions, cigars, and more. He was unchecked. Even President Clinton could not contain, restrict, or stop him. After all, he was an independent counsel.

In our case, on the second day Reed asked Rasmussen, if irregularities were uncovered, should they be investigated or simply reported? Rasmussen directed Reed to investigate.

Reed, another attorney, and an accountant began questioning our people while Bob Hensley and his team from Arthur Andersen began combing through our tax and accounting records. The process was time-consuming and a frustrating ordeal for our people. The independent investigation caused concerns among many team members, who were trying to do their jobs and respond truthfully to the questions. "You have the right to retain counsel," the lawyer would say solemnly. "I recommend you do have counsel." Within weeks, several dozen of our fine team members were interviewed.

On the second day of the investigation, Rich Ray and I called Joe Stegmayer, and then Bill Lomicka, to inform them on how the investigation was being handled. While Stegmayer's reaction was one of surprise and concern, Lomicka seemed indifferent as he suggested we allow Reed to continue. When we tried to tell Lomicka that Reed was talking to people who had no knowledge of sales tax, he said it was just part of the process.

I was disappointed in Lomicka's reaction. This director had been a dear friend.

Rasmussen informed the board several times that Reed would require additional time, since significant irregularities were being uncovered that required further investigation. Finally, Reed presented a list of a dozen items that he felt would concern the board. In my opinion, all of them were minor issues or were simply a result of his not understanding our business.

For example, one was the fact that computer programmers had access to "live data" making it possible for them to set up imaginary vendors, pay false invoices with company checks, and take the money. While that may have been theoretically possible, there was no evidence that a programmer had ever used live data for personal gain or to the detriment of CMH.

Another item: some alleged EEO complaints regarding inappropriate behavior violations in the workplace. While the company has always taken any personnel complaints seriously and investigates them with the utmost scrutiny, I dare say there isn't a public company anywhere without such a complaint. We've had a few, but all are promptly addressed and resolved with sensitivity and concern for the team member.

Another item on the independent counsel's list was fraudulent loans, which certainly got the attention of the management team. For a mortgage company to have fraudulent loans is the ultimate "horror story." After all, a mortgage company is dead without total credibility.

Vanderbilt's underwriting, audit, and other processes have kept our mortgages free from irregularities. How could the investigation find fraud in a few weeks when we have screen and filter processes in our mortgage compliance department that effectively look every day for even a trace of irregularities? This did not make sense to me.

Remember, all of this is happening to the same company that had received accolades from all major financial and business publications. On August 30, 1993, the *Wall Street Journal* said we were "one of the most successful mobile home companies in the country. Sales and earnings have set records every year since 1980."

On January 27, 1991, *The Tennessean* (Nashville) said about me, "He is President, Chairman, Chief Executive Officer and majority owner of Knoxville-based Clayton Homes, Inc., one of the top manufactured home builders in the country . . . stock grew 96.4 percent last year, ranking it the seventh-best performing stock on the New York Stock Exchange."

We asked for details, but Rasmussen and Reed declined, claiming that for management to know the details would make the information available to anyone who might sue the company—that darn privilege again. The investigation was expanded, and the costs continue to increase.

Bob Hensley brought in half-a-dozen computers and ran them day and night. Searching for statistical data to confirm their suspicions, the accountants focused on duplicate names, addresses, zip codes, and indications of fictitious loans.

Finally, we heard the investigation had found 110 fraudulent loans. We asked for details, but our request was denied. We pressed for information, but Rasmussen claimed he didn't know, and didn't want to know. He wanted the investigation to continue, even though we didn't know what they were investigating.

There was only one place to appeal. Calling Dan Evins, the founder and CEO of Cracker Barrel and a long-time CMH board member, we discussed our limited options. Dan and I set up a conference call with Rasmussen to urge him to get the details from Reed. Knowing that finding 110 fraudulent mortgages could be terminal for CMH, Dan was worried, but hadn't lost the faith.

Dan Evins is a likeable and well-respected person, and I believe Rasmussen liked and respected Dan. The conversation focused on surface issues involving the investigation, but soon Dan began to press Rasmussen to get the mortgage details. Reluctantly, Rasmussen said, "I'll talk to Reed and see what I can do." Dan promised Rasmussen that he'd follow up by phone the next day.

On the third day, Dan called and told me the only information he was able to obtain was that Vanderbilt had 110 mortgages all with the same name and address.

"Impossible," I said. "What is the name?"

Dan didn't know, but he did tell me it was a Birmingham, Michigan, address.

"Dan, that's Uniprop, we sell and finance them," I said.

Our view of the entire investigation changed completely with a quick call to Tim Williams, our mortgage group president. All I had to say was, "Tim, the 110 fraudulent mortgages are all addressed Birmingham, Michigan."

"That's our friends at Uniprop," confirmed Tim.

Tim and Vanderbilt's vice president, Paul Nichols, had approved mortgages for up to 10 homes in each of the Uniprop communities. The program had already been implemented in 11 of their fine communities. Multiply 11 by 10, and that's 110 homes and an equal number of loans.

Paul Zlotoff, their talented chairman, and the Uniprop team purchased 110 homes from Clayton, and they allowed us to finance the homes too. (By the way, Paul, thanks for the fine business. Sure wish I could ski half as well as you.)

Weeks of investigation had just confirmed that Vanderbilt did not have a fraudulent loan problem.

This was the sum and substance of the so-called "fraudulent

loans." (Tim, you are the best mortgage executive in our entire industry. Of course, that is already well known.)

When a board or audit committee is not satisfied with information provided by management about "fraudulent loans" or any other accounting, financial, or business matters, it has a number of resources available, including internal audit, corporate counsel, outside audit, and outside counsel. Any of these resources would have quickly, without disruption and significant expense, investigated the sales tax or any other issue of concern to the satisfaction of any reasonable board member.

Had Rasmussen chosen to do so, he would have found simply and quickly that the clerk did not say "fraudulent loans." She said "straw loans." There is a world of difference between the two. "Straw loan" is a buzz term for a loan on a home purchased by one person, but lived in by another; for example, parents buying a home for children who have no credit or bad credit. Another example would be children buying a home for their parents.

Since Wall Street investors require that Vanderbilt represent and warrant that our mortgages are owner-occupied, we underwrite and screen carefully to make sure the mortgage files are, and remain, extremely accurate. The internal audit department, currently headed by Greg Hamilton, is capably staffed with experienced accounting and finance talent. Carl Koella and Tim Rhoades, veteran Clayton team members respected for their technical and leadership skills, have managed the department.

With talent like this at an audit committee's disposal and no indication of involvement by upper management, there was no understandable reason for Rasmussen to "overkill" by retaining an independent counsel. Attorneys tell me they would not have accepted such an assignment as Brad Reed accepted here in view of the perceived or actual inherent conflict involved.

At Dollar General, it would appear that Cheek could have been considered to be in much the same position.

It is interesting to note that both companies enjoyed excellent performance at this time—also prior—also after. Both companies' shareholders lost huge sums as a result of the uncertainty involved during the extended investigations.

With some confidence restored, the executive team—Rich, Ty, Tim, Joe Stegmayer, and myself—made a decision to try to bring the investigation to a conclusion.

Joe Stegmayer did not know of the sales tax issues when we met at Bill Lomicka's estate in Louisville for a social weekend in late April 1993. I didn't have a clue, either. There, Lomicka and I talked Joe, who had served on our board for nearly a decade, into joining Clayton full-time as president and CEO. Joe joined the company in mid-July on schedule, just in time for the second confrontation with Rasmussen.

We had to replace Stegmayer on the Audit Committee since he was no longer an outside board member. Dan Evins agreed to take the position on the committee, but that would not give us another independent board member.

How do you recruit a board member when the company and its management are under investigation by the revenue department and by its own audit committee?

That's a difficult question, but the answer is simple.

A director candidate would have to know management and the company. That shortened the list considerably, and Dr. Warren Neel, dean of the College of Business Administration at the University of Tennessee, quickly topped the list. Warren knew us well; he conducted an in-depth strategic and succession plan for the company in 1991, and he readily volunteered to support the company and me.

To get Warren installed would require a board meeting—and what a meeting that would be. Individually, and as a group, the management team and directors tried to convince Rasmussen and Lomicka that this was the best way of moving forward. They did not agree.

Talk about a country boy being up a creek without a paddle

and in over my head!

Vanderbilt was making loans, writing checks, and "burning cash" to the extent of several hundred thousands of dollars every day. Merrill Lynch was standing by, ready to underwrite and distribute our mortgage-backed securities to Wall Street investors, as they do every quarter—except they'd have to disclose any information they, their counsel, and our accountants had that would bear on the financial position of the company. Various accountants, lawyers, and management must certify, represent, and warrant that all information has been disclosed. With the ongoing investigation, it was determined that many disclaimers would have to accompany each offering statement to an investor.

Would you buy a Vanderbilt bond backed up by mortgages under such circumstances?

We were running out of cash fast. Rich Ray was pulling his hair out. There were few doors, and all were locked tight.

At this point, there had not been a press release. Most CEOs would've listened to their lawyers and released statements like, "Independent Counsel Investigation Launched Over Various Unpaid Tax Liabilities." Or how about this one: "Audit Committee Launches Investigation Into Possible Fraudulent Mortgages And Inadequate System Issues." Investors would've loved this.

How could Rich and I get away without publishing a release? There were no material irregularities known. All cash was in the bank. No assets were missing. Earnings were the highest in history. The media continued to congratulate us. On November 12, 1992, *The South Bend Tribune* reported, ". . . he has just won the Wall Street Transcript's gold award for overseeing the most successful company in his industry for the fifth time in six years."

What's "material," anyway? Analysts argue about this. Generally, there is agreement that an issue of up to two percent to five percent of a year's income should be considered immaterial. For CMH, earning over $100 million annually after taxes, an issue would have to amount to over $2 million to be material. Here, the tax due by CMH amounted to less than $200,000. That is less than two day's income for the company, and clearly immaterial.

The date for the board meeting was set, and notices were sent. On September 29, one day before the board meeting, Joe Stegmayer and I visited Bob McCullough at the Baker-Worthington law offices in Nashville. Bob was the SEC counsel for Cracker Barrel and a close friend of Dan Evins. This was one of the most productive hours of my professional life. To have his legal expertise and calm demeanor present in that room may have been the glue that held my team together. Bob McCullough agreed to serve as secretary at the board meeting.

Encouraged after our visit, Joe and I walked three blocks to see Jim Cheek at Bass, Berry & Sims. Cheek was cordial and seemingly sensitive to our position, as he listened to us plead for him to intervene with Brad Reed. We wanted him to stop the investigation that we thought was hurting the company. We told him of our need for his firm to represent us in the pending Merrill Lynch securitization, and of our desire to have him and his associate, Mitch Walker, continue to be our SEC, NYSE, and public company compliance attorneys. Cheek declined to intervene.

Incidentally, several times over the years, I've bumped into Mitch Walker, who we had enjoyed watching mature as a fine lawyer. I always told him we missed him since we stopped using

Earnings Per Share

18% CGR
Compound Growth Rate

'83	'84	'85	'86	'87	'88	'89	'90	'91	'92	'93	'94	'95	'96	'97	'98	'99	'00	'01	'02
.04	.06	.07	.09	.10	.14	.15	.18	.24	.29	.37	.49	.59	.72	.80	.92	1.06	1.03	.77	.89

his firm. Mitch was always gracious and reminded me that he'd enjoyed working with the Clayton team.

Before we continue the investigation story, let me suggest that the reader may feel that I am being defensive. With this much smoke, you would expect there is one devil of a fire. Let me help you frame an accurate image of where CMH had been, was at the time, and would be going. On the previous page, look at the graph of the results up to 1993 and later. The defense rests.

Since Dan Evins, along with other board members, had requested a full report from Rasmussen on the investigation and the list of irregularities, we met at the law firm's office. On July 30, at nine in the morning, I called the board meeting to order in the Bass, Berry & Sims conference room.

In electing Dr. Warren Neel to the board and to the Audit Committee, Rasmussen and Lomicka objected. Though they knew Neel because of his planning and succession work for the company, they objected on the grounds that Neel and I had a personal relationship, that he was on the board of a bank in which I owned controlling interest, and that I was a major contributor to the university where he was a dean.

Despite the objections, Warren was elected to the Clayton board and would be a wonderful friend and supporter. He's currently in his 10th year of service. I appointed Warren to the position on the Audit Committee vacated by Joe Stegmayer, over objections by the same two dissenters. Rasmussen remained chairman, and Lomicka remained a member of the committee.

The independent investigation report, delivered by Mitch Walker, covered 12 items that, in my opinion, didn't amount to a hill of beans. Most of his time was spent urging the board to vote for Rasmussen's recommendation that the investigation be extended. Walker expressed the opinion that there could be significant accounting and other issues that could be identified only by allowing the independent counsel and the Arthur Andersen teams to proceed with their work.

Dan Evins blasted Walker and the group supporting him. This included Lomicka, Rasmussen, and Hensley. Dan asked for any information they had indicating that cash was missing, urged them to disclose any evidence of an intentional misstatement of income, and finished with a fist-banging demand for them to put up or shut up—either show the board that there is a material problem or stop the audit.

Dan, I will never forget that display of confidence and support.

Soon, it was time for my monologue. I covered the distractions, the disruptions, the fact that we were beginning to get questions from Wall Street, the imminent cash crunch, that Joe Stegmayer had been recruited by the board to enhance our financial and operational infrastructure, and that board requests had always been honored.

I then directed my closing plea to Rasmussen, urging that he and his team allow Stegmayer to take over and complete the investigation. I reminded him that he'd recommended Stegmayer for the president's position, and that I thought he was more qualified than Bob Hensley and Brad Reed to complete the sales tax and other audit functions.

Each member of the Rasmussen team spoke at length, opposing my recommendation. Dr. Neel called for the question, and I asked for a show of hands. Voting to continue with Brad Reed was Rasmussen and Lomicka. Voting to suspend the investigation was Joe Clayton, Ty Kelly, Rich Ray, Dan Evins, Warren Neel, and me.

We won, six to two.

The two dissenters resigned, but not quietly.

Identical letters of resignation, I suspect authored by our former SEC counsel, were sent to the SEC. The letters indicated *their investigation of sales tax and other matters had been blocked and that the company had serious financial irregularities of which management was well aware.*

That would be the last of Rasmussen and Lomicka at Clayton's.

CHAPTER 18

Succession Planning: New CEO

Since Rasmussen and Lomicka chose to file their letters of resignation with the SEC, a press release was now required. In our opinion, such a letter and its filing was completely inappropriate.

Since there were no material, financial, or other issues known, the statements made in their resignation letters were most unfortunate for CMH and its shareholders.

If they simply wanted to resign, they could've done so without injuring the company.

Normally, board and officer resignations, although technically considered material events, will be timed to occur and will be announced in one of the company's routine press releases.

Certainly, all parties normally do not want the company or the departing individual to be injured as a result of the announcement.

Here, however, the directors, and we believe Brad Reed, chose to file letters with the SEC, which contained extremely negative language. It would appear that the letters were filed knowing that CMH shareholders would suffer serious financial losses, which happened immediately. The vague and confusing language contained in the resignation letters, which appeared to be carefully chosen, alarmed investors. "The turmoil echoed on Wall Street," reported the front-page article in the *Wall Street Journal* on August 30, 1993.

The article, titled "Bump in the Road—Investigations Jolt Mobile Home Firm Jim Clayton Built," covered the events of the recent board meeting: "At a meeting July 30, Mr. Clayton persuaded the board to suspend the investigation, effectively firing the law firm and Arthur Andersen, whose services the law firm had retained. Messrs. Lomicka and Rasmussen dissented, arguing that the investigation should continue. Then, two weeks later, they quit, with resignation letters saying they doubted "any investigation can properly be limited to the sales tax matter.'"

The article quoted Rasmussen as saying, "I had no facts that there was any wrongdoing on Jim Clayton's part with the exception that he had the intermingling of company business and his own. I had always been against that kind of intermingling between company and personal business. Sometimes, you have to hit a mule on the head with a two-by-four to get their attention." We were able to use this Rasmussen quote to our advantage, calming Merrill-Lynch and their underwriting team. Rich Ray would wave the *Wall Street Journal* article at analysts, lawyers, brokers, and investors saying, "The person who started all this, we believe, and who we refer to as the devil himself, Rasmussen, told the *Wall Street Journal* that he knew of no wrongdoing by our CEO."

Also in the article, Rasmussen said, "The investigation we were conducting was cut off when (we) were gathering a lot of facts." He added: "I'm too damn old to go around being tainted."

Lomicka continued: "I can't tell you in any way that it's confined to one person. It may be one person. I don't know the answer. That's what we were looking into." Here, Rich, when answering questions about the alleged serious accounting irregularities at the company, would answer, "Rasmussen told the *Wall Street Journal* that he was cut off while gathering a lot of facts. Don't you think that if Rasmussen actually knew of even one material item of concern that he would have told the *Wall Street Journal?*" Again, this helped calm Wall Street.

The *Journal* article, written by Laurie M. Grossman, also said: "The company says that its problems are relatively minor and under control—an assertion that many observers, inside and outside the company, find believable. It says it doesn't expect any more surprises from investigators. Earnings are strong, and Clayton says there is no reason to believe they will be affected." It was the company and management credibility that allowed us to "save my scalp" and to protect CMH shareholders from possibly losing all their investment.

However this, at least temporarily, was a painful experience for management and for our shareholders, as Ms. Grossman summed up in her *WSJ* article: "The price of Clayton's shares on the New York Stock Exchange fell nearly 18 percent in the week following the announcement of the board resignations, $24.875 from $30.25. . . (closing) Friday at $25.75."

With a price drop of $6.50 on 45 million shares, CMH shareholders lost $242 million. The drop in price cost me personally $69 million, since I owned 28.5 percent of the stock. Ouch!

When Ms. Grossman met with Kay and me at our home, I was scared to death. She had asked to see me at home and to have me perform a couple of country songs before we "jumped into the story." Hard driving at first, she mellowed upon seeing the story in a different light. We never got around to playing the guitar.

I can't imagine a public company CEO relishing a front-page interview with the *Wall Street Journal*. To me that's roughly equivalent to being interviewed on *60 Minutes*. Sure, they both run positive stories, but all we tend to remember are the negative ones.

It was my view that this reporter understandably had her trap set for me. After all, with directors resigning and making public a letter containing the language: "Given the nature and seriousness of the facts and allegations that have come to our attention . . . investigation by management is likely to prove inadequate." She had every right to expect me to be the devil in disguise.

The reporter was tough, with piercing and penetrating questions from the inception. However, after viewing documents, the CMH financial record, the credentials of our current board, and Rasmussen and Brad Reed's background in these situations, she began to swing more toward a balanced and objective approach to the story.

The reaction to the story was mixed. Some readers who were familiar with the company saw it as being balanced, or generally positive. Some saw the negative quotes as being negative and wanted our explanations.

Particularly after that article, Rich Ray and Joe Stegmayer spent a lot of time reassuring investors, mutual fund managers, and other large institutional shareholders that we were stable and on track.

To placate Wall Street, the company had to complete the investigation. I recommended that Joe Stegmayer assemble a team of internal auditors: Jim Shelby from Arthur Andersen; Tom McAdams, our local counsel; and others as needed. This would be a creditable, expensive, and thorough process.

Warren Neel, our newly appointed Audit Committee chairman, insisted that his committee hire another independent counsel, and that they receive the support of an independent accounting firm. Here, Warren's "academic side" showed strongly, as he wanted to use the "textbook process" to complete the investigation. It was his call, and I reluctantly supported his decision.

Recognizing how urgent it was to give Wall Street some specific answers to questions that had been raised by Rasmussen and Lomicka, several board members, including Warren and Dan Evins, interviewed several large Atlanta firms, choosing Sid Nurkin at Powell, Goldstein. Sid was tough and independent, but had a reputation for being practical, reasonable, and thorough.

As for accountants, Warren chose to again use Arthur Andersen, but not Bob Hensley and the Nashville staff who worked for Brad Reed. Instead, the work was assigned to Arthur Andersen's office in Atlanta.

Warren, thorough as he was, still took some interesting business risks as he expedited the process. I insisted the team inform him daily on the investigation activity, requiring details from Arthur Andersen on every item where he and Nurkin felt CMH did not need the protection of the attorney-client privilege. Otherwise, on those few items that did require the privilege, he'd require Andersen to direct its findings to the independent counsel exclusively.

Dr. Neel soon had his independent investigative team well directed and anxious to start the process. After being held up for weeks as Brad Reed refused to hand over his notes, eventually the *handwritten notes* were made available, but not before a lawsuit was threatened. Warren Neel had to go to Jim Cheek for help in finally obtaining enough information from Reed's files to restart the investigation. Sid Nurkin then was on his way.

CMH board minutes dated November 10, 1993, reflects Dr. Warren Neel's final Audit Committee report on the investigation.

The report covered Sid Nurkin's findings on all of the issues raised by the former independent investigator. You would think the two firms had investigated two different companies. Nurkin's findings and his report indicated, in my opinion, that issues raised by Reed either did not exist, were immaterial, or that processes had been implemented to correct and prevent any reoccurrence.

The mortgage clerk was re-interviewed, and made it clear that she was speaking generically and not referring to a specific practice employed by our company when she mentioned "straw loans." She also said that, during the interview with her, she'd never used the word "fraudulent." The other issues involved were equally misinterpreted or misunderstood.

With two outside board vacancies, I had to do some recruiting. Kay and I, along with the Neels, flew my jet to Grand Cayman for a long weekend of relaxation and scuba diving. With us were Jim and Kathy Cockman. Though the trip was announced as strictly social, Warren and I had another motive. We wanted to recruit Cockman, the CEO of Ocean Fish Express, to our board.

When we finally found a phone on the island, it was a "soft shoe shuffle." Joe Stegmayer told us that, with the resignations, we couldn't take board action required for the Merrill-Lynch financing without Cockman's vote. So Warren and I did a quick close on Cockman. In fact, he couldn't say no. We voted him in and immediately asked him to vote for the Merrill-Lynch finance deal, miraculously crafted by Rich Ray. (Jim would serve several years on our board, and Kay and I made several trips to the Caribbean with him and Kathy. They are dear friends.)

Rich Ray, Joe Stegmayer, and Warren Neel *walked on water* in completing the Vanderbilt financing through Merrill-Lynch. What a position for a "Wall Street Darling" to be in! Here's what we faced: Wall Street needed comfort that the investigation and related findings were without material relevance; but with the investigation continuing, management and those conducting the investigation were not permitted, by Bob McCullough and Nurkin, to provide Merrill-Lynch or the underwriting attorneys information as to the findings.

After the state tax problems caused by Schede, it was no surprise that Dr. Neel and the Audit Committee recommended that we immediately hire a full-time tax officer.

Rich retained Doug Franck, of Boult Cummings, in Nashville, to replace Jim Cheek as our SEC counsel, and got them to interview Warren Neel to get the flavor of the investigation, if not the facts. Cummings, wanting to complete the transaction for us and hoping to get our future business, was willing to take considerable risk to get the deal out of the chute and closed. Reluctantly, they agreed, and based on the interview with Dr. Neel and his verbal assurance that he had not uncovered even one material financial irregularity (which he could not state formally), the comfort letter required to complete the financing was provided.

Rich got a check for $135 million from Merrill-Lynch.

In July 1994, we recruited another member who would make significant contributions to the CMH Board of Directors—Wilma Jordan, Knoxville native and co-founder of the 13-30 Corporation, which later became Whittle Communications. Wilma served as CEO of *Esquire* Magazine Group before becoming CEO of her own firm, the New York-based Jordan, Edmiston Group. Her firm, with clients in the U.S. and overseas, offers a full range of investment banking and advisory services for the publishing industry. Wilma and I became acquainted when we served as co-chairs on the University of Tennessee's fundraising campaign for its College of Business from 1990 to 1992.

It turned out that Warren Schede, who had started this whole mess by stonewalling and antagonizing the auditor from the Department of Revenue, had been embezzling money to the tune of $3.8 million over eight years. From me—not the company.

Schede had been writing checks on the bank accounts of two communities that I owned: one in Knoxville (Green Acres), and another in Tullahoma. He was supposed to deposit the checks, made payable to one James L. Clayton, directly into my master account at First American Bank.

Instead, he deposited the checks in his personal bank account at Home Federal Savings & Loan.

Joe Stegmayer confronted Schede, showing him a stack of canceled checks endorsed by Home Federal, where I never had an account. Within moments, Schede "had fled the building."

We informed the Department of Revenue, and federal authorities charged him with mail fraud and money laundering. Schede's plea bargain got him a free vacation in a federal white-collar facility for three-and-a-half years.

Schede's stealing affected many lives, including his family, friends, his colleagues at CMH who trusted him, and all the share-holders at CMH.

I filed a civil suit against him. After his home, cars, boats, and jewelry, which had been bought with my money, were sold off, I received $1 million, or nearly one-third of the documented amount stolen. I believe I have an agreement somewhere, requiring him to pay me another $1 million someday. Anyone want to bid $100 for it?

This wasn't a company issue, after all. Schede, who had been with the company for 10 years, stole money exclusively from me. (Though he had other responsibilities at Clayton Homes, I had paid the company a fee for Schede to handle my private accounting.) He did, however, apparently skip paying sales taxes on some company accounts, along with those in my businesses. Clayton Homes immediately paid those back taxes, plus interest and penalties, totaling $163,000. Without contest, I voluntarily paid back taxes in an effort to settle and to reduce penalties and interest. The amount was $175,000.

Unyielding, Agent Smith would still not settle and close the file—either with CMH or with me. This took months.

We recruited Amber Krupacs, a senior tax manager from Coopers & Lybrand. Her technical qualifications were just what we needed, and the entire team felt she'd be comfortable in the hard-working CMH culture. She came on board in December 1993, and for several years, devoted her time to CMH tax matters and administrative functions.

Today, Amber wears several hats, serving as vice president of finance, and is responsible for the mortgage subsidiary's securitizations and operations. She is a highly qualified professional in finance, treasury, benefits, and tax.

Yet another nightmare was over. Within a year and a half after the summer of '93, Clayton Homes stock had stabilized. Once again, adversity helped us become stronger.

Frankly, I have to be the luckiest darn guy in the world to get out of that one alive. To think we had been able to fire an independent counsel. *This simply can't be done.* Just ask Bill Clinton.

In reflecting back on the seemingly unrelated events that linked up to create a most unfortunate situation for CMH and for me—a mistake I made was not getting around to completing the separation of systems and accounting between family and CMH. I personally paid the company for a portion of Schede's time, and this had been properly disclosed to the board. Lomicka, Rasmussen, and other board members knew that the officer group had ultra conservative spending habits. There was no question but what shareholder interest had been protected.

Certainly, I ended up with the loss from the Schede fraud. To make sure that this did not ever happen again, I knew to recruit the best possible talent to exclusively handle the family bookkeeping, accounting, and taxes. This was turned over to two highly competent individuals.

For the past decade, Jeanne Campbell has been my amazingly efficient accountant. Before joining us, she spent eight years in the banking industry, working her way through a business administration degree from UT (majoring in accounting). Jeanne played an important role in the creation of the Clayton Family Foundation. As she has watched the Clayton family grow, we've seen her family grow. She and her spouse, Dennis, a Sevierville attorney, have one daughter, Kelsey.

Jeanne, interestingly, was raised on a peppermint farm. Her dad had more than 200 acres of peppermint, and the whole family pitched in during planting and harvesting season. They sold peppermint oil by the barrel to buyers all over the country.

Jerry Hollyfield was successful in sports, a winning all-round athlete: all-state, all-region and all-conference in baseball, basketball, football, and track for Pound High School in Virginia. His level of achievement was so high that his baseball jersey—number 13—was retired by the school.

Jerry signed to play professional baseball with the Baltimore

Orioles, spent three years in their farm system (and as a relief pitcher, compiled an excellent 7-2 record, with 32 saves and a 2.83 earned run average). Pitchers aren't supposed to be able to hit, but even there he did good—a lifetime .250 batting average.

After Jerry left the Orioles, he received his degree from the University of Virginia in accounting and financial management, and by 1978, he was CFO and on the Board of Directors of the Cody Equipment and Supply Company in Wise, Virginia. In 1980, he opened his own accounting firm, which he operated until attending UT law school in 1987. He was admitted to practice law in November, 1990.

Jerry became a part of my team in October, 1993, responsible for tax, financial and estate planning, and he is responsible for compliance matters. He lives with his wife Cindy in Farragut, Tennessee. Cindy was named the top graduate in the master's program at UT in 1998, and she's now working toward her doctorate. They've been married 27 years with one son, Jerod, a college freshman.

With the "Schede Fiasco" finally behind us, I was approaching age 60. My time to run the company was winding down as well.

Actually, we started retirement planning in 1989, when I was 55. At the time, I told the board that I would retire in another 10 years at age 65. (When I said that, I didn't realize that 65 would come so soon.) Essentially, the board's response was, "Are you sure?" In fact, at every board meeting for the next 10 years, that's what I'd hear: "Are you sure?"

Kay and the kids were even more skeptical. They simply did not believe I could retire and leave CMH. When I told them I was leaving the company at age 65, they'd say, "Sure," and chuckle.

Their doubt was understandable. It's not easy for the founder of a company to leave his baby. In fact, most founders "flunk" retirement. Most will not trust another individual to lead their company, no matter how many sharp, capable, and qualified people are available from within—and outside of—the business.

But I saw what had happened to some of my counterparts, CEOs of other highly successful companies who couldn't or simply wouldn't walk away. Many had to be carried away.

One example is Sheldon Coleman, who invented the Coleman Lantern. He tried to retire twice. I visited him when he was 84, just after he became CEO of the Coleman Company for the third time. He died three weeks later.

I enjoyed knowing this personable and talented entrepreneur. He had built such a great company and huge conglomerate. He should have been enjoying his retirement years, instead of dying in the saddle.

I also remember my father, who died at age 60 in 1972 as he was getting out of the shower and dressing for work. He was just weeks away from retirement.

I was motivated long ago to manage my career so that I too wouldn't die in the saddle. But I knew retiring was tough as heck, unless it was planned and executed perfectly.

Let me tell you about two retirements that *were* planned and executed perfectly, in my opinion. The two retirees? Ty Kelly—and *me*. I think many entrepreneurs could learn from our experience. I'll tell Ty's story first.

For over 20 years as president of the manufacturing group, Ty had built us into the best in the industry. By 1993, still serving as president of the group, he and Brenda had built their wonderful dream home on the Tennessee River, seven miles downstream from Knoxville. It is a picture-perfect setting, with a beautiful view of the river and mountains, and two boats ready to launch.

In September, Ty asked me to stop by after work to see his new 45-foot Sea Ray Cruiser, but knowing Ty, I fully expected other agenda items to soon surface. One did, and it was a big one. As we passed Turkey Creek, Ty told me that Jim and Kelly Gilligan were moving to Ardmore, Tennessee, to manage our plant there and to be near her family. For the last 12 years, Jim had successfully managed our Maynardville plant.

The Gilligan's leaving Knoxville? That shocked me. I knew them well. Kelly was a lawyer and a terrific vocalist. We had a lot in common. I thought they would be in Knoxville permanently.

I asked Ty, "Do you have a good replacement for Jim?" His response floored me.

"I think so, but you may disagree," he said. He went on to explain how much he enjoyed the people at Maynardville and wanted to spend the rest of his career working with that team, while, of course, enjoying his boating activities with Brenda.

"Okay," I said, "Ty, give me a couple of years to work that out for you."

But Ty was determined. "Jim, you don't understand. I want the Maynardville plant now," he said. "I'll give you two weeks to decide. Do I get the plant or do I retire?"

As Ty gave me those two alternatives, he reminded me that Clayton stock options and its 401(k) had served him well, and both of his boats along with the new home were debt-free. "I can retire right now if you won't give me the Maynardville plant. It's no problem," he said.

You guessed it. Ty got the Maynardville plant, and fortunately, Kevin Clayton was ready to take his job as president of the manufacturing group.

Ty immediately went to work as the new general manager of the old Maynardville plant, and he and his team made record contributions to CMH for the next six years. He had an absolute ball running the plant and still had time to play with his new boat, just as he and Brenda had planned.

It was a wonderful way for Ty to close out a great career.

On June 30, 1999, Ty retired, the same day that I did. Ty and Brenda are thoroughly enjoying his retirement. They spend summers in Knoxville and winters in sunny Tampa, Florida, enjoying his new boat.

This, to me, was a perfect way to execute a planned retirement, and I'm happy to report that my transition into retirement worked just as well—virtually seamless.

Here's how mine worked. As mentioned earlier, Dr. Warren Neel and Professor Mike Stahl facilitated a strategic and succession planning program for CMH as early as 1989. So as retirement began to loom over the horizon, I didn't feel pressured, since we had done the proper planning. That's the key—doing it gradually. That makes the transition almost invisible, and the retirement doesn't shock the team, the shareholders, or the board.

During our seven o'clock breakfast meetings prior to the board meeting, the outside members and I would discuss each senior manager and the backups for each position. Joe Stegmayer was my designated replacement for a few years, after he moved from board member to president and COO in 1993; however, he left in 1997 for a rich opportunity with our friend Walt Young at Champion Homes.

When Joe left, Kevin Clayton was named president and COO, and was penciled in as my potential successor.

He wasn't "given" the job because he was the "founder's son." Kevin clearly earned his stripes.

He began his career with Clayton Homes when he was seven as a floor sweeper and "gopher" for Max Nichols at the Halls manufacturing plant. His pay was 75 cents an hour. It wasn't long before Kevin, always anxious to supplement his meager allowance, eagerly took jobs all over the company during evenings, weekends, and summers. His early work experience throughout the company gave him a unique perspective on the Clayton culture, and I think that experience serves him well today.

The summer he was 11, Kevin and his brother Jimmy spent $1,000 to purchase a home in Green Acres from an insurance company. The home needed extensive repair, and the two of them learned a lot about product, materials, income, expense management—and the Green Acres community. They repaired the home and sold it for a profit of $1,200. They did that repair work nearly

30 years ago. Since then, the home has served two families, and it's still there.

As a youngster, Kevin often flew with me to visit our stores and plants. One story I love to tell happened when he was 10. We were on our way to Alabama, stopping off in Somerset, Kentucky, to pick up Larry Davidson, who was managing the sales center there. Soon after landing, Larry hopped in the plane, sat in one of the rear seats—and saw Kevin, sitting on two phone books in the "driver's seat," begin to taxi toward the runway! I was exchanging greetings with Larry while helping him with his seat belts and pretended not to notice.

As Kevin slowed near the take-off point, Larry became silent. He looked pale. He was trying to raise his right hand and point toward the windshield, clearly scared out of his wits. He thought I was going to allow Kevin to fly the plane during takeoff and the climb out.

I was.

By age 10, Kevin had been flying for three years, with more than 100 takeoffs and landings without assistance. On his 17th birthday, he earned his private pilot's license, and by age 21, he had his commercial license.

Today, Kevin usually travels in CMH's King Air B200 turbo-prop, the one Jake Butcher bought new during the 1982 World's Fair. Most of the time, Kevin is the pilot.

While a teenager, Kevin worked in financial services as an account representative, a credit manager, and a new systems coordinator. He received his degree from James Madison University, spent a year on Wall Street with Prudential-Bache, and then earned an MBA at the University of Tennessee. After that, he began working his way "up the ladder" at Clayton Homes, spending two years as the Southern regional manager of the retail group. He turned a difficult acquisition asset, destined for closing, into profitability.

Kevin volunteered for the toughest positions, taking assignments that were turned down by others, including Waco, Texas; Tallahassee, Florida; and Nashville. In Waco, Kevin's title was sales manager, but he bought everything from the stapler to the copy machine, interviewed each person on the start-up team, and set up lasting relationships with high-quality retailers to buy the new homes from the two plants that he and the team built. He also developed the Team Profit Sharing (TPS) incentive plan and the physical layout for manufacturing used by all of our plants.

Kevin was also able to travel all over Texas inexpensively by flying the CMH small twin Cessna 310 that he kept in Waco.

By 1992, Kevin was back in Knoxville, at corporate headquarters, running our human resources and benefits department. A year later, he became president of the manufacturing group (taking over for Ty Kelly). In 1995, he was promoted to president of financial services.

By the time Kevin was named president and COO, the company was servicing $2 billion in mortgages, an almost 50 percent increase in only two years. Now it's over $5 billion.

During that two-year period from the time Kevin became president of the company in 1997 until my retirement in 1999, we increasingly made decisions together. This gave him credibility and set the stage for the much-needed smooth transition.

Within five years under Kevin's leadership the Market Capitalization (value of stock) of CMH would grow to $2.2 billion—more than all other companies combined in our industry ($1.5 billion). See the graph on the next page.

Communicating with Kevin is just as easy as it was during my 20-year partnership with my brother Joe. In fact, when I'm talking to Kevin, I frequently slip and call him "Joe" by mistake. I can't seem to break that habit.

Also smoothing the transition, I made each position on the executive team increasingly responsible for planned results while steadily releasing control over the years. With responsibility came accountability, and I hope, appropriate compensation,

Market Capitalization
$ Millions*

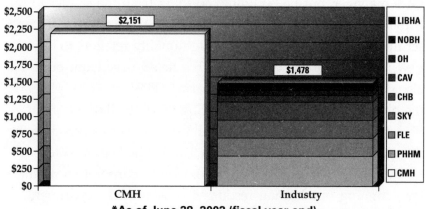

*As of June 28, 2002 (fiscal year end)

recognition, and autonomy.

Dr. Warren Neel and all the board, including Rasmussen, were great succession coaches. Their suggestions, which were often more like "demands," have proven to be insightful, although it sometimes took me a while to catch on.

For example, in 1994, when I turned 60, they asked me to start taking extended sabbaticals each year. I couldn't understand why in the world they would suggest that. After all, we were busy as ever. When I asked how long they wanted me to take off, they answered in unison, "at least a quarter."

Three months off? No way. But I did take a month off in March 1994. During the first week, my birthday week, I went skiing with friends in Beaver Creek and spent the rest of the month in Boca Raton, Florida, playing tennis and relaxing at our apartment.

Could a relentless, hard-charging entrepreneur like me enjoy a whole month off? You bet I could. I loved the month away.

Actually, I think Kay had more difficulty adjusting to the month off. As the end of March approached, she was anxious to return home to "touch her stuff." Truthfully, I would've loved another month in Boca Raton. But Kay was always happy to see the month end.

We result-oriented guys must always remember that our retirement can impact a relationship. Just being at home all day is such a change. You start getting—and asking—those questions: "Where are you going?" or "Where have you been?" or "When will you be back?" For both spouses, it's all new, and it can be quite stressful.

After successfully surviving my first "March Away," the board complimented me, and Kay and I have repeated the schedule each year since. This experience assured me that the board's succession plan would work, and that the management team and I could successfully play out our roles as required. By taking March off, I learned a lot about my relationship with (and my dependency on) Kevin and the senior management team of the company. My confidence level in them, always high, grew even more.

Yep, I would be leaving Clayton Homes in good hands.

During the transition period, I found it helpful to have varied outside interests, and I have plenty of those. Scuba diving, playing the guitar, singing, running—all have kept me from becoming bored even once.

Flying, of course, remains a joy. Tennis is another. When I began taking tennis lesson back in 1977, I knew even then this was something I could do as I got older. I've taken a lesson virtually every week for 25 years, except for a two-year layoff with tennis elbow back in the '80s. These days, I am scheduled three times each week with a great group of guys who play at Cherokee Country Club.

In 1999, I took two-thirds of the year off; this time, so Kay and I could build our dream home. It's near Neyland Stadium, overlooking the Tennessee River, and adjacent to where we had lived throughout our marriage. My friend, Raja Jubran, a commercial builder and a customer of my bank, shoehorned us into the new home in one year, as scheduled. Raja's $50,000 bonus, which was promised if the project was finished on time, was contributed to Habitat for Humanity and two other housing-related charities, just as we agreed. A word of advice: Don't ever try to build a big home in only 12 months.

Let me interject a story here that I love to tell. George and Joann Rothery live in the first house down the street from us, in sight from our bedroom. For years, we watched our lot remain vacant and were amazed as to why someone had not built on this large lot with a great view of the Tennessee River. Finally, Kay met Nancy, the daughter of Dr. Mose Howard, who had owned the land for years. We inquired about the land, and after a considerable time, bought the lot.

At the first meeting of our building crew, George came over, introduced himself, and chatted for a time. Anyone knowing George would know that 95 percent of the conversation was unilateral. As he turned to walk back to his home, I realized then the reason *why no one had built a home on the lot we had just purchased.* It was too late, we could not get out of our contracts, so we live next door to George Rothery.

I have fun telling that story. George probably tells it more than I do.

George Rothery is a very talented artist, and that rascal is getting better—even at his age. We really enjoy and appreciate our Rothery originals.

Kay and I moved into the house on June 30, 1999, the day I officially retired from the company.

Aside from the move, nothing special happened at Clayton Homes that day. There was no retirement party. I didn't want one. I felt that it would be too distracting and too expensive. Instead, I took the day off. Kevin and I wanted the transition to be smooth and as unnoticeable as possible.

Kevin, I'm still waiting on my gold watch.

CHAPTER 19

Buying Banks

By the mid-'90s, out-of-town banking conglomerates had bought most of the locally owned Knoxville banks, including Fountain City Bank, Bank of Knoxville, and Valley Fidelity Bank.

Customers enjoyed knowing their banking officer and, frequently, the directors and owners of the local banks. Disappointed that decisions were now being made across the plateau, on the other side of the mountain, or in Charlotte, Memphis, Atlanta, New York, or another out-of-town banking center, customers were shopping for new banking relationships.

Clayton Motors and later Clayton Homes depended on Fenton Kintzing and Valley Fidelity Bank, particularly during the early days of our businesses. In fact, had Fenton and Valley Fidelity not taken the time to know and trust us, Joe and I probably would have spent our careers in television.

First Tennessee Bank had purchased Valley Fidelity, and Fenton had been retired several years as the scene began to change dramatically. Joe, who was a long-time member of the Valley Fidelity Board of Directors, continued to serve on the First Tennessee Bank board.

A well-known career banker, Fred Lawson was CEO of the Bank of East Tennessee, which was built from "leftover pieces" of Jake Butcher's once powerful banking empire. Fred and a group of investors assembled assets purchased at huge discounts from the FDIC, formed a relatively tiny bank, and called it the Bank of East Tennessee. Within four years, BET became a $400 million local bank specializing in million-dollar small business and real estate loans to local entrepreneurs.

Bank of East Tennessee's success had not gone unnoticed. Union Planters Bank, a large public bank holding company with headquarters in Memphis, wanted to buy BET. Indeed, Union Planters was already performing its "due diligence," examining files and accounts to confirm the value of the bank.

During this process, Union Planters reviewed an acquisition that Fred Lawson had pending for the purchase of First Heritage Bank, with assets of $60 million and four branches in Loudon County and one in Knox. The price was less than $2 million, which would effectively grow to about $4 million with the immediate capital injection required by the regulators. Union Planters insisted that Lawson abort the acquisition, even though Fred had made a commitment to Lee Congleton, the owner of First Heritage Bank.

This was a tough spot for Fred. First Heritage had a troubled loan portfolio. Congleton had presented a number of prospective buyers to the regulatory officials, but each time, the deal fell through. The officials now gave Congleton a very limited amount of time to inject additional capital in First Heritage. Otherwise, they would close it. Congleton, a respected business leader, was like many of us—he'd lost a bundle in the Jake Butcher downfall. He'd recovered significantly, but decided to sell rather than invest additional capital in this bank.

Dr. Warren Neel, my good friend and a member of the Board of Directors of Clayton Homes, was also on the board of Fred Lawson's Bank of East Tennessee. Recognizing that both Lawson and Congleton were in a difficult position, Warren suggested that I might want to bid on the Bank of East Tennessee. The deal was just too rich for me. I would've had to use debt and liquidate a lot of securities to fund the purchase. Besides, BET was pretty much a "done deal" at this point, and indeed, Union Planters closed on it within a few weeks.

A few days later, Warren came back with another suggestion— buy First Heritage Bank and let Jim Caulkin, Fred Lawson's nephew, manage it.

So we did. Thanks to Fred Lawson, "due diligence" on the bank had already been done by BET; his staff had analyzed every loan and reviewed the securities and investments records. With Caulkin at the helm, we had a good CEO in place to show the regulatory people. Without him and Warren, I wouldn't have bought the bank. We put $1 million at risk to convince the regulatory people that First Heritage Bank and Lee Congleton had a buyer this time that could and would perform—one who wouldn't go away.

With audits done and management in place, the approval by the Tennessee Department of Banking and the FDIC was a simple matter of completing half a ton of paperwork. First Heritage Bank was ours, and I owned 100 percent—for a short time.

Jim Caulkin, absolutely terrific as he began marketing, operating, and training team members at First Heritage, was someone with whom I was comfortable. Jim's Uncle Fred, though under contract with Union Planters for six months, would be a great resource to the extent allowed by the contract.

Interestingly, when Fred completed his contract with Union Planters, he agreed to become our CEO at First Heritage. At the same time, Caulkin announced he would devote full-time to his real estate, broadcast, and other investments in Sevier County.

There was one small decision Fred wanted to make immediately with our help—a new name for the bank. None of us liked the name First Heritage. Shortly after the acquisition, all the bank's officers, along with Warren Neel, Tim Williams, Rich Ray, and myself, held a "sticky note session," also known as an identity exercise. Basically, we all sat around the table and brainstormed, writing down names for the bank on Post-It notes. Dr. Neel facilitated.

About three dozen names were considered. Half of us wanted the name to be 21st Bank, for the upcoming 21st Century. But our side lost. Lawson liked the other top pick—BankFirst.

The name BankFirst served us well until December 27, 2000. In six years, our fine team expanded that little five-branch, $60 million dollar bank to $800 million with 36 branches throughout Knox and adjoining counties. Along the way, we acquired additional assets, either by purchase or merger, including First National Bank of Gatlinburg ($200 million), Curtis Mortgage ($20 million), and First National Bank of Athens ($200 million).

The other name, though not used for the bank, turned out to be the perfect name for a new manufactured housing lender. Tim Williams grabbed it immediately after the meeting and uses it successfully today at 21st Mortgage.

Actually, I liked the name BankFirst, except that it's used by banks in other regions of the country, so it can't be used nationwide. (Besides, do we really need more banks that have "First" in its name?)

Fred began assembling a splendid team of veteran bank executives who brought blocks of business with them: Bob Sullivan, Steve Hagood, Mike Bryson, Missy Wallen, Jerry L. French, and others who'd teamed at Fred's Blount National Bank. The startup, as Fred opened in Knoxville and Maryville, was amazing.

With previous investors, Fred had to sell additional stock as the bank grew. But I promised him we'd keep BankFirst well capitalized. Warren Neel and I saw that our team would exceed growth and profit plans, which made it all the more important to hold ownership and the expected profit close, to benefit our board, executive officers, and customers.

Besides, since only a handful of people were involved back

when the risks were high—Lawson, Neel, me, the popular investor Fred Langley, along with a few others—I couldn't imagine bringing in other investors. In fact, when two highly respected, high net worth investors asked us about our needs for capital, I recommended they look for an investment that would provide more flexibility and a higher return. We let them keep their investment and our group happily kept a very high return on our BankFirst investment.

Over six years, the initial investors realized a 40 percent return. I am very appreciative of Lawson's leadership, Neel's guidance, and Langley's creativity. It made this venture a happy investment for our team.

Not only did Fred Langley invest early on, he added to his investment when we purchased the Gatlinburg bank. That was an interesting transaction. Without Fred's support, it probably wouldn't have happened.

Both the president and a director had left First National Bank of Gatlinburg. Reportedly, the FDIC terminated them and banned them from the banking industry. Rumors suggested the problem related to a poorly managed loan portfolio. According to the story, the director had been given options down through the years and thought the options were valid, but the bank's attorneys and accountants were adamant the stock options were no longer valid.

I made an offer for the bank, but was told that the bank's attorney, Jerry Becker (Lockridge & Becker was the firm that represented Kathy during our divorce), recommended the bank find a better offer. As a result, I began to buy the bank's stock. I called a number of stockholders who wouldn't sell to me, but since they'd bought CMH stock when we went public, they were happy to vote for me to take over their bank. I gathered far more votes than Becker and the board thought possible.

Even Denny Bortoff, the CEO of First American, Clayton's lead bank, made an offer for FNB, though he first called me to see if I would mind. Darn right I would mind! But his offer was in the newspaper the next morning. Denny had been Pat Harrison's boss and a good friend. We still are friends, but his offer sure offended most of my bank team. Still, I understand that friends can bid against each other. That's just business. We have to compartmentalize such issues.

Denny and I are on another NYSE board and see each other at least every quarter. I keep asking Denny why he did not go away when I told him I had the votes. Surely he knows I made good grades in arithmetic. Denny didn't come close to making his deal.

Thanks to Langley's creativity and my risking a couple of million, we soon had the director's options and sued the bank to force Becker, the divorce lawyer who represented the bank, and the board to issue the stock represented by the options. The Judge ruled for the director; we got the stock; Becker was discharged; and finally, I had the opportunity to communicate directly with the chairman and vice chairman that I'd been fighting with for the last year.

I instantly liked them both, Charles Earl Ogle Jr. and Geoffrey Wolpart. We became the best of friends and have enjoyed great times together, at board meetings as well as social events. In fact, Charles Earl is my vice-chairman on the local BB&T advisory board, and Geoff remains a board member. Geoff, his wife Pat, and I ski at Beaver Creek (our place) and Deer Valley (their place) together several times each year. We've also traveled extensively on scuba diving vacations.

With three acquisitions after buying First Heritage and forming BankFirst, we were large enough to take the banks public.

All of the acquisitions and the public stock offering were relatively easy. With Fred Lawson supplying his great team, Warren Neel giving us great strategic advice, and Fred Langley as a great cheerleader and deal maker during the very difficult Gatlinburg acquisition, it sure was painless for me.

The stock symbol was BKFR, and the offering was over-subscribed. Our managers, now with a market for their stock, were even more motivated to grow the bank and increase shareholder value because they too were owners.

Warren and I recommended that we allocate stock and options to the senior executives, a move that surprised Fred Lawson. I've never seen a more appreciative group of officers, as the value of their holdings multiplied. Later, some told me that they made more money in six years with that package than they'd made over their entire careers.

Before ending this section on BankFirst, I must issue some special thanks to Fred Lawson, Tennessee Commission of Banking; Stephen Hagood, senior credit officer; Jerry French, retail banking; David Allen, McMinnville County executive; David Butler, Sevier County executive; Bob Sullivan, Blount County executive; Michael Bryson, Knox County executive; Martha Wallen, small business banking; Jessica Rich, regional operations; Sharon Woods, private banking; all BankFirst senior officers; and those in senior regional positions with BB&T.

Likewise, special thanks go to the BankFirst corporate board, including, again, Fred Lawson; Charles Earl Ogle Jr., vice chairman; Andy Walker Jr., Scott Mayfield, Geoffrey Wolpart, David Sullins Jr., and Warren Neel, chairman of the Audit Committee. I was chairman of the board.

In 1995, while attending the Tennessee Banking Convention, I was introduced to Burney Warren III, the manager of acquisitions for BB&T, a large banking conglomerate based in Winston-Salem. BB&T was aggressively acquiring banks and wanted BankFirst to consider joining them. I wasn't interested. But Burney stayed in touch with me—no pressure, just always inviting me to Winston-Salem to tour the BB&T facilities.

I watched BB&T expand geographically while growing their earnings. In 1999, I agreed to accept Burney's long-standing invitation. We'd likely be able to gather some information that we could bring back and use. Fred Lawson and Warren Neel went with me. Even then, I told Burney that I wasn't interested in selling BankFirst, but I'd heard so much about BB&T that I thought I might learn something and would enjoy seeing their operations.

BB&T flew us to Winston-Salem in their King Air, and all three of us were instantly impressed with BB&T—its culture, values, focus, and commitment. In particular, we liked the fact that they practiced "localizing" those functions, impacting their customers, while centralizing systems and functions where control and economies could be better realized.

The six-person senior management team, headed by Johnny Allison, their chairman and CEO, was very impressive. With Allison's knowledge, experience, and leadership qualities, along with the support of Kelly King, the bank's president, and other members of the executive team, it was easy to see how they achieved success.

They made it clear that decision-making would remain on our side of the mountain, rather than at headquarters, which is what you'd normally expect in a merger. Since BB&T has such a unique culture and does so much training, they trust local people to make the larger decisions. We liked that a lot.

In short, the merger made sense to us. With BB&T, we could provide Knoxville's largest companies with any banking service they needed. For the first time, such services as personal and commercial insurance, investment banking, factoring, and international and municipal finance products would be available to our customers.

After visiting other large regional banks that were acquisitive, the decision to complete the BB&T transaction was easy to make. It was completed in December 2000, and the name change, from BankFirst to BB&T, took effect at all the branches in July 2001.

At the time of the transaction, which was valued at $216 million, I owned over 40 percent of the bank. Over the next six years, I'd continued to add capital with each acquisition.

For the position of regional president, Johnny Allison promised us their very best candidate. In particular, Fred Lawson appreciated that, since he was near retirement age. In fact, when we purchased the first bank, Fred told us we'd get three to five more years from him before he retired.

Allison came through with his promise, giving us Lars Anderson, whom we liked instantly. He was cut from the same mold as Allison and Kelly King, someone with a very impressive focus, work ethic, and people skills.

Lars was well seasoned and had been with BB&T since 1984, serving in numerous retail and commercial lending management positions, including BB&T's executive for Charleston, South Carolina, and Greensboro, North Carolina.

Lars accepted the regional president position of East Tennessee in March 2001. I'm proud to be his chairman and on the board and the executive committee of BB&T in Winston, Salem, which owns the banks in Tennessee.

The BB&T merger made me the largest individual shareholder of the 12th largest bank in the country.

It was October 2001, when on my answering machine, there was a voice I hadn't heard in half a century. The message went something like this:

"Jim, we haven't spoken in 50 years, but we were in the 11th and 12th grades together at Chester County High School. I rode a motorcycle. We played pool together a few times, and I lived just up the street from Bobbie Jo Maness, whom you dated in high school . . .

The caller went on:

"First State Bank is about to be sold at a cheap price. Wouldn't it be neat to own the 'Main Bank' in our old hometown? Please call me back."

The message was from my old friend, Dr. Steve Ellis, now living in Greenville, South Carolina. When I called back, his wife Billie Lou answered, another voice from the past. I remembered her immediately—Billie Lou Tarpley, our class valedictorian at Chester County High School, the "brain" in school, as I reminded her in our conversation. At the time of the call, she and Steve had been married nearly 46 years.

For the next few minutes, "Blue," as family and friends know her, filled me in on the times of their lives:

Steve and I were married in December 1955, in the middle of his senior year at Washington University in St. Louis, while I was completing an internship in Dietetics at Barnes Hospital. After Steve got his degree in chemical engineering, we lived in Saginaw, Michigan, where I worked at Saginaw General Hospital, and Steve worked for Dow Chemical in nearby Midland.

When the Russians launched Sputnik in 1958, we decided Steve would go back to Washington U to get his doctorate and help "win the Space Race" against the Russians. Steve's doctoral dissertation was titled, "Gaseous Diffusion at Elevated Temperatures," which dealt with keeping spacecraft from burning up when re-entering the atmosphere.

While in graduate school, Steve got interested in computers, and in June 1962, went to work for IBM in St. Louis.

In 1965, IBM moved us to Lancaster, South Carolina, for two years, then to Charlotte, North Carolina, for three years, then to Greenville. After that, we decided we didn't want to move again. Steve opted to be an IBM salesman in one place.

Steve was with IBM for 25 years, took an early retirement option in June 1987, and became a college professor at Clemson University for the next nine years. He retired when he turned 62 in May 1996.

We still live in the middle of 20 acres of woods. Our time is occupied with our four children and seven grandchildren, who all live nearby.

Steve came in from his chores, got on the line, and quickly explained the situation. The offer to buy First State Bank in Henderson, already accepted unanimously by the FSB Board of Directors the previous month, was from Jim Ayres of the First Bank organization. Ayres was offering $172.84 a share.

Since Billie Lou now owned stock in First State (inherited from Steve's uncle, Burl Smith), the two of them had studied the prospectus outlining the acquisition, mailed to every stockholder, and called for a special meeting to ratify the board's vote. They concluded the $172.84 per share offer was too low.

Steve, knowing that I was BB&T's largest individual shareholder and that I'd been the principal investor and chairman of BankFirst, merging it with BB&T, was now suggesting I buy First State Bank.

I didn't even know FSB was for sale. I was interested, certainly. First State was a desirable acquisition, maintaining a solid customer base and over a 70 percent share of the market. But it sounded like it might be too late to get in the game. After all, the FSB board, and officers, had already approved the acquisition. Was this indeed a "done deal"—or was there an opportunity to place a late bid?

Steve had determined there were three large shareholders who owned about 51 percent of the bank. With a combined vote of their shares, those three could determine the outcome of the shareholder vote required to confirm the board's decision to sell First State Bank.

Before the death of Paul Barret Jr. in December 1999, he had been the largest FSB stockholder, with 34 percent. Steve, contacting the Probate Court Clerk of Shelby County, obtained a copy of Barret's will. He learned that Barret, who was not married and had no known heirs, left everything to a charitable trust fund, making it almost certain that his interest in First State Bank would be sold.

After speaking with me, Steve reached John Douglas, the co-executor of the Barret estate, and was assured that the First State Bank acquisition was not a done deal. Steve also discovered precisely who held the controlling interest along with the Barret estate—Barret's sister, Rebecca Matthews, with 12 percent, and Trustmark Bank, with 5 percent. (Another Paul Barret bank had originally owned the 5 percent, but Trustmark acquired the interest when it bought that bank.)

Thanks to Steve's persistence, we now knew who the three majority stockholders were, and better yet, learned that all three parties were definitely interested in a better deal. We had a shot at getting an opportunity to bid.

Now I began doing my homework. I knew that, under the leadership of Jack Bulliner, the President and CEO of First State since 1970, the bank had experienced steady growth and enormous customer loyalty, in part because of the company's culture, and management's long-time personal approach to the needs of its customers.

I began to formulate a strategy to buy out the "Big Three."

We contacted the attorneys for the majority stockholders and offered to buy the bank for $191 a share, about $20 a share over the original offer. Ayres countered with a matching offer. I increased mine to $200 a share, agreeing to purchase the shares of all 100 smaller shareholders at the same price.

Before the vote, Steve and Blue, along with several of their cousins, contacted most of the minority shareholders, making sure they knew to vote "against" the Ayres offer in order for me to win. They came through. Only about 5 percent of the minority shareholders did not vote "against." There was also one vote to abstain from our friend Paul Matthews.

We're not angry, though. Some people are just born with a double dose of contrariness.

I bought First State Bank in December 2001. There are three branches, all in Henderson, with current assets of $147 million. I am the sole owner.

On January 25, 2002, at the regular stockholders meeting of First State Bank, I was welcomed by the officers, directors, staff, and shareholders. I had a wonderful day meeting with them; seeing friends and family; and enjoying a celebration dinner on the way back to my plane with Jack and Patsy Bulliner, their daughter Randi, Steve and Billie Lou Ellis, and Matt Daniels, the president and COO of FSB Holding, which holds the bank. Also with us were Clayton and Linda Skinner (Clayton, my cousin, joined the FSB board, where his father, Charlie Skinner, has served for two decades).

First State Bank has a long and distinguished history. It started back in 1889 as Farmers and Merchants Bank. In 1931, it merged with Chester County Bank to form FSB. In 1985, when the movie theater in Henderson closed, Jack Bulliner purchased the building in a 30-minute transaction, and today, the place where Henderson citizens once watched movies, ate popcorn, and smooched is now the home of First State Bank. Jack's office used to be the lobby, where the popcorn was popped.

Incidentally, Jack, who started working at First State at age 16, has now been at the bank for more than half a century. Actually, Jack was ready to retire to spend more time with his wonderful wife Patsy, gorgeous daughter Randi (an attorney), and grandson Adam, but he graciously agreed to stay on "just as long as you need me," to help smooth the transition for our customers and team members.

Most investors would have immediately recruited a high-powered CEO. In turn, the CEO would have brought in his or her own senior officers. Often, a new team "points fingers" at the departing group, writing off everything possible to make the next several quarters look better. This would've made Jack and his team look bad, while the new CEO would appear to be a hero.

Instead, at First State Bank, Matt and Jack recruited three outstanding vice presidents: Jeff Baker as CFO, Teresa Eubanks as HR/Tech manager, and Steve McCormack as senior loan officer. These three executives, along with our other officers at the bank, will soon be searching from within, or on the outside, for a CEO who subscribes to our values and beliefs.

All of us involved in the CEO recruiting process, including our three new VPs, will individually vote only for a candidate that we can commit to support in every way possible to be successful. The new CEO, in turn, will be urged to accept the role only if he or she can commit to assisting and supporting our management team to be personally and professionally successful, both individually and collectively.

One word about Matt Daniels, the COO of FSB Holding: He is 24 years old, the son of a minister and public schoolteacher, a magna cum laude graduate of UT, past president of Sigma Phi Epsilon (my fraternity), and married to Megan, who teaches fourth grade. Eight months after joining FSB, Matt was part of a team that implemented a new data processing system, reduced delinquency by over 5 percent, initiated risk-based pricing, and instituted performance-based compensation.

Matt's younger brother, Michael, has been working for me as a personal intern since May 2000 and is completing his degree as this book is printed.

Both of them exemplify a key ingredient in the Clayton culture—flexibility. Without it, you won't be successful, no matter what the job is. In particular, if you don't display flexibility doing small tasks, you won't get the opportunity to handle greater responsibilities.

CHAPTER 20

The Dream Continues

Now that we're approaching the end of the book, it might be a good time to throw out some "bouquets" to the people around me who have given so much of their time and talent down through the years. I only hope that everyone understands that, as much as I'd like, I can't list all of the people who deserve mention. If I did that, this book would be at least 5,000 pages!

Earlier, in Chapter 18, we had the opportunity to recognize Kevin, my son and CEO of Clayton, for his education, leadership, and accomplishments. Now permit me to toss a few bouquets to other members of the CMH senior management team.

David Booth has been president of the Clayton Retail Group since 1990. For 300 of our managers and 1,000 of our salespeople, David is head cheerleader and chief disciplinarian—with a keen sense for recruiting and retaining the best people.

From 1977 to 1987, David was with Conner Homes Corporation, our competitor for many years. By the time he was 35 years old, he was an executive vice president of the company.

Until David joined us, it was a standard belief in the industry that it was impossible to successfully manage more than 100 sales centers. But with the 1991 acquisition of 20 Country Squire sales centers in Georgia and South Carolina, the number of Clayton retail stores jumped to 123.

Several companies, including Mobile Home Industries, Conner Homes, and River Oaks Industries had grown past the 100-store barrier. But within a few quarters, all had failed. There were several common factors which appeared to cause their failure—all were undercapitalized, lacking in systems, inadequately staffed, expanding into new geographic regions, and attempting to grow over 50 percent each year.

With those factors addressed at CMH, our board was comfortable approving David's request to complete the acquisition.

Of late, three of our vertically integrated competitors—Champion, Fleetwood, and Oakwood—have closed many of their stores, purchased at very high prices. Champion has about 116 stores open and has closed over 160, while losing close to $400 million over the past three years, far more than their net worth. Fleetwood's numbers are not significantly different. In fact, their loss is just over $400 million in only the last two years. Our friends at Oakwood have also reported losses of $400 million over the past three years, but the number of store closings are now at 216, while they are now operating 196.

Integrated Companies

COMPANY	STORES	PLANTS
Clayton Homes	290	20
Oakwood Homes	196	19
Palm Harbor	152	15
Fleetwood Enterprises	135	27
Champion Enterprises	116	37

Numbers as of October 2002, based on company news releases.

Store Closings

COMPANY	PEAK	CURRENT	CLOSED
Clayton	318	290	28
Fleetwood	244	135	109
Champion	280	116	164
Oakwood	412	196	216

Numbers as of October 2002, based on company news releases.

These numbers and the trends would indicate that we will have far less competition next year.

By 1995, David successfully managed our retail growth to 200 company-owned stores. As of 2002, we have 287. Supported by a seasoned home office team, together with talented regional and sales center managers, David continues to defy industry trends.

David's leadership has allowed the retail group to upgrade our retail leadership academies. He and his senior managers bring in more than 500 team members each year for training. He also championed the use of LINK in 1999, which connects all of our team members whether they are at home, traveling, or even out of the country. LINK uses inexpensive local Internet providers to connect our offices and people. Data can be transmitted two-way for credit applications, approvals, income statements, and delinquency data, instead of using dedicated long-distance lines.

The entire industry agrees that David is the best in the world at leading a retail manufactured housing group.

Rick Strachan has had a truly outstanding career. He began with Ford Motor Company, where he helped launch the Mustang in the '60s, as an engineer and management trainee.

In 1969, he became general manager and director of sales for Golden West Mobile Homes. Later, he was vice president of manufactured housing operations for Atco Industries, followed by a five-year stint as senior vice president, and then president, of

Ryland Modular Housing. From 1989 to 1994, Rick was president and chief operating officer of the Visador Company, which specialized in building materials.

Then Kevin Clayton recruited Rick to join the CMH team. Rick was named regional operations manager of the manufacturing group in 1994 and became its vice president and general manager in 1995. A year later, when Kevin left manufacturing to head financial services, Rick was promoted to president of manufacturing, where he remains today.

After Kevin introduced TPS (Team Profit Sharing) at our Waco manufacturing operations, Rick has since rolled this out nationally to all CMH plants. TPS, an extension of open-book management, teaches and motivates all team members to make daily decisions that maximize profitability over the long term.

This provided an opportunity for Rick to introduce the "Buy Off" Support System, or BOSS program, part of a six-sigma quality process that has led to Clayton Homes having the lowest service costs in the industry, at 2.5 percent.

Even during 2001 and the worst industry turndown in more than 25 years, the Clayton Manufacturing Group remained profitable. Under Rick Strachan's guidance, Clayton Homes did not close a single plant, a remarkable accomplishment in an extremely cyclical industry.

Active Manufacturing Plants

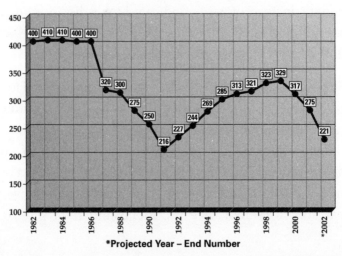

*Projected Year – End Number

Rick has a passion for adding value to the homes we build. This has helped set us apart in the industry.

Incidentally, when Rick introduced BOSS, he partnered with his operations manager, West Point graduate Rick Boyd, a licensed engineer with superb leadership abilities.

Our CFO, John Kalec, joined us in 1996 after holding senior financial positions with Philips, the Dutch multinational company. He had been with Philips for 20 years, including a four-year stint in the Netherlands as managing director of finance and accounting for the company's worldwide components division.

He and his family had just returned to the States, and were living in Princeton, New Jersey, when I received a call from Pam Jordan, my former secretary. Pam described John as very talented and anxious to relocate his family back to the area. (John once held a senior financial position with Philips-Magnavox consumer electronics in Knoxville).

I knew John would not know our industry, but it appeared he had the education, experience and intelligence to learn fast. Later that month, I met him in New York during an investor conference, and I was impressed with the manner in which he represented his company. Back in Knoxville, I talked with a number of people who knew John and his wife Karen. The feedback was all positive. We quickly extended an offer, which was accepted. His impact on the company was immediate, as he facilitated the implementation of a comprehensive strategic planning and budgeting process.

After a couple of years with us, John had an offer from an Oak Ridge technology company. It was an extraordinarily difficult decision for him, but John decided to leave us and was not looking forward to giving me the news. Later, he told me it was one of the toughest days of his life.

"When I approached you that day, I figured one of three things would happen. I would be asked to leave that morning; I would be asked to clean out my desk and say goodbye after lunch; or, best case, maybe I would be allowed to stay until the end of the day. Needless to say, I was prepared for the worst."

But the "worst" didn't happen. I knew John had done his homework and had made a tough call. I told him I understood, respected his decision, and asked him to consider joining the Clayton Board of Directors.

When John left as CFO, I took some risk and did not fill his position for three years. Instead, we assigned a variety of the CFO functions to several others, including investor relations to Carl Koella, vice president of accounting to Amber Krupacs, and reporting and controller to Greg Hamilton.

Wall Street readily accepted this structure, but only because they knew John left us with a truly outstanding staff.

For three years, all of us on the board enjoyed John's valuable insight in his director role. Then, recovering from "Internet fever," John called and invited me to Shoney's for breakfast where he told me that he'd be available to us in a few weeks. I was delighted. "As soon as you are ready," I said.

Our people were excited to have him back too, though there was some concern that John "might not be John" after the whirlwind life he'd lived for three years on the Information Highway. But after John met with Kevin and David, they quickly saw he hadn't changed. Once again, John had universal acceptance.

Incidentally, our senior management was recognized by the New York Stock Exchange with the opportunity on August 12, 1998, to "ring the bell" to start the trading day. Presidents, prime ministers, and kings have been among those who've had the chance, but on this day it was this "hillbilly" and his team from Tennessee who were center stage.

The ringing of the bell takes place at 9:30 A.M. eastern on the dot. If you watch the market during the day, you know that the financial networks like CNBC show the event live, and it's flashed all over the world. CNN also carried the event live. Since it was Friday and a slow news weekend, they kept replaying the tape over and over again all weekend.

People that I had not heard from for years called to let me know that they saw the event. Friends, team members, and shareholders told us they watched. Participating with me in the ceremony were David Booth, Rick Strachan, Allen Morgan, Kevin, and Kay.

Carl Koella, our vice president of investor relations, joined us in June 1991 after graduating in the top 10 percent of his class from the University of Chicago's MBA program. This after graduating from Duke University—Phi Beta Kappa, no less—and two years in the finance division of First Tennessee Bank's corporate headquarters.

Among other things, Carl focused on self-insurance programs for the retail group and the partnership program as CMH director of special projects; led a financial services group process improvement team that designed over 100 new programs for our insurance operations; and, as insurance marketing manager, began a successful MBU to market an extended warranty program.

In 1996, Carl was promoted to investor relations manager. His relationships with analysts at Goldman Sachs, Merrill Lynch, First Boston, Prudential Securities, and others have been of enormous benefit to Clayton Homes. On our equity road shows in New York, Boston, and Chicago, portfolio managers frequently tell me Carl is the best person in investor relations that they've dealt with at *any* company.

Carl won well-deserved national recognition—the 2001 *Barron's* Magazine Investor Relations Award for Best Communications with the Retail Market.

Carl became an officer of the company in 1998.

Jess and Linda Haun, two of our wonderful Clayton team members, work together at the Norris Homes sales center in Nashville. When Jess joined us back in 1969, he started at the Clinton Highway location. During one December, when business should have been slow, he closed 23 of the 28 homes sold from the sales center that month.

"I probably wasn't as polished as some of the other guys, but you don't need polish," he says. "You need drive, desire, and willpower."

I saw that Jess had those qualities in abundance and sent him to Athens and Jackson to open new sales centers. In Jackson, he met Linda, and on their first date, they went to visit one of Tennessee's most famous bootleggers. But not to buy whiskey, instead, Jess was trying to sell the bootlegger a home!

Over the years, Jess has been named Clayton's Manager of the Year half a dozen times. His sales center consistently tops $5 million in sales. In 1986, Linda, then the manager of a Cracker Barrel gift shop, joined Jess at the sales center after he suffered a heart attack. It was supposed to be temporary, but Linda sold 23 homes in her first month on the job. She was named Salesperson of the Year for 1986.

Today, all five children work in the industry; Jess and Linda have used Clayton bonus money to furnish their spacious home in Hermitage, a Nashville suburb; and they go to Cancun every chance they get.

"We've just about worn that place out," laughs Linda.

"If you follow the Clayton retail manager program, the money's naturally there," says Jess.

Here's something about Dick Rector that won't surprise anyone who knows him: At the sales center he runs with his fine team, there has not been one customer complaint from the thousands of homebuyers that Dick and his superb staff have serviced over the years. That's an enviable—and incredible—record.

I could write another book on Dick and Loraine, who have unselfishly given so much of their time to the company. Dick, as an instructor for hundreds of Clayton classes, has served as a mentor to so many of our people.

Dick and Loraine have been together more than 40 years. It has been my pleasure, and Kay's, to travel the world with them as well as spend time at their beautiful estate on Fort Loudon Lake.

Incidentally, Dick was recruited to Clayton by his wife's wonderful sister, Marjorie.

You'll recall Marjorie and her husband Jim Ausmus were mentioned earlier in the book regarding Jim's former fear of flying, which was "cured" when he began working with us as finance manager at the car dealership in 1969.

In December 1972, Jim opened the Greeneville sales center and has been there ever since. He and Marjorie have two daughters, Jimmie Sue and Janet, and one granddaughter, Logan.

Since I taught Jim to fly in '69, he has flown about 7,000 hours in the six airplanes he has owned.

Remember the old saying from the TV commercial: When E.F. Hutton talks, everyone listens? Well, when John Moore and his wife Doris talk about picking stocks, choosing investments, and managing money, we at Clayton Homes listen.

Of all the CMH sales center managers, John is believed to have the highest net worth, and for the past 20 years, he and Doris have been major landowners of hundreds of acres in the Jackson, Tennessee, area.

John was recruited to us by Jess Haun and began work at the Jackson sales center in 1974. He'd be the first to say that Doris, who operates her own tax office, has played a huge role in their financial success. The two of them have also done a wonderful job mentoring our new Clayton managers.

Their oldest son Jay is a team member at the Jackson store, where he does the "set-up" of our homes. Their youngest, Jake, a junior at Lexington High, loves the guitar.

John and Doris had a wonderful daughter, Misty, who they lost to cancer in 1993. What a beautiful and courageous young girl. When she passed away, our entire company comforted this popular, much beloved couple during that tragic time. Particularly on occasions like this, our Clayton team members are so much like family.

Larry Yantz started with the company in 1976. A high school basketball star married in 1966 to Mary Ann, they have three wonderful sons.

While working in Kentucky for a casket company in 1976—that's right, a casket company—Larry drove down to Somerset, Kentucky, to deal on a repo that he saw me hype on *Startime.* It was there that he met Larry Davidson, who preached some Clayton to him and showed him the awards and travel incentives that he had won over the years. Suddenly, Larry Yantz wanted to quit that casket company.

For three years, he managed the service department at the Somerset sales center and delivered record numbers. At one lot promotion in 1980, he sold more homes during a weekend than all of the other salespeople combined.

In 1987, Larry realized his dream to return to his hometown in Stanford, Kentucky, and open a Clayton store.

Since then, he has operated an exemplary business—over 50 percent of his business is referral, and his advertising expenses are zero. He and Mary Ann have been to Hawaii four times on our incentive vacations, along with trips to the Caribbean and Europe.

Jerry Moses, one of our most valuable team members, has been with the company since January 1974. Ty Kelly recruited him for the Halls plant at just the right time. Jerry's wife Carol didn't like the tornado-prone Oklahoma flatlands.

During the '70s, Jerry opened a sales center in Harold, Kentucky, then returned to Knoxville and began setting up retailers in Virginia and West Virginia. In the '80s, as a sales representative, he shipped over $20 million in new homes from our factories to his independent retailer friends. Upon Ty Kelly's retirement in 1999, Jerry became general manager of the Maynardville plant. Today, instead of retirement, he works directly for Rick Strachan, our president of manufacturing, on a variety of special projects. Many of our new models are beautiful and price-competitive because of Jerry. He has an excellent eye and feel for pleasing homeowners.

We believe Jerry has sold more manufactured homes than any person on Earth! He is the best.

Eddie Venable started with us in 1972. For 27 years, he has managed our sales center in Middlesboro, Kentucky. He started with Clayton's at age 19, and I'll never forget the first time we met.

Eddie was working for an independent dealer as a third-year college student with plans to become a lawyer. I happened to be on his lot, just looking around and checking out the competition with another Clayton manager.

Eddie recognized me from TV, since he'd been watching *Startime* for years. I asked if he'd mind showing me some of his display homes. He was very nice, a good salesperson, and just for fun, he gave me a "closing statement." I laughed and said, "Y'know, I like this house," and he said, "I tell you what, let's just fill out an application, and I believe I can get it for you." I laughed real big, and we parted until the following Saturday.

As my manager and I got back in his car, I said, "Johnny, don't let the sun go down until you've hired Eddie."

Three hours later, Johnny and Eddie went to lunch. The following Saturday night, Eddie, his wife Brenda, Mary, and I enjoyed a nice dinner at Regas. Eddie and Brenda were sold.

In preparing this book for publication, Brenda said that Eddie, who lost his mother and father at an early age, considered me a father figure. I am deeply touched and flattered.

On November 2, 2002, we celebrated Eddie's 30th anniversary with the company at my home, with about 50 of us old-timers.

I must say a few words about my wonderful children here. I've already bragged on Kevin, but I still have Karen, Jimmy, and Amy to go.

As mentioned earlier, Karen is married to Gordon Davis, who is the chief pilot and aviation manager for Clayton Homes. They live near me, with four wonderful children: Flynt, 23; Kevin, 21; Reed, 16; and Chris, 14. Flynt is in law school now, and Kevin is majoring in marketing at the University of Tennessee. (He also works part-time at the Clayton corporate office in telephone marketing of specialty mortgage and insurance products.)

Karen received the bachelor's degree in interior design from the University of Tennessee, which is easy to understand when you see their beautiful and elegantly decorated home. Beginning in October 2000, she, along with business partner Hanely Testerman, began doing "trunk shows" for the New York clothing line Etcetera.

As I discussed earlier in the book, Karen sang with me for years on *Startime*. We had a ball singing the old songs from the '60s at my last birthday celebration in Beaver Creek. She is a wonderful mother and homemaker—and a beautiful person.

Jimmy and his wife Lisa have three wonderful children: Craig, 11, Corey, 9, and Chase, 6. Jimmy received his degree in finance at the University of Tennessee and is currently managing a credit unit for Vanderbilt.

He has worked in numerous roles within the company, including regional management, retail and community management. Five years ago, Jimmy took a year off from operations to manage the construction of our unique corporate headquarters building.

Amy, our youngest, is married to John Stevens. They live in Virginia. Both have master's degrees in education from William and Mary, and both teach high school. He's a coach. She teaches English literature. They have one daughter, Maren, who is very special to me. Maren was born on July 4th two years ago, the first granddaughter after a seven card straight of boys.

When Amy was two, she sang "Twinkle, Twinkle Little Star" on *Startime*, and in November 2002, she was still singing. She was marvelous, as she had the starring role in a large, regional musical production.

Istill have dreams. I dream that I'm 90 years old, still playing tennis with Kay, and enjoying my grandchildren and great-grandchildren. I'm flying my helicopter, or jet, or possibly my glider, and it's my 90th birthday. With the glider, it's real "basic flying"—it's relaxing to see the countryside from the aircraft. The ridges below look familiar as I fly over the Tetons in Wyoming—or is it the mountain range at the southern tip of Maui? What a way to see God's green Earth.

That said, we are at the finish—of the book, that is.

The real journey never ends. You never get "there." Perhaps that's the way it should be.

You see, it's not where you wind up that's so important. It's what you did along the way—the lives you touched, the work you did, the people you loved, and the dreams you lived.

I've drafted several versions of these last few paragraphs. None I liked as well as a CMH newsletter article, "The Road Ahead," which I penned a few weeks before handing over the CEO position to Kevin on July 1, 1999.

Please flip the page to read the article.

Epilogue I

Tonight, as I write this, I am in a small but shockingly expensive hotel room in Boston with Carl Koella, our investor relations director. I miss Kay. She normally travels with me, but she stayed behind this trip to pack for the move into our new home. It would be good to have her here to help me plan and organize, as tomorrow morning the first of six investor meetings starts at 7:30. By the time Carl and I leave for Knoxville, we will have retold the Clayton Homes story to portfolio managers and analysts at Fidelity, Putnam, and to other large CMH shareholders. This is my 15th year of "show and tell" as your CEO.

With a 7:30 meeting and a long day tomorrow, I must get some words into the laptop before I hit the "hay." For me, starting is the hard part of writing, and I always procrastinate, just as I did in preparing for law school exams years ago. However, when I finally get started, it flows fast, and I enjoy the process. After all, it is good therapy to pause and reflect back on your life. It seems I do more of that nowadays.

This article is special, at least to me, as it is my last one as your CEO. By the time this is published, Kevin will have taken the reins, and I will be your retired, non-executive chairman.

Where did the time go? How did I get to age 65 so fast? It seems only yesterday that I sold an old car through a classified ad from the fraternity house. That was in 1953. That endeavor led to a tiny car lot on Clinton Highway, where, with the help of my brother Joe Clayton, our company began in 1956. WOW! That doesn't seem like 46 years ago, but if my math is correct our company has been around that long.

How can this be... me, retired? After all, I am blessed with good health and most days, I feel young. A lot of thought and planning have gone into this decision over the last decade. Too, I have discussed the subject numerous times with family, board members, your senior management team, and, of course, Kay. Is this what I want to do? The answer is a strong "No!" Then why retire? I am frequently asked that as of late.

The answer is, it is the right thing to do for me, for Kay, and for the company. How do I know that? Because it was 10 years ago when the board started asking about succession plans. I confess, I did not listen much at first, but it was soon evident that they were dead serious about having a plan in place and were not about to let the subject drop. Any chairman knows that the board can make life real difficult when they remain concerned about an issue. Seeing they were determined, I began sketching a plan and seriously dialoguing with them. In fact several times each year, for 10 years now, I have met privately with the members of our board, separately and as a group. There, we talk about succession for me and for each member of the executive team.

Ten years ago the board helped me happily implement a plan for my retirement to take place at fiscal year end following my 65th birthday—and here it is.

Over the years, some of the names on the succession chart have moved around, but I could not be more pleased for CMH, and for me, as to the way that this has played out.

I was helped along in this process by watching founders of other companies as they addressed this same issue. Some retired at normal retirement age. Some did not. Some returned to grab the helm again and again. Clearly, companies have fared better when the founder retired at or near age 65; carefully planned for the departure; and, most importantly, *stayed* retired. My sense is that some did not stay retired for one primary reason: the process was not executed over an extended period in accordance with a carefully crafted plan or clear vision.

Founders of successful companies tend to work very hard and enjoy it, as I have—and I think it shows—and refuse to retire until the day of their funeral. That just doesn't benefit the share-holders, the family, and most certainly the individual.

After all, the world's rate of change is increasing. Businesses change; consumers change; and leadership must change to be able to seize current opportunities. That is often difficult when you are age 65 and beyond.

Having a great CEO in place, ready to succeed me, has been a major focus of your board for several years. Now that it's done, your chairman and the entire board is proud to have Kevin ready and happily willing to assume this responsibility. He is an exemplary leader with high values, in-depth experience, educa-tion, and the support required to carry out this increasingly demanding role. Kevin and the executive team are the most sea-soned, talented, capable, and respected senior executive team in our industry. I am so proud of this team for many reasons, but none more important than the fact that they are simply great, hardworking people who share high values, aspirations, and vision for our great company.

There are several factors that make me optimistic about all this. First, at Clayton, we have a wonderful senior executive team—the best. Second, I have been through this process several times, in that I have been privileged to lead several business units and then turn the reins over to very capable leaders. Joe

Clayton took over the automobile dealerships back in 1968; Ty Kelly led the manufacturing group starting in 1973; Tim Williams headed Vanderbilt Mortgage Company in 1981; and David Booth began guiding our retail group in 1990. Those were gratifying experiences for me, to say the least. This transition will, like those, produce excellent results for all involved.

My role will be to chair the board for another five years and to encourage and support them in their vision, strategic planning, and, for the short term, to assist the legal department. Our current communications tools will allow me to adequately support our small, but talented, legal staff part-time. I embrace involvement in these compliance, planning, and defense activities.

I look forward to time with Kay in our new home, hitting tennis balls, skiing powder in Colorado, getting to know seven wonderful grandsons, seeing new ocean life through our scuba goggles, learning to pick and sing some new songs with friends, and devoting more time to exercise and fitness. Too, there is two-thirds of a book written that must be finished, others that need to be read, travel to be done, and time to be devoted to the Clayton Charitable Foundation. Will we stay active and busy? You bet.

Clayton Homes has been so good to me, as well as to my family. It is wonderful to be at this point in life and to have a great corporation, people, and programs supporting us. Clayton is a unique and interesting company where we appreciate and take care of our homebuyers and each other. With 7,500 team members in 32 states, it's important that we continue to care for and support the team and each team member in the same manner as we have throughout the years. To the extent possible, we still must think, work, act, and spend as a small company.

For 43 wonderful years filled with unforgettable memories, this is one sharecropper's son who will be eternally grateful to our God, our country, our industry, our company and its people, for the opportunity to work, learn, grow, and share a wonderful life with some truly amazing individuals.

It will be my pleasure to tell your story to some of your largest shareholders in the morning. I like that. What an honor it is to represent 7,500 great people in this manner.

For this, I am very appreciative.

Jim Clayton
June 14, 1999
Boston, Mass.

NOTE TO THE READER.

This is where I ended *First A Dream* in 2002.

What's happened since?

The following chapters cover two busy years of amazing *Happenings*.

Please turn the page.

CHAPTER 21

Happenings

"Jim, this is Warren Buffett.

"I read your book over the weekend and enjoyed it very much—you did a good job on it. I've followed your company for several years and congratulate you on taking it to the top of the industry.

"Give me a call. I'd like to get your views on the industry."

Warren Buffett calling me! Can you believe it? Now that is a *Happening*.

First A Dream—New Edition is all about *Happenings*.

The *Happenings* concept was a gift from *Roots* author, miniseries pioneer, and a truly great American, Alex Haley. We met in 1986 at a Knoxville Museum of Art unveiling and quickly found we had a lot in common. We were both the same age, born in West Tennessee, and single—that is, divorced.

Alex moved to a farm 25 miles north of Knoxville after meeting John Rice Irwin, a friend I admire a great deal. Invited by Governor Lamar Alexander, Alex and John were included in a group of 25 notable Tennesseans asked to plan the state's bicentennial celebration.

Both had spent most of their lives researching and recreating their respective roots. They were destined to be great friends.

Alex soon toured John's Museum of Appalachia and enjoyed a weekend with him and his neighbors. Hesitant to leave, he made an ardent request.

"Find me a retirement home—I want to spend the rest of my life as your neighbor, John Rice Irwin."

Gesturing to the rolling expanse of hills that surrounds the museum, John Rice happily replied, "One of these farms will be yours—give me a month."

Construction began a month later on Alex's farm and retreat— a mile away from John Rice's home and the Museum of Appalachia.

Soon the farmhouse had been restored. John Rice donated the logs from an ancient cantilevered barn, and they were quickly assembled along the winding picturesque drive to the main house. Suites to accommodate 30 guests were contained in the various buildings scattered throughout the complex—two favored suites were in the cantilevered barn.

I am so pleased that John Rice recently invited me to join the museum foundation board.

Alex's dream, or vision, of introducing the world to Appalachian traditions as he had for African-American history with his book and mini-series—both major *Happenings*—was now ready to become reality.

But, it didn't happen.

Inviting 30 dignitaries from his global list of notable friends, he staged an event that he thought was certain to produce a *Happening*.

Sometimes these events turned into *Happenings*. Sometimes not. That wasn't enough for Alex. We discussed this the night we met. Leaving the museum, we shook hands as he invited me to attend his next event.

A few days later, I received a call from Alex. With meticulous detail, he asked that I arrive promptly at 6:15 p.m., adding with a smile in his voice "exit your helicopter carrying a guitar and be sure a lovely young woman is at your side."

It was now time for Alex's guests to enjoy authentic country cook'n—some for the first time.

Moving to the lodge, former Governor—now Tennessee's esteemed Senator—Lamar Alexander was playing "Rocky Top" and "Tennessee Waltz" on the piano. John Rice Irwin accompanied him on the mandolin, and I joined in with the guitar. This was the first exposure to *hillbilly* music for some guests.

Sometimes the event is a *Happening*—but not every time.

Alex still wasn't satisfied.

He called me saying, "I want all of my events to be a guaranteed *Happening*. You've heard my speeches where I say you can't guarantee a *Happening*." He then explained his new plan to invite one notable guest with the understanding they would invite 30 of their friends to join the *Happening*.

He called Oprah. She happily accepted. It was a *Happening*. Oprah and her friends had a ball, and Alex was elated.

As I loaded my guitar in the helicopter that evening, Alex explained, "Jim, we've got it. This plan guarantees a *Happening*—just watch."

I have such wonderful memories of the *Happenings*—and of Alex.

In my own life, I look for *Happenings*.

Thanks, Alex, for the lesson.

This new edition is about *Happenings*, all of which occurred because the first edition of *First A Dream* was actually read. How about that?

Even I, the proverbial optimist and dreamer, could never have imagined how many significant *Happenings* would unfold over these two years.

All because I—with a lot of encouragement and help from family and friends, after four false starts and a dozen years of procrastination—finally finished *First A Dream.*

Too, I think you would agree a telephone call from Mike Tedford from his 43,000-foot-high office aboard Air Force One triggered a *Happening*—again because of my first book.

On a Friday afternoon in early July, I was alternating between tasks—writing this book and preparing for an American City Bank board meeting (acquiring that bank is another *Happening*.) The phone rang, interrupting my concentration.

"Hi, Mr. Clayton.

"This is Mike Tedford calling from Air Force One."

The call caught me off guard, but I knew instantly that I should recognize the name belonging to that enthusiastic, friendly voice. Before I could ask, I remembered.

The *Chester County Independent* frequently chronicled his exciting 28-year Air Force career. Mike Tedford is a favorite son of Chester County in central West Tennessee—from where Eddy Arnold and I hail. For the past eight years, as chief of communications for Air Force One, he served President Clinton and now President Bush.

Dropping by to see his banker and friend Jack Bulliner, my chairman of First State Bank, he picked up a copy of *First A Dream.*

"We haven't met," Mike told me, "but my grandmother Blanche Tedford worked with your mother Ruth for 17 years at the shirt factory. I have been looking forward to meeting you ever since I read your book."

"If you have some time Monday, I'd like to show you where I work. I'll give you a tour and buy your lunch—on Air Force One."

WOW! Who would have thought I would ever get a call from Air Force One *and* a tour *and* lunch?

But that's just one of many amazing *Happenings* resulting from *First A Dream.*

More on this *Happening* with Mike later.

The most far-reaching *Happening* began with a simple voicemail message left for me by the *Oracle of Omaha,* the man whose renowned advice is sought after by the highest-paid CEOs in the nation and from royalty and high-ranking government officials around the world—Warren Buffett.

My introduction to the CEO of Berkshire Hathaway came by way of his friend, UT Associate Professor of Finance Albert Auxier and Michael Daniels.

Michael was completing his three-year tenure as my intern and was one of Dr. Auxier's fortunate students in the renowned investment class at UT. There, Dr. Auxier details meticulously and lauds extensively Buffett's investing and corporate management philosophy.

During one of his lectures, Dr. Auxier discussed entrepreneurs and strong corporate executives. I was pleased to learn that he referred to me as an example. He ended the talk with, "These are the type of leaders Warren Buffett appreciates."

Looking back, did Auxier *at that moment* plant the seed that would grow into the CMH acquisition?

Believing that his favorite professor and I shared mutual interests, Michael arranged for the popular professor and me to meet over lunch.

Dr. Auxier's enthusiasm and knowledge of the Buffett investment style impressed me.

"How in the world did a professor from the hills of East Tennessee develop a relationship with Warren Buffett?" I had to ask.

He recounted that, in 1994, *Barron's* magazine published an article he authored titled, "Happy Birthday, Benjamin Graham: A Century After His Birth, His Legacy Lives On."

Buffett, who is Graham's most accomplished disciple, sent Auxier a congratulatory letter.

The two became penpals and later, friends.

Being an avid Graham investor and teacher, Professor Auxier found himself adopting his new friend's modernized version of Graham's value investment style. Soon the professor's UT finance presentations had more references to Buffett than to Graham.

Applying his updated Buffett–Graham principles to managing money provided by TVA in competition with 19—later increasing to 25—other universities, the Auxier students took home the trophies and prizes year after year. Since 1998, they've won prizes totaling $100,000 for both single and three-year performances. For six years, the students have beaten the S&P 500 Index.

Buffett watched the student portfolio managers' success and in letters to Auxier cheered on the students. He eventually issued a standing invitation for the professor and his students to visit his Berkshire Hathaway headquarters each year.

The young men and women who take this annual pilgrimage to *Buffett Land* will tell you it's an unforgettable, life-changing experience. See page 370-C for a photograph of some of the students who presented a copy of *First A Dream* to Warren Buffett— and contributed to the Clayton acquisition.

Each year, Auxier and the students search for an appropriate appreciation gift for their esteemed host. In the past, gifts had been a jersey signed by Peyton Manning, a basketball autographed by Pat Head Summitt, the winningest coach in women's basketball, and a football signed by Phil Fulmer, UT's national championship coach.

This year the gift would not be orange.

Michael, who had tolerated me throughout the six-month final edit of *First A Dream,* grabbed two copies when the books arrived.

Michael had participated in Professor Auxier's annual trip to Omaha in 2002 and knew the protocol of expressing their gratitude to Mr. Buffett with a gift.

Holding a book in each hand, Michael excitedly asked, "Will you autograph these—one for me and one for Mr. Buffett?"

"You gotta be kidding," I said, smiling. Realizing he was serious, I happily obliged.

Michael continued, "Dr. Auxier and I want to present your book as our gift to Mr. Buffett for this year's visit to Omaha."

The first of the 15,000 copies of *First A Dream* was autographed to Warren Buffett on December 6, 2002. The *Wizard of Omaha* would be presented the book on the next annual pilgrimage to the Berkshire shrine on February 3, 2003.

Auxier and Michael are admittedly visionaries, but surely they could not have foreseen the *Happenings* they had just put into motion.

Dr. Auxier would receive this note from Buffett less than three months after the Omaha visit.

> Al,
> I'm glad you gave me the book instead of another basket-ball or football. Tell your students that they have firmly established their credentials as dealmakers. Next year I'll come to Knoxville.
> Best regards.
> Warren
> P.S. Unless, of course, the students prefer to come to Omaha.

Tennessee's two respected senators, Bill Frist and Lamar Alexander, chose to recount the same story on the Senate floor. See the Appendix H-1 & H-2 for the text from the framed addresses I proudly display on my vanity wall.

But, I'm getting ahead of the story that I've enjoyed telling hundreds of times.

By the time the annual trip to Omaha rolled around in February 2003, Michael had graduated and joined the highly successful Dugan McLaughlin Wealth Management Group at UBS Financial Services as a financial advisor. Other Auxier students have gone on to become analysts and fund managers at recognized investment firms.

Before leaving the internship program, Michael very ably handed off his responsibilities to Richard Wright, another Sigma Phi Epsilon fraternity brother. (More on my talented and successful interns later.)

As Richard was my current intern, Dr. Auxier selected him to present the autographed copy of *First A Dream* to Mr. Buffett.

After arriving for their long-awaited, whirlwind day in Omaha, the students toured two of Buffett's favorite Berkshire Hathaway companies.

Now spread across 75 acres, the Nebraska Furniture Mart was established in 1937 by Rose Blumpkin, a Russian immigrant. With $500, she started a second-hand clothing shop in her basement.

Much has been written about Buffett walking into the now-famous Furniture Mart in 1983. Approaching Mrs. Blumpkin, he asked if she were interested in selling. "Name your price," he said.

"$60 million," was her response after a short pause to see if he was serious.

"It's a deal, but only if you stay," he stated. Her grandson Ron runs the business today. Rose was actively involved until her passing in 1998 at 104 years old.

I wish Buffett had allowed me to *name the price*. Otherwise, our deal was much the same.

Impressed with the success, business savvy, and impeccable reputation of the Blumpkins, a handshake sealed the deal.

Early in his reign, Buffett wanted former owners, now his managers, to retain some ownership. Buying 90 percent, Buffett insisted that Rose and her sons retain a share and continue to run the Nebraska Furniture Mart as their own.

I would like to know—and maybe I'll ask him one day—why his philosophy changed. In the Clayton Homes purchase, and others in more recent years, he insisted on buying 100 percent.

"I don't do that anymore," he said without an explanation.

Buffett is unconventional. Some say I am too.

He buys companies without "kicking the tires."

Heck, he doesn't even look under the hood.

In buying banks—I'm up to three and one-fourth now—we did not visit a single location before consummating the acquisitions.

All three banks have been happy purchases for me. The former owners, who are now our managers, say the same.

For another real-life, up-close example of Buffett's acquisition decisions, the students visited Borsheim's Jewelry Store.

Borsheim's, home of the world's largest faceted diamond, the 545-carat "Golden Jubilee," was the second stop for the enthusiastic students.

Buffett's guests were not surprised to learn that he approached the purchase of Borsheim's with the same philosophy—no audit, no inventorying of goods, just a keen awareness that he was getting good value.

Thus, another well-known American icon belonged to Buffett.

Before seeing Buffett, the students made a memorable stop at the Oracle's home, which he bought for $31,500 in 1958. Simple tastes and frugal habits have kept him living in the same home ever since.

The UT group gathered in the Cloud Room atop Kiewit Plaza for the much-anticipated meeting with Buffett.

Classic and Cherry Coke were served, the latter being Buffett's favorite beverage. He owns 8 percent of Coca-Cola. "Buy what you like" is one of his investing mantras.

A hush fell when the tall, gray-haired gentlemen bounced into the room. The moment had arrived. The students rose to their feet.

"Hello everyone, welcome to Berkshire Hathaway and Omaha, I'm Warren Buffett," he said.

Except for the frequent laughter as their idol delivered his one-liners one after another, the students sat spellbound by his pragmatic philosophy of life, success, business, and finance.

I would soon see this self-deprecating style first-hand.

"Hit me with your questions, the harder, the better," Buffett challenged his audience.

"With a sharp decline in 2002's manufactured housing shipments, what should a company do to lead the recovery cycle?" asked Richard Wright, adding, "How can the industry learn to provide investors with acceptable and predictable returns?"

Richard said later that he could not believe Buffett's swift and detailed response.

Buffett gave a brief history of the cyclical manufactured housing industry and then turned to the oversupply that started about five years ago when factories were producing 350,000 homes per year, as opposed to the normal 200,000.

He spoke of eager salesmen shaving off commissions to close deals. Financing became too loose, causing owners to default on mortgage payments, leading to repossessions and a build-up of distressed inventories. Now homes that sold for $50,000 were repossessed, refurbished like new and resold for as low as $20,000.

Conseco, holding $20 billion in mortgages, and other industry lenders were forced to tighten underwriting standards. Sales and new loan originations dropped to near all-time lows.

The entire industry went into a tizzy—and still is.

"It was obvious Buffett had read the Clayton Homes annual report," Richard recalled.

Buffett shared his thoughts on the requirements for a company to become, and remain, an industry leader.

Since most manufactured homes are, in effect, a commodity, a successful company must build a high-quality product at a competitive price to motivate a homebuyer to walk next door to buy.

The industry leader must "build a moat around themselves," to use one of Buffett's favorite phrases. By creating brand loyalty, a company enjoys a distinctive competitive advantage.

Halfway through the Q&A, Dr. Auxier rose to his feet and signaled Richard with a *thumbs up*. It was time for the student's gift—my book—to be presented to their prophet.

What a *Happening*!

A photograph was snapped. Months later, this photograph would be published around the world as Buffett lauded the students as deal makers.

Waving the book, the Oracle quipped, "Now Jim Clayton is one CEO who deserves a raise. I've watched this fine company for years."

CHAPTER 22

The Deal Is ON

The first sign of spring finds me every year on March 2nd skiing at Beaver Creek in celebration of my birthday. For decades, 50 friends, half of them CMH managers, have joined Birthday Boy for some of the best intermediate skiing in the world. The culinary offerings are equally delightful.

Although I have skied every slope on the mountain, by mid-afternoon my *one-year-older*, burning muscles and aching bones were crying for a rest. I needed a break at McCoy's, the popular watering hole at the mountain's base.

After a birthday toast of Chardonnay with Kay, I got my second wind and decided to dispel any confusion as to my being completely *over the hill* by catching up with the group for a couple of fast runs before the lifts closed.

Yet, I paused for a moment evaluating the alternatives—another Chardonnay with Kay or hit the slopes again with the young Clayton executives and friends? While deliberating the decision, I remembered that I had not had a voice-mail hit all day.

I hurriedly dialed the ancient pay phone, and there it was, the message that changed my life, while altering the future of everyone connected with Clayton.

The voice asking me to return his telephone call belonged to Warren Buffett.

Without hesitation, I pressed the *forward* button saying, "Mr. CEO, you will certainly want to return this call."

Grabbing my ski gear, I made a dash for the chair lift determined to keep up with my 50 or so friends and family members for the final runs of the day.

At the risk of appearing defensive, let me stop and cover a point that to me seemed rather unimportant; however, it appeared to be very surprising to early-draft critics. (After typing the first draft, I e-mailed it to select friends imposing on them for edits and comments.)

My friends can't believe—and it's hard to convince them—that I did not personally return Warren Buffett's call.

Let me assure you—not once did I think of returning that call.

After all, in line with succession plan commitments, I had publicly announced I was turning over the CEO responsibilities to my son Kevin on July 1, 1999, some three years before Buffett's call.

I had referred significant calls and issues to Kevin, increasingly so for a decade, as mandated by the CMH succession plan. Heck, all the company's high finance and Wall Street relationships were long ago handed off to Kevin, my well accepted successor.

Kevin and I get high marks for a well-crafted CMH succession plan from everyone, internally and externally—he, for his excellent leadership, and me for staying out of his way.

To this day I have never called Warren Buffett.

Likewise the *Sage of Omaha* has never called me—unless you count his voice-mail message, the recording that started this amazing chain of events.

"What's it like to do business with Buffett?" I'm often asked. Or, "I hear you and Buffett are really good friends."

They expect me to have spent time with Warren Buffett.

The truth is, I never spoke to him one time through all the negotiations.

He never came. We never went. No one from either side even

met. Kevin and Warren talked every day. John Kalec and Marc Hamburg, the CFOs, talked frequently. Tom Hodges and Berkshire attorneys communicated constantly. Charlie Munger, vice chairman of Berkshire Hathaway, also an attorney, was coaching from the sidelines.

Isn't it amazing that the universally admired chairman, Warren Buffett, and vice chairman, Charlie Munger, remain hands-on to the extent that they personally devote the time and attention to all the details of a fast-moving, complex merger?

What a duo!

Warren Buffett's sniffing around the industry over the last several months had not gone unnoticed.

Having purchased most of the DIPs (debtor-in-possession bonds) of Oakwood—"flawed thinking," he later told me— Buffett entered the bidding war for Conseco, the world's largest manufactured home lender, which was also bankrupt. The *Oracle of Omaha*'s interest in buying Conseco ultimately cost the winning bidder, Cerberus, $200 million. Retaliatory shots directed at Buffett would not leave Clayton Homes unharmed.

I was about to learn more about Delaware corporate law than I ever wanted, and the cost of that education would be exorbitant.

Assuming Buffett wanted to discuss lending opportunities, loan servicing, delinquencies, loss history, and the state of the industry in general, I continued to enjoy the remaining hours of a perfect annual birthday ski retreat.

Stay tuned.

Monday morning I was securely belted in the captain's seat of my high altitude, very fast Citation Ultra jet with the Global Positioning System tuned to Knoxville. (This is our eighth year travelling in this wonderful flying machine. From its 40,000-foot cockpit, Kay and I have enjoyed viewing of most of North America many times.)

As an Airline Transport Pilot-rated captain, the highest rating issued by the FAA, I am armed with a 50-page document from the renowned and expensive Flight Safety International (coincidently owned by Warren Buffett). This certifies that I am exempt from the second pilot requirement.

With Kay in the co-pilot's seat and nine of our CMH friends back in the cabin, we were back in two hours, comfortably and safely, in Knoxville before lunch.

On the drive home from the airport, I couldn't wait any longer for a voice-mail update. Listening to Kevin's enthusiastic voice, he detailed the earlier phone conversation with Warren. They had talked at length about CMH and the industry in general.

Interestingly, he demanded during their first conversation that they use first names. Warren is full of surprises.

That says a lot about the bigger-than-life icon.

Warren discussed with Kevin, in detail, the battle for Conseco and his investment in Oakwood bonds. (Later, using *Buffett Cash*, Kevin would leverage these bonds into a front row seat at the Oakwood bankruptcy auction.)

Aware that Warren had $35 billion in cash and headed one of only eight AAA-rated companies, Kevin asked if he would like to invest in securities issued quarterly by CMH's Vanderbilt Mortgage.

Kevin thought, and I certainly would have agreed, that those securities, totaling almost $2 billion annually, would be an excellent use of cash for the *Oracle*.

Kevin Fed-Ex'd a standard investor package as Warren requested. They agreed to talk again the next afternoon.

At exactly 4 p.m. the next day, Kevin called Buffett's direct line and, after exchanging pleasantries, Buffett pointedly stated: "Kevin I wouldn't be interested in buying your mortgage bonds. I don't want to just be your banker.

"Why don't we talk about bringing Clayton under the Berkshire umbrella?" he asked.

With a smile in his voice, he added, "I think you would like being a Berkshire Hathaway CEO.

"You guys have built a great company, and I admire you." the *Oracle of Omaha* repeated.

CMH stock traded at $11 that day, recently up from $9. On May 17, 2002, the price had peaked at $19.60.

Warren told Kevin that it would be hard for him to come up with an offer that would properly compensate for all the years of hard work and the company's position in the industry. He added, "My *preliminary analysis* indicates we could probably make an offer around $12."

Relaying Kevin's report to CMH board members individually, I alerted them to the fact that a significant and unexpected blip—in the form of Warren Buffett—had appeared on our radar screen.

These conversations were quite casual and none of us had an inkling of the *Happenings* that would soon rapidly unfold. To be sure, the industry's rapid deterioration had concerned us, but a merger had never been top-of-mind.

After all, CMH was among the few industry stalwarts still standing amid a firestorm of bankruptcies, loan defaults, and plant closings. CMH had spurned making acquisitions in recent years because industry assets had been selling at high premiums.

Soon those same assets sold for a song as all but a handful of smaller companies were saddled with backbreaking debt, delinquent loans, and sagging sales.

At the Clayton helm, Kevin and the industry's brightest managers deliberately and steadily executed their plan, choosing to ignore the industry recession. As a result, not a CMH plant was closed and our company continued to earn around $100 million each year after tax.

Warren Buffett own Clayton Homes? NO WAY!

Buffett's overture was hard to believe, but as our board realized, a serious offer was on the table. They had a fiduciary responsibility to go into an evaluation mode.

Would such an offer be in the best interest of the CMH shareholders?

Management had recently presented the board a detailed update on the continuing downward spiral of the industry, including the following:

- CMH stock value is more than all other competitors combined.
- CMH earnings are more than all others combined.
- The largest retail competitor, Oakwood, is bankrupt.
- Conseco and Oakwood Acceptance were bankrupt, leaving a serious void in customer financing.
- Chase, CIT, Deutsche Financial, Bombardier, GreenPoint, and others exited manufactured housing lending—permanently.
- Fleetwood had closed 117 sales centers and 20 plants.
- Champion had closed 202 sales centers and 28 plants.
- Oakwood had closed 325 stores and 20 plants.

Industry shipments had declined more than 200,000 homes over four years from 373,000 in 1998 to only 168,000 in 2002. They would fall even further to 131,000 in 2003, a 41-year low!

Kevin and I conferred with our board of directors via telephonic conference, and advised Buffett that the board would evaluate and give consideration to an offer of $17.

Buffett acknowledged that he understood and stated that a price in the range of even $12 would be above the eight to nine multiple of earnings paid for the last several Berkshire transactions.

Before the conversation ended, Buffett had pegged his non-negotiable offer at $12.50.

"That's my final offer," he said.

In a telephone board meeting Kevin relayed Buffett's firm offer. The board authorized Kevin to go back and communicate that the board was interested in considering $15.

There was a board consensus that the industry fundamentals suggested an offer providing shareholders a significant premium should be considered.

Two Sig Ep interns "brokered" the deal. (Left to right) Jim, Michael Daniels, Richard Wright, Warren Buffett.

Warren with his wallet quipped, "It's lighter now!"

Days after the sale was announced. Jim, Warren and Kevin. April 8, 2004.

Dr. Al Auxier and Warren Buffett.

Gift of book sparked transaction

Richard Wright, a University of Tennessee senior, **presents** Warren Buffett a copy of Jim Clayton's autobiography, "First A Dream," last month. UT professor Al Auxier has taken students to visit with Buffett for the last five years at his Omaha, Neb., headquarters.

BY AMY NOLAN
nolana@knews.com

University of Tennessee financial professor Al Auxier has traveled five times to Omaha, Neb., with students to meet with Warren Buffett.

This year, Auxier presented the legendary investor with Clayton Homes founder Jim Clayton's self-published memoir, "First a Dream."

Knowing Buffett's penchant for reading – he buys stock in virtually all publicly held companies to get their annual reports and recommends students read up on the best business leaders – Auxier thought he'd enjoy the book chronicling Clayton's journey from a West Tennessee sharecropper's son to an entrepreneur who created a $1.2 billion manufactured-housing company.

That March 2 exchange set off a series of telephone calls, faxes and meetings that culminated in the Tuesday announcement of Berkshire Hathaway's $1.7 billion offer to purchase Clayton Homes.

See **DEAL** on C2

Intern Richard Wright and Warren, with the book that caused the deal. Made the press around the world.

Wednesday

NEWS SENTINEL

Knoxville · KnoxNews.com

Today: Mostly sunny and warm.
High: 75
Low: 50
Details: B2

50 cents
Final edition
April 2, 2003

CONVERSION OF CARDINAL
Rick Ankiel's role as a reliever starts with the Tennessee Smokies. **D1**

POPULAR PIZZA
Out-of-the-ordinary toppings are hot. **E1**

Buffett to buy Clayton

Berkshire Hathaway will pay $1.7 billion for Blount-based manufactured-home maker

BY AMY NOLAN
nolana@knews.com

Legendary investor Warren Buffett's Berkshire Hathaway Inc. has agreed to buy Blount County-based Clayton Homes Inc. for $1.7 billion in cash, or $12.50 per share, the companies announced late Tuesday.

Clayton Homes founder and chairman Jim Clayton and the Clayton Family Foundation, who together own 28 percent of

Jim Clayton

Buffett

Clayton Homes stock, support the merger. The company's board of directors approved the agreement Tuesday.

Clayton Homes' management and 6,800 employees — 2,500 in the Knoxville area — will remain in place after the merger and business operations will continue as planned, the announcement stated.

"The fact that Warren Buffett has chosen to invest in the future success of Clayton is a strong statement of their belief

and recognition that our people are truly exceptional," said Clayton Homes CEO Kevin Clayton. "Clayton's proven industry success coupled with Berkshire's AAA credit rating and financial resources will assure our continued success."

Berkshire Hathaway is a holding company with $42.3 billion in annual revenues from a wide range of businesses. The investment insight offered in Buffett's annual shareholder letters has

earned him the moniker "Oracle of Omaha." Buffet said Tuesday, "Clayton Homes is far and away the premier company in the manufactured housing industry with high quality products and outstanding leadership and personnel.

"By retaining discipline, Clayton Homes is the lone tower of strength in an industry battered in recent years by the consequences of lax financing practices," Buffett said. "Clayton Homes will be a great addition to the Berkshire Hathaway group of businesses."

Business writer Amy Nolan may be reached at 865-342-6342.

COMPLETE COVERAGE IN BUSINESS

■ **The deal:** What it means for the company, its employees and shareholders. **C1**

■ **Behind the scenes:** A professor's gift spawns a merger. **C1**

■ **The players:** Snapshots of Berkshire Hathaway and Clayton Homes. **C1**

■ **Timeline:** How Clayton Homes grew. **C2**

■ **The money:** What will Jim Clayton do next? **C2**

Surprised the world.

Warren presents Ph.D.s (Phenomenally Hardworking Dealmaker) and Berkshire stock to 40 UT students. Buffett said, "Bringing the deal...lowest Broker fee I ever Paid."

After paying $1.7 billion, *Mr. Sunshine* greets *his* CMH managers.

Warren and Kevin (center) visit the Appalachia plant with Rick Strachan (left) and Ronny Robertson (right).

Clayton postpones sale vote

A Clayton home *stars* at the Berkshire Hathaway annual meeting, May 1, 2004.

Kevin Clayton – a Berkshire Hathaway CEO.

My Sig Ep interns: (Standing left to right) Matt Bobrowski, Richard Wright, Michael Daniels, Kelly Williams. (Seated left to right) Matt Daniels and Tom Hodges.

Air Force One with
Mike Tedford.
A *Happening*
because I penned,
First A Dream.

The Charlie Chase
Show with Kelly in
Nashville after
First A Dream was
released.

Side-chick Elizabeth
Jane Chedester and
side-kick Darrell
Puett *singing and
"picking"* at a book
signing and fund
raiser.

Interview with
Norris Dryer at WUOT,
January 2003.

370-E

Great fun! The Hallerin Hill
show, "Anything is possible."

With Kevin signing books in Nashville at
MHI Convention.

Look! There's four of
us. Jim, Jim, Jim and
Jim, signing books at
Barnes & Noble.

Back home in Henderson,
Tenn., Eddy Arnold and I
receive honorary Ph.Ds at
Freed Hardeman University,
where I delivered the
commencement address.

Family members present for the honorary Ph.D ceremony at FHU. (Standing left to right) Joe, Kay, Chris Davis, me, Craig Clayton, Gordon Davis, Karen Davis. (Seated left to right) Jim Jr. and Kevin.

Jack and Patsy Bulliner delighted to see Eddy Arnold (left).

A quote from the book was used in her eulogy – Ms. Maness read the book just before her passing. "She was sweet, patient, and completely in charge."

Quoted from *First A Dream*
Copyright ©2002 by James L. Clayton

"Ms. Ward taught me how to read and write, and I think a lot more. I was lucky to have her —— sweet, tolerant, patient, yet completely in charge. Instead of trying her patience, every student tried very hard to please her.

I knew I was Ms. Ward's favorite student. Later on, I would learn that each of her students felt the same. She had the ability to stay in tune with each person."

(James Lee Clayton was a first-grade student of Mattie Lou Ward, when she was teaching at Finger Schools)

Mattie Lou Ward Maness
March 20, 1916   January 21, 2004

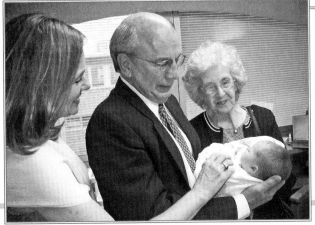

Ella on Day One with Kay and Ruth Browder Clayton, her great-grandmother, April 23, 2003.

370-G

New addition to the family, Laddie the Labradoodle, Kay's designer dog. Christmas 2003.

Chelly and Ella meet Laddie with Santa Jim. Christmas 2003.

With happy grandparents Jim & Kay. Jeb was born September 24, 2003, our eighth and newest grandson.

We flew Amy & Tim Williams to the Bahamas for their wedding in April 2004.

Peter Breazeale, chief pilot and bank facilities VP, and his wife, Amanda, our interior designer.

Matt and Megan Daniels skiing at Beaver Creek.

Carl Koella, senior VP, Clayton Bank and Trust, and wife, Beth Koella, customer service manager at 21st Mortgage.

Annual birthday celebration with friends at Beaver Creek. (Left to right) Matt Daniels, Donie Wood, Shari Wood, Megan Daniels, Warren Neel, Annelle Neel, me, and Kay. March 2, 2004.

Laddie, first mate and me, pilot, on my Sea Ray in Boca Raton, Fla.

What a match! (Left to right) Donie Wood, Jim, Islam Ulhaq (my Boca Pro) and Tim Williams, in Boca. Islam and I beat 'um.

George and Elwanda Vibbert get their Clayton Cash (formerly Buffett Cash) on May 28, 2004. George passed away in September. He is sorely missed. Elwanda joined our board in November 2004.

George S. Vibbert, Jr
BIOGRAPHICAL INFORMATION

- Chief Executive Officer and President of American City Bank since 1979
- Bachelor of Science Degree from MTSU
- Graduate of the Graduate School of Banking of the South, Louisiana State University
- Graduate of Tennessee Bankers Commercial Lending School at Vanderbilt University
- Graduate study in Engineering Management at University of Tennessee Space Institute
- 1971 Jaycee's "Young Man of the Year"
- Worked at ARO, Inc., from 1966 to 1974
- Past President of Tullahoma Kiwanis Club
- Tullahoma Noon Rotary Club Member since 1980
- Former Director of Tennessee Bankers Association
- Taught Bank Marketing and Consumer Lending courses at Motlow State Community College
- Board of Directors of Bankers Advisory Board, Conference of State Bank Supervisors
- Former Director of Tennessee Valley Economic Coalition
- Former President, Tullahoma Chamber of Commerce
- Former Mayor of Tullahoma-(Five consecutive terms from 1972 to 1982)
- Former Chairman of Tullahoma Industrial Development Board
- Former Chairman of the Coffee County Joint Industrial Development Board
- Former Trustee of Motlow College Foundation
- Former member of Tennessee Valley Aerospace Region Board
- Former Chairman of Tullahoma Utilities Board
- Former Director of Upper Duck River Development Association appointed by former Governor Winfield Dunn
- Former Director of the Tennessee Municipal League
- Former Chairman of Federal Policy Committee of the Tennessee Municipal League
- Former Director of Middle Tennessee Health System Agency
- Former Director of the South Central Development District
- Former Chairman of Tennessee Vocational Training Program in Manchester
- Served six years in Tennessee Army National Guard
- Longtime member of First United Methodist Church, Sunday School teacher, served six years as Chairman of the Administrative Board and a member of the Board of Trustees
- Co-author, "Easy Money....How to Get a Bank Loan"
- Married to the former Elwanda Sawyer-lives at 119 Kingsridge Blvd in Tullahoma
- Hobbies: Golfing and World Travel

George is survived by his wife of 41 years, Elwanda Sawyer Vibbert, brother Gerald and wife Holland Vibbert, brother-in-law Marvin Norman Sawyer, sister-in-law Rebecca Stynchula, sister-in-law and brother-in-law Dr. Tulio and Mary Figarola, brother-in-law Sam and wife Dianne Sawyer and several very special nieces and nephews and great nieces and nephews.

George and Elwanda at Tennessee Bankers meeting, at Breakers in West Palm. They were guests at our home in Boca, June 2004.

Dr. Frank Glass, chairman of ACB, and wife, Kathy, attended Horatio Alger ceremonies with us in Washington D.C. April 2004.

(Left to right) Matt Daniels, Troy Martin, and Carl Koella at Tennessee Bankers meeting in Palm Beach. Three excellent executives on our CBT team.

Madyline White, ACB executive assistant and Jeanne Campbell, Clayton family office manager deliver the American City Bank shareholders their *Clayton Cash*. May 2004.

Two Presidents, Paul Priddy (left), president of Bank of Friendship, and Matt Daniels.

Barry Rich, CFO of First State Bank.

(Left) Barry Rich and Matt Daniels, CFO and CEO at First State Bank.

Kay and Jim with (left to right) Jack and Patsy Bulliner, Linda and Clayton Skinner. Jack, chairman, Skinner, board member, at First State Bank.

(Left to right) Jim and Kay, Laddie (seated), Matt Daniels, Patsy Bulliner, Beth Koella, Jack Bulliner, Carl Koella, Troy Martin, George and Elwanda Vibbert. Leaving Boca after the Tennessee Bankers meeting.

About to vote.

Dollar General board members with founder, Cal Turner Sr. (seated center). (Standing left to right) Reginald D. Dickson, Jim Clayton, John B. Holland, Wallace N. Rasmussen, William S. Wire, II, David M. Wilds. (Seated left to right) Cal Turner, Jr., Barbara M. Knuckles.

Signing a limited edition of First a Dream for friends Scott and Ann Northcutt in Boca, Summer 2004.

For chairman Clayton, 'life changes' again

BY AMY NOLAN
nolana@knews.com

Jim Clayton, dubbed the richest man in Knoxville by Worth magazine last year, will be out of a job this summer.

If Clayton Homes shareholders approve the company's merger with Berkshire Hathaway, a Clayton Homes board of directors will no longer exist and its founder will no longer serve as chairman.

"Life changes, companies change and roles change," Clayton said in an interview.

Clayton retired as Clayton Homes' CEO in 1999. He spends little time at its Blount County headquarters. He participates in some awards banquets for employees and in quarterly board meetings.

He acknowledged a little sadness regarding the proposed merger of the company he founded 47 years ago but noted he'd been down that road before.

As the chairman and the largest single shareholder of BankFirst, which he built by acquiring banks and expanding the business, he approved its merger with BB&T, one of the 20 largest U.S. banking conglomerates based in Winston-Salem, N.C.

"I was melancholy, too, as a I processed the BankFirst transaction, but I've really enjoyed serving on BB&T and getting to know its (local) CEO, Lars Anderson."

Clayton's net worth, pegged by Worth at $620 million, won't change much but will include much more cash – $459 million before taxes if the merger is approved.

The Clayton Family Foundation will gain $21 million before taxes. The Clayton family has made contributions of more than $1 million to Baptist Hospital and the Knoxville Museum of Art.

"The foundation will grow and be much more liquid," Clayton said.

Business writer Amy Nolan may be reached at 865-342-6342.

Après-skiing at Beano's Cabin. (Left to right) Megan Daniels, me, Kay, Bob and Georgia Hatcher, Michael Daniels. New Year's 2004.

Steve Michaels and Tim Williams. Reunion of old friends at Boca. Summer 2004.

Joe and Jim –without my beard people say we look like twins. "Which one is older?" The answer depends on which of us you ask.

Our new Citation XLS Jet delivered February 2005 – in the air and signing the bulkhead on the assembly line September 2004.

First State Bank board of directors, October 2004. (Standing left to right) Clayton Skinner, Burton Williams, Joe R. Stanfill, Carl Koella, Kenneth Stumph, Edwin Morrison. (Seated) me, Matt Daniels (CEO), and Jack Bulliner (chairman)

CBT BancShares board of directors. (Standing left to right) Joe Clayton, Dr. Frank Glass, Tim Williams, and Kevin Clayton. (Seated left to right) Matt Daniels, Kay Clayton and me. October 2004.

Newest branch of FSB in Jackson, Tennessee. Opened October 2004.

Buffett responded again with, "$12.50."

A motion was made for the board to seek a fairness opinion, essentially a detailed appraisal of the company by an investment banking firm.

Sensitized by the Sarbanes-Oxley legislation, designed to cure corporate ills, the board was cautious. The highly publicized scandals at Enron, Tyco, and WorldCom were viewed by board members as a shot across the bow.

Being a $1 billion company, the board wanted a Wall Street icon to provide the fairness opinion. Should the transaction trigger a lawsuit, the directors reasoned that a high net worth investment firm would be more able to defend its fairness opinion.

I reminded them that fairness opinions contain so many waivers, disclaimers, and outs of all kinds that investment bankers rarely have to pay up. In fact, only in cases involving willful and flagrant fraud are investment bankers slapped with a judgment.

I asked my intern (remember Richard Wright?) to research fairness opinions for hours to find one case where the issuer of a fairness opinion had to pay up.

He found none.

Taking suggestions from our well-connected board members, John Kalec lined up four firms to make presentations to the full board. Two were smaller, but respected, regional firms; the other two were Wall Street giants.

It took all I could do to keep the regional firms in the running.

After all, with a CFO like John Kalec and his emphasis on strategic analysis, "economic-value-added methodology" and detailed planning, he had at his fingertips much of the data that the successful firm would need to hurriedly develop and render a fairness opinion.

Knowing that this quality information and support would be readily available, BB&T and Morgan Keegan offered a price of $150,000 to produce the fairness opinion. Wow! I liked that–the

Wall Street nameplates wanted $1.5 million for the same work.

It was pointed out that the more seasoned professionals from the two respected regional firms would be as credible as a document prepared by young MBAs typically carrying the banner for their big-name New York firms. On a witness stand I would prefer the former—any day.

Dead serious, our board members, without exception, worked diligently to fulfill their fiduciary obligations and were at all times mindful of their responsibilities to shareholders. At no time did any director show any indication that they were not focused on making the best possible decision for CMH shareholders.

Interestingly, none of our thoroughly experienced board members could remember seeing a fairness opinion that didn't generally support the contemplated transaction.

Like real estate appraisals, the final product tends to support the position of the firm paying for the opinion.

In this case, management knew a thorough analysis of the industry and the company would confirm $12.50 was within a justifiable price range.

In summary, John Kalec and his team had produced internally their own abbreviated fairness opinion for the benefit of our board's consideration.

I urged the board to retain Bill Tyson and his impressive team at BB&T. Their analyst John Diffendal knew the industry inside out and would have enormous data to support the quick turn requirements.

I was outvoted. The board, sensitive to my relationships with BB&T, retained Morgan Keegan. However, they delivered an excellent document on time—and for $150,000, a savings of more than $1 million.

Warren told Kevin the next day, "When I need a fairness opinion, I'm calling Jim."

Again, the board reviewed current and projected financial data on CMH and the industry, discussed the offer by telephone, and instructed Kevin to reply with $13.50.

Buffett responded, "$12.50."

"Even if all the capital and stock markets shut down, you can still bank my $12.50 price," Buffett emphatically confirmed to Kevin.

He was final and firm, promising to fund the $1.7 billion purchase price—in cash—immediately upon a positive vote from shareholders.

CHAPTER 23

I Thought My Shareholders Loved Me

Packing my files on the transaction into three briefcases, Kay and I pointed the jet 180 degrees south for Boca Raton and our tenth annual March sabbatical. We were a few days late departing, but were pleased to be keeping our CMH succession plan commitment. (See page 303.)

Unlike past years, I was talking several times a day to Kevin and John. Indeed, a voice-mail from Kevin was waiting as soon as we landed.

"Dad, Warren and I talked about the risk of the stock price running up if there should be leaks to the press.

"We shouldn't talk to anyone."

Only Kevin, the board, John Kalec, and I knew.

Discussions were moving fast. If information leaked to the media, a formal press release would be required. The stock price, access to money markets, and SEC compliance would all become significant issues.

Confidentiality at the Clayton home office was difficult. Secrecy is not part of CMH behavior. The culture is all about openness. There are no private offices—everyone works in cubicles. Even the CEO and CFO sit at desks inside low-walled cubicles.

While I worked at my home in Boca looking out across the sun-bathed Atlantic beach, John and Kevin brought me up to speed on the first draft of the merger agreement.

Kevin asked, "Mr. Chairman, how's the sunshine down there?" John said, "To maintain confidentiality we need a code-name. What do you suggest?"

After a brief pause, I replied, "Kevin you just said it— Sunshine."

"I like it!" said John, as Kevin interrupted, "Book it."

Until the merger was announced, the project was called Sunshine. Warren was nicknamed *Mr. Sunshine.*

Quickly reading everything in sight about Mr. Sunshine, Kevin ordered volumes from Amazon.com. With specific approval from Warren, he talked to a couple of Mr. Sunshine's CEOs.

We wanted to be sure this transaction would benefit all the company's stakeholders—shareholders, employees, customers, and the communities where they live and work.

I called John Holland, the respected CEO of Sunshine's Fruit of the Loom. Since 1988, John and I had served on the board of Dollar General. He and I served on the audit committee, John as chairman.

After asking Holland about the SEC investigation and class-action lawsuits (see page 290), I continued, "John, what's it like being a Berkshire CEO?"

The quiet, intellectual gentleman's voice suddenly became animated and filled with enthusiasm. "He leaves us alone. I talk to him about once a month. Some CEOs talk to him weekly. It's our choice."

Without telling him about the pending Clayton transaction, John and I talked at length about Warren's style, the companies owned, how quick and decisive he is, and the direct communication between Warren and his CEOs. This conversation gave me considerable insight into Berkshire.

Three lines of communications were informally established as the deal progressed at lightning speed.

Kevin talked to Warren. CMH and Berkshire accountants collaborated—at the same time lawyers were drafting an agreement.

As negotiations continued and the price firmed, the capital markets related to manufactured home financing were rapidly disappearing.

Selling to Buffett was becoming more attractive.

CMH was the only company that still was able to garner any investor interest in its mortgage-backed securities. Even then, it was at such a yield that we were being priced out of the market. We were having to retain more and more of the issues ourselves, a situation that, if continued, would gradually strip the company of the strong cash position we had enjoyed for over a decade.

CMH had considered loading the balance sheet with tons of debt to raise mortgage fundings, but this raised a whole new set of issues, and would provide only temporary relief. With $1.3 billion in equity, the balance sheet would only support $3 billion in debt, enough to last 18 months.

We explored selling homes under a lease-to-own program, thinking this type of alternate structure would be of interest to investors.

Morgan Keegan, on March 28, delivered its fairness opinion, an extensive presentation setting forth the firm's evaluation of CMH from a variety of perspectives. The conclusion? $12.50 was a fair price for our shareholders.

The board agreed on April 1, 2003, after careful and long discussion and deliberation.

Budgets, planning documents, projections, evaluations, assumptions, and other data were thoroughly reviewed.

Finally, armed with a consensus and board support, Kevin communicated the acceptance of the Berkshire no-contingency offer to Buffett.

Without Warren visiting Clayton Homes, or meeting Kevin or

me, we signed a definitive agreement.

On April 2, 2003, four weeks after the first telephone call from Warren Buffett, the *Knoxville News Sentinel's* front page trumpeted the news, "Buffett to buy Clayton." (See page 370-B)

Photographs of me and the world's second richest man accompanied the lead story. I was smiling. Buffett was smiling.

The evening before the story broke, I called John Holland to explain the real reason for my earlier call. Congratulating me and obviously pleased, he laughed in delight.

What a *Happening*!

In daily talks, Kevin continued to educate Buffett on CMH structure and operations. Upon learning that CMH was about to go to Wall Street to fund a large pool of home-buyer mortgage originations, Buffett asked, "When? How much?"

Kevin explained that we had been using Wall Street investment bankers to raise $300 million per quarter, but this offering would be about $360 million.

Buffett said, "I can save you some money. Berkshire has excess cash and this would be a good short-term use of it, even if the acquisition should blow up."

Three days later, Berkshire's accountant sent a simple, three-page loan agreement to fund up to $1.8 billion. Roughly $690 million was drawn on that credit line over the next few months. The savings on legal, accounting, and investment bank fees were significant.

Amazing!

I have used the same process in buying my last two banks.

It works. Taking the unnecessary "noise" out of a transaction sure reduces the legal costs and expedites the close.

Six days after the sale was announced, Buffett came to Knoxville in person to meet the young bright executive who would soon be CEO of a Berkshire Hathaway subsidiary—Clayton Homes Inc.

The agenda included a welcome for Clayton Homes to join his stable of seemingly unrelated, but high-performing, businesses. He asked to see a factory production line, a retail sales center, a residential community, and to take a handshake tour through the home-office and Vanderbilt Mortgage.

Kevin wanted Buffett to address the corporate staff. I suggested that Knoxville's community and business leaders would love to hear Buffett speak over lunch.

Kevin came to my home the night before Buffett's visit to fine-tune the itinerary.

"Buffett wants you to pick and sing with him," Kevin announced.

"You gotta be kidding," I responded. Seeing he was serious, I exclaimed in shock, "What songs? When do we rehearse?"

Dialing the phone, Kevin said, "Let's call Warren now!"

That wipes me out. This kid of mine is dialing Warren Buffett late at night. And on my phone!

Warren answered, and that was my first conversation with the world's greatest investor who was buying the company Joe Clayton and I started 37 years ago in 1966.

After exchanging greetings, I asked him what songs and what keys. He replied, "I am likely to sing the 'Coke Song' ('I'd Like to Teach the World to Sing') and 'Take Me Out to the Ball Game,'" but he said he didn't know the keys.

I listened as he sang over the speaker-phone and quickly found the chords to accompany him on the guitar. I layered in a high harmony vocal on some phrases. He seemed adequately impressed, but it was apparent that Warren Buffett knew even less about music than I do.

Luckily, he sang both songs in one of the easier keys for the guitar, the key of C.

Warren "wowed" the crowd. Their enthusiastic questions used up all the time so I missed my once in a lifetime opportunity to pick and sing with Warren Buffett.

He forgot all about my guitar on the stand beside him.

Give our new friend Warren a microphone and he forgets all about time. He loves the audience just as much as they love him. It was a wonderful event. He told stories and delivered one-liners as he entertained questions from a couple hundred of Knoxville's most influential government and business leaders.

I have a file folder stuffed full of thank-you notes from the grateful attendees. They appreciated the complimentary photographs of themselves with Warren.

One of Knoxville's best-known businessmen wrote, "I would not have changed my schedule even for a meeting with the President of the United States. I happily did so to have lunch with Warren Buffett."

He shows off his picture with Warren to every visitor to his office, telling them, "I know Warren Buffett. Jim Clayton introduced us."

We thought this was going to be a simple, quick deal—all cash.

The price gave shareholders a 12 percent premium over the price quoted on the New York Stock Exchange the day the deal was announced. I had contracted to vote my shares—those in trust to my family members and those owned by our foundation, totaling 28 percent of all shares—in favor of the transaction.

Shareholders couldn't believe this family-owned business with a rich heritage was being sold. They were shocked. Some feared the CMH headquarters would be moved to Omaha.

Berkshire Hathaway, the holding company, employs only 15.8 people at its home office. Warren Buffett only buys companies with excellent leaders who agree to continue to manage the business.

Having communicated publicly our succession plan (see Chapter 18), flawlessly executed over the past 14 years, shareholders and the community expected the company to remain in the family for generations, certainly through Kevin's tenure.

However, current trends in our cyclical industry were not typical and threatened the fundamental structure of our business. Conseco, the 800-pound gorilla, was bankrupt. So was Oakwood. Now US Bank, Fannie Mae, Freddie Mac, credit unions, and others were entering the business with low-cost funds, skimming off the high quality loans.

Depending solely on the asset-backed securitization market to provide mortgages for its customers, Clayton's sources of mortgage funds were becoming uncertain and expensive.

As site-built home mortgage rates dropped below 6 percent, we had to price our mortgages as high as 12 percent. Our long-term Wall Street investors were finding our mortgages more and more unattractive, even at the current high rates. They were smarting from the losses they were experiencing from their Conseco and Oakwood investments.

It was a *sea change* for the industry, and most money managers and investment firms listened and seemed to understand our analysis of why Buffett's offer was fair and the risk to CMH in this shifting environment was assumable.

In early May, a Bermuda money manager who owned about 5 percent of Clayton Homes stock launched a full-scale campaign to derail the merger.

Orbis Investment Management's William Gray was outraged. It is my guess that he has allowed his and his investors expectations to be unrealistically high—and in turn had failed to realize the current industry fundamentals.

Later, when Kevin and I met with him, he would not listen to the facts and research we presented.

Gray was not interested as Kevin explained, "Capital sources for our industry have become scarce and expensive, and we are giving you irrefutable data that CMH has to charge customers almost double the rates paid by site-built homebuyers—an impossible situation long term."

William Gray was not impressed as he suggested he knew

investors would be happy to buy our homebuyer mortgages.

I wanted William Gray, who is a charming, educated, and very nice man to, "Show me the money."

Of course, he couldn't.

With a shareholder vote pending, Clayton Homes executives were in a quiet period and could not issue information not included in the SEC required, acquisition proxy statement.

We were gagged. Our hands were tied.

Contrast that with Orbis' William Gray, who retained a New York public relations firm to solicit support. They were able to circulate statements from other investment managers criticizing the merger—based on what we believed to be flawed data.

Gray soon filed a petition with the SEC and a lawsuit with the Delaware Chancery Court. He wanted to prevent family and management votes from being counted; he sought a rule change for the upcoming shareholder election—claiming our votes were self-serving. He petitioned the court to allow only "independent" shareholders to vote in the election.

William Gray worked feverishly in court and in press releases, as he personally called institutional shareholders urging them to vote against the merger—no doubt an expensive campaign.

On June 3, Gray sued again in Delaware. He demanded a specially called shareholder meeting to replace the current Clayton board of directors and for the shareholder vote to be postponed until the new directors were in place.

His complaint alleged that CMH did not give proper notice required by Delaware law for its annual meetings for 2000 and 2002. Gray alleged that the proxy statements for the annual meetings were not mailed on the required date.

Had the judge ruled against CMH, Gray could have nominated his own board of directors, taken control, and aborted the acquisition.

The Delaware chancellor ruled on June 27, 2003, that shareholders received *exemplary notice* from the company. The meetings were well attended, meaning shareholders had to have been well informed about the meeting date. Therefore, they were not confused or injured by the inadvertent technical mistake.

Having been involved, as a board member, in dozens of poorly attended annual meetings, I find them typically boring and uninspiring. Reading from a lawyer's prepared script, the chairman reads the SEC boilerplate precisely, and the secretary announces the vote. The meeting adjourns, and that's about it.

A Clayton annual meeting amounted to a mini festival with entertainment and refreshments. They were informative and always well attended.

I, as chairman, conversationally wrote and delivered the required information. Senior managers enthusiastically joined me in responding to questions and comments as we thanked shareholders for their continued support and involvement.

Unconventional? Yes.

In 1999, Kevin welcomed our shareholders, and introducing me, said, "Here's your Founder and Chairman—Jim Clayton." The podium remained empty as a baritone voice and guitar echoed over the sound system.

From the back of the meeting hall, strolling toward the podium I sang the first verse of John Denver's "Country Road." At first one, then a few, then all turned to discover their singing chairman. Before the chorus, I invited my favorite audience to sing along. "Country road, take me home, to the place where I belong ...."

They did—and what a great sound!

It was an effective and fun meeting, exemplifying the casual Clayton culture. We made the front page locally, and the national press loved it too.

When the Delaware chancellor ruled in our favor, Kevin announced that earnings would be down 20 percent, or 5 cents to 7 cents, from the prior year's 25 cents per share, and that industry production was already down 26 percent for the year.

Still, Gray would not give up.

On July 1, he issued a letter to shareholders urging them to vote against the merger.

Clayton Homes countered each issue Gray raised.

The industry environment, at least on the surface, was now working against us.

Buffett's involvement in the industry coupled with new lending capacity from US Bank and others had generated investor enthusiasm and had pushed stock prices up.

Fleetwood announced the hiring of additional workers to meet anticipated demand for recreational vehicles and manufactured houses. Stock prices spiked higher.

In early July, industry stock prices increased almost daily. Champion and Fleetwood Enterprises stock increased 23 percent in one month!

As stock prices rose and Orbis sustained its campaign, CMH research confirmed that industry fundamentals were continuing to deteriorate. Investors were bombarded with contradictory news releases and letters appealing for their support.

Institutional Shareholder Services, a well-respected proxy advising firm, gave its blessing to the deal on July 7. Its lesser-known subsidiary, Proxy Voting Services, issued a report concluding just the opposite.

Just when we thought this simple, straightforward transaction could not get more complicated, Cerberus Capital Management, named for the mythological three-headed dog guarding the gates of Hades, roared onto the scene.

In classical mythology, this watchdog of Hell is described as possessing a hurtful nature and is known to plot brutal and sudden mischief.

The dog came barking at our door, actually Borders' door, in Nashville where I had been invited to autograph *First A Dream* on the evening of July 10.

Kevin telephoned.

"Cerberus' managing director, Frank Bruno, has sent a letter—

he released it to Wall Street and the media—indicating he wants to raise Warren's bid for Clayton Homes."

My life as chairman of a public company just got even more stressful.

In the Bruno letter, he asked us to sign a confidentiality agreement and to allow Cerberus to begin due diligence immediately "with access to all company non-public information."

The letter indicated they wanted to buy the company and were prepared to pay a higher price.

The letter referenced Cerberus' recent acquisition of Conseco, a bankrupt lender in the manufactured housing industry.

Was Cerberus really this interested in biting off another slice of the industry pie, or was this simply an attempt to get even with Buffett, who had raised their bid for Conseco by a few hundred million?

Cerberus' letter, in my opinion, did not amount to an offer because it contained no details of price, terms, or conditions. My livestock-trading, circuit-riding Grandfather Clayton would not have given a second thought to such an offer.

In the current environment of intense scrutiny of public company governance, however, CMH management had to acknowledge the communication.

"Show me the money," was my response published around the world.

Interestingly, if this had been a real offer and determined to be in the best interest of our shareholders, Warren Buffett would have walked away with a $35 million break-up fee—paid by the new buyer.

Warren didn't go away. The day before the shareholders' meeting, he issued a clear, concise statement in the form of a press release detailing his offer, our agreement, and reiterating the industry's negative trend.

True to style, his statement went straight to the heart of the matter.

"Berkshire will not raise its price now or in the future." (See Appendix G-1.)

Warren's press release went on to say that Berkshire would not lend in the industry except through Clayton and that the fundamentals of the company and the industry were appearing bleaker, not brighter.

What a credible validation for our company and staff. Warren consistently referred to Clayton Homes as "the best company in the industry" and Clayton management as "the best in the business."

"Nevertheless Berkshire hopes that Clayton shareholders accept our offer. But it is not one that we will renew," Warren said with finality.

Orbis would not give up. Gray continued with full force urging shareholders to vote against the deal.

The Cerberus letter cast a cloud of uncertainty over the proceedings.

Deliberating late into the night before the meeting, directors concluded they needed more time to evaluate the tentative Cerberus letter. Was it an offer? Was it simply an expression of interest? Would Clayton shareholders be best served by pursuing a transaction with Cerberus? Would Warren extend his offer to allow time for the directors to negotiate with Cerberus?

The directors asked Kevin to check with Warren to see if he would support a delay of the shareholder vote and extend his contract for adequate time for Bruno to prepare an offer. Kevin did not believe Warren would agree to this.

Why should he? With a desk piled high with offers from company owners eager to get their hands on *Buffett Cash,* he could easily move on to less complicated deals.

Kevin pointed out to the board and our attorneys that a number of shareholders were interested in evaluating the interest of Cerberus or any other suitors. There were interesting discussions about how to accomplish a recess or postponement. It appeared to be an unusual request.

Should we attempt to accommodate those shareholders, and Warren Buffett, who wanted the matter resolved as scheduled? Should we be sensitive to those shareholders who insisted on giving potential bidders, if any, more time?

Did Tennessee or Delaware law apply? Could the board make the decision? Was a shareholder vote required?

The CMH directors were overworked and underpaid in 2003—for sure.

On the morning of July 16, shareholders, employees, lawyers, and the media packed the CMH auditorium. Gray was there, with his New York public relations representative.

Leaving Kevin in conference with Warren and the lawyers, I called the meeting to order. Alone in the hot seat, I fielded questions from the crowd for over an hour.

The shareholders needed to vent.

Some challenged the Buffett price emotionally. After all, they had been bombarded with information from the Orbis campaign.

But many of the shareholders were sad that their relationships with CMH might end. Some ties dated back to public stock offering in 1983. My great friend, a true statesman, Senator Ben Atchley, said privately to me, "This is my 21st shareholder meeting, never missed a one. I will miss them."

He and so many others believed in us and expressed their willingness to remain patient and stick by us until the industry rebounded.

Their confidence was gratifying.

Finally, we broke for lunch, during which I chaired an interesting and intense board of directors meeting.

Needless to say, the food went untouched.

When the meeting reconvened, I introduced Kevin for the first time that day.

Kevin announced that Berkshire Hathaway had graciously agreed to a two-week extension. This would permit time for Cerberus to present a definitive offer and for the board to analyze the possible higher-than-Berkshire bid.

"Mr. Frank Bruno has assured us that he and his team, starting immediately, can accomplish due diligence and deliver a detailed offer within that two-week period," Kevin informed the shareholders.

"Mr. Buffett's offer will remain available," Kevin stated, adding, "His fee for granting the extension will be $5 million."

Kevin and Warren had talked several times each day regarding shareholder concerns about the price. Although they were convinced no one would pay a higher price, both respected the directors' obligation to diligently determine if Cerberus, or anyone else, would present a better offer.

Even if a higher offer materialized, Warren would walk away with both the break-up fee plus the extension fee, totaling $40 million. Either way Berkshire would realize a profit.

Our Delaware attorney had uncovered an interesting statute.

Those shareholders in attendance were eligible to vote on a recess, while those shareholders absent but represented by proxy were not.

Gray and another money manager, Carl Tash of Cliffwood Partners, argued forcefully that management was attempting to undermine the will of the shareholders.

Kevin countered just as forcefully that it was in the shareholders' best interest to determine if Cerberus or anyone else could make a better offer.

I called for a vote.

After the votes were tallied, I announced that the shareholders had voted overwhelmingly for the meeting to recess for two weeks until July 30.

With this unexpected turn of events, the board reconvened before the shareholders—scratching their heads in amazement—filed out of the building.

The decision was made to hire Bear Stearns to evaluate the Cerberus letter and to perform a new full-scale fairness opinion, if needed. Their meter would tick off over $1.5 million before they left two weeks later—the going rate for blue chip firms.

Talk about extreme Wall Street greed!

That very expensive fairness opinion would never be used.

The following Monday morning, Bruno's army of accountants, lawyers, and consultants showed up at Clayton Homes' door.

Joining them were executives with The Blackstone Group, Texas Pacific Group, and Credit Suisse First Boston—definitely enough firepower to potentially fund a higher price than Warren's $1.7 billion bid.

Why would they devote these resources, spend tens of thousands of dollars each day, and loan high-level executives to the effort, if they weren't serious about buying the company? Every indication was that our shareholders would soon be celebrating a higher price, and CMH would belong to Cerberus.

We gave them total cooperation and a terrific working environment. The CMH management team had worked the weekend preparing detailed financial schedules and the other items from their long request list. Our army matched theirs in number.

The CMH board and attorneys directed our team of professionals to treat the visitors with utmost respect, and to respond with complete candor to every question. Our guests were to be treated as business professionals and in the same manner as we would have received any other potential bidder.

The team cooperated completely, but couldn't forget that this potential suitor, if successful, would take a far different approach in directing the company's future. These Cerberus-type venture funds are often called "vulture funds" because they load their acquisitions with debt, lay off staff, and sell assets to pay down the debt.

Cerberus attempted to put a friendly face on its presence by dispatching the organization's ambassador, its chairman of global operations—former Vice President Dan Quayle.

He spent the morning of July 23 at the home office, meeting with management, shaking the hands of employees and talking to reporters. Quayle was pleased when several employees said they voted for him in two presidential elections.

Business Week even noted the former VP's visit. "We asked Dan to go make sure Clayton knows we are serious," the Cerberus COO was quoted as saying.

As the work of the two teams proceeded, it became apparent that the information gathered was sobering to the Cerberus group. Drilling in on the negative industry trends and decline in CMH financial results, they increasingly focused on the huge capital requirements of our mortgage unit.

The Cerberus team left late in the day on Friday, July 25. As Kevin drove Bruno to the airport, Bruno confirmed that he would fax his offer Monday morning.

Did they leave as optimistic as they came? No way. It was obvious.

Speaking by phone conference with Cerberus' Bruno late on Friday night from his home in New York, it sounded as if his interest level had faded.

Come Monday, Bruno faxed "for discussion purposes only" a term sheet titled "Clayton Recapitalization—Sources & Uses." Somewhat like his earlier letter "expressing an interest," the faxed offer did not amount to a definitive offer as we had expected.

CMH executives huddled over the fax–the price was a whopping $14 per share. Wow! The shareholders would love that.

The rest of the story certainly was not appealing. In the fine print, "shareholders would receive only $9 in cash; $5 would be paid in recapitalized CMH stock."

The newly capitalized company would be saddled with $200 million in bank debt and $300 million in senior unsecured notes. Bruno would raise another $650 million by auctioning CMH assets. The Cerberus group would pay only $755 million in cash.

In effect, the stripped CMH would be paying most of the $2 billion purchase price–*for itself.*

It was clear to management that a sale to Cerberus would place the company at risk. By contrast, Buffett's deal would elevate the company to a Triple-A-rated powerhouse. However, the board was required to consider only the interest of shareholders.

Monday afternoon from New York, Bear Stearns dialed into the already lengthy board conference call. The Wall Street giant predicted capital markets would not react favorably to the highly leveraged balance sheet of the new CMH. With its credit rating lowered, the company's ability to provide mortgage funds for CMH homebuyers would be severely limited. Without adequate mortgages at favorable rates, the company could not sell enough homes to keep the factories running.

Comfortable with the Bear Stearns conclusions, the board voted unanimously to endorse the Berkshire Hathaway bid.

The attorney in me surfaced. I insisted that we preserve the paper trail documenting the board's decision-making process. The Bear Stearns presentation was key to confirming the fairness of the price.

With lawsuits pending and Gray's opposition campaign continuing, we needed hard proof that the Cerberus team had been allowed a bona fide look at the company, and that we had not *chased them away.*

Late Monday evening Kevin, and I, placed a call to Frank Bruno with the board's decision.

Bruno was gracious. There were no ill feelings.

Thanking him, Kevin and I asked him to convey our appreciation to his team for their professionalism and cooperation during their intense week in Knoxville.

I suggested that a press release issued by him stating that he had declined to make an offer would be well received—by the press and especially CMH shareholders. He readily agreed.

I, with assistance from Tom Hodges, the Clayton general counsel, quickly drafted the release and faxed it to Bruno for his approval. I also faxed a draft letter from Bruno to Clayton Homes Inc. confirming that the Cerberus team had received appropriate cooperation.

Bruno suggested only small edits. Minutes before midnight

and in time to make Tuesday morning media deadlines, the signed letter was in hand along with the press release. (See Appendix G-2.)

The Bruno letter read, *"We want to thank you and the many outstanding people in your organization who facilitated our due diligence review. We appreciate the cooperation received in what we know was a compressed time frame, requiring a substantial effort from all concerned. The level of professionalism and expertise which we encountered is a tribute to the company's leadership and reflective of the company's outstanding historical performance and premiere position in the industry. We wish you every continued success."*

Clearly we had solid evidence that the Cerberus due diligence process had not been sabotaged. CMH legal eagles were pleased to have this important bullet for their defense guns.

And we would use those defense guns.

CHAPTER 24

Dodging Bullets

On Friday, July 25, arguably the nation's largest class-action securities litigator, Milberg Weiss Bershad Hynes & Lerach, slipped into Blount County Circuit Court. The firm filed derivative and class-action claims, ostensibly on behalf of their *client* and *all* CMH shareholders mirroring allegations that had been heard and dismissed by a Delaware judge repeatedly.

Perhaps one of the investigators, researchers, or assistants employed by Milberg Weiss spotted a Bloomberg, Reuters, or other national news reports covering the Buffett-Clayton transaction. Seeing the potential, you would expect a meeting was held, a consensus reached, and someone said, "Go get 'um".

How odd that a pension plan, the last remnant of a union which ceased to exist years ago, would surface as injured client in this case. Shareholder records did not contain any reference to the Denver Area Meat Cutters and Employees Pension Plan *ever* owning our stock.

The following Monday, Milberg Weiss sought a temporary restraining order to force shareholders to vote on the Berkshire offer that Wednesday. Delaying the shareholder vote again would not be an option.

CMH attorneys countered that the legality of the recess had already been exhaustively litigated in Delaware. Our attorneys appealed to Blount County Circuit Judge W. Dale Young to allow the Delaware court to continue its oversight, thus blocking Milberg Weiss from inappropriate forum shopping.

Strangely, Young granted the injunction, with the caveat that if CMH directors should attempt a second recess, they would have to seek his court's approval. This was the first of a series of surprising and difficult to understand rulings from Judge Young.

Remember Judge Dale Young from the Frozen Embryo case?

The shareholders meeting reconvened on Wednesday, July 30. Kevin was more confident than I was that shareholders would vote in favor of the Buffett offer. I expected the vote to be very close.

Calling the meeting to order promptly at 11 a.m., Kevin joined me at the podium to respond to questions and comments from shareholders anxious for details.

This could be the last time for this Chairman and this President to represent shareholders who had invested billions in our dream.

Orbis' Gray was there again, although noticeably quieter. The fact that the Cerberus offer did not materialize must have taken the wind out of his sails.

Lee and Lovella Richardson were among the long-time shareholders who spoke. He managed investments for a local college; she, the family finances.

He would vote against the sale; she would vote in favor.

"I feel like we've sort of gotten the impression that Clayton Homes will go down the tubes if we don't sell to Berkshire Hathaway and I don't believe that for a minute," Mr. Richardson said.

Mrs. Richardson countered, "If we can't finance them, we can't manufacture them, and we can't sell them. I think we've got a good deal going, and we probably should go ahead and vote on it."

Kevin nudged me, whispering, "Dad, I've done all I can do to communicate the issues and to address shareholder concerns. Let the cards fall where they may. I'm comfortable leaving it up to them.

"Let's count the votes," the young President said as he stepped to the podium.

Kevin responded to a final question, and I announced that all votes had been counted.

The inspector of elections gave his report, "Fifty-two percent of the shareholder votes are in favor of selling the company to Berkshire Hathaway."

The vote was close, but surely enough margin to discourage a recount—we thought.

You would expect this vote to end the debacle and restore the peace. Kevin and his executives could again focus on managing the CMH operations.

Shareholders believed and the media confirmed it was a done deal. All that stood between shareholders and their *Buffett Cash* was some routine paperwork.

The peace was short lived.

William Gray's lawyer was standing by. The lawsuit was filed the next morning in Delaware challenging the election. Accusations of ballot tampering were included in his complaint. After a round of hearings, the judge allowed Gray to audit the entire voting process.

The proxy management specialists were directed to use a fine-tooth comb to examine and recount all of the ballots, an expensive *touch every ballot* procedure. To guard against any improprieties, CMH hired its own specialist firm to monitor Gray's auditing process.

In the first batch of ballots, they zeroed in on one representing 9,175,411 shares. Gray's specialist claimed the ballot was faulty.

Like in the 2000 presidential election fiasco, changing only a few ballots could reverse the election results. Any ballot with a blemish, tear, crease, or smear the Gray specialists singled out to challenge in court. The more ballots they challenged, the more would be disallowed—*they thought*.

Expecting the 9-million-share-ballot to be from a large institutional shareholder, imagine our surprise upon learning that the ballot held my signature. The Orbis election consultant challenged my right to vote those shares.

The ballot represented shares owned by the Clayton Family Foundation.

A few days later we received by fax a copy of the ballot. Inadvertently, I had neglected to add my title of president on the signature line.

It was my view the small technicality would not present a legal issue. Receipt of the proxy had been confirmed. The vote was properly counted. Surely the judge would agree.

Thousands of other votes were challenged for similar insignificant or immaterial reasons. Both sides were spending hundreds of thousands of dollars on lawyers and election experts.

Gray seemed to believe he could reverse the vote with a few successfully challenged ballots. Remember how anxious our nation was over the hanging chads? Votes were challenged. The U.S. Supreme Court had to rule on the merits of the arguments as to which ballots were valid.

Florida all over again—the Clayton Homes version.

Without deliberating, the Delaware court ruled from the bench. The election results were valid. Gray had spent tens of thousands of dollars in vain. CMH had to spend a similar amount to preserve the integrity of the election.

Finally, Warren could "show me the money." No! Not yet.

Instead, Milberg Weiss renewed the battle in Blount County. Joining with Orbis, the formidable legal team on August 4 sought a temporary restraining order to prevent us from consummating the merger. The firms wanted a special master appointed to take possession of the ballots and conduct a recount. They even floated some names.

No doubt Milberg Weiss did not join the battle to simply support Orbis in its effort to block the deal. These hunters were after bigger game.

These combative, hyperaggressive, and take-no-prisoners style lawyers frequently receive huge fees by settling lawsuits on behalf of shareholders. Their clients, in many cases, receive little if any of the settlement.

The defendant company has to eliminate legal harassments, millions in defense attorney fees, disruption of business, embarrassment, and indeterminate risk. It is a cost of doing business—a tax—and we all pay the price in the goods and services we buy.

A gainst Dollar General, Millberg filed a class action lawsuit on Monday, April 30, 2001. The drop in total shareholder value that day was $2.5 billion, according to Yahoo!Finance. This indicates just how devastating their presence is perceived to be by the market.

Millberg Weiss's fees were $33 million, according to a *Forbes* article titled "Mr. Class Action" and dated February 9, 2004.

That same article stated, "Now their own methods are under federal investigation." In referring to the attorneys, the article said, "grizzled and intimidating...flamboyant, sharp-elbowed showman." The article went on, "The firm is so pugnacious."

The settlement for Dollar General shareholders was a few pennies per share. Many would agree their check wasn't enough to buy the gas to get to the post office.

The *Forbes* article went on, "....they have bullied corporate America out of $30 billion in damages and counting...their mission has been unbelievably profitable—especially for themselves." A lawyer referring to Mel Weiss called them "manipulative, deceptive, ruthless."

I magine a West Tennessee kid raised in the cotton patch up against such a formidable foe.

The investigation and restatement of earnings by Dollar General was introduced back on page 290. I am pleased to complete my 16th year as a member of this great company's board of directors.

On August 6, ruling in Clayton's favor, Judge Young allowed the merger to proceed. It appeared this lawsuit was over, and finally shareholders would be paid for their stock.

Yes, the ruling was in our favor. However, the wording of the judge's order would haunt us soon.

With the stay lifted, thanks to Judge Young, our Delaware attorneys were waiting at the door of the Secretary of State's office at daybreak on August 7, 2003.

At 7:30 a.m. sharp, the first order of business for the Secretary of State was to certify the merger. The Certificate for the Berkshire Hathaway-Clayton Homes sale was finally filed.

Ticker tapes worldwide announced the merger. Seeing the news, officials of the New York Stock Exchange halted trading at 8:09 a.m.

Thinking their check was *in the mail*, shareholders were not concerned as they received news of the halt in stock trading as a non-event.

CMH stock would never trade again.

Rushing to the Tennessee Court of Appeals, Milberg Weiss sought a temporary restraining order blocking Berkshire's settlement with shareholders.

Milberg Weiss argued that the certificate of merger was filed knowing that Young's ruling would be challenged. They alleged the merger was filed in Delaware to circumvent the Tennessee appellate court.

Can you believe the firm went so far as to allege the directors had committed fraud! Those irresponsible and reckless charges hurt. As accusations of fraud bounced around the national media, Kevin especially bristled.

We had spent 37 years building the reputation of Clayton Homes. Indeed, our credibility and integrity were among the attractions for Buffett.

Proving fraud was the only legal avenue to void the merger. Milberg Weiss was faced with the dilemma of having to unwind a completed Delaware merger involving two corporations domiciled there. This would be an uphill battle, and they knew it.

On August 8, the Tennessee Court of Appeals stopped everything. Shareholders could not be paid. The court stated, "The purpose of this order is to maintain the status quo of the current state of the merger, whatever that status may be."

Knowing that any decision would likely be appealed—eventually to the Tennessee Supreme Court—the court insisted on a well-written and properly documented record supporting Young's decisions.

To keep shareholder payment from being delayed indefinitely, the court expedited the proceedings. "Due to the time sensitive nature of the matters at issue in the proceedings currently before this Court and the Trial Court on remand, the Trial Court is further instructed to resolve the remanded issues within 14 days from the date of this Order."

It's deposition time in Tennessee! And Nebraska! And California! And Delaware! The depositions were conducted over three days in a dozen cities to meet the 14-day, court-mandated timeline.

Milberg Weiss delivered an 18-page request for documents as attorney fee meters kicked into overdrive, to prepare for a full-blown jury trial.

Directors and CMH officers spent hours in depositions. Staff had to produce a truckload of documents. It appeared the primary objective was to drive up our cost and motivate us to pay a couple of hundred million dollars for a ticket to send Milberg Weiss back to California.

Milberg Weiss is reported to have flown in 22 lawyers, assistants, researchers, and the like, and signed six-month leases for nine luxury condominiums at a cost of $97,200. When you add the travel, catering, and other expenses, you can imagine what the firm invested as they geared up to take us down.

In the meantime, *our* costs were escalating.

We had lawyers defending CMH in Delaware and Tennessee. Buffett deployed professionals from partner Charlie Munger's firm to protect Berkshire Hathaway's interests.

My efforts to keep the fees and cost of this transaction to a minimum now became ineffective. We were spending serious money. Once it starts, the process takes on a life of its own. If anyone has control, it's the lawyers. Driven by attorney-fee-generating greed, the behavior of aggressive and adversarial attorneys fuel the runaway train.

When one of these class action lawsuits takes off, it's a *Happening*. Yes, *Happenings can be nightmares too*!

Milberg Weiss uses scorched-earth tactics when pursuing corporations, hurling insults, threats, and stacks of legal motions with the aim of getting the enemy to surrender without the added cost of a trial.

Our legal team consisted of Hunton & Williams' Richmond and Knoxville offices; Richards, Layton & Finger in Delaware; and Kizer and Black in Maryville.

Milberg Weiss deposed me, CMH director Dan Evins (Cracker Barrel founder), Kevin, and Carl Koella, our vice president of investor relations.

Ed Fuhr, our litigator from Hunton & Williams, was at my elbow as the bright, young Milberg Weiss attorney stated the ground rules for the battering I was about to receive.

Fuhr prepped me—a buzz-phrase for a long session designed to keep the witness brief. "If the question is clear and you can answer with a yes or no, then do that and shut up. If you don't know for sure or don't definitely remember, then answer, *I don't know*, or *I don't remember*, and *shut up*."

Having been deposed a half-dozen or more times—and being a lawyer—I know the process. Nonetheless, I had to listen to his lengthy sermon with his *billable hour* meter running.

Rules prohibit the witness's attorney from speaking, but early in the deposition, Ed's body language indicated he was not happy.

It's difficult for a witness to keep from volunteering information. The questioning attorney plays to that. That's their role. Sure, I volunteered some facts as I justified "yes" or "I don't know" type answers. But it was benign. At least that's my view.

Soon, Ed said annoyed, "Don't you need a break?"

Ed was taking me out back to the woodshed!

Quickly steering me to an empty office, he shut the door, shook his finger in my face, and demanded, "You've got to answer the questions in the manner I instructed. Don't be forced to volunteer information. Period."

Back in the hot seat, Milberg Weiss fired the same questions.

I answered as directed this time.

In the court reporter's printed copies, my deposition had generated over a hundred pages of "I don't know" and "I don't remember."

Early in the grueling session, the youthful, but highly trained Milberg Weiss attorney saw how the deposition was unfolding and he played to it.

Boy, did he!

Going through his notes, he skillfully fired question after question, phrased to assure a series of "I don't know" responses.

This new breed of young class-action attorney is superbly trained. Firms budget large sums for it. Despite his youth and lack of experience, the opposition outplayed Fuhr, at least that day.

Should the case go to trial, and they never do, their attorney would beat me up with that deposition.

I certainly don't agree with Judge Young's ruling, but I can see why in his August 18, 2003, merger-halting opinion, he wrote the following:

"Many (but not all) of the Deponents responded with: 'I don't know,' 'I don't recall,' 'I don't remember.' The answers given by said Deponents may be the absolute truth and the Court does not question the truthfulness of said Deponents."

He said, "This Court presumes every witness gives truthful testimony until the contrary is shown. However, these answers might be considered by a jury in connection with other evidence that tends to prove fraud."

OUCH! I hate that *fraud* word. Sure I'm generally critical of litigators. They have a need for control and tend to trip over their egos. Fueled by their often unproductive and combative behavior patterns, hostilities escalate, and so do billable hours.

Ed bothered me on two issues, three if you count the chartered jet and exorbitant fee.

First, his advice caused me to look bad in the depositions.

Second, he muzzled me.

I was in my office preparing the Chairman's report for the upcoming BB&T executive committee meeting when Kevin called. "Ed Fuhr insists that you stop talking to the media. He'll be the CMH media spokesperson and retain Cynthia Moxley's public relations firm to help him."

Kevin explained that Ed wanted conversations with the media *privileged.* (I touched on this back in Chapter 17.) Certainly, I understood the frequently overused attorney-client *privilege,* which enables the attorney to perpetuate control. I had been cautious with our media communications.

If the company talks directly to the media, the conversations are subject to discovery, but an attorney's communications with the media cannot be used in court. Ed's plan to hire Moxley would preserve the attorney-client privilege.

Previously, I had submitted CMH quotes to the media for Kevin, sometimes for John Kalec, the CFO, and only occasionally from me.

Ed Fuhr appointed himself the CMH media spokesperson.

Talk about driving up billable hours! His quotes suddenly appeared in news wires, business press, local papers, and television around the world. Did the media stop calling? No way! "Who is this guy?" or "What does this mean?" The reporter would ask.

Did I stop talking to the press? Nope! Within a few days, Ed's media stardom had been short lived, and I was providing background and quotes daily.

The *News Sentinel* had been instrumental as a communications resource. Thousands of shareholders, fans of Warren Buffett, friends and family, and especially CMH personnel depended on their generous and detailed coverage.

At the risk of appearing contradictory, I must state for the record, the Hunton and Williams law firm represents us well. Sure, on some days I've had issues with Ed Fuhr, who I admit is bright, creative, and experienced. Give him a few years and he may be one of the best in his field. Allen Goolsby, their senior attorney from Richmond, is an amazing negotiator and a highly professional corporate SEC specialist. You see Allen quoted often in the national press.

Judge Young's second ruling on August 18 prevented shareholders from getting their money—again.

In reversing his earlier ruling, the judge froze the merger and ordered the lawsuit tried before a jury. Possibly reacting to the Appellate Court's reversal of his earlier ruling, Judge Young ordered the lawsuit tried before a jury.

Young reversed his earlier ruling, and the judge allowed the most high-stakes lawsuit of his career to proceed. He froze the merger and ordered the lawsuit expedited.

Imagine the shareholder frustration! This was an unprecedented *Happening.*

We CMH shareholders were in a heckuva fix.

Shareholders voted for the merger. The Delaware court upheld the election. The merger was filed in Delaware. The New York

Stock Exchange stopped the trading of CMH stock—and the local court blocked the shareholder settlement.

Freezing the merger caused harm to Clayton Homes and to thousands of institutional and individual shareholders.

There was no market for the stock. Ownership of the company was unknown. We were in an unprecedented legal no-man's land.

Our attorneys assured us the merger was complete and Berkshire owned the company.

The tension escalated with each day's headline.

Read on.

Briefs for appellate courts must be very carefully drafted and redrafted. Ed was busy in depositions and hearings and leaving the drafting of briefs to young associates in Knoxville and Richmond.

My former intern and CMH's General Counsel Tom Hodges and I recognized the importance of these briefs and the short time allowed by the Tennessee Court of Appeals for preparation.

We forwarded the rough drafts to Tom McAdams, respected Knoxville lawyer and a CMH director—who, of course, had been following the case daily—and asked for his word wizardry.

McAdams polished the briefs and provided talking points in outline form that allowed Fuhr to organize his brief in a smooth logical manner.

It worked.

With Tom Hodges and Kevin's support, I urged Fuhr to use McAdams' suggested draft.

When the Tennessee Court of Appeals on September 3 ruled strongly in our favor, its opinion contained several quotes originating verbatim from McAdams' brief.

The Court of Appeals' detailed and rational opinion rejected every claim that Milberg Weiss put forward.

The Court waded through all the mud and painted a clear picture of the *Happenings* related to the CMH sale.

Finally our actions over the past six months were vindicated. How wonderful it was to see Judge Charles Susano's words printed around the world.

"There is not a scintilla of evidence in this record demonstrating that a single vote was voted in favor of the merger because of any fraudulent act of the defendants or that the vote count was not as certified," this fine judge wrote on behalf of his brethren on the bench.

Milberg Weiss had too much invested to give up, and turned to the Tennessee Supreme Court for a ruling from the appellate court.

Without an additional hearing, the Supreme Court on September 25, 2003, unanimously denied the Milberg Weiss appeal—exactly the ruling we requested.

The agony we experienced between the shareholder meeting and the Tennessee Supreme Court's ruling made eight weeks seem like eight years.

We were confident that the law was on our side—we had already won every battle in Delaware. However, our score in Tennessee was 0 for 4. We remained fearful that the merger somehow could be undone.

If the merger had been unwound, our stock, which had not traded for eight weeks, would be active again on the NYSE. How would Wall Street react?

The Asset Backed Securities market had turned its back on funding the manufactured housing industry. How would we raise the funds to provide mortgages for our homebuyers?

The opposition made what I considered to be an unsupported allegation, crying fraud and breach of fiduciary duty. Would anyone, including shareholders, want to associate with Clayton Homes in the future?

We'll never know.

On September 30, 2003, $1.7 billion was paid to shareholders in *Buffett Cash*.

Now over a year later, the lawsuit is still open, with occasional settlement discussions.

Buffett was determined not to pay the class action attorneys even one penny. That's his philosophy. Mine too. At the time of this writing, no payment has been made. However, the directors and officers insurance company has other thoughts on the subject.

"What would Clayton stock be selling for today had Warren Buffett not read your book?" I am frequently asked this question when I speak at civic clubs and conventions.

During the 20 years CMH had been a public company, I was often asked a similar question, "What will a share of CMH be worth a year from now?"

My answer to both questions was the same. Stocks go up and stocks go down. Over the year, CMH could be up 50 percent–or down by half. That's how the stock market works, especially for a cyclical industry. There is no way I or anyone else can be certain. I believe CMH would be *much* lower than $12.50 had not Warren Buffett opened his billfold to the industry.

CMH stock sold as low as $9.23 on October 7, 2002—the year before the New York Stock Exchange halted trading. Some shareholders realized as much as $14 on August 27, 2002.

Clayton Homes stock today would not be selling for more than $12.50.

I believe that.

But, being a lawyer, I have to plead my case further.

Some shareholders couldn't budge from their firm belief that CMH would be higher than $12.50 if we hadn't sold.

They argue the following. "The stock went up after the announcement and would have continued to rise." They also maintain, "Industry stocks advanced after the sale was announced, and CMH would too."

My response was that the stock price of a company being acquired tends to go up after the announcement of a merger.

Why? A higher bid is anticipated. Also, word of the sale caused Wall Street to believe Warren saw an upturn in the industry. That was not the case.

Just the fact that Buffett validated the industry by buying CMH, and later Oakwood, has added a nice premium to most competitors' stock prices.

Tracking the price of industry stocks since the merger leads to erroneous conclusions. Had Buffett not validated the industry by bidding on Clayton, or if shareholders had rejected his offer, the industry would not enjoy his shining halo effect. (See Marty Lavin's discussion on this in Appendix E-1.)

With ONLY one source of capital for mortgage lending; with greatly increased regulatory cost to build and install; with the increased cost of consumer litigation; with an acute shortage of good sites in many markets; and with greatly increased competition from the large track mega-builders, then a reasonable cash price from a credible buyer made solid sense to the CMH management and board.

Over the 15 months since our sale to Buffett, the total industry funds raised on Wall Street would not finance CMH homebuyers for even one quarter.

Some believed that US Bank would bail out the industry as their newly opened lending office was announced. I assure you that US Bank will be cautious. There is no way these astute bankers will offer the liberal underwriting standards the industry became addicted to over the past decade.

When General Motors set up shop, many thought this premier lender would fill the void created by Conseco's bankruptcy. GM's excellent underwriting platforms will not accommodate the industry's appetite for liberal lending.

Chase, leaving the industry in spring 2004, reduced lending capacity more than US Bank and GM will accommodate.

But for Buffett's supporting the industry with his AAA credit rating and virtually unlimited lending capacity, manufactured housing would be up the creek without a paddle.

Since most manufactured home buyers require a mortgage, the reality is several factories are running today because of the Clayton Homes sale to Berkshire Hathaway.

Industry-wide, just under 200 factories are operating today, down from 330 in 1998, and this year 131,000 homes will be produced. Over $5 billion will be required to fund homebuyer mortgages, creating an opportunity for the Clayton mortgage units to employ *Buffett Cash.*

Vanderbilt Mortgage provides financing for the Clayton and newly acquired Oakwood sales centers. Homebuyers purchasing from competitors enjoy financing through 21st Mortgage, founded by Tim Williams–now a wholly owned subsidiary of CMH.

Remember Tim from Chapter 13? For more than 21 years he built and operated Clayton's Vanderbilt Mortgage unit before leaving in 1995. I convinced Tim on allowing CMH to own 25 percent of 21st Mortgage, which he and former Clayton CFO Rich Ray founded.

Homestar, a Texas-based manufacturer and retailer, owned 50 percent of the new company but bankrupted in 1997. At the liquidation auction, Tim purchased an additional 25 percent of 21st Mortgage, as did CMH.

With management by Tim as CEO and Rich as CFO and supported by CMH capital, 21st Mortgage has become a premier lender in only nine years.

Now Berkshire owns this fine company also. Tim and Rich have a wagonload of *Buffett Cash,* much of it managed by our First State Bank Trust Group.

Being on the board of FSB BancShares, Tim sees first-hand that FSB offers a unique low-cost approach to estate planning and investing.

Tim and Rich are phenomenal business leaders. They have a great staff and solid systems. The landscape is littered with skeletons of those who attempted to do what they do so well. The experienced team manages risk and mitigates losses, and maintains steady growth unruffled by the industry's vicious cycles.

With the serious void in manufactured housing mortgage financing, Tim is buying portfolio after portfolio of loans at significant discount from lenders retreating from the industry. The excellent staff gives the newly acquired customers terrific personal attention, and delinquencies and foreclosures are dramatically reduced.

Kay and I recently flew Tim and Amy to Green Turtle Key in the Bahamas for their wedding. They let us stay for the honeymoon. What fun!

CHAPTER 25

Buffett Cash

Now I had a wagonload of *Buffett Cash*. I received $480 million in cash from the world's greatest investor for my stake in Clayton Homes, and the revenuers scooped up $60 million. (See Appendix G-4.)

Ouch!

I have been blessed with the ability to make far more money than I deserve. I am grateful.

Jerry Hollyfield, a lawyer and accountant, files our tax returns. Jim Shelby, a brilliant CPA, has guided the family with excellent estate planning counsel for 40 years.

The two agree that combined personal and corporate income thus far amounts to more than $1 billion.

Deduct a third for taxes and it's still an enormous sum.

I envisioned that we would give back to the community, even in the early years as brother Joe and I struggled to build the business.

Cash was not available until I sold stock at the Clayton Homes' initial public offering in 1983. With my sweat equity transformed into a popular Wall Street trading security, I began to gift cash or stock to a wide range of charitable efforts.

Forming the Clayton Family Foundation in the early 1990s, we increased our support to recognized charitable organizations. A broad base of agencies focusing on education, the homeless and disadvantaged, art and culture, health, and youth are recipients of annual gifts.

Assets of the foundation soon increased to $20 million through conservative investment and additional gifts of CMH shares. Stock was sold each year to fund $1 million in annual giving.

In 1993 as family office manager, Jeanne Campbell, and I completed our estate plan update, the decision was made to gift 8 million CMH shares to the foundation. The Berkshire Hathaway merger turned that gift into $100 million of *Buffett Cash*, making our foundation the largest in the region.

The Clayton Family Foundation today has $120 million in invested assets.

The foundation provides an effective structure that will allow the family—for generations—to continue supporting the communities where we live and conduct business.

God led me into banking, I believe, primarily to support the foundation and its charitable initiatives, although I didn't recognize this early on. I feel directed *now* to grow our banks and contribute the earnings to the foundations. The newly formed bank trust group will manage and conserve the foundation in perpetuity. That's my dream.

It seems to me that vastly different skills are required to effectively give away huge sums of money. In fact, I think it is easier to earn money and preserve assets.

Giving demands an enormous amount of time and just plain hard work. There is so much noise out there in fund raising. More and more groups launch capital campaigns, while all organizations continuously solicit operating funds.

In a business environment, you simply find a prospect and deliver a product or service. These decisions, after due diligence and screening, tend to be logical and clear-cut.

In philanthropy, evaluating carefully planned, well-prepared and scripted presentations designed to evoke emotion can be extremely difficult.

Saying no is hard. That's the intent.

Traditionally, foundations solicited and readily accepted grant applications. However, the current trend is for large donors to proactively seek out promising beneficiaries. Donors are involved in developing program plans. Progress is monitored, and results evaluated. Focusing on accountability, this process is labor and time intensive.

This is the major reason I give at the highest level to the United Way. They tell us our family is the second largest supporter of the agency in the East Tennessee area. We trust United Way to make sound decisions in selecting beneficiaries and to hold them accountable for the desired results.

Examples of gifts made by the Clayton Family Foundation include the following: $3.25 million to the Knoxville Museum of Art; $1 million to Baptist Hospital to fund the Clayton Birthing Center; $1 million to the University of Tennessee's Clayton Center for Entrepreneurial Law; and $1 million to help fund the University's Clayton Chair of Excellence in Finance.

Proceeds from the sale of the first edition of *First A Dream* raised directly and indirectly $800,000 for the beautiful restoration of a Knoxville treasure, the Tennessee Theatre.

That's an interesting story. Expecting a mention in the *Knoxville News Sentinel*, I sent a review copy of the book to publisher Bruce Hartmann. He scanned it that night and the next morning he handed it to Amy Nolan, the seasoned business writer who followed CMH. He said, "Amy, let's serialize Jim's book."

Now folks, that's a *Happening*. Imagine my opening the newspaper every day and seeing from one to four pages devoted to my new book—with pictures. You couldn't miss it.

You can see the entire serial on the *News Sentinel* Web site at www.knoxnews.com. They've already asked for permission to serialize this *New Edition.*

Of course, I approved.

I got hundreds of phone calls. Bookstores clamored for the book before we could stock their shelves.

Recognizing immediately that the book was going to sell, I looked for a worthwhile charity needing immediate funds. I did not want to realize any income from the book. That's why I self-published.

I chose the Tennessee Theatre Foundation because their fundraising to restore the historical landmark was stalled.

In Henderson, the book receipts are donated to First State Bank's major charitable cause, Relay for Life, an annual celebration recognizing and honoring cancer survivors and benefiting the American Cancer Society.

All proceeds—not just the profit—from the sale of this new edition will be donated to the same respected charitable efforts.

Recently we gave Freed Hardeman University back home in Henderson a large donation.

I love the background behind that gift.

After the book was published, I received a lot of invitations from universities and civic clubs to speak. One of the more memorable speech *Happenings* resulted from accepting an invitation from Freed Hardeman University.

Dr. Milton Sewell is a great Christian leader and the university's dynamic president.

Over lunch in the university's cafeteria, he said, "We'd like to confer an honorary Ph.D. at our upcoming commencement."

I respectfully declined for two reasons: the calendar wouldn't accommodate—and I knew a significant contribution would be expected.

Folks, honorary Ph.D.s are not free.

Dr. Sewell is wonderful, but he is persistent. Visiting in our home a few weeks later, he again brought up the topic. "Eddy Arnold has agreed to accept an honorary degree if you will, too." He then added, "Mr. Arnold insists you deliver our commencement address."

I'd managed to say no to Sewell, but not to Eddy Arnold.

Oh boy! Here comes another honorary Ph.D.

The receiving line wrapped around the University gym and extended a few hundred feet down the street. Sitting on stools for two hours, Eddy, Alice Arnold, Kay and I greeted warm fans. Granted, most had not come to see me. It was such fun to hear "I knew you back in high school" or "we are distant cousins."

Eddy must have autographed 200 commencement programs for admiring fans. Happily, I signed a dozen or so books brought to the occasion by my family and childhood friends.

After Eddy signed the last autograph, staff ushered us to a private dining room. Over a fine dinner, Dr. Sewell and Burton Williams, the University's director of financial and estate planning, graciously related stories about the rich Freed Hardeman tradition.

It was wonderful getting to know Burton, who is one of the sharpest and most personable young men I know. Between courses, Burton enthusiastically said, "Please give me every detail you remember about my grandfather and great grandfather."

In 1950, his grandfather, James Williams, my high school principal, had persuaded Burton's great grandfather, Uncle Tom Williams, to audition me for his popular Saturday morning radio show. (That story is back in Chapter 3.)

Matt Daniels and his wife Megan had joined us for the elegant dinner, as had Burton's beautiful fiancée Nicole. The young couples were already great friends.

As we talked, it was obvious that Matt and Burton shared a common interest in banking and finance. Leaving the dinner I whispered to Matt, "If you agree, ask him to join our bank board." Matt agreed. Burton accepted.

Reconnecting with Burton's forefathers—powerful figures in

my early development—was gratifying. This remarkable event occurred because I asked Eddy Arnold to endorse *First A Dream*.

The entire day was an unforgettable *Happening*.

Now I have four honorary Ph.D.s. Freed Hardeman gave me the fourth and last.

Man, they're expensive—you'll see what I mean.

On January 14, 2004, Dr. Sewell set up a meeting at Eddy Arnold's Nashville office. Included were Eddy, Henderson's Mayor Eddie Patterson, Sewell and me.

After a warm welcome, Eddy proudly gave us a tour of his office.

Every inch of every wall was filled with treasures documenting his unparalleled career. His memorabilia included gold records, photographs, and letters from famous people and adoring fans.

As we settled into our chairs, Eddy said, "Now what can I do for you nice people?"

Handing him a presentation folder, Dr. Sewell described his vision for a new Fine Arts Center at Freed Hardeman.

Quickly thumbing through the 12-page folder, Eddy interrupted, "Dr. Sewell, you know this is going to cost an *awful* lot of money. I'll bet $10 million."

Dr. Sewell replied with a grin, "Actually it's only $9 million."

"Well," Eddy responded in his deep, resonant voice, "I can't do that Dr. Sewell. My money is *working*. It's all tied up at the bank. I can't *disturb* that."

Eddy's *pushback* was the best I've heard, and one that I now use. It works. Thanks! Eddy.

Dr. Sewell went home empty handed—this time.

A few weeks later at my home in Knoxville, Dr. Sewell persuaded Kay and me to write a $1 million check for his arts center.

I bet Eddy will happily match it. I hope so.

Freed Hardeman also will benefit from my $5 million pledge for construction of an airport and adjacent industrial park. These resources will foster economic development and job creation in the area.

The new airport will encourage affluent alumni to visit their university more frequently. Dr. Sewell believes that the convenience of a new airport will make the University more accessible to world-renowned researchers and scholars. The speakers and guests traveling to his premier Advisory Board Benefit Dinner, an annual $1 million fund raiser, will enjoy the nearby facility.

Flying in to speak this year is legendary CBS news anchor Walter Cronkite. Past luminaries include President George H. W. Bush, Prime Minister Margaret Thatcher, Senator Bill Frist, Senator Elizabeth Dole, and celebrity TV host Regis Philbin.

Our First State Bank is a proud sponsor.

CHAPTER 26

BACK HOME AGAIN

I enjoy visiting back home. Occasionally when in Henderson, I drive the eight miles to Finger and reminisce. Only a few landmarks remain standing.

Dad and Mother's old home where I was raised from age 10 to 18 is still there. A new red brick house stands where my Clayton grandparents lived.

A square dance is still held every Saturday night in the old gym, while the four-room schoolhouse has been gone for years—but not the memories.

I especially recall the smallest of the four classrooms where I spent the first grade with Mattie Lou Ward, my teacher. (See Chapter 1.)

Over the years, when driving by the site, I have remembered Miss Ward fondly and how much I loved school that year. I've often thought about how nice it would be to thank her for teaching me that learning can be fun.

One of the great pleasures resulting from *First A Dream* is reconnecting with those from back home, but reuniting with Miss Ward would be only through my book.

She read the book a few weeks before her death on January 21,

2004, according to her daughter Linda Autry. Calling Kim Burnett, Clayton's center manager and my good friend in Amarillo, Linda asked for permission to quote from the book at her mother's memorial. (See page 370-G.)

Moving to Texas, Miss Ward gave up her beloved teaching career in 1947 to marry Troy Edward Maness. They moved to Texas.

She will be remembered for her love of children and of teaching. Indeed, she is remembered in the book *First A Dream*, printed in 2002, authored by Jim Clayton, one of her first grade students. He wrote the following:

"Ms. Ward taught me how to read and write, and I think a lot more. I was lucky to have her—sweet, tolerant, patient, yet completely in charge. Instead of trying her patience, every student tried very hard to please her.

"I knew I was Ms. Ward's favorite student. Later on, I would learn that each of her students felt the same. She had the ability to stay in tune with each person."

Linda told me her mother had enjoyed the book and looked forward to a reunion. Gosh, what I would have given for that.

Now, my calendar sends me *back home* every month where Jack Bulliner expertly chairs the board meetings for my First State Bank in Henderson.

Remember Jack and Patsy Bulliner and how we purchased their fine bank? The story is in Chapter 19.

Thanks, Jack, for giving us the following update.

In October 2001, fate was about to weave some mighty powerful magic. I received a call from our beautiful daughter, Randi.

"Daddy, is it too late for Jim Clayton to enter a bid for our bank?" I could tell she was excited as she added, "Mr. Clayton will up the Jim Ayers bid."

That set into motion a process that led to Jim's becoming the owner of First State Bank.

I am so pleased that ownership remained in the hands of a native son.

Jim's support has been meaningful to our staff, customers and community—and has allowed FSB to move quickly forward. Patsy refers to Jim as a "master genius."

After three productive years, loans are up 50 percent while delinquencies are at record lows. Our staff and customers enjoy our new systems and up-to-date technology.

The new branch in Jackson is "humming," and our trust department is at $100 million—after one year.

Patsy and I are pleased American City Bank joined our organization. When I was president of the Tennessee Bankers Association in the '70s, ACB President George Vibbert and his wonderful wife Elwanda became close friends of ours.

Spending time and traveling again with George and Elwanda, are unforgettable memories—thanks to Jim.

We sorely miss George, a great person and a talented community banker of the highest order.

The acquisition of the Bank of Friendship, having branches in Lexington, Covington, and North Jackson, will increase capacity and broaden our customer base.

Acquiring 26 percent of the stock in Merchants and Planters Bank in Toone should evolve into a synergistic relationship. I would expect their board and management to eventually welcome our support.

I confidently handed over my president and CEO responsibilities on January 1, 2004, to Matt Daniels, an amazing young leader. Never have I seen a quicker study.

Teaming with Barry Rich, our respected CFO, Matt's leadership has inspired our team members to embrace change and support our acquisitions and new product announcements.

First State Bank is much larger now, but Patsy and I still proudly call each individual Friend.

It has been my great pleasure to serve as chairman during these exciting years.

And–the best is yet to come.

Jack Bulliner

The bank's board under Jack and Matt's leadership is exemplary. They are a positive community interface and conscientious in their approach to regulatory responsibilities. Without their active and enthusiastic support, First State Bank would not own an extraordinary 70 percent share of the market.

With his finance education and experience, Burton Williams' fresh perspective has been well received by the board.

Clayton Skinner, my first cousin, who joined the board soon after purchase, represents the bank well. Interestingly, his father, my Uncle Charlie, served on Jack's board for 15 years until his death in 1975.

Kay and I truly wish we could spend more time *back home* with our old and new friends and family. The board, the Skinners, the Bulliners, the Daniels, and so many others have made us feel welcome.

With our room reserved in their comfortable home, we never have a motel bill when spending the night in Henderson, thanks to the Skinners' hospitality.

Thanks to my favorite cousin for contributing the following:

I was thrilled when Jim asked me to join the board at First State Bank where my father had enjoyed serving for years. Already a long-time customer of First State Bank, I respected Jack and his board.

I remember well meeting Matt Daniels at my first board meeting. Jim had borrowed him from CMH for the day to make a presentation to our board. Matt shared an impressive economic and marketing analysis he had assembled on the bank's trade area.

Matt showed his last slide and answered our questions. "Don't you think Jack should offer Matt a job?" Jim chimed in.

We agreed—unanimously!

Linda and I are amazed at how fast our bank has grown since Matt arrived.

We were pleased to have them stay for a year in my mom's little house next door. What a treat to see the delightful young couple each day. We treated them like our own.

Matt and Megan renovated an older home with a huge lawn and lots of tall oaks and a flower garden. It's at the edge of town and only five minutes from the bank. The gifted 4th grade school teacher's drive is little more.

Moving day was bittersweet.

I completely supported Jack's decision to appoint Matt president and CEO of FSB. At 24 years old he had more banking knowledge than most bank officers who are 30 years his elder.

First State Bank has supported our wonderful community for 116 years. We are very fortunate.

Clayton Skinner

Remember Mike Tedford invited me to lunch at his office on Air Force One.

I wrote the following at the request of Mike's hometown newspaper—mine too— the *Chester County Independent*. The editor didn't change a word.

Mike Tedford Flies High

At the Knoxville Air Guard facility I mingled with the press and watched the President wave as he climbed into the limousine. As the entourage sped away for the President's speech at Oak Ridge, I felt a tap on my shoulder.

"Hi Mr. Clayton, I'm Mike." As I turned, he added "Welcome to Air Force One." It was Mike Tedford's friendly voice.

Mike grabbed my hand and said, "Let me show you where I work." I felt like I had known him all my life. Actually, his grandmother, Blanche Tedford, and my mom, Ruth Browder Clayton, worked at the Henderson shirt factory for 17 years together.

Mike showed me every nook and cranny of this majestic ship and allowed me to sit at the President's desk. I chatted—one ATP pilot to another—with the captain Colonel Mark Tillman and sat for 15 minutes in the pilot's seat. Although the mighty aircraft first flew President George H. Bush in 1990—actually there are two exactly alike—it is remarkably well equipped, as you would expect. Interestingly, the planes will not have a "glass cockpit" until 2008. My 1994 Citation Jet has it.

As chief of communications for the Air Force One team, Mike sits alongside his two assistants in the command center—immediately aft of the cockpit. Mike hand delivers, personally, every e-mail or fax for the President.

When President Bush decided to take his surprise trip to Iraq for Thanksgiving 2003, only five people including Mike and the President had knowledge of the daring flight. Two days before the trip, Mike was allowed to bring one assistant into the plan. Only one member of the White House staff would know.

The President and the select crew lifted off from Crawford, Texas, at 7:27 p.m. on Thanksgiving eve. With Mike carefully monitoring CNN Asia, the pilot was prepared to abort the flight at the first hint that the President was not with his family back at the Crawford ranch.

Mike proudly said, "Our President left his loved ones back in Crawford in the same way our fighting men and women leave their families—with little notice.

At 5:30 p.m. on Thanksgiving Day, just after dark, the mighty ship made one circle over the huge Baghdad airport starting from 20,000 feet. Diving 5,000 feet per minute in a perfect spiral, the captain landed and quickly taxied to a vacant corner of the air base.

On the ground, the happy President greeted thousands of surprised service men and women. Two hours and 12 minutes later, the President departed for Crawford before the rest of the world knew.

Climbing 5,000 feet per minute at 600 miles per hour, Mike called out the minutes. As he reached 10, the crew cheered. They were out of missile range.

Twenty hours later the elated President and his select team were home with their families celebrating Thanksgiving.

Flawlessly executed, the only blip in the entire scheme involved a British Airways captain. Over London he radioed the controller asking, "Isn't that Air Force One at our nine o-clock?"

The controller relayed the question to Air Force One. "No! We are a Gulfstream," was Colonel Tillman's calm response. With a "Roger" from the airline pilot, the colonel was convinced that his story had been accepted.

We reminisced about two farm lads growing up in Henderson—the old school, our Principal James Williams, the leadership training in FFA, and our meaningful mentors A.C. and Alma Jones. (See Chapter 2.)

As we shook hands, I said, "Mike I look forward to seeing you back in Henderson." Then I added, "Want to help me with the bank when you retire?"

Chief Tedford retires from the Air Force after 30 years in 2006.

Mike and his lovely wife, Katrina, stopped by First State Bank as I was walking out of the August board meeting. They had just enrolled their beautiful daughter, Shannon, in nearby Union University. Smiling at Katrina I said, "I told Mike he'd make a great community banker."

Visiting with the happy attractive couple, I am optimistic about spending lots of time with them over the coming years.

First State Bank is rich in tradition and I wish space would permit me to relate story after story associated with the bank and its people.

As Matt and Jack grew the bank, a CFO became increasingly necessary.

I'll let Barry Rich tell this one.

I had been a partner in the accounting firm, Philhours, Rich & Fletcher for 10 years. In February 2000, Jim Clayton, Matt Daniels, and their director, Clayton Skinner, made an appointment and came to see me.

A few weeks earlier, Jim had purchased First State Bank, which had never been audited by an independent CPA firm.

I was immediately impressed with the dedicated trio. They were exactly the type of entrepreneur-bankers that I like to serve.

The meeting went well. I expected to be retained.

Jim's letter arrived three days later. He decided to stay with the large regional firm that he used at BankFirst.

I called Matt and thanked him for considering our firm, and said, "Matt, feel free to call anytime you have a question." Notice the emphasis on free.

He did—and I didn't mind. I liked Matt a lot.

Checking in from time to time, Matt would ask about various accounting, regulatory, and other issues. He was quick and did not waste my unbilled time—much.

During one of these chats, I suggested, "Matt, with your optimistic growth plans, you better be looking for a good CFO."

It did not occur to me that I would soon solve that issue for him.

Later Matt asked if I'd heard that the FDIC was auctioning the Bank of Alamo's loan portfolio in Dallas.

I quickly responded, "I have. You know that's the first Tennessee bank to fail in years. It made the headlines in Jackson. They were my client a few years back."

Matt engaged me to help and we were at Jackson airport the next morning ready to board when Jim's sleek jet taxied up.

Obviously familiar with the plane, Matt quickly unlatched the door and gestured me up the steps into the cabin.

"Hi Barry, good to see you again, thanks for going with us," came the friendly voice from the cockpit, as Matt closed the jet's door.

It took me a minute to recognize that the voice belonged to Jim. "He is our pilot?" I wondered. Matt had not told me Jim was a pilot, too. Was I nervous? Yes, a little.

After take-off, Matt explained that Jim holds the highest rating issued by the FAA for jet flight. In addition, he carries a special exemption that allows him to fly without the normally required second pilot.

Matt handed me a copy of First A Dream. *I scanned a few chapters during the brief flight and was impressed with Jim's story and the values he expressed. His basic business philosophies were mine—exactly.*

In just over an hour, we had safely landed at Love Field in Dallas, near the FDIC regional headquarters.

Over the next two busy days we pored over the Bank of Alamo loan files. Many I recognized from auditing the bank a few years back. Matt and Jim appreciated the process I used in evaluating file after file of bad loans.

I enjoyed the two long days of hard work with them. Over dinner, we talked about pricing the loans, and about trends in the industry. A bond of mutual respect was developing.

Back at the Jackson airport, Jim autographed my copy of his book as he said graciously, "Thank you for assisting Matt on this project. I hope you will help us again soon."

A few days later I stopped by First State Bank on the way to a client appointment in nearby Selmer. At lunch Matt shared his and Jim's vision for the bank.

I was impressed with Matt's optimism and focus. We shook hands as I said, "Sounds to me like your team is going to need a top notch CFO to support all those acquisitions. When it's time, let's talk."

My phone rang the next morning. A friendly voice said, "Barry, this is Matt. Jim and I want you to be our CFO."

Leaving the firm was the toughest decision I've made. But, I needed to prove that I could execute the tax, accounting, and compliance programs that I had recommended for the past 20 some years.

Elsewhere in the book, you will see that I have had a very busy, rewarding, and fun year and a half.

Barry Rich

The first acquisition for Barry Rich after joining our team was the Bank of Friendship closed in December 2004–as this book went to press. It is a story most of which is best left untold. The media had reported the huge loan charge offs and resulting regulatory problems.

Fortunately, Paul Priddy, an experienced bank executive, had been recruited as chairman and president. After Paul hired capable lenders, he turned it around and produced a profit for the second quarter 2004.

With the bank's results improving, a large shareholder came to see Matt Daniels. Matt heard the complicated history of the troubled bank. Plagued with shareholder disputes, lawsuits between the bank and former officers, and disagreements over the owner-ship of a building, we knew the price would be low.

We negotiated an acceptable price and teamed with the new CEO in dealing with numerous and complex issues. Over many months Barry, Matt, and Steve Eisen, our bank attorney, worked through most of the conflicts.

With the bank's reputation tarnished, we merged Friendship into First State Bank and will operate Friendship's four offices as branches.

Our investments in community banks are now over $40 mil-lion—near half of our planned allocation of *Buffett Cash*.

Kay and I visited the Bank of Friendship where we welcomed and chatted with each friendly person.

After meeting and greeting all the staff, Paul drove us to lunch in Jackson. Matt and Barry joined us at Suede's where we met the owners, Debbie and Bart Swift.

I was pleased to learn that the affable Bart Swift who greeted us was the son-in-law of the late Carl Perkins. Remember the gui-tar picker on my radio show 52 years earlier. (See page 43.) Suede's is named after Carl's huge hit song "Blue Suede Shoes."

Two tour buses had just unloaded, and there was not a table in the main dining room to be found. Bart greeted us personally—he and Barry had served on the Boy Scouts board—and he quickly set us a table in the banquet hall.

Barry gave him a copy of *First A Dream*, and we reminisced about Carl helping me with my radio program. He was an engag-ing host. "He could teach our bankers about customer service," I told Barry.

A few weeks later, Bart applied for a position at the Bank of Friendship. Paul Priddy, our president, happily received my favorable vote for Bart. Barry and Matt had already approved his application. A city councilman and tireless worker in the com-munity, Bart is going to be a great leader and ambassador for our team.

The book launched another *Happening*.

CHAPTER 27

Banking in Retirement

Today, FSB BancShares, our bank holding company, is the proud parent of 3.26 banks—and more in the pipeline. They are: First State Bank, Henderson (100 percent); American City Bank in Tullahoma and Manchester (100 percent); and Bank of Friendship of Lexington, Covington, Jackson, and Friendship (100 percent).

We also own shares in Merchants & Planters with offices in Bolivar and Toone (26 percent). Buying this minority interest from several shareholders, we were assured that the majority would soon welcome our support.

We underestimated the influence of their recently appointed chairman, Arthur McCarver. He is an effective leader who loves his job. I have to admit, he is a much better salesman than I am—at least on his home turf.

The holdout board members convinced shareholders that we did not pay enough for our shares. Believing that operating results can be improved over the next two years, shareholders are holding out for higher price.

If the chairman's predictions do materialize, we are likely to make a profit on our shares. If they don't, our price of $125 per share will be attractive to the shareholders.

We look forward to the day that attorney fees stop and we can either team with M&P, or sell our stock and exit. After all, we can quickly build new banks, *de nova*, in their markets. We will remain flexible and work toward a positive outcome—for all involved.

The American City Bank acquisition was quick, pleasant, and involved complete cooperation at every step.

The bank's president, George Vibbert had retained Steve Eisen, partner in the Baker Donelson law firm, to explore a potential sale of the bank. Steve confidentially contacted Jim Ayers and Stan Puckett. Stan was immediately interested.

When talks with Puckett slowed, Steve mentioned, again confidentially, to Barry Rich, our CFO, that we should look at ACB. After Barry analyzed the Tullahoma and Manchester markets and researched the public information on the FDIC web site, he recommended that we take a look.

I asked my assistant, Tina Adkins, to look for a time when I would be in Nashville for a Dollar General board meeting, or other opportunity to meet with Steve and Mr. Vibbert.

She advised that on December 5, 2003, I was scheduled to be in Nashville to tour MidCountry Financial's small loan offices. They wanted me to invest. Later in the day, I was to meet with the owner of an interesting mortgage origination boutique. Matt would be with me.

I had scheduled a visit with Pat at *Wine:30* without telling Tina—and was reluctant to cancel our happy hour routine. Let me stop and digress.

Pat had called a week earlier. The conversation went something like this. "Jim, my calendar indicates you are in town on Tuesday. Can we meet at W*ine:30*?"

"Book it," I said.

Let me translate. *Wine:30* means 90 minutes—sometimes more —of swapping *vintage war* stories over a bottle of *young* wine at a watering hole near the airport.

Pat Harrison has been my friend and banking mentor for over 40 years (see page 205). We schedule *Wine:30* several times a year when I'm in Nashville.

Wine:30 is a special occasion for me—and I think for Pat, too.

No one celebrates CMH success more than Pat. He loves to recall his difficulty in keeping Commerce Union Bank sold on Clayton—early on. Beginning in the 1960s Pat believed in, and trusted CMH and its management.

It would take another book to thank Pat for his role in my life.

"Pat we'll re-schedule *Wine:30, soon.* Sorry to cancel—I've gotta go see a man about buying a bank."

Precisely at 4:30 p.m., an immaculately dressed couple appearing to be in their 50's approached the reception desk of Mercury Air. Matt introduced himself—then me. While I showed off my jet to the Vibberts, Matt confirmed that the conference room Tina had reserved was available.

After introductions all around, George, Steve, Matt and I took our positions around the large table.

Steve had sent the well-respected banker a copy of *First A Dream.* George pulled the copy from his briefcase saying, "You have to autograph this for me." Much to my surprise, George had not only read it—he had memorized it.

For some 10 minutes, George focused on the book, pointing out all the people he knew in the 32 pages of pictures. When he pointed to a picture of Jack Bulliner, Matt and I elaborated on the First State Bank story and how we had come to know Jack and Patsy.

George had met Jack, the popular president of the Tennessee Bankers Association, in 1977 and 1978. They had become friends as had their wives, Elwanda and Patsy.

He wanted to talk about Warren Buffett and his acquisition of my company. From newspaper accounts, he knew that I had received cash for my stock and that CMH management would continue to run the company.

Fascinated with the unusual transaction, he asked, "Did Buffett really buy your company without a face to face meeting? And, he didn't visit your facilities?"

He asked me to confirm what Steve had told him—that we were interested in buying ACB in the same manner.

Having experienced weeks of due diligence, site visits, and inquiry with his current prospective buyer, he was not looking forward to initiating a similar process with us.

I assured George that, subject to agreement on price, we would buy ACB, *all cash,* just as Berkshire Hathaway had bought Clayton Homes—and there would be no site visits or due diligence.

Leaning forward, I said, "Buffett bought Clayton because of reputation and credibility—mine and Kevin's. I will buy your bank based on its reputation and your credibility."

As you would expect, George had kept his salary at a modest level and most of their estate was concentrated in ACB stock—even his retirement plan. No one could ever accuse George Vibbert of "not eating his own cooking."

I explained, "Yes, Mr. Vibbert, we would be primarily paying for a relationship with you, your board, and the fine customers of American City Bank."

Getting down to business, Steve and George briefly hit the high points of the Puckett offer—it was well above the average recently paid for community banks.

George was comfortable with the Puckett price, but he was uncertain that his older shareholders would support the sale if they were paid in stock.

He explained.

"If we are paid in stock, it may go down when the acquisition is announced—that often happens. During the two-month wait for the shareholder vote it could go down more. Then, as we begin selling the thinly traded stock, it is likely to drop even further."

Matt said, "The nice thing about selling to Jim is that you and your shareholders will know exactly what you are going to get."

I outlined our plan to invest $100 million of my *Buffett Cash* in community banks like his—over the next 24 months.

George later stated, "At that point I lost all interest in the Greene County offer."

On the way out, he complimented me on writing a good book. Chatting with Elwanda, I said, "Make George write his autobiography—and the history of your great bank."

We shook hands and agreed to talk again. I urged George to call the Bulliners at First State Bank. George said he would.

Barry and Steve began to prepared a formal offer the next day.

ACB had been and is currently very successful. The Stan Puckett offer of stock and a little cash was priced aggressively. We would have to pay the shareholders a sizeable premium.

I asked Barry and Steve to draft a creative offer giving the ACB shareholders—in *Buffett Cash*—close to the same price offered by Green County in stock. However, $10 per share of the price would be escrowed for a year and paid if the bank met reasonable performance standards.

The requirements to receive the bonus were based on the bank's business plan George had shared with us. If management delivered the planned results, the shareholders would receive an additional $10 per share.

George and his chairman, Dr. Frank Glass, were pleased—the agreement was signed on April 21, 2004.

The more time Kay and I spent with George and Elwanda, the more we liked them. We flew the Vibberts and Bulliners to the bank convention in June. They stayed with us in our new winter home in Boca Raton—the memories from the trip are priceless.

It would be our last time together.

George looked great and participated fully in all the busy Florida activities.

At our first meeting George had told me about his significant health problems–two years earlier.

I saw him last at Nashville's Baptist Hospital on August 24, 2004. Visiting with him and Elwanda for an hour, I gave him an update on another successful ACB quarter.

He held my hand as I was leaving and said, "I've been blessed with great shareholders—but Jim, you are the best."

I will never forget that moment.

My wonderful friend passed away on September 5, 2004.

A few days after his memorial Elwanda related to me, "George was so happy and optimistic to not be constrained by limited capital. He was looking forward to adding new branches and additional products."

Then she added, "Oh how I wish George could have had five years with you."

George gave us a wonderful staff, committed management, and a great chairman, Dr. Frank Glass, who provided this account of the ACB *Happenings.*

George Vibbert, our revered president, called on the way back from meeting Jim Clayton in Nashville.

He exclaimed, "Mr. Chairman, he has the CASH." We laughed frequently during the busy weeks that followed over that lengthy conversation—all six words of it.

This was the first I heard about the upcoming sale of ACB.

Later at the office, George gave me the copy of First A Dream *that Jim Clayton had signed for me and shared details of the meeting.*

Having followed the Clayton Homes-Berkshire merger and knowing that the local Clayton sales center was a valued ACB customer, I already knew Jim by reputation.

After hurriedly reading the book—when I could get it away from Kathy, my bride of 38 years—I was comfortable selling to Jim.

The book would prove to be a valuable resource at ACB. George gave copies to bank customers and community leaders who received it with interest and enthusiasm. Everybody who reads it connects with Jim in some way—relating some part of his story to their lives.

In a few days, our lawyer had drafted an agreement. George and Jim quickly approved—the announcement made the headlines.

Jim did not retain separate counsel—isn't that amazing? He must know that the more lawyers, the slower and more costly the process.

Soon it was time for the shareholders to vote their approval. We all looked forward to meeting our new investor.

Remember, only George had met Jim—one time for 40 minutes.

The staff, officers, board, and shareholders—the whole town—was excited as Jim landed his helicopter in the bank's parking lot. He obviously knows the importance of a first impression.

With him was Jack Bulliner who had sold his First State Bank to Jim two years earlier. It said a lot that Jack was smiling from ear to ear.

They brought a small group of sharp, friendly, and professional bankers. A shareholder asked, "Which of you will be coming here to work with us?" They answered in unison. "NONE! When Jim buys your bank, you run it."

After the shareholders voted 97 percent for the transaction, George V. introduced our guest to the board and officers of the bank.

Jim spoke briefly about his hands-off plans for the bank—to support but not manage.

Jack Bulliner nodded his head in agreement.

Interaction with Jim's staff and their response to our questions gave us insight into the Clayton culture, values and vision.

They were diverse in age and personality, but similar in their dedication and commitment to sound banking and to working as a team. From this beginning, the merger has been filled with energy and excitement.

Before departing, Jim and his group attended a reception at George and Elwanda Vibbert's new home and then on to a memorable dinner at a favorite restaurant, Emils. My wife, Kathy, joined us there—surprising Jim with her detailed questions about his book.

It could not have been a happier meeting.

As I look back there were early concerns—there always are with change. "Will we be replaced? Will he bring in new people? Will ACB be so different we won't like working here anymore?"

The transition was well handled—so smooth and seamless.

During George Vibbert's last days he thanked me for supporting his decision to sell to Jim. George loved working with him.

Me too. I am pleased to be his chairman.

Dr. Frank Glass

On September 16, 2004, Chairman Glass announced that the ACB board of directors had elected Troy Martin President and CEO of ACB. Having worked closely with George for three years, Troy will continue the George Vibbert tradition of caring for community, customers and staff.

The 2004 Christmas party at BB&T will be memorable. John Allison, chairman and CEO, and Kelly King, president and COO, will nicely remind me I have been on this earth for 70 years—the mandatory retirement age for BB&T board members.

As my board tenure comes to an end, they will recognize me with a certificate and a thoughtful farewell gift. That's all grand, but, why remind me of my advancing age?

My BB&T experience could not have been more positive. This management team has the highest possibly values. They work hard. Their credibility is above reproach. Their enviable performance is world class.

BB&T ranks 212 in the *Forbes* list of the 2000 World's Largest Companies—based on assets, sales, profits, and market value.

Based on long- and short-term performance, according to *Forbes*, BB&T is ranked 85th on their list of the Best 500 Companies.

Forbes places BB&T at number 227 on the list of 400 Best Big Companies.

Chairing the executive committee and serving on the board of a $93 billion bank—the tenth largest in the country—has been a productive learning experience. Witnessing merger after merger accomplished smoothly helped me gain a perspective on integrating acquisitions. The benefit of that experience is serving us well at FSB BancShares.

Seeing the former owners of banks acquired by BB&T enjoy

their new relationship has given me insight into the importance of a well-executed merger process.

I could have used this back at BankFirst to help us avoid some merger related issues.

It was considerate of them to allow me to acquire banks while my non-compete was in effect. I signed the agreement when I sold BankFirst to them.

I have informed John and Kelly in advance of each acquisition—all outside their marketing area. I would never want to surprise or disappoint them.

When the CMH sale closed, my *Buffett Cash* was wired to my friends at BB&T.

Remember the first meeting that triggered the ACB acquisition. Matt and I had toured offices of MidCountry Financial. I'm proud to be involved with them as a board member and significant shareholder.

Here is that story.

I got to know Bob Hatcher on the way to BB&T board meetings. Bob and I would fly our planes to the Winston-Salem airport where a BB&T car waited for us.

On the short drive to the $93 billion bank's corporate headquarters, this likeable banker and I typically chatted about airplanes and the BB&T board agenda.

In December 2002, I gave Bob a copy of *First A Dream*.

When we met at the Winston-Salem airport for the January meeting, Bob said, "I had to read your book to learn that we both are in Beaver Creek at the same time every year—I just got back."

"Me too—we've celebrated New Year's Eve there for the past 26 years," I replied. It turns out Bob had a home there for 20 years and is a member of the Beaver Creek Club.

Come to find out, Bob and I had a lot of common interests.

After a successful 20-year career with SunTrust, Bob was recruited in 1988 to save the troubled Liberty Bank in Macon, Georgia.

Alpha Companies, an Alabama insurance holding company, was the lead shareholder. As a 40 percent owner of Liberty, they badly needed a leader who could resurrect the near worthless investment.

Bob quickly assembled a strong management team, turned Liberty Bank around, and positioned it for years of steady growth.

In 1999, Bob sold Liberty to BB&T and joined their board. I would join the board in early 2001. He chairs the BB&T Trust Committee, and I chair the Executive Committee.

Over a few months, Bob brought me up to speed on his vision to make MidCountry a broad based financial powerhouse practically overnight. They were looking to build MidCountry by acquiring companies in banking, specialty finance, insurance, and mortgage.

Bob told me BB &T had waived his non-compete, clearing the way for him to form MidCountry. BB&T CEO, John Allison, had approved my purchasing First State Bank earlier.

Bob and I have disclosed to BB&T every move we've made in building our new banking organizations—they have and will continue to support us. We value our relationship.

Heights Finance, based in Peoria, Illinois, with 100 small loan offices in five states, was the first MidCountry purchase. BB&T supported with $19 million of the needed $125 million operating line of credit—the remainder was participated out to other large regional banks.

Bob closed the purchase of Heights in August 2002.

Matt Daniels and I visited four Heights offices around Nashville on December 5, 2003, with Bob and his new Heights president and CEO, Tim Stanley. (Same day, I met George Vibbert to discuss buying ACB.)

A few weeks later, I invested $10 million and accepted a seat on the MidCountry Board.

Today, Bob's organization consists of the finance company plus three banks acquired in 2004.

Imagine, from zero to $1 billion in assets in two years—that's amazing. MidCountry has strong leadership and dedicated board members—most involved in the Liberty turn-around—who have been working together for two decades.

When the third and largest bank was acquired in Illinois, I purchased stock in the second-round offering. I am the largest individual shareholder of MidCountry. Alpha Companies is the largest overall shareholder.

Sharing information about our mutual banking experience is meaningful. Admittedly, I get the best end of the deal.

Thanks, Bob and team, for another book *Happening*.

We plan to invest $100 million—*Buffett Cash*—in community banks. We are about halfway, with 3.26 banks—and more in the pipeline. I'd love to tell you about our acquisition candidates. But we promised confidentiality.

Want to sell *your* bank? Know someone who wants to sell *their* bank? Call right away! We expect to reach our investment goal in 2006—maybe sooner.

Our holding company, FSB BancShares (we are considering renaming it Clayton Bank & Trust) consists of 3.5 people—three full-time plus my part-time intern Matt Bobrowski. It's important that we retain excellent staff and management.

Please talk to the bankers who have joined our team. You'll like what you hear.

At BankFirst, we made several acquisitions. Within a year, almost half of our people were competing against us at other banks. Their leaving impacted performance. When BB&T acquired BankFirst the staff happily adapted.

What was the difference? The management team and I like to talk about this.

Here are my views.

At BankFirst we rushed the process and omitted some key steps.

The bank names were changed, systems were altered, new products were introduced, and policies were re-written. Sure, we had the best of intentions, but rapid changes without proper training and adequate communication overwhelmed the staff.

Contrast that with the BB&T-BankFirst acquisition. The day we announced the acquisition, John Allison, president and CEO of BB&T, flew over from Winston-Salem and addressed the board, management, and supervisors. He outlined the BB&T integration process. "It will take a year—and will not be easy at times," he said.

Recognizing the importance of good communications, John urged each person to take a copy of BB&T's acronyms and sayings.

He explained that everyone would be assigned a personal *acquisition mentor,* or buddy. Their buddy would be on call 24/7 and pleased to answer questions—*or just to talk.*

What about? Any subject!

John added, "Your mentor joined BB&T when we acquired the bank where they were employed. Having lived through an acquisition, they will understand your concern—and tell you how *they* resolved it."

On two Wednesdays, John and I visited our 39 offices where he shook hands with 350 BankFirst people.

Training, constant communication and follow-up are key components of the BB&T process—and it works.

I've discussed our First State Bank and American City Bank acquisitions. Management and staff remained and performance has exceeded plan. We've implemented our version of the BB&T integration effectively. Mainly, like Warren Buffett, we stay out of management's way.

Our intent is to eliminate change and to make the integration seamless to the staff, management and, especially, to customers. We say, "Don't shock the system."

With only 3.5 people at the holding company, you won't see "experts" from the home-office. We'll attend your board meetings and banking programs—and love to be involved in community events.

Supported by our Clayton Family Foundation, your bank will deliver substantial increased annual giving in the community without impacting performance. Bank management will evaluate giving opportunities and present the foundation checks. The organizations where your staff and customers are involved will be favored.

After watching BB&T's acquisition integration process, and more recently, Warren Buffett's, we have found that less is more.

Berkshire Hathaway is only 15.8 people. Warren Buffett, without hesitation, emphatically states that management must remain and continue to run the acquired company. He depends on current management and staff—period.

We learn as much as we teach—sometimes more. Leveraging best practices from one of our banks improves results for all.

American City Bank is a pristine bank and we are implementing some of their best practices already. I am pleased that American City Bank is enjoying learning from our splendid team at First State Bank. The goal is to enhance this concept with each acquisition.

We like to pay with *Buffett Cash. That's clean, simple and quick.* If deferring capital gains is important, we can incorporate a variety of tax-management strategies. We'll consider funding with BB&T stock, shares of our bank, or listed stocks and bonds.

Availability of capital will not be an issue as your management achieves their growth and expansion plans.

I have mentioned *Buffett Cash* several times. Normally we think *cash* is *cash.* Is there a difference? It seems so.

The Warren Buffett *persona* should not be underestimated. Could my wagonload of *Buffett Cash* be more meaningful in buying banks? George Vibbert and I talked about this. He assured me an offer promising *Buffett Cash* would be more appealing than a plain vanilla cash offer.

Why?

When a cash deal contract is signed, it usually depends on the buyer's being able to go out and borrow or raise the funds. Sometimes they can, sometimes they can't. A contract for a cash sale frequently *falls through the cracks*.

George reminded that he and his 55 shareholders received a *Buffett Cash* offer without contingencies. The transaction was, in fact, clean, simple, and quick. George and Elwanda were elated.

"When you told me we'd get *Buffett Cash* and no contingencies, I forgot about my other offer." George said referring to the 30 minute meeting the night we met.

On the way home, according to George, Elwanda asked, "Honey, are you sure?" He said, "Warren Buffett read Jim's book and paid him $1.7 billion *all cash* for his company. I read Jim's book and I want him to pay us $27 million of that *Buffett Cash* for our bank."

Was it the *certainty*? Was it the perception of *credibility* that came with Warren Buffett's attraction to the company I founded? Was it the no contingency provision? Was it the Buffett *mystical aura*?

Possibly, it is all of the above to some extent. I guess that is true, but I can't logically arrive at that conclusion.

Yes, not plain cash, but genuine extra special *Buffett Cash*.

Our bank will expand by acquisition and by opening *de novo*. The first branch in Jackson, Tennessee, opened in October, 2004. Matt promised it would be open April 15—notice I said it was "our first branch." Matt learned a lot. We all did. Seriously, we made terrific improvements to the design, well aware that the opening would be delayed.

We learned a lot about building codes, bias against modular construction, and how plan changes delay completion. This new south Jackson branch is a Clayton modular building. It looks great and Matt expects to replicate it across the state over the next five years. (See page 370-P.)

Great job, Matt and team. I know you'll open the next one on time.

Our next branch will be in downtown Knoxville. No! This will not be in a Clayton modular building.

We repurchased the old Bank of Knoxville building where Clayton Homes and BankFirst shared buildings for two years. Remember, BB&T acquired BankFirst from me to spread their growing footprint into Tennessee and used the building as their headquarters until recently.

The Clayton Family Foundation and the East Tennessee Foundation, where I'm a member of the board of directors, have offices in the building formerly occupied by BB&T.

When Clayton Bank & Trust—CBT—opens in 2005, one of our most aggressive competitors will be the newly opened BankEast. It's next door and Fred Lawson, my former president of BankFirst, is the organizer. BankEast is in the old Valley Fidelity Bank building. Joe Clayton and I banked there with Fenton Kintzing for decades.

Notice the similarity between BankEast and BankFirst. Using the same layout and green coloring, at a glance they are the same. I thought about opening BankNorth, but ruled that out. Wonder who will?

Would you deal with a bank named "Bubba Bank?" Type into your browser BubbaBank.com and you'll find that domain has been reserved for three years—by me.

I've had a ball bouncing the BubbaBank concept off my friends for several years. Some get excited. Some turn away shaking their heads. I even talked to a couple of marketing consultants.

Kay repeatedly said, "There's no way I'd bank at a bank named Bubba."

Matter settled. Long live Bubba! Anyone want a domain name? Bubba.com is for sale—cheap.

I never thought about using the name *Clayton* on a bank. I wish I remembered who made the suggestion. It was around the pool with friends at Boca.

They are right, of course. Clayton is an established brand. Talented Clayton men and women have invested over one hundred thousand *man-years* in developing the Clayton brand.

Jim, Joe, Kevin, Rick, Mark and other family members have achieved success carrying the Clayton banner—beyond wildest dreams.

We will focus more toward consumer, installment, indirect auto, and manufactured housing lending. First State Bank is successfully providing loans supporting manufactured housing community owner-operators. Loans are collateralized by the real estate, receivables from resident home purchases, home inventory-for-sale, and homes for rent. The new Knoxville office will add significantly to this growing portfolio.

Matt already has acquired $20 million of MH mortgage portfolios from banks and specialty lenders exiting the industry. He'll continue to add to this business-line by opportunistic purchase. The portfolios he buys are too small to be of interest to Clayton or 21st Mortgage.

Contrast our ACB transaction with the normal process in which a bank, or other business is sold. The buyer typically makes the selling banker an overly optimistic, or *would-you-take* offer that the seller can't refuse.

The *tentative* agreed price is inserted into a contract with more holes than a block of swiss cheese. Dozens of "OUTS" and the ever present catch-all phrase "subject to due diligence" are designed to later weaken the selling bankers negotiating position.

The stressful process has just begun—especially for the seller.

The buyer sends a list of information items and data required for the examination to the owner. This takes days of long staff and management hours to compile.

Then the buyer brings a large team to comb through the banks books, minutes, and records. All accounting records are audited. The loan files are examined. The fixed assets are evaluated. The real estate is appraised.

The poor owner and his staff are worn out by the time the process comes to an end, with the owner receiving a disappointing low-ball offer—much less than the buyer had offered earlier and far below the owner's expectations.

However, fearing that the bank management and staff would have to go through the process again, the owner reluctantly accepts.

That process is not pretty to watch—definitely not a pleasant experience for the seller.

For American City Bank we offered George a firm price near his expectations plus a 10 percent shareholder bonus or "true up" if the bank met its one-year earnings goal—and if the senior management team remained intact.

With that agreement, we were comfortable examining only the required public information posted on the FDIC web site. George was kind enough to provide a dozen pages listing salaries, fixed assets and the real estate owned.

That's it. We never saw the bank's four offices—never met again with George or any of his staff—until the required shareholders meeting. Weeks after the merger contract was signed,the happy shareholders gave us 97 percent approval—no hanging chads.

Recently, I recruited an educated, experienced and hardworking young man. I've always admired his professionalism. He will play a significant role in managing the foundation and our banks. Carl Koella spent thirteen years—a third of his life—at Clayton Homes (see page 363). Here are his words.

Before the ink dried on my University of Chicago MBA, Jim Clayton recruited me as a fast-track-special-projects trainee.

When tickets to new opportunities were being passed out, I ran to the front of the line. Starting as a research analyst, I moved to internal audit —which took me to the four corners of the organization.

In insurance I got a taste of operations, as my team successfully launched a new product and grew it into a million dollar business unit.

For three years I was VP of investor relations.

I was thrilled to tell the CMH story to investors all over the world— first with Jim and in later years with Kevin. For this work, I was privi-

leged to win the Barron's Magazine *Award for Excellence in Investor Relations.*

The opportunity allowed me to spend time with Warren Buffett, support innovative CEOs, Jim and Kevin Clayton, and team with world class CFOs, John Kalec (CMH) and Marc Hamburg (Berkshire). I watched in amazement as John and Marc quickly drafted simple documents to support the multibillion dollar complex transaction.

*Oakwood and 21st Mortgage acquisitions were unique second wave merger challenges resulting from low cost capital—*Buffett Cash *again.*

Seeing Jim's recent success in banking I remembered assisting him in 1994. We purchased a tiny bank and Jim transformed it into a regional powerhouse. In 2000 he sold his interest to Branch Bank and Trust Company, the tenth largest bank in the country—for $80 million.

Noting his BankFirst success, I watched with interest as he purchased and expanded First State Bank—I wanted a closer view.

Careful to be politically correct, I told my CFO and CEO at CMH. John and Kevin understood and volunteered their support. Over lunch Jim and I penciled an agreement on a napkin.

Dusting off my banker's suit, I checked into my new office next door to Jim.

Today my role is to help Jim invest $100 million of Buffett Cash *in quality community banks and to assist in giving away $100 million to worthy charities.*

Carl Koella

Thanks, Carl. I have been privileged over the years to work with great people.

CHAPTER 28

Relationships

W e've talked about the *Happenings* resulting from the publication of *First A Dream*. Even as I write this new edition, the *Happenings* continue.

Such was the case this summer when six terrific young men gathered at our home. All are members of Sigma Phi Epsilon—my college fraternity—and all interned with me.

I wanted you to know how proud I am of these outstanding leaders and to show them off in a group photograph. (See page 370-D.) The meeting was scheduled as a half-hour photo shoot, but it turned into an all-afternoon reunion–a *Happening*.

The close knit group of Sigma Phi Epsilon brothers now number six—and counting. At fraternity alumni events, I saw them receive recognition for their leadership contributions.

There's no job description for the *interns*. They do yard work, network and computer maintenance, research, travel and meetings, and, in general, are involved in all of my family and business activities.

These savvy young men learn so much so fast. Within a few months I come to rely heavily on their rapidly developing skills.

The job is often tough, but quitting is not an option. How could they tell their fraternity family, or the prior graduates of our program that *it does not work*?

Knowing up front that expectations are high, they accept responsibility fast. I ask a lot from them—and they conscientiously deliver.

Sigma Phi Epsilon, locally and nationally, has cited our program as an exemplary mentoring program. The fraternity encourages successful alumni executives to establish similar intern initiatives.

I encouraged my brother Joe, also a Sig Ep, to hire an intern. Last year Jeremy Shannon, a junior at UT in finance, joined Joe at his auto dealerships. Joe is as excited as I am about the program.

Each intern recommends and trains their replacement—that's the program.

The tradition began in 1991 with Kelly Williams (see page 283). We met when Kelly presented the local chapter's scholarship report. As trustee of the Tennessee Alpha chapter scholarship foundation, I and all the trustees were impressed. Handing him my card, I said, "Kelly, call me. I want to talk about your career."

His remarkable career took off after graduation when he joined me at CMH. Moving through retail and financial services as a trainee, he progressed to general manager of the company's commercial housing division—which he pioneered.

"We met the most interesting people and did the coolest stuff—but we couldn't let that go to our heads. We had to do some crappy jobs, too," Kelly recounted at the *Happening*.

Tom Hodges, referred by Kelly, was the fraternity's president (see page 243). Today Tom is VP and general counsel of Clayton Homes. His leadership role at the fraternity and his experience as my part-time legal assistant opened an accelerated career path.

When Tom graduated with a degree in psychology, he entered the CMH fast track management program full-time. After a year, I urged him to work with me part-time—and go to law school full time. Upon graduating as president of his class, Tom was promoted to CMH corporate counsel—at age 26. Four years later, as

VP and chief legal officer, Tom helped lead the CMH litigation team through the headline-grabbing, difficult Berkshire sale.

Matt Daniels, another president of SPE, followed Tom as my intern (see page 334). Now, at age 25, Matt is president and CEO of First State Bank. He is the youngest bank president in the state, we are told.

He is a mature leader at a very young age. Designated as my successor, when—or if—I should decide to retire again, Matt will become the CEO of our Bank Holding Company.

"Among the lessons I learned was the importance of coming into an organization and contributing value immediately," Matt said. "Also, you have to be flexible and committed. I've mowed the lawn in the morning and *jetted-off* with Jim to a board meeting in the afternoon."

President Daniels and I talk often about how we can replicate the intern program in our banks. The key is to find young, educated men and women who share a common bond. We believe the young officers training program and our developing culture of mutual support will foster and reinforce teaming, positive behavior and commitment.

Some of this culture was inherited from CMH. The fast-track sales and management programs developed by Kevin, Rick Strachan, Allen Morgan, and David Booth produce outstanding business leaders. The recruiting and training initiatives at CMH are supported by a teaming atmosphere—and especially by the entrepreneurial culture.

The results are exemplary—ask Warren Buffett.

At our *first annual* summer intern reunion, we laughed as Matt recalled his first assignment. Driving a ditch-witch and laying miles of PVC pipe, he helped develop a drainage and irrigation system for our new house on Fort Loudon Lake.

That evening, Matt and his brother, Michael, were with me at a political fund raiser rubbing elbows with Senator Fred Thompson, the Governor and other Tennessee luminaries.

Matt ably trained brother Michael (see page 334), who planted ivy—in the pouring rain—on his first day. Later, he was a capable roadie—setting up and operating the sound system while keeping me supplied with books at dozens of speaking and musical *Happenings* resulting from *First A Dream*.

Michael and I had a lot of fun selling and signing books at conventions, churches, and county fairs—all for charity.

Richard Isaacs, the managing partner of the UBS investment office, recognized Michael's ability as he trained the Isaacs to operate the security, sound, and lighting gadgets we had enjoyed in the condominium they purchased from Kay and me.

Michael is a financial advisor with the UBS Dugan McLaughlin Wealth Management Group, where he manages my personal account.

Richard Wright began tagging along with Michael when we began the *First A Dream* road shows. After Michael graduated, Richard assumed the responsibilities smoothly.

A 2005 MBA candidate at Vanderbilt, Richard works part time and summers at First State Bank with Matt. Graduating in May, he will join Matt at FSB as an officer-in-training.

You have to replace yourself with someone with high values and integrity—who will make you look good," Richard told the group during our summer intern *Happening*.

Richard spent considerable time grooming his successor and my current intern, Matt Bobrowski, a junior in finance at UT. Matt has been my chief research assistant for this new edition. He is an excellent *Google-izer.*

They are all different, but have a lot in common. Early on, I learn how they think, process, and behave—under stress and when relaxed. I know their strengths, weaknesses, and motivations. Some are best flying by the *seat of their pants* on short-term rush projects. Others thrive on structure and detail. All are sharp, crisp, get-to-the-point, and results oriented communicators—with well-developed writing skills.

At the *Happening,* Kay fondly referred to the outstanding group as "my boys."

We all agreed the first annual intern reunion was indeed a *Happening*.

I am blessed with four amazing children and ten remarkable grandchildren.

Karen, my firstborn, gave me four grandsons.

Flynt, 25, will receive his law-MBA degree in 2005 from Saint Thomas University. Kevin II, 23, is graduating now from UT-Knoxville.

James Reed, 17, will enter Arizona State in September 2005, while his younger brother Chris graduates from middle school (Webb) in June. Both are avid golfers like their dad.

When CMH built a factory near Scottsdale, Arizona, Karen accompanied Gordon Davis—her husband and Clayton's chief pilot—when an empty seat was available. Falling in love with the desert, they decided to retire there. Karen, a professional decorator, is now carefully selecting décor and furnishings for their new Arizona home—as she did last year for her sister Amy's new Virginia home. Her use of bold and unusual colors is original and tasteful—and homes she's decorated have been featured on HGTV and in other media.

In May 2005, they will move into their dream home now under construction—thanks to *Buffett Cash*.

"Now, Gordon, you can eliminate the golf handicap you've blamed on me over the years—for making you pilot too much."

My son Jimmy is back at UT developing his skills as a professional artist. A painter in oil and other media, he has exhibited and sold early works. Degreed in finance, Jimmy contributed to the growth of CMH in various groups over the years. At age 44, Jimmy is an all-star dad with three sons growing up very fast.

Craig, Corey and Chase attend Webb School—they make this old grandpa proud.

Kevin, now 41, married his beautiful wife Chelly seven years ago. They were delighted to learn in 2002 that they were expecting a child.

Five months later, Chelly's obstetrician referred her to Dr. Perry Roussis, a high risk pregnancy specialist for a series of tests. Kevin and Chelly were devastated when Dr. Roussis delivered the terrible news. Their little girl didn't have a heart beat.

Instead of dismissing the loss, he began a research and testing program for Chelly. "I don't subscribe to the theory that these things just happen. There's always a reason—finding it is my job," he assured the concerned couple.

After analyzing the test results, Dr. Roussis announced to Kevin and Chelly that she had a genetic blood disorder that had contributed to the loss of their first baby.

A few months later, Chelly learned she was pregnant with Ella. They rushed to tell Dr. Roussis who expertly prescribed a daily injection of Lovenox.

If Chelly's difficulties and Kevin's around the clock responsibilities in the Berkshire saga were not enough, the anxious husband came down with a stress related case of the shingles.

Bravely Chelly followed Dr. Roussis's exercise and medication regimen to the letter. On April 23, 2003—the eve of her great grandmother's (my mom's) 88th birthday—Ella was born happy and healthy.

Her grandparents think she's perfect. Kevin and Chelly insist she is an angel and a genius.

That was 2003, a never to be forgotten year for Kevin and Chelly. Kay and I enjoy babysitting Ella. Recently, as they started for the car with the proud father carrying their sleeping angel, Kevin and Chelly said in unison, "This is the best year ever for our family."

Amy, a high school drama and English literature teacher, is taking time off to be with the children. John Stevens, a high school teacher and winning soccer coach, is an avid sailor.

Their delightful independent firecracker, Maren, was born July 4, 2000. She's my first granddaughter after a seven card straight—all boys. Maren adores her little brother, Jeb, who just celebrated his first birthday.

John just built his beautiful family a new home on the Chesapeake Bay—more thanks to *Buffett Cash*.

I happily live with three girls—Kay, my wonderful wife for 11 years; my loving and understanding Mother, who at 89 is bright and healthy; and the third is Laddie, our one-year-old Labradoodle—a mix of Poodle and Lab. Kay calls Laddie a *designer dog*.

Mom cooks, reads two daily newspapers, knows far more sports trivia than I, and joins me in singing hymns for our guests. We built her a new home on our property in 1999 as we built our retirement home. However, she spends nearly all of her time with us. She is afraid Laddie will be neglected. Those two are inseparable.

Although mom cooks frequently, she and Joe have a standing date for dinner every Sunday.

Kay is busy with charitable activities and family. As a board member of our FSB BancShares, she takes the position seriously.

Pushing the "Send" button to transmit the manuscript will be a *Happening*. When the first pallets of books are unloaded, that will be a *Happening*. When the newspaper runs excerpts, that will be a *Happening*. With the new edition, Christmas shopping will be done and that will be another *Happening* for *me*.

Many of the invitations to speak arising from the book's release will amount to a *Happening*—for me and, if you are in the audience, hopefully for *you*.

If you sell us your bank or join our banking team, we will do our dead-level best to make that a *Happening* for *you*.

Epilogue II

T
hat's my story—so far. After a bit of success in cars, then housing, now I'm a banker. I love it. Come to think of it, I've loved all my jobs.

Clayton Homes is an incredible learning laboratory. It was for me and for thousands of people I've been privileged to call *friend* there.

It's been fun to prove that the same entrepreneurial principles and values that fueled our success at the first used car lot transferred perfectly to housing and more recently to banking. This special culture attracts amazing, hardworking, loyal and lasting friends to our team.

The same principles and values will work for you too—*whatever* your profession.

Having been asked to include a step-by-step formula for building a winning organization, I wrote a chapter on success and motivation. I trashed it—after realizing, each topic was more than adequately addressed in current books and magazines.

The plain and simple truth is, "I don't have a *magic formula*."

However, listen to Chairman Jack Bulliner and he will convince you that the growth and success of First State Bank with

Matt Daniels as his president is pure *magic*.

How do they do it? Hard work, while artfully avoiding mistakes, is the key ingredient to the *special* developing culture.

Plain and simple, it's all in the execution. Its not what you know, it's what you do. It's how much you *care* about your company, your team and your customers.

Entrepreneurs make it look easy—too easy—it is not.

Take a special look at the last eight chapters. I've tried to share my activities and my thoughts—that occurred over the last two years. "How did you have time for it?" I am often asked.

As these new chapters reflect, I have been involved in many critical decisions. Selectively I have been in the middle of the action. However, the credit goes to our splendid team. Because of them, I have the freedom to schedule tennis three times per week, ski every slope in Beaver Creek dozens of times, relax with Kay in Boca, travel worldwide, and spend countless hours involved in philanthropic activities.

Luckily, I can do what I do from anywhere in the world as I am a cyber-nut. I have the added advantage of a management team that knows when to involve me.

Success involves a process. Recruiting and retaining the best people is crucial. At times, I've kept non-performers too long. That is a costly mistake—for them and for the team. Without an experienced staff—the culture and the process—the entrepreneur will not *have a life*.

Selling Clayton Homes, my baby, was a traumatic experience. Was it the right thing to do? Yes, Yes, and Yes!

For me. For the team. For the shareholders—definitely!

Then why am I building Clayton Bank & Trust at my age— three score and ten?

I love to see young people grow and become great leaders. It's been my pleasure to tell you about a few of them.

The "Clayton Maxims and Sayings" come from a lifetime of

observing what we do and say at work every day. They reflect what effective leaders use as a guiding light down life's path to success. I included a copy of these on page A-1(c) in the Appendix.

Many of you have been kind to tell me you presented a copy of *First A Dream* to someone you love. Thank you for the follow-up letters and e-mails. It is nice to hear that something they read in my book inspired them to perseverance, second-effort and success.

I am credited with having the ability to make money—and then to grow it by making good investments. It appears that my calling is to create wealth in my lifetime for the benefit of others. Kay and I will never spend a penny earned by the banks. The value created will channel through our foundations to benefit worthy charities.

I love it when I learn of Kevin's or Matt's frequent and generous statement, "We are here because of the creative vision, ambition and dedication of our founder. It's remarkable that he is influencing the organization's bright future—just as he did half a century ago."

Acknowledgements

This is the place in the book where I have the opportunity to mention those special people who helped make *First A Dream* a reality.

After aborting more than half-a-dozen earlier drafts, I'm past the final night's deadline and must release the entire book now into "cyber space." It's just as well, because everything I've written as a way of recognizing family, co-workers, lenders, vendors, shareholders, directors, and friends has been so inadequate. I must now write something quickly before I have to press the "Send" key.

To Kay, my family, and our friends who have tolerated my absence and silence during the final four week crunch, thanks for your support and understanding. Special thanks to Kay for the long hours combing through several attics and many cartons for pictures. Her insistence on adding the second 16-page picture section (and a third for the *New Edition*) was a great decision. The weekend Kevin Clayton spent submerged in the CMH photo archives was meaningful and is sincerely appreciated.

For six months of calm and understanding support from my collaborators, Bill Retherford (*First Edition*) and Amy Nolan (*New Edition*), I am appreciative.

It is easy to see why Bill won an Emmy for TV news. He is a quick study. Over the long Labor Day weekend 2002, our interviews in Knoxville sold Bill on our quality friends and team members. Without his focus, responsiveness, and professionalism, we would not have made our Christmas deadline.

In March, Bill and I spent four days in Boca Raton, with me tethered to a tape recorder—for 16-hour days. Working out of a large trunk filled with drafts from earlier writers, Bill and I took off on the six-month marathon. He was my collaborator on organization and editing via e-mail. Our work together was a pleasure.

There would be no *New Edition* but for Amy Nolan. As a business reporter for the *Knoxville News Sentinel*, she reported CMH *Happenings* for several years. She broke the Berkshire Hathaway story to the world and devoted full time as it developed. Conscientiously covering every court hearing, the two visits by Warren Buffett, and both shareholder meetings, she meticulously researched every legal angle while interviewing all participants.

Amy's invaluable help evenings and weekends over September and October made the project possible. Digging through her voluminous files collected over the long year of the Buffett saga, she extracted the meticulous details that I wanted to convey—warning that the reader might find them overly meticulous.

Jim Wells, our production manager for both books, is forceful, demanding, and uncompromising, yet at every turn, he is also "Mr. Nice Guy." The team members Jim assembled are amazingly talented individuals, including Yvonne Loveday, who, with patience and caring for every sentence, corrected spacing, typos and proper name misspellings. And we were fortunate to have Dwayne Hickson handle all graphic production and design responsibilities. He is multi-talented and in every respect a highly versatile and productive team member. Many thanks to all for the long hours devoted to both editions.

My intern, Matt Bobrowski, and his predecessor, Richard Wright, proved to be invaluable researchers. Their Internet skills are superlative.

I began writing the *New Edition* early in 2004. In August, I saw the possibility of having a new book out for Christmas—again. I called Linda Weaver, who had helped me on the *First Edition.* I said, "Linda please help me! We've got another Christmas deadline—like two years ago. You're the only one who can make it happen." After spending full days at her UT office, she was at my elbow long into the night for 30 days. She is truly amazing!

Back in 1990, when I thought writing a book would be quick and easy, I enjoyed support from Cynthia Moxley, who, fortunately, interviewed 50 significant people.

I'd be remiss if I didn't thank all the "volunteers." At every stage, I have enjoyed talented cheerleaders who have advised, recommended, and encouraged. Warren Neel hammered me draft after draft on the first book, reminding me to add feeling and emotion along with the facts. Tom Gunnels and Les Lunceford are seasoned writers who recommended our production manager and were faithful readers of each draft.

To Stoney Stonecipher and Ray Rose, the glue who held *Startime* together, I thank you for your reflections and historical detail on our amazing show. I only wish I could thank every Kountry Kings band member and every guest who stared into the *Startime* camera lens over the 17-year run of the show.

Thanks to Pat Harrison, Wallace McClure, George and Joann Rothery, Sharon Kennedy, Geoff Wolpart, and Sam Furrow for detailed research on proper spelling and details relating to people and places.

Steve and Billie Lou Ellis, thanks for your highly detailed Chester County research; Jim Shelby, Jim Early, Rich Ray, and Tim Williams, thanks for your great recall of CMH people and events. Thanks to Tom McAdams, John Kalec, Joe Clayton, Kevin Clayton, and again, Warren Neel, for their generosity of spirit as they provided numerous "special reads" of selected topics.

To the staff, board, and members of the Horatio Alger Association—many thanks for encouraging me to, also, write my story.

Thanks to Martin Lavin of Mobile Home Lending Corporation and George Allen of GFA Management, Inc. for the generous reviews (see Appendix E-1 and Appendix E-2). Sales at Amazon.com spiked after each writing. Your insight into the historical and the current industry activity is unequalled. I was honored by your generous endorsements.

To Bruce Hartmann, I thank you for the opportunity to participate in the renovation of our historical treasure, Tennessee Theatre. Your serialization of the first book—and agreement to do the same for the *New Edition*, was generous and especially meaningful.

The understanding of Matt Daniels, Jack Bulliner, Dr. Frank Glass, Troy Mann, and Carl Koella, for my not being available during October was terrific and appreciated. Tina Adkins, my assistant for more than a decade, I thank you for keeping my schedule clear.

And to those dear friends who endorsed *First A Dream* with their kind comments, I wish to give special thanks to all of you, including Eddy Arnold, Fred Thompson, Art Linkletter, John Allison, Bill Frist, Ed McMahon, Dolly Parton, Wilma Jordan, Wink Martindale, Wayne Huizenga, Louise Mandrell, William Schreyer, John Duncan, Red Poling, Robert Schuller, Dan Evins, Tom Harkin, and Peter Jannetta.

My thanks go to Steve Michael and Scott Northcutt, meaningful friends and business colleagues from the past—and now our new Boca friends—for your creative suggestions for this book and for what you and your wonderful wives mean to Kay and me.

To those many people who are important to me and who have great stories that I so wanted to tell, but time and space kept them from getting "inked," please accept my apologies, and know that I'm deeply grateful to you for being part of my life.

Now, I truly have to hand over this somewhat-perfect creation (I wish) and overcome my reluctance to give it up—as I press the "Send" button.

Clayton Homes, Inc. Timeline

- **1956** First Used Car Lot on Clinton Highway
- **1961** Bankruptcy + New Company + Law School
- **1966** First Retail Store Opens on Clinton Highway
- **1968** Clinton Highway Sales Center Largest in the Industry
- **1970** Manufacturing Opens Halls Plant in Knoxville
- **1974** Financial Services Group Begins as Vanderbilt Mortgage
- **1976** Revenues over $16 Million; Net Income over $1 Million
- **1983** Initial Public Stock Offering with Prudential and Bradford
- **1984** CMH Listed on the New York Stock Exchange
- **1987** Revenues Over $185 Million; Net Income Over $10 Million
- **1988** Communities Group Starts with Seven Properties
- **1988** 10th Plant Opens in Waycross, GA
- **1990** 100th Company-owned Store Opens in Walterboro, SC
- **1991** Purchased $110 Million Odessa Portfolio
- **1992** Vanderbilt Mortgage Issues Asset Backed Securitizations
- **1994** Appalachian Plant Begins New Manufacturing Concept
- **1995** 200th Company-owned Store Opens in Shelby, NC
- **1997** Revenues Surpass $1 Billion; Net Income Exceeds $115 Million
- **1999** 300th Company-owned Store Opens in Kodak, TN
- **1999** Kevin Clayton Named CEO; Jim Clayton Remains Chairman
- **2000** 20th Plant Opens in Hodgenville, Kentucky
- **2001** Market Cap More Than All Similar Competitors Combined
- **2002** Mortgage Servicing Balance Exceeds $5 Billion
- **2003** Berkshire Hathaway buys 100% of Clayton Homes
- **2004** Clayton Homes purchases Oakwood Homes
- **2004** Mortgages serviced exceed $10 billion

Clayton Bank & Trust Timeline

- **1889** First State Bank chartered as Farmers and Merchants Bank
- **1904** Friendship Bank founded
- **1905** Merchants & Planters Bank established
- **1970** Jack Bulliner elected President of First State Bank
- **1974** American City Bank began operations
- **1979** George Vibbert elected President and CEO of American City Bank
- **2002** Purchased First State Bank in Henderson, TN
- **2002** FSB Bancshares, Inc. incorporated in TN
- **2002** Matt Daniels elected COO at First State Bank
- **2002** Paul Priddy elected CEO of Friendship Bank
- **2003** Barry Rich elected CFO
- **2004** Matt Daniels elected CEO of First State Bank
- **2004** Carl Koella elected Secretary of FSB Bancshares
- **2004** Purchased 26% of Merchants & Planters Bank in Toone, TN
- **2004** Acquired American City Bank in Tullahoma, TN
- **2004** Troy Martin elected CEO of American City Bank
- **2004** Opened South Jackson Office of First State Bank
- **2004** First State Bank acquires Friendship Bank
- **2005** FSB Bancshares becomes Clayton Bank & Trust

CLAYTON MAXIMS and SAYINGS

- Always exceed customer expectations.
- Attitude, Atmosphere, Action – Jim's 3 "A" Speech.
- Bought right is half sold.
- By failing to *prepare*…you *prepare* to fail.
- Decisions: (90/10 rule for exceptions) 90% Individual, 10% support, team, partner.
- Do what works (use policy and rules with judgment – be flexible).
- *Expect* <u>only</u> what you are willing to *Inspect.*
- First loss is the least loss.
- *First*, we will be best, then we will be *first.*
- Five F's: *Fast-Focused-Flexible-Friendly*-and-*Fun.*
- Frog on a fence post – did not get there by itself.
- Get our circles together and keep our circles together.
- Good people in good homes on good sites.
- Happy Customers, Happy People, Happy Stockholders.
- If we can't please them when *we have the home*…how can we please them when *they have the home*?
- If we do what others do…we get their results = average.
- If you see a turtle on a fence post, you know it didn't get there by itself.
- No Surprises – communicate.
- Our lives work only to the extent that we are ***willing*** to keep our agreements.
- People don't *care* what you know until they know that you *care* – establish rapport first.
- Perception is Reality. It is what it is.
- Performance + Values = Excellence (P + V = E).
- Rapport, Relate, Reassure, Remove (4 R's).
- Retail is Detail – the devil is in the detail (*execution*).
- Rising creek hides a lot of stumps.
- *Someone* is doing well in every market – we must be that *someone.*
- Stir what you got. Love the one you're with.
- The **<u>Choices</u>** we make lead to the **<u>Habits</u>** we form that define our **<u>Character</u>** and our ultimate **<u>Destiny</u>** – in business and life.
- The *strength* of the pack is the wolf…the *strength* of the wolf is the pack.
- Together Everyone Achieves More (*TEAM*).
- We are no stronger than our weakest link.
- We are rarely a poor *victim* (accept responsibility).
- You can't play the game if you are *always* watching the scoreboard.
- You don't have to work all of the time…but you must be *willing* to work all of the time.

Clayton Mission and Values

Our Mission:

...Create and market high value products and services for the benefit of Clayton stakeholders:

- *customers*
- *shareholders*
- *team members*

Our Values
We, at Clayton's:

- are people who:
  - **enthusiastically strive to exceed customer expectations**
  - **value the significance of family**
  - **emphasize our strengths in a positive environment**
  - **deliver quality and excellence through continuous improvement**
  - **achieve desired results through hard work**
  - **believe that <u>T</u>ogether <u>E</u>veryone <u>A</u>ccomplishes <u>M</u>ore**

- endorse and practice open communication
- encourage leadership that fosters prompt decision-making at all levels
- believe we can only expect what we are willing to inspect
- embrace change and leverage it as a strategic advantage
- know our lives work only to the extent that we are willing to keep our agreements
- support our local communities with leadership, time, and money
- respect and protect the rights and dignity of one another

News Release

For More Information
Investor Relations
Phone:423-380-3202
Fax:423-380-3780

FOR IMMEDIATE RELEASE
Contact:
June 23, 1999

CLAYTON HOMES PROMOTES
KEVIN T. CLAYTON CEO

KNOXVILLE, Tenn. - - Clayton Homes, Inc. – (NYSE: CMH) today announced that Kevin T. Clayton has been named Chief Executive Officer effective July 1, 1999. Currently, President and Chief Operating Officer, he has served in all groups of the Company. Starting part time in high school and continuing as a college intern, Mr. Clayton has been a Credit Manager, Community Manager, Retail Regional Manager, Manufacturing Sales Manager, President of the Manufacturing Group, and President of the Mortgage Company. Kevin holds an MBA from the University of Tennessee.

Stepping down as CEO, James L. Clayton, who will remain Chairman, stated, "the Board of Directors and I began succession planning ten years ago. Kevin's leadership qualities and performance in a wide variety of positions made him the Board's and the management team's choice. Now that I have reached age 65, it is gratifying that Kevin has eagerly accepted the challenge to lead the most outstanding management team in our industry; thus fulfilling the plan."

Clayton Homes is a leading vertically integrated company in the manufactured housing industry with 51 consecutive record quarters of revenues and net income. Employing more than 7,100 people and operating in 32 states, the Company builds, sells, finances, and insures manufactured homes, and owns and operates 75 residential manufactured housing communities.

News Release

Contact Investor Relations

FOR IMMEDIATE RELEASE   Phone:423-595-4727

January 12, 1998   Fax:423-595-4703

Clayton Homes, Inc. (CMH, NYSE) elects Kevin Clayton Director

Kevin T. Clayton, President and Chief Operating Officer of Clayton Homes, Inc., was elected to the Company's Board of Directors today announced Chairman and Chief Executive Officer, James L. Clayton. "This change reflects Kevin's commitment, leadership, experience, and support from team members at all levels and is consistent with the company's succession plan approved by the board of directors." Kevin Clayton has held various positions including President of the Manufacturing Group, and President of Vanderbilt Mortgage.

The board seat filled by Mr. Kevin Clayton was vacated by the resignation today of Joseph H. Stegmayer, who left to pursue other interests. Mr. Stegmayer had most recently served the Company as Vice Chairman and Director. Mr. Stegmayer said, "I have enjoyed 5 years with this very capable executive team following 6 years as an independent director. We grew the Company past the $1 billion revenue level exactly as planned, and I am proud of the excellent management team and strategic plan now in place."

Clayton Homes, Inc. is a vertically integrated manufactured housing company engaged in manufacturing, retailing, financing and insuring homes, and operating manufactured housing communities. Other board members include: James L. Clayton, B. Joe Clayton, James D. Cockman, Dan W. Evins, Wilma H. Jordan, Thomas N. McAdams, and C. Warren Neel.

My Bottle Empire

Thanks to those of you who have asked me to continue writing personal articles in *Clayton NOW*. I appreciate the opportunity it gives me to reflect on significant events in my life that have molded my attitudes and the way I process issues. Here is one of those relatively insignificant stories that seems to have made just such a difference in the person and businessman I have become.

I grew up in a sharecropping family. We operated a small, red-clay cotton-farm just four miles outside the tiny town of Finger, Tennessee. Our hours were long, the work hard. Shortly after the end of World War II, Dad purchased the Clayton General Merchandise Store, located in downtown Finger, from my Uncle R.C. Dad played the dual role of merchant and farmer for a little over two years, after which he returned to full-time farming until his retirement in 1968.

It was the summer of 1945. I had recently turned 11, but was already looking for opportunities to earn money. I built fires and swept the floors at the Church of Christ and at the junior high school. I earned enough selling Grit newspapers to make my first major purchase—a little red Radio Flyer wagon.

My little red wagon became my business vehicle. I know that when I found bottles along the road, if I took them to our store, Dad would just put them in the bottle pen. However, if I took them to the Guy Bishop Hardware Store, they would pay me one cent for each bottle—in cash.

The only problem was that my method of finding bottles along the road did not prove to be a very reliable supply system. One day after completing a two-hour search for empty bottles, I counted only seven in my wagon and immediately came to the conclusion that what I needed was more bottles and less walking up and down that hot road. My solution: cash-in on the empty bottles that were sitting idle in Dad's bottle pen.

Dad's bottle pen was a small area on the side of the store built of chicken wire and two-by-fours. Dad kept it locked; however, climbing over chicken wire was no feat for an 11-year-old. I selected six Royal Crown and seven Orange Crush bottles. Combined with the seven I had already collected, my business transaction at the hardware store promised to be a lucrative one.

Mr. Bishop paid me 20 cents and thanked me for bringing the bottles. Then he picked up the phone receiver, cranked one long ring, and told Mabel Henry, who, with her sister, ran the central switchboard from their home, to connect him to Dad. Mr. Bishop told him about my four recent hauls and that he thought it peculiar I was pulling my wagon the extra distance to his store for the conversion of bottles to cash. He thought Dad might want to check into the situation.

Dad met me half-way on my journey back and asked me what I knew about the bottles missing from his pen. In one brief moment, like a lightning bolt hitting me, I not only realized that those bottles weren't mine to take, but that admitting to taking them would mean certain dire consequences.

Taking a giant gulp, and mustering the most innocent face I could, I looked up at my father and meekly asked, "What missing bottles?"

Without hesitation, he grabbed my right hand, and brandishing his belt, leather began to make considerable and frequent contact with my rear-most anatomy. After 10 or 12 strong licks he stopped, and said "That was for stealing my bottles. Now this for lying to me." At that time, he grabbed my left hand and began laying more leather on my tender backside.

Can you imagine my embarrassment? I got two spankings right there beside the road and in clear sight of Jane Rankin's bedroom window. (She was the prettiest girl in town.)

The walk up the hill to the sanctuary of home and the empathy of a loving mother was long and hot. Guilt now weighed heavily on my conscience. Needless to say, I closed my bottle empire at once.

Dad added a final component to my punishment and rehabilitation. I had to clean and straighten the bottle pen the next Saturday afternoon.

After carefully cleaning the bottle pen as instructed, I went inside the store and saw Dad behind the counter. "I've finished cleaning the bottle pen," I told him.

Dad reached over the counter and took my right hand. In it he placed two packs of Kits, my favorite candy. While still firmly holding my hand, he said, "I love you."

I was one happy kid. I knew everything was okay. Dad was not going to throw me out of the family. I was safe, secure, and still in the fold.

Many years have passed since I folded my bottle empire. As I look back, it wasn't the punishment that left the lasting impression; it was my father's love and desire to instill solid values that have resonated throughout my life. I am thankful that Dad taught me to consider the consequences of my actions, and I have worked to pass this same lesson along to my own children. It is heartwarming to see these values and qualities in my seven beautiful grandchildren.

Enjoy your family this holiday season, and to each of you, a safe and happy New Year.

The Stovepipe

In considering my message for this issue of *Clayton NOW*, I was looking for a way to engage you, my audience, in an examination of business principles. My wonderful life partner, Kay, always insightful, suggested I share one of my mother's favorite stories.

Now those of you fortunate enough to know Ruth Clayton are quite taken with her many endearing qualities—kindness and patience being just two of them. Perhaps it is her demeanor that makes the telling of the "Stovepipe Story" all the more entertaining. Certainly nobody tells it like her. With her blessing, I share it with you now.

It was a typical Friday. I trekked the half-mile from the red brick, four-room schoolhouse to arrive some 30 minutes before Mom came home. She spent her days at the shirt factory, hovering over a commercial sewing machine, earning sweatshop pay. Little did either of us know that the next hour would provide Mother with a test of her tolerance for me, an inventive 10-year old, and give her a story that, 55 years later, still evokes tears of laughter from all who hear her tell it.

Let me preface the story with a bit of history. I was seven when my Uncle R. C. Clayton gave me a Sears and Roebuck guitar. In four years time, I had learned all the major chords used in country and gospel music and found that I was being asked, with some regularity, to "bring the guitar" to family and neighborhood events.

By 1944, I was a budding Eddy Arnold, and like my idol, I needed a microphone and speaker. I managed to acquire an old microphone and an amplifier-speaker with money I'd earned from building fires in the schoolhouse and church, along with "egg money" contributed by Grandmother Clayton.

But after many performances, I soon found the tiny speaker in that old amplifier was limiting my audience's full appreciation of my young, developing voice. The solution arrived in the form of a powerful speaker I removed from an old Philco console radio that I repaired for the Finger Railway Station manager. (He was my first customer after completing Part 1 of the National Radio Institute Correspondence course in Radio Repair.)

Not only did I collect 50 cents for my efforts, but Mr. Naylor gave me the old and once-powerful speaker.

Later, while exploring the inner workings of the speaker, I discovered an open coil in the electromagnet. It only took a few turns of the coil until I found the break. I soldered the broken connection and happily completed a successful test of the ancient speaker.

With the speaker working, I now needed an enclosure larger than my original amplifier case. When I entered the kitchen that afternoon, I saw an easier and quicker alternative to building a more conventional wood box enclosure for the speaker. It was in the ceiling.

You see, the family had used a wood burning cook-stove until just a few weeks earlier. Mom's new GE electric range did not require a stovepipe, so Dad placed a tin pie pan over the opening in the ceiling vacated by the stovepipe. I estimated the size of the hole in the ceiling to be approximately the size of my newly repaired Philco speaker. Wow! My old, but powerful speaker would sound *great* in the kitchen ceiling cavity. I quickly removed the pie pan, inserted the speaker, and carefully attached the small speaker wires.

I heard Mother's arrival in the family's 1937 Ford just as I was connecting the opposite end of the speaker wires to my guitar amplifier's speaker leads. When Mother walked in from her grueling eight-hour day of sewing, I quickly loaded the 78 RPM turntable with Eddy Arnold's big hit "Any Time."

"Hi, Mom!" I blurted, as she entered the kitchen. "Look at this."

Hardly able to contain my excitement, I showed her the record player, the amplifier, the wires to the stovepipe speaker, and told her of my good fortune in being able to repair Mr. Naylor's speaker.

Mother did not share in my enthusiasm, but she did pause to take a quick look at my contraption as I placed the needle in the record groove. Apparently, I had the volume up a little high; the bass was cranked to the last notch to accommodate the small speaker normally driven by the little amplifier.

Simultaneously, the room filled, not only with the resonant voice of Eddy Arnold and his studio recording band, but with a thick cloud of rich, black soot, surging from the stovepipe outlet. Soot billowed across the kitchen, into the living room and the bedroom, and filled every crack and crevice with the jet-black powdery substance. Not exactly the pyrotechnics of a modern-day concert, but you could say the effect was riveting.

For years, my Mother has taught me to appreciate music of all kinds, but on this occasion, she was somehow unable to fully appreciate Eddy Arnold's rich harmonics and the wide range of sounds emanating from my recent electronic invention.

"Turn that thing off and help me clean this place before your Dad sees this mess," she said.

The silent recovery effort took some time. She, of course, was tired after having awakened at the usual 4:30 a.m. to tend the chores, cook breakfast for the family, go to work, and then drive home to be greeted with my disaster. On this particular Friday morning, she had devoted extra care to tidying the house, since it was our turn to host the clan of grandparents, uncles, aunts, and cousins for the weekend.

I don't think that Dad ever learned the details of this episode. He knew only that Mother had experienced a difficult day and that she had decided not to prepare her normal "supper" of fried chicken, potatoes, beans, cornbread, milk, and honey. Perhaps he may have noticed how I quietly stayed in the background and was unusually attentive to Mom for the weekend.

How does this story relate to the basics we follow at Clayton? In our business, we have to carefully test a new concept before we take it up to full speed. We have to use proven, basic techniques that have been tested and perfected. Risk has to be minimized. Enthusiasm and creativity have to be tempered so that we may consider the impact of our actions on others.

When I created my new speaker case, I failed to follow the basics and disaster followed. Overcome by my own excitement, I neglected to test the concept, reduce the risk, and consider Mother's reaction.

Often times, people are tempted to short-cut essential elements of business to win the contest, be number one, make more commissions, or only accommodate the customer in the short-term. No team member at Clayton can afford to take these risks. Why? Our jobs, our security, our benefits, and our future depend upon following the basics. CMH customers, shareholders, and team members rely on us to do that.

We must protect a credible record of over 43 years of superior service to customers, vendors, lenders, shareholders, and ourselves by doing what we've always done—following the basics.

My Brother Joe

As Joe and I were growing up, we fought like most normal brothers. But as a child, when Mother, Dad and the two of us were huddled around the fireplace one cold night, Joe—stepping in-between us—fell, turning over a cast-iron tea kettle filled with scalding water. The accident caused scars that he carries even today. When it happened, I cried even louder than he did. I did the same thing when he dropped a disc from a farm implement and severed his big toe.

As we finished high school, we found little to argue about (and have had no arguments since). I graduated one year before Joe, and immediately took a job in Memphis, where I was encouraged to enroll at Memphis State. A year later, Joe registered at Draughen's Business College in Nashville. Both of us had all of the farm work, with its meager returns, that we could stand.

We would meet in Memphis, Nashville, or at home in Finger whenever our busy schedules would permit. After finishing pre-engineering, I transferred to the University of Tennessee at Knoxville; as soon as Joe graduated from Draughen's, he joined me. Later, Mother and Dad would migrate east and also make Knoxville their home. The Clayton family has called Knoxville their home ever since.

While attending UT, Joe and I both worked nighttime at local radio and television stations. We placed a classified ad to sell my old Kaiser – which caused numerous car salesmen to break out in laughter when it was suggested they place some value on it as a trade on a more acceptable car. But two buyers answered the ad, resulting in us helping another student working with us at the TV station. He was also stuck with a car that seemingly no one wanted – a Studebaker. Our commission for facilitating that deal was $50. We were hooked, and soon were selling a car almost every week, and earning more than we were paid at our other jobs. Sure, the hours were long, but it was fun and profitable.

A state licensing agent insisted that we operate with a license, phone, sign, service facility, and display yard. As an alternative to fines and potential jail sentences, we leased a corner of a service station on Kingston Pike. Now we were in business with overhead, and all that goes with operating a small family business. That was in 1956, as Clayton's was born.

Actually, Joe worked for me, as I had been the owner of that old Kaiser and had written that first ad. But to see Joe washing those cars, changing tires, placing ads, taking buying trips to auctions and new car dealers for inventory, and selling too—all between classes at UT—you would've thought he was an owner.

We enjoyed a lot of success, and by 1961, had a 50-person team and three locations with both new and used cars. Then, a business failure. We were wiped out. Even Joe had taken notes and IOU's for most of his commissions. One morning we had a thriving business, and by nightfall, the doors to Jim Clayton Motors, Inc., were closed in bankruptcy.

With a great deal of hesitation, I made Joe an offer. If he would work full-time in rebuilding the business, I'd work part-time while getting my law degree. And I would give him half of everything I had.

All I had was the business – and it was flat broke and bankrupt. Without hesitation, he said, "Deal." Armed with a law degree, we thought that we could avoid ever being bankrupt again. You know, it worked. Neither of us has been bankrupt even one time since.

Now we were 50/50 partners. It took just over three years for us to be confident that the business would be a success – and for me to get my law degree and pass the state bar exam.

Joe worked unbelievable hours, spending much of his time building good parts, service and body shop facilities, along with accounting and even data processing systems in the early '60s. I watched over sales. When there was cash available, we took equal salaries. Later, when we could afford a bonus at year's end, ours were exactly equal. For 20 years, until 1981, we were equal partners—the kind of partnership/team that maximizes synergies, so that 1 + 1 = 11. (Notice 1+1 *can* make 11. In this case, it really did.)

Oh! Did I tell you that we paid every creditor every cent owed by the old business? I think anyone who knows us wouldn't be surprised to learn that we had to pay every vendor. Before, during, and after the business failure, we paid everyone. That is the kind of people the Claytons have always been.

Joe and I never kept score, even though we shared airplanes, vacation homes, and cars, while having our personal residences as the only separate assets for 20 years.

By 1966, it was apparent that Joe and I had the management capacity to take on additional responsibility. It was recognized that the automobile business did not lend itself to "cookie cutter" expansion. I'd enjoyed our Manufactured Home on Norris Lake, and I had enjoyed the one we lived in while in college (and sold to buy six cars for inventory when we leased the service station). I'd also watched Taylor Homes across the street, tying up traffic on Clinton Highway with all their deliveries, so we decided to test the concept. It worked!

Joe, along with our father and Clarence Cole, our service supervisor, started the first factory in a building that had been our body shop. By the time they had the first home finished, they discovered the garage door was too small to get it out of the building. That was soon fixed, and the first home was "born" in January 1970.

But the building was too small for our big ideas, and the present Halls plant was acquired. In that same month, Lincoln-Mercury offered us the local dealership. Joe and I flipped a coin to see who would take on the new car dealership, with the other to be responsible for the new factory expansion. I forgot who won the toss, but Joe took on the Lincoln-Mercury challenge. Jim Ausmus and I took on the factory and recruited Jim Early, who had handled advertising and communications for us, to be General Manager. (Max Nichols replaced Jim when he had a health problem later in the year.)

Fast-forward to 1981. Joe and his sons were focused almost entirely on the car business, which was very successful. But Joe also spent untold hours on the housing accounting and data processing systems. I spent all of my time on the housing retail, finance, parks, and manufacturing.

With our sons becoming more and more involved in the business, it was natural that we would need a structure that would give them an ownership interest. These discussions resulted in Joe and I each owning 100 percent of the automobile and housing businesses, respectively. We carved apart very complex business interests and never had one strained moment. How about that? That is the kind of person my brother Joe is.

There's more. In two years, we were able to take CMH public. My interest was multiplied more than 10 times. Joe was never jealous, not one time, or resentful of my good fortune. He supported me by agreeing to serve on our Board without asking for any ownership interest. Of course, he has done very well on his standard Board member options. And his automobile businesses have been very successful too.

Joe possesses a most unusual set of business and human relations skills. Just some of them include computers—he wrote the basic general ledger and other programs that we used until two years ago. He wrote the mortgage-servicing program that we use today. He is good at accounting, sales, human resources, service, finance, and golf (he hid that from me until we separated the businesses). He served on the Board of Valley Fidelity Bank, later First Tennessee Bank, and has been of enormous support as a valued Board member of Clayton Homes, Inc.

Joe and his two fine sons, Rick and Mark, and daughter Debby, own and operate Volvo, Nissan, and used car dealerships in Knoxville, and Mercedes and Volvo dealerships in Columbia, S.C. They are very successful, by any measurements of growth, profitability, market-share, and especially, customer service.

When I look at the current CMH Mission and Value statements, I see Joe Clayton and our parents in every item. Exceeding customer expectations, delivering quality, expecting what we inspect, keeping open communications, doing the hard work, making prompt decisions, following the "Together Everyone Accomplishes More" philosophy, keeping agreements, acknowledging the significance of family, and respecting the rights and dignity of others—yes, that's my brother Joe— our co-founder. Thanks, Joe. I can never repay you.

ANALYSIS

THE BERKSHIRE EFFECT

By Martin V. Lavin

I turned on my computer to check what e-mail came in overnight, coffee in hand and eyes still a little bleary early in the morning of April 2. My eye quickly caught the headline of an e-mail sent by BB&T's John Diffendal that read, **Berkshire Buying Clayton Homes**.

My heavens, could this be true? I checked to see it wasn't April 1, so I wouldn't be a fool. No, this was real all right. The greatest investor of this generation, Warren Buffett, "The Oracle of Omaha," was buying Clayton Homes of Knoxville, Tenn.

Wow! Warren Buffett!

Not too long after that came the torrent of phone calls and e-mails. Everyone had two things on their minds:

1. Why did this happen?
2. What does it mean for the industry in general and the Claytons in particular?

I chatted with many pundits and people of influence in factory-built housing. Many called to see if I had a different take or inside information of any sort. Let me be clear, everything I know is a matter of generally available information. I know and like Jim and Kevin Clayton, but I am not a confidante on these matters. That said, I was as shocked as everyone else about this impending sale.

Nuts and bolts

Last November, industry stalwart and one-time high-flyer, Oakwood Homes of Greensboro, N.C., had gone into Chapter 11 bankruptcy. Through a financial transaction, Buffett's investing arm, Berkshire Hathaway (BH), wound up effectively controlling Oakwood with debtor-in-possession financing. The control of Oakwood is more important than the details, as is the desire of BH to get involved in the factory-built housing business at any level.

Why were they there? At the time, many (me included) wondered if this was a precursor to further investment moves by BH in this industry. Shortly after the Oakwood announcement, however, they seemed to drop from sight for a while.

Oakwood went about the business of sorting out their affairs in an attempt to right themselves in a very stormy industry. Little was heard from BH for months with regard to any concrete industry-related news, although there were persistent rumors.

About a month after the Oakwood announcement and in a huge bind thanks to over-aggressive lending practices, Conseco Finance (formerly Green Tree Financial)—the one-time leader among industry-based financial institutions—filed for Chapter 11 bankruptcy protection too.

CFN Investment Holdings, a group of financial investors, appeared to be controlling the purchase of Conseco Finance. While other bidders were mentioned, little if any mention was made of BH's interest in Conseco Finance in news reports.

Then, at the Conseco bankruptcy auction held in early March, the news broke that BH had in fact bid on Conseco and, for a time, even seemed to be the leading player. But, in an apparent change of mind after battling aggressively over the rights to Conseco Finance, BH seemingly exiting the bidding process.

A complex offer they made to the bankruptcy court in Chicago was rejected as being too conditional to be viewed as real. It looked like CFN won the bidding as BH dropped out that day.

The next day, BH reemerged to make strong moves in an attempt to gain control of Conseco Finance, but the court ultimately ruled in CFN's favor. Disappointed, BH retreated, but not entirely without rancor, angry their bid had not prevailed.

What did all this mean? Was it a matter of one more financial intervention into a bankrupt company by BH to profit short-term from the disabilities of Conseco? Or, was it an attempt to purchase value with the servicing-of-loan rights Conseco retained to a $24 billion industry portfolio and maybe even return to loan originations?

That answer was unapparent to observers based on what was made public at the time. Most believed BH simply saw a short-term advantage to those huge servicing rights Conseco had, and little more. (Insiders have told me this is true.)

But clear evidence of BH's real intentions in factory-built housing became fully apparent shortly after their failed bid for Conseco about a month later. When BH announced the Clayton Homes deal, they emphasized this was the purchase of the premier company in an industry whose assets are generally vastly undervalued.

The classic Warren Buffett approach to investing was evident, swooping up a successful and profitable company run by people of integrity carrying out a clear and simple business enterprise understandable by a 10-year-old, and purchased at a price with a margin of safety to boot. That is a pretty acceptable investment philosophy. I'm sure Buffett's mentor, Ben Graham, would have been proud.

The Conseco effect

Why did the Claytons do this? Jim and Kevin don't ask for my consent, so this is mostly my speculation based on careful observation of the facts.

First and foremost, there can be no question the stock short-sellers (people who put up money gambling that stock value will go down) have been beating up on Clayton stock unmercifully for quite some time, banking on it going down in value, at one point driving it down to about $9 per share. The thinking of the "shorts" has been Clayton shouldn't be doing well in an industry in which everyone else was floundering and their turn would come to pay the price.

Never mind that Clayton had continued strong earnings, suffered the least in terms of loan portfolio losses and was continuing to gain market-share even as the industry shrunk dramatically, down 55 percent from the last top.

All great food for thought, of course, but the short-sellers weren't buying—or eating it. They didn't believe in Clayton and kept up the pressure right to the end (the one-time share price of around $11 reflected the short-selling pressure).

Meanwhile, the asset-backed securities (ABS) market—our industry's lenders' lenders—also were suffering from the "Conseco effect" that punished all securitizers of loans sold by our industry lenders to investors, because of portfolio losses. This made loan sales difficult and even unprofitable for most, although not for Clayton.

As you can imagine, Clayton Homes' lending subsidiary Vanderbilt Mortgage and Finance (VMF) soon began to fear the "Conseco effect" too. That punishment for the sins of others endangered the future of what had been orderly business plans at Clayton. Though they had kept their loan noses clean, VMF was concerned they could be punished right along with the worst of them.

Clayton is a fairly substantial company, with a strong balance sheet, of which they should be proud. But, the company wasn't made of gold, the last time I looked. The prospects for less-than-clean future securitizations into a very troubled ABS market were a cause for some concern.

Jim Clayton, the hard-driving businessman he is, had built a vast fortune doing things right in an industry famous for various defects. Jim must have wondered if he was going to be sacrificed at the altar of industry excesses, in which he did not engage. Or, that he would be victimized by the very industry to which he had made many positive contributions.

Were that to happen, endangering the enterprise and the Clayton family fortune, it would have been unfair in the extreme, but the damage would have had potentially devastating effects for the company, its investors, the Claytons and their 6,800 associates.

All those things considered, if you were the Claytons and Warren Buffett put an offer on the table for your company, I'm sure you'd seriously contemplate it.

Meanwhile, Jim Clayton, approaching 70, had given way to his son Kevin, who is about 40 and an extremely talented and engaging young man running the business very successfully during this terrible industry downturn. (A good future for Clayton Homes would portend a good future for Kevin, so that must have been on their minds as well.)

And lastly, if you haven't been to Maryville, Tenn., you haven't met their talented, motivated and enthusiastic cadre of employees, all of whom seem to bleed "Clayton Blue" when it comes to their company.

I'm not alone in this observation. You cannot help but be impressed with the morale and efficiency of this group.

That attitude tells you something about how the Claytons do things. Make no mistake, Jim and Kevin are demanding and this is **their** business, but their associates respect and like them, and vice-versa. In the long run, Kevin says this sale was very, very good for the Clayton Homes "team." I know this was a major consideration in the sale, in doing something to perpetuate the company's growth, profits and success that bring on even greater opportunities to the team.

So, Jim turns his major asset into cash and goes on to the things he likes doing, proud of his accomplishments. The sale locks in a fair value for Clayton Homes investors considering the industry downside and short seller persistence. Kevin gets to sell his share of the stock advantageously and, more importantly, remains in charge of the company, as is the Buffett way. And, the Buffett balance sheet brings Clayton a new liquidity unmatched by any other industry player, save Chase, which allows the entire enterprise to exploit the market even further. As one wag told me, "as if Clayton Homes needed more help..."

All of this preserves and encourages the Clayton Homes team to grow and prosper. In turn, Buffett gets the premier player in the industry with 40 years of culture and accomplishment, at the price he offered. If this thing isn't win-win for most involved, I can't imagine why, based on what I know.

I hear some investors would like to have seen a greater premium over the stock offer price of $12.50 per share. That's certainly understandable, but I'm sure Oakwood and Conseco investors would have been happy to have gotten anything for their stock.
(continued on page 20)

Appendix E-1

Although Clayton Homes isn't like either of those companies, with industry conditions as they are, the war and the general economy, this could quickly be a $8-$9 stock as well. I suppose the short sellers weren't doing handstands either, as many got hurt financially.

The industry upside?

The BH move was good for most of the cast of characters I've discussed so far, but what about the impact of the transaction on the industry as a whole?

Let me leave no margin for misunderstanding that this is wonderful news for the factory-built housing industry, especially the HUD Code, chattel-financed portion of it.

Clayton Homes, along with its VMF subsidiary, is essentially a modest housing, chattel-financed provider of shelter for the entry-level home buyer. They make no apologies for that business plan and have been diligent in not overselling or exploiting their ability to finance clients through their own framework. They don't "over-finance" homes for too long a term, destroying the buyer's investment and impairing their company's loan quality.

From where I sit, the industry is following Clayton's lead now more frequently as the surviving lenders get on the same winning page.

The lending world is a monkey-see, monkey-do world. In this latest lending episode, it became rather obvious to me as more industry lenders exited the market, even more followed suit. **Nobody** wanted to offer lending to the factory-built housing industry.

Never mind that the last couple of years, for a disciplined, highly liquid lender (like GMAC), this industry has presented one of the all-time opportunities to get into this sector, choose from the very best loans and take charge of an industry's lending that was ripe for the picking. But it was generally perceived there was an inability to profit because others were struggling within the industry.

Forget that those struggling had hardly loaned on a rational basis, and should have expected loan problems, which they got. New lending institutions would not have had to deal with that overhang of problems, clearing the way to lead. However, this all presumes strong liquidity on the part of any who would be the leader, to say nothing of having pretty large nads.

The lenders in today's industry constitute two classes:

• Those who want to step up and lend properly but aggressively, but don't have the juice to do it.

• Those with the juice who didn't want to loan aggressively, not really believing in the market and waiting for it to have a crystal clear direction.

There are few rewards for the latter course and only better liquidity can cure the first. Clayton, through its VMF lending arm, pulled it off better than anyone, lending properly, but aggressively. Still, the company finally grew increasingly concerned about ABS markets failing to provide the kind of liquidity Buffett does. As a result, Clayton is about to have the ability, desire and liquidity to do it right, big time!

As you read this, corporate officers in boardrooms of various companies are probably having conversations that go something like this: "Have you seen what Warren Buffett did with Clayton Homes?" "Yes, I heard. What do you make of it?" "Well, I think there must be an opportunity in financing 'trailers' and we ought to look into it. Look into it."

I expect significant interest from the investment community with the potential to bring fresh, new money to the industry. I have always believed this would happen on its own, but this could really accelerate it, helping to turn the industry into a growth mode once again.

Investors have been following Warren Buffett around for a long time. The people at Clayton Homes using Buffett's money are sharp, experienced operators, so I'm not concerned about them. Will the rest of the money and the people attached to it following Buffett's lead into the industry be as smart? We'll see.

I believe the message Buffett sent this industry was that chattel-financed, modest homes are what he is banking on. Those who firmly believe that the industry needs to leave this tier of HUD Code housing behind should know they are doing so for BH and Clayton Homes to exploit and control.

These two seem comfortable for the present to remain in that position and, based on the success of each, perhaps giving the industry pause to contemplate the breadth of product necessary to make a success.

There's one more thought about this pending deal that needs to be voiced: Before the announcement, it never crossed my mind Clayton Homes needed to be "saved" or that they were looking for a savior. Cer-

tainly, Clayton didn't need it. The company saw about $120 million in cash generated by operations in 2002. That type of money will keep Clayton Homes bubbling at a good business clip with strong prospects for success.

Although everyone in business faces challenges from time to time, the Knoxville Boys have an uncanny knack of taking advantage of the misfortunes around them to create greater profits for themselves. They are a sound, well-run company with good future prospects.

The BH umbrella has turned them into a HUD Code home juggernaut with incredible potential to truly capitalize on the market they now serve and future potential for other excursions for growth. Moreover, forgetting the upside potential, the sale foreclosed the "bad case" scenario for Clayton Homes investors and associates. It just seems like a no-brainer to me. What's to question?

As I write this, that's how the world looks to me. Many things could change by the time you read this. Nevertheless, many of the things I've discussed here have currency whether Buffett goes to Knoxville or decides to stay in Omaha.

As Yogi Berra said, "It ain't over, till it's over," and this is not a done deal. But the contemplation of it all, at least for the moment, is delicious in the extreme. □

Martin V. Lavin is an attorney and 30-year veteran of the factory-built housing industry, with special emphasis on lending. He lives in Burlington, Vt., and is a consultant and expert witness to the industry. Lavin serves as chairman of MHI's Financial Services division and sits on the group's Executive Committee and Board of Directors. He also represents Mobile Home Lending Corp. Lavin also publishes a free industry newsletter, News and Notes. To receive his newsletter, contact him at 802/862-1313, or by e-mail at MHLMVL@aol.com.

APPENDIX E-2

Review of Jim Clayton's Autobiography "FIRST A DREAM"

Sat 06/21/03 08:09:34 pm
by GEORGE ALLEN

Someone truly significant within the manufactured housing industry has given us a detailed look at his personal and business journey through life; creating at the same time, an enduring and valuable legacy for family, friends, business associates and peers.

In several ways, Jim Clayton's *First A Dream*, is a near perfect example of why, when, and how to effectively pen one's memoirs.

Why an autobiography? To recall and describe, from his perspective, a full life as an entertainer, successful entrepreneur, amateur pilot, generous philanthropist, and banker. To share intimate, practical, poignant, and timeless 'lessons learned' along life's journey, that'll inspire and educate future generations of his family and CMH team members.*1

When? Best penned at the productive-turning-reflective apex of one's life and career, before memories wane; and while present day plans, decisions, and activities continue to hone the wit and wisdom of the teller.

How? In this instance, with assistance of an able, experienced and motivated journalist/collaborator.

The **substance** of *First A Dream*, based on Jim Clayton's early life as a sharecropper's son, student, fledgling pilot, country singer, and young entrepreneur; and ultimately, successful businessman and banker, highlights **four categories of his insights and sageness:**

• Jim's general, personal, and business lessons, tips and principles

• Pithy insights relative to marketing and sales 'the Clayton way'

• Inside manufactured housing revelations unavailable elsewhere

• CMH-specific concepts and programs worthy of emulation

But first; what was **'the dream'** that inspired Jim's early life and direction? In his own words: *"I'm standing on center stage, performing at the Grand Ole Opry. Singing. Picking my guitar. Promoting my latest hit record. Awash in adoring fans. Bathed in bright lights. Drenched in applause. There I am, the consummate entertainer, taking it all in stride, totally at ease with my fame and fortune."* P.19. Furthermore, his **youthful goals** were "as grand as they were generic" - "I wanted to be recognized (respected) and I wanted to be rich (secure)." P.20.

As Jim matured, so did his views. In essence, *First A Dream* was penned to demonstrate that "...hard work and commitment does pay off - if you balance it with faith in God, concern for others, integrity, a passion for learning, and a positive mental attitude. By dreaming dreams based on sound values, and sometimes realistic expectations, and working hard while remaining focused, we can succeed and accomplish most of the important goals we dream for ourselves." P.xii.

The **'ageless concepts'** he carried from his boyhood home include: "Self-discipline. Willpower. Perseverance. Realizing that disappointment is not defeat. Knowing that problems often present opportunities. Obstacles may get in the way...But the human spirit can triumph... Adversity breeds resilience and can build character. It is possible to survive, even prevail." PP. 17 & 18.

At times, Jim's homespun wisdom is flavored with humor. About **planning**: "A bad plan is more likely to work than no plan at all." P.69.

About helping one's **competition**: "It's never smart to shine a light on your competition, not even a candlelight." P.110. And, **a simple truth**: "My experience tells me that high moral and ethical values can't be taught." P.243.

Moving from general, personal, and business lessons onto Jim's insights relative to marketing and sales, here's what he writes about hiring salesmen and women: "I believe introverts, those with a quieter, more thoughtful approach, sell more than extroverts do. Introverts listen better." P.90. And if you haven't heard this opinion by now, "One more comment on advertising, I don't think much of the Yellow Pages. Never have." P.105. How about **'mirroring'**? Here's how it works in the Clayton scheme of things: "Our salespeople are trained to be aware of and adapt to the tone, style, and manner of our prospects. If they talk fast, we talk fast. If they lean forward in the chair, we lean forward in ours. Whether they're monotone or animated, we do the same. These presumably small nuances are actually wonderful communication tools, a nonverbal way to say, 'I understand. We're on the same page.' P.252. Now, those three marketing and sales lessons, according to Jim Clayton, work very well at CMH, but are absent form many contemporary training resources. What does that tell you?

Then there are some pretty heady filled-in-the-blanks observations the author makes about manufactured housing. This is as succinct a description of our industry's umbrageous practice of 'packing' as you'll read anywhere: "Here's how it works: a retailer buys a $30,000 home from the manufacturer, but asks the manufacturer to add a pack, or rebate, to the invoice for $5,000. This could be labeled as marketing support, display materials, or even a furniture package. The invoice has now grown to $35,000. The manufacturer, after receiving payment, rebates the $5,000 to the dealer." P.84.

And this is Jim Clayton's succinct summary of what happens too often within our segment of the factory-built housing business. "...the industry becomes euphoric at the first sign of increased sales. Lenders rush in after seeing CMH earns more than $100 million after tax each year, also because they believe the higher yields will offset poor underwriting, aggressive advances, and weak servicing. The lender looks like a hero for three years as the portfolio builds. Early warning signs are ignored because the next downturn is still three years down the road." P.85.

Then there are the CMH specific concepts and programs Jim proudly describes in his book. The acronym **TEAM** has been around for a long time. While generally accepted to mean *'Together Everyone Achieves More!'* the **CMH variant** is *'Together Everyone Accomplishes More!'*

Every company should have a **BUBBA program!** Initiated in 1990, **B**uying **U**nder the **B**i-Weekly **B**udget **A**dvantage mortgage program has proven a boon for CMH homebuyers. "BUBBA is easy, fast, with no checks to write, no mail to send, and a 20 year loan can be repaid in 12 years." How? "BUBBA homeowners pay half the mortgage every two weeks, or bi-weekly. Instead of paying a $400 mortgage on the first of the month, a BUBBA participant pays $200 every two weeks, electronically, through a no-fee checking account." P.282.

And how bout the **MBU program** (Million Dollar Business Unit) program initiated by Kevin Clayton. "Basically, anyone in our organization with an idea for a new product or service can make a presentation to senior management to sell the concept. The idea must be able to produce a net profit of $1 million a year by the third year. If the program is approved, CMH will support the concept with start-up capital, a full-time staff, and a board of directors versed in accounting, legal, marketing, computer systems, and administration." P.283. What a terrific employee motivator!

With that said, this reviewer found the first 285 pages of *First A Dream* to be an easy, energizing, educational, inspiring 'read'! And up to that point I'd heartily recommend the autobiography to every young and aspiring business person or manufactured housing aficionado.

The exception? **A dual treat really**. Jim's thoughtful and thorough preparation for eventual retirement, and Kevin's rise in the CMH organization, are together, nearly as encouraging and inspiring as reading of Jim's early life as a sharecropper's son. In the first instance, most middle aged readers will likely come away inspired to begin similar planning for their retirement; in the latter instance, I gained additional respect for Jim's son Kevin, as the able exec I've watched him become at Manufactured Housing Institute meetings and other industry events during the past several years.

With all that said, and written, *First A Dream* concluded, leaving one posed but unanswered question: **'When will Jim Clayton receive his gold** (retirement) **watch?'** P.320.

Everyone who earns a paycheck, or receives a dividend check, from any HUD Code manufactured housing related business should study this book! At the very least you'll read of individuals, firms, and entertainers you've heard of or read about over the years. And at best, you'll come away impressed and inspired by the life experiences of one of the greatest businessmen to hail from Tennessee!

Box # 47024

Indianapolis, IN 46247

Dr. Auxier's Deal Makers
February 3, 2003

Richard Wright, my intern, presented *First A Dream* to Warren on behalf of Dr. Auxier and his UT students – triggering a series of *Happenings*, including the CMH sale to Berkshire.

Michael Daniels, my previous intern who made the annual pilgrimage to Omaha in 2002, and Dr. Auxier *dreamed up* the gift idea for Warren.

A Peyton Manning jersey, a basketball signed by Pat Head Summitt, and a football from Phil Fulmer had been Warren's gift on prior visits.

If the gift had been *orange* in 2003, Berkshire would not own CMH – and this *New Edition* would not be.

Ronald Allyn	Adam Johnson	Colin Rochford
Albert Auxier	Steven Kariuki	Daniel Ruble
Maria Bellenger	Seth Kehne	Charles Shaffer
Chris Campbell	Andrea Kiltau	Jennifer Sullivan
Michael Daniels	Derrick King	Samuel Tibbs
William Ellison	Elizabeth Kirk	Justin Walker
Michael Faris	Jonathan McKee	Justin Waters
Chirs Faris	Natalie Nelson	Jason Watson
Jeremy Hamilton	Corey Neureuther	Doug Webster
Christopher	Cort Neureuther	Jonathan Webster
Hammond	Benjamin Newman	Gary (Michael) Willett
Sara Hill	Angel Norman	Clayton Williams
Natalie Hunt	Jayme Place	Wesley Wright
Ryan Johnson	Carolyn Quinn	Richard Wright

BERKSHIRE HATHAWAY INC.
1440 KIEWIT PLAZA
OMAHA, NEBRASKA 68131
TELEPHONE (402) 346-1400
FAX (402) 346-0476

WARREN E. BUFFETT, CHAIRMAN

To Whom It May Concern:

I am writing on behalf of Michael Daniels, an outstanding young man that I have come to know through an interesting chain of events.

We first met in my Omaha office when the Tennessee Valley Authority Investment Challenge team from the University of Tennessee, came to visit. Usually university guests give me a football or other native object as a nice gesture. This time, my ambitious new friend, Michael, presented me with an autographed copy of Jim Clayton's recent autobiography "First A Dream" telling me, "these are your kind of people."

Reading the book that weekend caused me to immediately offer $1.7 billion dollars for Jim's company, Clayton Homes, Inc. A month later, I acclaimed Michael a "deal maker" during my press conference in Knoxville, TN as we announced the fine acquisition he had brought to my attention.

He is the type of person any company or institution would be lucky to have. When looking for management, I search out those that jump out of the bed in the morning excited about taking on the day. I see that Michael is this type of person.

With a high level of energy, intelligence, and integrity, qualities that are prevalent in Berkshire managers, Michael has a very exciting career ahead.

Sincerely,

Warren Buffett

BERKSHIRE HATHAWAY INC.
NEWS RELEASE

FOR IMMEDIATE RELEASE   July 15, 2003

Omaha, NE (BRK.A; BRK.B) — Tomorrow, shareholders of Clayton Homes meet to consider Berkshire Hathaway's offer to acquire their company. Clayton shareholders should be aware of the following facts:

(1) Berkshire will not raise its price now or in the future.

(2) Berkshire will not become a lender to the mobile home industry except through Clayton. Berkshire made a bad investment several years ago in Oakwood Homes and learned the hard way of the dangers in mobile home finance. Indeed, these dangers have become manifest at Clayton, even though it is – in Berkshire's opinion - by far the best company in the mobile home industry. The 8-K Clayton recently filed indicates that both delinquencies and loss severity have increased substantially in the past year. In the first half of 2003, the average loss incurred in repossessions was 49.2% of the contract amount.

(3) This staggering loss experience is in stark contrast to the experience of lenders financing site-built homes. Simply put, the value of mobile homes has often plummeted after purchase, while traditional homes have appreciated. The industry's troubles have in large part occurred because of this difference in resale experience. The result: Sales of mobile homes have fallen dramatically and consistently during the past few years while sales of site-built homes have been strong. Industry observers have regularly predicted turnarounds in mobile home sales during these years. They have been wrong: Low interest rates have caused housing to thrive – but new mobile home sales continue to sink. Clayton is no exception.

(4) Berkshire believes the spread in financing costs between site-built homes and mobile homes will not narrow should interest rates rise. The spread results from the high losses that occur when the underlying asset depreciates in contrast to the general appreciation in site-built homes. In Berkshire's view, the industry-wide decline in mobile home sales during the past few years would have been even more severe had interest rates not fallen.

(5) Berkshire values the Clayton management – in our view the best in the business – but has no special deals with them, as some have insinuated. If the transaction is completed, their compensation with Berkshire will be similar to what they would have earned if independent.

CERBERUS
Capital Management. L.L.P.

July 28, 2003

Mr. Kevin T. Clayton
Chief Executive Officer and President
Clayton Homes, Inc.
Clayton Homes Headquarters
5000 Clayton Road
Maryville, TN 37804

Dear Mr. Clayton:

This letter is to advise you that Cerberus Capital Management, L.P. has determined not to proceed with an offer to acquire Clayton Homes.

We wanted to thank you and the many outstanding people in your organization who facilitated our due diligence review. We appreciated the level of cooperation we received in what we know was a compressed time frame requiring a substantial effort from all concerned. The level of professionalism and expertise which we encountered is a tribute to the Company's leadership and reflective of the Company's outstanding historical performance and premier position in the industry.

We wish you every continued success.

Very truly yours,

Frank W. Bruno
Managing Director

450 Park Avenue • New York, NY 10022

Illustrative Capital Structure for Discussion Purposes Only

Clayton Recapitalization – Sources & Uses

$14.00 per share offer (minimum $9.00 per share in cash, depending on shareholder election)
($ in millions)

	PRO FORMA
Sources	
Excess Cash	$32.7
Bank Debt (Communities)	200.0
Senior Notes	300.0
Proceeds from Securitization	850.0
Cash Equity Required	387.4
Total Sources	**$1,770.1**
Uses	
Cash Portion of Purchase Price [1]	$1,236.1
Refinance Debt	91.0
Berkshire Payout	368.0
Transaction Costs	75.0
Total Uses	**$1,770.1**

Pro Forma Credit Statistics [2]		
Total Debt / EBITDA [3]		2.4x

Pro Forma Ownership	Stand-alone	
Clayton Family / Management	29.1%	18.5%
Cerberus and Co-investors	–	36.3%
Other	70.9%	45.2%
Total	**100.0%**	**100.0%**

(1) Based on 137 million fully-diluted shares outstanding.
(2) Excludes liabilities associated with securitization.
(3) LTM EBITDA of $854.5 million.

Delaware

PAGE 1

The First State

I, HARRIET SMITH WINDSOR, SECRETARY OF STATE OF THE STATE OF DELAWARE, DO HEREBY CERTIFY THE ATTACHED IS A TRUE AND CORRECT COPY OF THE CERTIFICATE OF MERGER, WHICH MERGES:

"B MERGER SUB, INC.", A DELAWARE CORPORATION,

WITH AND INTO "CLAYTON HOMES, INC." UNDER THE NAME OF "CLAYTON HOMES, INC.", A CORPORATION ORGANIZED AND EXISTING UNDER THE LAWS OF THE STATE OF DELAWARE, AS RECEIVED AND FILED IN THIS OFFICE THE SEVENTH DAY OF AUGUST, A.D. 2003, AT 7:29 O'CLOCK A.M.

A FILED COPY OF THIS CERTIFICATE HAS BEEN FORWARDED TO THE NEW CASTLE COUNTY RECORDER OF DEEDS.

Harriet Smith Windsor, Secretary of State

2697207   8100M

030514583

AUTHENTICATION: 2569639

DATE: 08-07-03

☐ **JAMES L. CLAYTON**

67-816/642
40703

BB&T
BRANCH BANKING AND TRUST COMPANY
ALCOA, TENNESSEE

CHECK
NUMBER

008472

PERSONAL ACCOUNT
5000 CLAYTON RD.
MARYVILLE, TN 37804

PAY ****************44,825,120 AND 00/100 DOLLARS****************

DATE
Apr 15 04

AMOUNT
*$44,825,120.

TO THE
ORDER
OF   Us Treasury

JAMES L. CLAYTON

67-816/642
40703

BB&T
BRANCH BANKING AND TRUST COMPANY
ALCOA, TENNESSEE

CHECK
NUMBER

008473

PERSONAL ACCOUNT
5000 CLAYTON RD.
MARYVILLE, TN 37804

PAY *THREE HUNDRED EIGHTY NINE THOUSAND EIGHT HUNDRED FIFTY AND 00/100 DOLL

DATE
Apr 15 04

AMOUNT
$389,850.00

TO THE
ORDER
OF   Tennessee Dept Of Revenue

AUTHORIZED SIGNATURE

JAMES L. CLAYTON

67-816/642
40703

BB&T
BRANCH BANKING AND TRUST COMPANY
ALCOA, TENNESSEE

CHECK
NUMBER

008474

PERSONAL ACCOUNT
5000 CLAYTON RD.
MARYVILLE, TN 37804

PAY ***********FOUR HUNDRED THOUSAND AND 00/100 DOLLARS*********

DATE
Apr 15 04

AMOUNT
$400,000.00

TO THE
ORDER
OF   Us Treasury

AUTHORIZED SIGNATURE

Congressional Record

United States of America

PROCEEDINGS AND DEBATES OF THE *108th* CONGRESS, FIRST SESSION

Vol. 149   WASHINGTON, FRIDAY, APRIL 11, 2003   No. 59

Senate

JIM CLAYTON

Mr. ALEXANDER. Madam President, I rise today to pay tribute to an outstanding Tennessean, James L. Clayton, better known as Jim.

Jim Clayton is the son of a sharecropper and was raised in West Tennessee. This impressive Tennessean has lived the American dream of Horatio Alger. From his most humble beginnings, he has gone on to become one of the wealthiest men in the United States. Mr. Clayton is the entrepreneur behind Clayton Homes, Inc., a $1.2 billion manufactured-housing company, which is one of Tennessee's great economic treasures.

Last week, Warren Buffett, the widely respected head of Berkshire Hathaway, recognized what we in Tennessee have long known about the quality of Clayton Homes by offering $1.7 billion for the purchase of Clayton Homes' manufactured-home empire.

Mr. Clayton has served as chairman of the board of Clayton Homes, Inc., since he founded the original Clayton auto sales companies in 1956. In 1966, he expanded and branched out into manufactured housing and sold his automobile dealerships in 1981. The Clayton Homes corporate headquarters is located in the county of my hometown, Blount County, TN. Clayton Homes employs 2,500 Tennesseans who work in its sales centers and factories in excellent jobs. Thousands more Tennesseans are employed in good jobs as a result, direct and indirect, of Clayton Homes. And I am pleased to say that as a result of the negotiations, Berkshire Hathaway has agreed to leave Clayton Homes and its employees in Tennessee.

I want to say a few words about Jim Clayton, who is a good and long-time friend. Mr. Clayton received his college degree from the University of Tennessee in 1957 and his law degree from the University Of Tennessee College Of Law in 1964. He has received several honorary doctoral degrees and numerous business awards, including many Wall Street Transcript Gold Awards, Silver Awards, and a Bronze Award as the top chief executive in the manufactured-housing industry. Forbes, the business magazine, has named Clayton Homes, Inc., one of its 200 Best-Managed Companies at least nine times. Clayton Homes has received the Platinum Award for being one of the top companies in the United States. Just this year, Worth magazine recognized Jim Clayton as one of Tennessee's wealthiest residents. Mr. Clayton's amazing story from sharecroppers' son to America's business elite can be found in his fascinating autobiography, First a Dream.

Mr. President, not only is Jim Clayton outstanding in the business arena, he is also an outstanding member of the Knoxville, TN community. He has made generous contributions to many charitable causes, including $3.25 million for construction of the Knoxville Museum of Art; $1 million for the University of Tennessee College of Law for its Center for Entrepreneurial Law; $1 million to start the Clayton Birthing Center at Baptist Hospital; and many grants to K-12 educational programs, most of which were given anonymously.

Mr. Clayton also generously donates his time to various committees and community organizations that work to improve Knoxville and its surrounding communities.

I know Mr. Clayton and count him as a friend. Despite his great wealth and success, I know him to be a warm and humble person. But my colleagues need not take the word of one of Mr. Clayton's friends. Many other Tennesseans have told me over many years of how helpful, kind, and approachable Mr. Clayton is, what a perfect gentleman he is. Mr. President, compliments do not get much better than that.

Mr. President, this brief statement cannot capture all the strengths of Jim Clayton and his manifold good works for his employees, his customers, his community, and his State. I did want to bring to my colleagues' attention the accomplishments and legacy of Jim Clayton, and I am honored to recognize his contributions to Tennessee and America as a whole.

Presented by Senator Lamar Alexander

FRIST REMARKS ON UNIVERSITY OF TENNESSEE FINANCE STUDENTS AND WARREN BUFFETT

Floor Statement -- Remarks as Prepared for Delivery

March 12th, 2004 - Dear Mr. President, I rise to call your attention to the 2003 Annual Report of Berkshire Hathaway, Incorporated. It was released to shareholders on Saturday, March 6th. Berkshire Hathaway, as you may know, is the $42 billion firm led by the greatest stock market investor of modern times, Warren E. Buffett. I call the annual report to your attention because it contains an unusual story involving 40 students and a professor from the University of Tennessee.

For the last five years, Professor Auxier has led his finance class on a field trip to Nebraska to meet with the legendary Oracle of Omaha, as Mr. Buffett is known. The meetings can last as long as two hours as students pepper the investor with questions on everything from finance to life lessons. At the end of each meeting, the group presents Mr. Buffett with a gift of appreciation. Professor Auxier tells my office that his pupils always leave the meeting exhilarated and inspired.

At last year's meeting, the Tennessee group presented Mr. Buffett with the autobiography of Knoxville home builder, Jim Clayton. This would not be particularly noteworthy, except for the fact that Mr. Buffett became so interested in Jim Clayton's story and his successful venture, Clayton Homes, that Mr. Buffett bought the Knoxville company for $1.7 billion. He closed the deal last October.

The story gets even better. Mr. Buffett was so appreciative of the students putting him on to the Clayton Homes investment, that this past October he presented each of them with a share of class B stock in his company. Those shares are now worth roughly $3,100 each. He also gave the professor a share of class A stock, which was worth, as of yesterday, $94,790. Professor Auxier tells my office that when Mr. Buffett unveiled the surprise gifts, everyone was "flabbergasted."

All of this is recounted in Mr. Buffett's Annual Report to his shareholders who now include 40 very lucky students and a tremendously appreciative University of Tennessee professor.

Mr. President, there are, I believe, two lessons to be learned from this delightful story. The first is to be interested in other people. Mr. Buffett read the autobiography of a fellow businessman and was so impressed he ended up buying a company.

Likewise, the Tennessee students took the opportunity to fly to Nebraska to meet a world-renowned expert in their field, and had the good fortune of getting his advice. And are now $3,100 richer for the experience.

Which leads me to the second lesson to be learned: Make sure you always give a thoughtful thank you present. It's the right thing to do–and you never know where it may lead.

Presented by Senator Bill Frist

Clayton Homes' future 'as good as it gets'

A year after the deal, Berkshire's backing has solidified Blount company's No. 1 spot

By BILL BREWER, brewerb@knews.com
September 26, 2004

It's been one year since Berkshire Hathaway paid $1.7 billion for Clayton Homes, and Warren Buffett's hunch about getting into manufactured housing appears to have been right.

During Berkshire's annual meeting in May, thousands of stockholders and others stood in long lines to go through a top-of-the line, double-wide Clayton model home displayed at the meeting in Omaha, Neb.

It was Buffett Nation's introduction to manufactured housing, and it turned a hunch into a cinch for the Oracle of Omaha, whose reputation for stock-picking and company-buying has created a financial cult following.

The first-time display was a "huge hit," Buffett said, estimating that between 4,000 and 5,000 people waited in line to walk through the house. He joked that he may sell tickets next year.

Buffett is banking on similar reactions everywhere a Clayton home is sold. And with his Berkshire Hathaway holding company's deep pockets, the country's leading producer of manufactured houses has a friendly financial backer and no longer is reliant on temperamental Wall Street.

In a year of upheaval marked by changing ownership, acquisition of a major competitor and an industry still in disarray, Clayton Homes' new financial muscle restores the 38-year-old company's clout and position atop the manufactured housing industry.

With the $373 million purchase of Oakwood Homes in April, Clayton immediately grew from 20 manufacturing plants, 304 sales centers and 6,750 employees to 32 plants, 395 centers and 11,200 workers covering 49 states.

Calling it a "huge pickup," Clayton Homes President and CEO Kevin Clayton said the addition of Oakwood increased the amount of loans his company is servicing from $5.6 billion to $10.5 billion.

"Those locations came in and contributed to profitability overnight," Clayton said, emphasizing that sales have doubled. "The merger has worked out better than we dreamed and hoped it would."

It's a partnership that both Buffett and Clayton are valuing more as their companies' union moves beyond the honeymoon.

"The bride and the bridegroom are getting along terrifically," Buffett said in an interview last week. "Kevin is a delight to work with."

Clayton also relishes the new arrangement, which includes call forwarding to the home of America's second-richest man. They talk on average once a week but never exchange e-mails. Buffett eschews electronic correspondence.

Clayton gets calls from Buffett while sitting in his corner cubicle at the manufacturer's Blount County headquarters, discussing topics like the buyout of Oakwood, which at one time was larger than Clayton Homes before going bankrupt.

And when he calls Buffett, he said, "Ninety percent of the time he answers the phone. It's kind of like the Bat Line."

Some changes at Clayton Homes have been subtle, such as a Buffett-endorsed wellness program for employees.

Others have been more radical, such as the closing of Clayton Homes' retail centers on Sundays to give sales employees more time with their families.

Wanting to more closely adhere to a mission of balance in employees' family, health, spiritual and work lives, Clayton in February began closing its retail sales centers on Sundays - a major shift in operations from a financial and personnel standpoint.

"We are genuinely concerned about the wellness of our team members," Clayton said. "Being closed on Sundays really captures the spiritual part of our business. It's easier to staff, and (workers are) much more rested to begin the week."

Clayton said 95 percent of the company's store managers supported the decision. "We think ultimately it is not going to cost us any business, and it promotes family," Clayton said.

A 60,000-square-foot, $4.9 million expansion to the headquarters is nearing completion. It will add office space to accommodate the Oakwood work and doubles the sizes of the full-service cafeteria and fitness center. The company plans to add nearly 500 employees in the next three years, putting its headquarters work force at about 1,500.

The company, founded in 1966 by Kevin's father, Jim Clayton, has manufacturing operations from North Carolina to Oregon, and its most profitable sales center and plant are located in California.

Clayton Homes is exploring modular construction of its homes, where main parts of a house are constructed in a plant and transported to the building site and assembled. . . .

Oakwood already had a foothold in the modular business, prompted by easier financing from banks that prefer lending for site-built homes and shy away from manufactured housing.

The manufactured housing industry has nearly collapsed because companies and industry lenders made too many questionable loans, and while Clayton Homes' Vanderbilt Mortgage division was unmarred by the massive loan defaults, the industry's woes chased away billions of dollars in Wall Street capital needed to secure loans.

That lack of money threatened Clayton's entire operation and made the Berkshire deal appealing. . . .

How good does Clayton Home's future look now, 13 months after reaching its lowest point?

"It's as good as it gets," Clayton said. "I would suggest that our future looks real bright with the financing and the people we have in our organization."

To underscore his point, Clayton recalls what Buffett advised when he was consulted about the Oakwood deal.

Buffett's response, according to Clayton, was, "You guys are going to have to make that decision, but rest assured we have plenty of capital."

Buffett, who takes a hands-off approach in overseeing his holdings, said Berkshire Hathaway is proud to own Clayton Homes and sees good things ahead as the company moves past its troubled peers.

"It's going to be a big field over time and we'll be a dominant part of that," Buffett said. "(Clayton Homes is) a very logical, rational workplace and that hasn't been a very rational industry."

While change has defined Clayton Homes over the past 12 months, employees say they hardly notice.

A team atmosphere is back and stress created by the company's uncertain ownership is gone. Clayton said it's remarkable for a new owner to step in and keep the management team intact. Posters and fever charts of sales goals again motivate employees. Worries about pink slips have been replaced by thoughts of bonuses.

Worries and costs from being a public company are also gone, something Clayton doesn't miss. He said the company was spending $7 million to $10 million a year to be publicly traded.

Being public made the company ripe for takeover as it tried to work out a sale to Berkshire Hathaway.

"In 2003, there were so many stressful days among our team members. We weren't sure who was going to own us for a while," Clayton said. "Berkshire brought a sense of security. It's very comforting to all our team members."

Employees at the Blount headquarters say little has changed in the past year except they are busier than ever, which contributes to job security. . . .

Clayton said he never had a grand illusion of what the Berkshire merger would be, adding that there have been no surprises, no disappointments, but further confirmation of the person Warren Buffett is and the kind of company Berkshire Hathaway is.

Again quoting Buffett, Clayton likes the billionaire's belief that Berkshire Hathaway companies can lose money, "even a lot of it," but can't afford to lose their reputations.

"Run your business as you would if it was the only asset of your family that took over 50 years to build," Clayton quoted Buffett telling his managers.

"Of course that's easy for me because it's reality," Clayton said.

To My Father on His 70th Birthday

I was thinking of a way to celebrate 70 years of your life and I began reflecting on the 46 years that You and I have shared.

We have had many fun times together as you taught me your love for music. You took me under your wing as your child apprentice and taught me how to type, answer a switchboard, assist in retail sales, sing, entertain and work with adults. You also taught me a strong work ethic and that anything worth doing is worth doing to the best of one's ability. I learned the value of the dollar by working and having my own financial spending decisions to make. I appreciate that opportunity.

I was too young to know that you had suffered bankruptcy. All I knew as a child was normalcy and security through what must have been such a difficult time. I respect you for the courage it must have taken to get up and keep living when everything in your world seemed to be falling apart. Few would have faced that reality with the steadfast determination that you showed. I learned that courage is the strength to do what is necessary even when confidence is lacking.

I'll never forget when you taught me to drive on Sharp's Ridge in a stick shift. You made sure I could handle any hill and it worked. It was always a lot of fun whenever you would surprise us with a golf cart, sewing machine or pony that you had taken in trade on a home. You did this for your children's delight and we were always excited!

I know that I was a difficult teenager at times and made some poor choices in my young adult life. You had the courage to let me fail and learn from my own mistakes. Not until I became a parent did I realize the strength and sacrifices it takes. You have shown me what it really means to be strong and hard working and it has marked my life.

The quality of my life and the substance of my character are largely of your making. The sacrifices you made to invest in me will affect my children and my children's children. For all that you are and all that you have done, I love you dad. Happy 70 years. May God bless you with good health and happiness for many more.

I love you,

Karen

Index

Clayton Bank & Trust
625 Market Street
Knoxville, TN 37902
Phone: 865.525.2858
Fax: 865.525.4991
info@claytonbank.com
www.claytonbank.com

First State Bank
101 East Main Street
Henderson, TN 38340
Phone: 731.989.2161
800.894.4402
Fax: 731.989.7280
info@FSBtn.com
www.FSBtn.com

Trust Department
101 East Main Street
Henderson, TN 38340
Phone: 731.989.2161
800.894.4402
Fax: 731.989.7280
trust@FSBtn.com

American City Bank
340 West Lincoln Street
Tullahoma, TN 37388
Phone: 931.455.0026
888.209.7373
Fax: 931.455.7329
customerservice@americancitybank.com
www.americancitybank.com

Friendship Bank
574 Main Street
Friendship, TN 38034
Phone: 731.677.2151
Fax: 731.677.2709

Clayton Homes, Inc.
5000 Clayton Rd
Maryville, TN 37804
865.380.3000
Fax: 865.380.3750
www.clayton.net
info@clayton.net
careers@clayton.net

32 Manufacturing Plants, 400 Retail Sales Centers, 88 Communities with 23,000 sites, and 340,000 mortgage customers with $12 billion in servicing.

Vanderbilt Mortgage & Finance, Inc.
500 Alcoa Trail
Maryville, TN 37804
800.970.7250
Fax: 865.380.3750
www.vmf.com

21st Mortgage Corporation
620 Market Street
Knoxville, TN 37902
800.955.0021
Fax: 800.210.0164
www.21stmortgage.com
RecruitingManager@21stmortgage.com